38 Goebels propaganda
39 Zambia no negotiation 1964
40 Endaba 1964
44 Udi not by force but by bluff
20 (crucial) no serious move to settle R until
Ian Smith threatened UDI.

68 Mar 1968 comprehensive mandatory sanctions
73 international politics a sham
114 Africans ready to help
59 British passports to Africans
90-91 Kerby Wilson's advisor on Russia and
interpreter KGB
119 Portuguese hint of abandonment
of Mozambique 1972
160 South Africa with greatest strength
or weakness for Rhodesia
161 Subtle obscure Un own

190 1977 the whole of Rhodesia is a
operational area Walls in newspapers,
210 ay illusion they were fighting a
war not known was shortlived

114 never dared recruits
69 Bournewood

navy 1977
rejected

number of ... 128-29

157 RF pursuit of 'apartheid an
embarrassing anachronism', Vorster

158 'But hypocrisy is not one
of the Afrikaner hosts, zeal
on faith are...'

SERVING SECRETLY

262 majority of
... 1960 ...

SERVING SECRETLY
An Intelligence Chief on Record
Rhodesia into Zimbabwe
1964 to 1981

KEN FLOWER

JOHN MURRAY

To Olga,
who suffered the locust years

© Ken Flower 1987

First published 1987
by John Murray (Publishers) Ltd
50 Albemarle Street, London W1X 4BD

Typeset by Fakenham Photosetting Ltd,
Fakenham, Norfolk

Printed and bound in Great Britain
by Butler and Tanner, Frome

British Library Cataloguing in Publication Data

Flower, Ken
Serving secretly: an intelligence chief
on record: Rhodesia into Zimbabwe, 1964
to 1981.
1. Intelligence service – Zimbabwe
I. Title
327.1'2'0924   JQ2925.A5516

ISBN 0-7195-4438-6

Contents

Illustrations

Sources: 4, Camera Press; 5, 6, 7, 8, 10, 11, 12, 14, 18, National Archives of Zimbabwe; 13, 16, 20, 21, 22, 23, 24, *The Herald* (Harare); 17, *Evening News* (London); 19, Directorate of Public Affairs, Metropolitan Police.

Maps

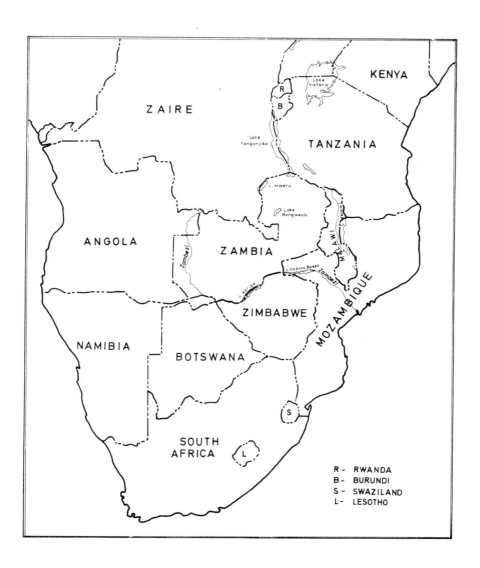

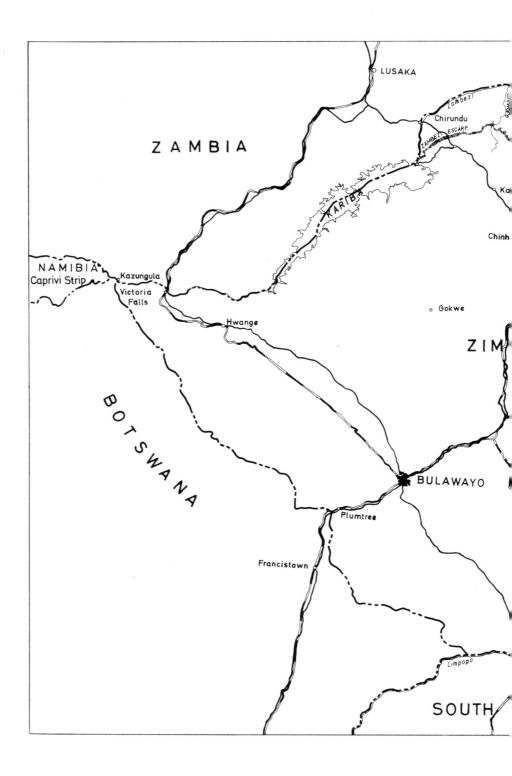

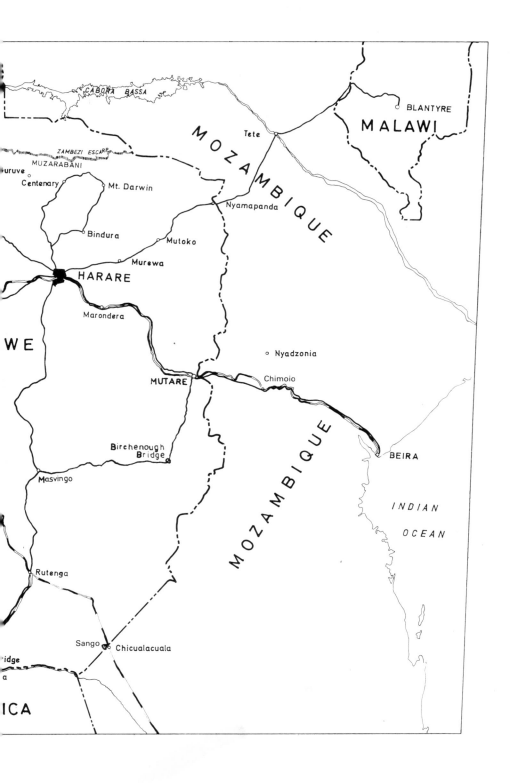

Acknowledgements

I am indebted to those who have helped me in transforming my, sometimes specialist, experiences into something readable by the general public. In particular, I wish to thank Kay Sayce, Dr John Hargrove and Professor Idris Parry who spent much time in improving the presentation of my manuscript; and General Sam Putterill for his assistance in elucidating some of the mysteries of military strategy and tactics. I must also thank those members of my family – Joyce in particular – who helped in the typing, or suffered my uneven temper over the past five years whilst this book was taking shape. The facts, the inferences drawn from them, as well as any errors, are my own.

Note on Place Names

Current spellings and names are used on the map on pp viii and ix, but in the main text, pre-1982 versions will be found. Below is a key to the two versions of places on the map.

Current	Pre-1982
Chinhoyi	Sinoia
Guruve	Sipolilo
Gweru	Gwelo
Harare	Salisbury
Hwange	Wankie
Marondera	Marandellas
Masvingo	Fort Victoria
Murewa	Mrewa
Mutare	Umtali
Mutoko	Mtoko
Muzarabani	Mazarabani
Sango	Vila Salazar

Foreword

I am delighted to have been invited to write a foreword to this fascinating book by my friend Ken Flower, as his whole life has been dedicated to the service of our country. As an indication of his ability and dedication, he has been Chief of the Intelligence Service under five consecutive Prime Ministers, who have held widely differing policies. The Intelligence Service was organised by him under instruction from Prime Minister Edgar Whitehead; it was developed by Winston Field in the hope of achieving national unity; it passed to Ian Smith in the service of a Government implacably opposed to black rule, when much of Ken Flower's advice was politically unacceptable; then to Bishop Muzorewa; and was finally inherited by Robert Mugabe who requested Ken Flower remain in service.

This surely is enough to show that all these Prime Ministers had complete faith in his ability and genuine desire to do his best for the country. Ken Flower had the advantage of being on friendly terms with the most important contacts both within the country and also externally in those states concerned with our progress and development. To each of our Prime Ministers he has put forward advice which he felt was in the best interests of the Country rather than what he believed would be acceptable to them.

Many books have been written on the period of our history which he covers and many incorrect impressions have been created, but no one is in a better position than Ken Flower to put the record straight. We should all be grateful that he has taken endless trouble to do just that. This book's manifest truths should correct the distortions of the past and illuminate such lessons as may be learnt – particularly in South Africa – before history is forced to repeat itself.

Sir Humphrey Gibbs

Harare
December 1986

Chronology

1888   Cecil John Rhodes obtains Rudd Concession from Lobengula, King of the Matabele, whose ancestor, Mzilikazi, had fled Tshaka in Zululand and trekked northwards to settle in the western area between the Limpopo and Zambezi rivers, naming his capital Bulawayo. The Concession gave Rhodes the mineral rights to Lobengula's territory (Matabeleland, with claims over Mashonaland).

1889   Rhodes establishes the British South Africa Company, incorporated under Royal Charter.

1890   Rhodes forms the BSA Company's 'Pioneer Column' in Bechuanaland, comprising 200 white settlers and 500 BSA Company Police. The Column reaches Salisbury on 12 September and occupies Mashonaland in the name of Queen Victoria.

1893   BSA Company forces invade Matabeleland in what became known as the 'Matabele War'. Bulawayo occupied on 4 November and Lobengula flees.

1894   Lobengula dies.

1895   Matabeleland and Mashonaland renamed 'Rhodesia'. Dr Jameson makes abortive raid into the Transvaal in December – harbinger of the Anglo-Boer War. His entire force of 400 surrenders. Less than 50 mounted police left behind in Rhodesia.

1896   Matabele Rebellion, crushed within the year. The 'Mwari' or 'Mlimo' cult of an oracular god played a prominent part in the Rebellion. Uprising in Mashonaland.

1897   Mashona Rebellion ruthlessly crushed. The 'Mhondoro' cult prominent. Spirit mediums Nehanda and Kaguvi captured and executed. One tenth of white population killed or wounded – considerably more than in other revolts in Africa, e.g. Kenya, Algeria.

1898   British Order-in-Council becomes the established governing instrument of the re-named 'Southern Rhodesia', representing a compromise between Imperial and Company requirements.

1899   Legislative Council for Southern Rhodesia established. Outbreak of Anglo-Boer War; white Rhodesians heavily involved against the Boers.

1902 Anglo-Boer War ends. Peace of Vereeniging. Rhodes dies.

1907 White settlers form majority in the Legislative Council.

1914–18 World War I. Rhodesian troops engaged in German South West Africa and fight a bitter campaign under General Smuts in German East Africa.

1918 British Privy Council rejects case for African and Company ownership of land and rules that 'unalienated land' belongs to the Crown.

1922 Referendum favours 'Responsible Government' rather than Union with South Africa.

1923 'Company Rule' is terminated. Southern Rhodesia becomes 'Self-Governing Colony'. General election results in Sir Charles Coghlan becoming first Prime Minister.

1927 Death of Coghlan. H. U. Moffat becomes Prime Minister.

1930 'Land Apportionment Act', approved by Britain, divides country into African and European areas.

1933 Chartered Company sells its mineral rights to Southern Rhodesia government. Moffat replaced as Prime Minister by G. Mitchell. Dr G. Huggins wins general election and becomes Prime Minister.

1934 First African National Council (ANC) formed under Aaron Jacha.

1939 Huggins wins another general election and forms war-time government.

1940 Empire Air Training scheme begins in Southern Rhodesia.

1945 Strike by African railway workers. ANC revived under leadership of Rev Thompson Samkange.

1948 First general strike by African workers. General election: Huggins returned as Prime Minister.

1949 Victoria Falls Conference proposes Federation between Southern Rhodesia, Northern Rhodesia and Nyasaland.

1953 Referendum approves Federation of Rhodesia and Nyasaland. Huggins becomes first Federal Prime Minister. Garfield Todd Prime Minister of Southern Rhodesia. First disturbances in Nyasaland.

1956 Sir Roy Welensky succeeds Huggins (Lord Malvern) as Federal Prime Minister. African National Youth League (ANYL) replaces City Youth League, and organises bus boycott leading to detention of 200 nationalists.

1957 Youth League and ANC merge under name ANC, with Joshua Nkomo as President and James Chikerema as Vice-President.

1958 Todd ousted in Cabinet revolt, replaced as Prime Minister by Sir

Edgar Whitehead. ANC meetings prohibited in rural areas. Dr Hastings Banda returns to Nyasaland after 40-year absence and assumes leadership of Nyasaland African National Congress.

1959 Widespread nationalist agitation in Northern Rhodesia and Nyasaland. Troops and Police from Southern Rhodesia sent to quell disturbances. Banda detained. Southern Rhodesia ANC banned and 500 members detained.

1960 Monckton Commission recommends that Federal territories be given right to secede. National Democratic Party (NDP) formed under Michael Mawema – later Nkomo. British Prime Minister, Harold Macmillan, makes 'winds of change' speech in Cape Town.

1961 Agreement reached on a new Constitution for Southern Rhodesia under chairmanship of Duncan Sandys. Nkomo later repudiates the agreement. After sporadic violence the NDP is banned and the Zimbabwe African People's Union (ZAPU) formed.

1962 Whitehead launches multi-racial 'Build a Nation' campaign. Serious disorders in Salisbury. ZAPU banned. Whitehead discusses formation of Security Intelligence Service. The Rhodesian Front (RF) formed and wins general election with Winston Field as Prime Minister.

1963 Zimbabwe African National Union (ZANU) formed under Ndabaningi Sithole from ZAPU members dissatisfied with Nkomo's leadership. Nkomo forms People's Caretaker Council (PCC). Months of faction fighting follow. Field appoints author to establish Central Intelligence Organisation (CIO). First recruits of Zimbabwe African National Liberation Army (ZANLA) go to China for training. Federation of Rhodesia and Nyasaland comes to an end on 31 December.

1964 Evan Campbell appointed High Commissioner in London. Field, reluctant to seize Independence, resigns as Prime Minister, succeeded by Ian Smith. ZANU decides in secret session to decline further negotiations with whites and to pursue the 'armed struggle'. PCC follows suit. Both factions banned, and their leaders including Nkomo, Sithole and Robert Mugabe detained. Rhodesia Party (RP) formed under Whitehead and Welensky who loses by-election in October. Smith visits Salazar in Lisbon and goes on to London. Operations Co-ordinating Committee (OCC) formed. Major-General Jock Anderson, Commander of the Army, forced to resign. Succeeded by Major-General Sam Putterill. Chiefs' 'Indaba' at Domboshawa unanimously supports 'cutting of strings'. Referendum gives overwhelming support to RF policies. Labour win general election in UK. Malawi and Zambia independent.

1965 Arthur Bottomley, Secretary for Commonwealth Relations and Lord Gardiner, the Lord Chancellor, visit Salisbury to discuss

independence issue. First guerrillas of the Zimbabwe African
People's Revolutionary Army (z i p r a) enter from Zambia. r f wins
all 50 'A' roll seats at general election. Campbell replaced by
Brigadier Andrew Skeen as High Commissioner in London. Smith
visits London and Harold Wilson visits Salisbury in October.
Wilson abjures the use of force. Unilateral Declaration of
Independence (u d i) on 11 November. Sir Humphrey Gibbs ignores
u d i and remains as Governor and Queen's representative. Press
censorship imposed. Clifford Dupont appointed Acting Officer
Administering the Government. Wilson sends threatening message
to Smith via Gibbs. Britain applies selective economic sanctions and
announces an embargo on oil and petroleum products. Rhodesia
introduces petrol rationing.

1966 Commonwealth Prime Ministers in Lagos uphold Britain's refusal
to use force. 'White spaces' in newspapers (denoting censorship)
forbidden. 1965 Rhodesian Constitution becomes law. Informal
Anglo-Rhodesian talks begin in April. Small group of z a n l a killed
at Sinoia (Chinhoyi) by police. The u n Security Council declares
Rhodesia's actions a 'threat to world peace' and Britain imposes
naval blockade of the port of Beira. Wilson and Smith meet,
unsuccessfully, on h m s *Tiger.* United Nations Security Council
imposes selective mandatory sanctions. Wilson announces policy of
'No Independence Before Majority Rule' (n i b m a r).

1967 First serious guerrilla incursions (Operation 'Nickel') by z i p r a and
South African (s a a n c) forces. South African Police (s a p) arrive in
Rhodesia. Constitutional (Whaley) Commission established. Wilson
announces new initiative on Rhodesia, using Gibbs as intermediary
in re-negotiating *Tiger* proposals. George Thompson,
Commonwealth Secretary, holds discussions with Smith in
Salisbury.

1968 Rhodesian Security Forces have marked success in Operations
'Cauldron' and 'Griffin'. Sir Alec Douglas-Home visits Rhodesia.
Rhodesia Appeal Court dismisses appeal of three captured guerrillas
convicted of murder; Queen's reprieve ignored and guerrillas
hanged (The 'Constitutional' Case). United Nations impose
comprehensive mandatory sanctions (May). Whaley proposals
rejected by r f. William Harper, Minister of Internal Affairs, resigns
at Prime Minister's insistence. Rhodesian government accorded 'de
jure' status by Rhodesian judiciary. Bottomley returns to Salisbury
for discussions. Smith and Wilson meet aboard h m s *Fearless*
(October). Post-*Fearless* talks in Salisbury between Thompson and
Smith fail and Rhodesia announces rejection of *Fearless* proposals.
Facing defeat, z a p u / z i p r a resort to press-ganging Zimbabweans
living in Zambia.

1969 Sithole sentenced to six years' imprisonment for plotting to
assassinate Smith, but denounces 'Armed Struggle', leading to his

subsequent removal as ZANU President. There is a marked lull in guerrilla incursions out of Zambia. New proposals for Republican Constitution overwhelmingly supported in referendum. Sir Humphrey Gibbs relinquishes post as Governor. Closure of Rhodesia House in London and of British Residual Mission in Salisbury. ZANU meet FRELIMO to request access to Rhodesia through Tete province of Mozambique as part of re-assessment of ZANLA strategy. In December Roger Nicholson and Trevor Gallaher sentenced to imprisonment for economic spying.

1970 Nicholson and Gallaher released and deported. Rhodesia declared a Republic in March. RF win general election and Dupont sworn in as President. Britain and United States veto United Nations resolution on tougher sanctions. CIA representative leaves Salisbury. South African Prime Minister, John Vorster, visits Rhodesia in May. Conservatives win British elections in June, with Douglas-Home as Foreign Secretary. Guy Clutton-Brock deported. The lull in the terrorist war continues.

1971 Death of Lord Malvern. Petrol rationing ends. Lord Goodman, Britain's special envoy, visits Rhodesia for discussions. Douglas-Home and Smith reach agreement on constitutional settlement (November). UANC under Bishop Muzorewa activated to oppose the proposals. The lull in the terrorist war continues but the Portuguese position in Mozambique has become precarious.

1972 Commission led by Lord Pearce arrives in January to carry out test of acceptability of constitutional proposals. In May the Pearce Commission announces proposals not acceptable to Rhodesians as a whole. Rhodesian sportsmen and women banned from Olympic Games in Munich. US Senate votes against re-imposing sanctions on Rhodesian chromite. Widespread infiltration by ZANLA guerrillas out of Mozambique – 'politicisation' of the rural population in north-eastern areas marks new phase of the guerrilla war. Attacks on white-owned farms start in late-December.

1973 Smith closes border with Zambia in January, offers to re-open it in February but Kaunda keeps it closed. Operation 'Hurricane' gets under way in north-eastern areas. 'Protected Villages' and 'Cordon Sanitaire' implemented. Peter Niesewand deported in May. Smith begins negotiations with Muzorewa in July. Military component of Selous Scouts introduced in November.

1974 Portuguese government in Lisbon overthrown in military coup staged by middle-ranking officers. Moves to withdraw Portuguese presence in Mozambique, thus weakening Rhodesia's hold on Mozambique border. Guerrilla war escalates. Extended military call-up of territorials affects the Rhodesian economy. Intensification of raids into Mozambique and Zambia.

Smith wins all 50 white seats in general election (July). Smith/

Muzorewa negotiations break down. Vorster pursues policy of detente and persuades Smith to release African Nationalist leaders for discussions in Lusaka. Nhari rebellion (ZANLA) occurs in Mozambique and Zambia. Smith announces ceasefire but it fails to take hold. Ineffectual 'Declaration of Unity' under Muzorewa (UANC) signed in Lusaka by Nkomo, Sithole and Chikerema. Portugal hands over to FRELIMO in Mozambique (September) without holding elections and dissatisfied Mozambicans flock to join the Mozambique National Resistance (MNR) developed as 'eyes and ears' for CIO in Mozambique.

1975   Herbert Chitepo, chairman of ZANU (PF) assassinated in Lusaka on 18 March. Zambian authorities detain scores of ZANU leaders and act against hundreds of their followers. An 'International Commission' investigates the death and draws the wrong conclusions. Mozambique gains independence under FRELIMO (June). Abortive Victoria Falls Conference between Rhodesian government and nationalist leaders set up by Vorster and Kaunda. Mugabe appointed leader of ZANU. Smith starts negotiations with Nkomo: they sign 'Declaration of Intent' to hold a Constitutional conference.

1976   Guerrilla infiltrations out of Mozambique extend from Tete to Manica, to Gaza provinces. Rhodesian forces raid deeper into Mozambique. Samora Machel closes Mozambique border (March). Selous Scouts attack Nyadzonia/Pungwe camp resulting in 1000 killed and wounded. Smith's negotiations with Nkomo fail.

Vorster increases his pressure on Smith, including the withdrawal of SAP. US Secretary of State, Henry Kissinger, and Vorster persuade Smith to accept majority rule within two years. Conference to establish interim government opens in Geneva in October. Kaunda releases detained ZANU leaders to attend. Conference adjourned in December without re-assembling. Nkomo and Mugabe form Patriotic Front (PF). Rhodesian Security Forces 'kill rate' increases steadily but cannot keep pace with guerrilla recruitment. Policies of 'Safe Return' and Psychological Action Unit (PSYAC) ('to win hearts and minds') extended.

1977   Dr David Owen, British Foreign Secretary, together with US Assistant Secretary Andrew Young, launch new Anglo-American initiative. They insist that PF must be part of any settlement. Smith rejects their proposals and resumes negotiations for 'Internal Settlement' with Muzorewa, Sithole and Chief Chirau.

OCC advise Government that the war is being lost and a political settlement is essential. South African attitude towards Smith improves after US Vice-President Mondale tries to browbeat Vorster, but Pik Botha tells Smith 'a peaceful settlement is no longer possible and there will have to be losers'. British Field Marshal Lord

Carver makes an abortive visit and OCC is replaced by Combined Operations (COMOPS) with Lieut General Walls as Commander, Combined Operations.

Guerrilla war continues to escalate and Rhodesian Security Forces intensify attacks in Mozambique, including attacks on camps at Chimoio and Tembue, in December.

1978 Conference in Malta attended by Owen, Young, Nkomo and Mugabe while Smith signs agreement (3rd March) with Muzorewa, Sithole and Chief Chirau for Transitional government leading to majority rule, but Nkomo and Mugabe vow to destroy the Transitional Government. Conference in Dar-es-Salaam attended by US Secretary of State, Vance, Owen, Young, Nkomo and Mugabe.

The Transitional Government fails to stop the war or curb guerrilla recruiting. Muzorewa loses authority when Minister Byron Hove resigns. The guerrillas intensify their campaign of terror – Elim Mission massacre in June, and destruction of Air Rhodesia 'Viscount' in September when survivors are massacred. Smith describes this as a 'stroke of fate' that ends his secret negotiations with Nkomo. White Ministers demand retribution and Martial Law – General Walls threatens them with a 'Military Junta'. Peter Mackay is deported against the wishes of black Ministers. Rhodesian forces carry out daring ('Green Leader') attacks in Zambia on ZIPRA bases; but Kaunda re-opens Zambia's rail route through Rhodesia.

1979 White referendum accepts majority rule constitution. Second 'Viscount' shot down. Muzorewa wins internal elections in April. Conservatives under Lord Lennox-Boyd report the elections as 'free and fair' but Front Line Presidents oppose and international recognition withheld. On 1 June Muzorewa assumes office as the first black Prime Minister of Zimbabwe-Rhodesia.

Conservatives, under Mrs Thatcher, win general election in May and renege on election promises to Muzorewa. Queen and Mrs Thatcher attend Commonwealth Conference in Lusaka. Agree to convene constitutional conference at Lancaster House which opens on 10 September. Zimbabwe-Rhodesian delegation accepts British proposals on 21 September and Muzorewa agrees to stand down as Prime Minister against his delegation's wishes. Conference breaks down in October but Samora Machel coerces Mugabe into acceptance of British proposals. PF accept pre-Independence arrangements and British publish ceasefire proposals.

Lord Soames sent to Salisbury as British Governor on 11 December. Agreement signed at Lancaster House on 21 December. Legality is restored and sanctions removed, but Soames dependent on Rhodesians to hold the ring whilst the guerrillas assemble and arrangements are made to hold elections.

1980 ZANU (PF) and ZANLA ignore ceasefire and intimidation is widely practised. Lord Soames faces serious problems and the Rhodesian Security Forces are re-deployed. Nkomo returns on 13 January and Mugabe on 27 January. Soames assumes wider powers but ignores Rhodesian requests to ban or restrict political parties practising intimidation or continuing to break the ceasefire.

COMOPS stages confrontations with Soames and British officials. Muzorewa considers trying to reverse the trend of events by force if necessary, but Rhodesian officials say matters must now take their course.

Mugabe escapes assassination attempts. Elections are held over five days commencing 27 February. The results announced on 4 March show Mugabe as winning 57 seats, Nkomo 20, Muzorewa 3 out of 80 African seats in the 100-seat Parliament. Soames, Walls and Mugabe appeal for calm. Nothing untoward happens and Zimbabwe becomes Independent on 18 April.

Abbreviations

OCC   Operations Co-ordinating Committee

PATU   Police Anti-Terrorist Unit

PCC   People's Caretaker Council – formerly ZAPU

PF   Patriotic Front – an alliance of convenience between ZAPU and ZANU

PIDE   Policia Internacional é de Defésa do Estado – Portuguese Security Police – subsequently DGS

PSYAC   Psychological Action (Unit) – to win 'hearts and minds'

PV   Protected Village – the 'strategic hamlet' of Malaya

RAP   Rhodesia Action Party

RAR   Rhodesian African Rifles – black battalion with white officers, as in the King's African Rifles (KAR)

R & R   Rest and Recuperation – rest period between call-up for military service

RF   Rhodesian Front

RP   Rhodesia Party

RLI   Rhodesian Light Infantry – all-white regular battalion

SAANC   African National Congress of South Africa

SADCC   Southern Africa Development Co-ordination Conference

SADF   South African Defence Force

SAP   South African Police

SAS   Special Air Service – on same lines as British SAS

SB   Special Branch – a branch of the Police, incorporated in CIO

SCCI(A) or (M)   Serviço de Centralizacão e Coordenação de Informação – civil Intelligence service in Angola (A) and Mozambique (M)

SDECE   Service de Documentation Extérieure et de Contre-Espionage – French Intelligence Service

SWAPO   South West African People's Organisation

TANZAM   – Railway, subsequently TAZARA, Tanzania–Zambia Railway

TTL   Tribal Trust Land, previously Native Reserve

UANC   United African National Council – under Muzorewa

UDI   Unilateral Declaration of Independence

UNITA   National Union for the Total Independence of Angola

ZANLA   Zimbabwe African National Liberation Army (ZANU)

ZANU   Zimbabwe African National Union. Leaders: Ndabaningi Sithole and then Robert Mugabe

ZANU(PF)   ZANU within the alliance of PF

ZAPU   Zimbabwe African People's Union – pre- and post-PCC. Leader: Joshua Nkomo

ZAPU(PF) ZAPU within the alliance of PF
    ZIPA Zimbabwe People's Army
   ZIPRA Zimbabwe People's Revolutionary Army (ZAPU)

Prologue

On 25 May 1980, just over a month after Zimbabwe had become an independent nation, I received a telephone call from the Minister of State for Security. 'I think you should come to see me about a report made to the Prime Minister concerning yourself.'

Half an hour later I was shown into the Minister's office. After scant formalities he said, 'The Prime Minister wishes you to know that the Commissioner of Police has reported to him that you have been spending much of your time recently trying to murder him.'

'Was I named? And, if so, who else?'

'You were clearly named, and certain officers working for you.'

The Minister was watching me closely and the thought flashed through my mind that I was then and there on trial for my reputation, perhaps for my life.

'Does the Prime Minister expect me to defend myself, or justify my actions before him?'

'No, he merely wishes you to know what a colleague of yours has reported concerning yourself.'

'But how can I leave it like that? And how can I justify my actions? For instance, did the Commissioner explain that some of those implicated are officers in Special Branch which is part of the Police and under his command? Or that we have always insisted on collective responsibility at the top?'

'No, he indicated that you were in charge of the men concerned and that they were acting under your orders.'

'Who else heard this report, and what do you intend doing about it?'

'I was present – no one else. The Prime Minister does not intend doing anything other than to advise you.'

'And what, if I might ask, do you believe?'

'I was astounded, personally, that whites would want to shop each other like that.'

'Yes ... Of course, I can be accused of many activities, authorised and unauthorised, and in many countries that I know I could expect to be put against a wall and shot.'

'That is not why you are being advised. In fact, the Prime Minister told the Commissioner that he was surprised – not at the occurrences, because he has been nearly killed on several occasions – but he made it clear that we have declared an amnesty; our policy is reconciliation and we are not interested in what happened before we assumed power.'

'I appreciate what you say, but I feel I must see the Prime Minister nevertheless.'

'It is not necessary to see him about this. He understands better than you might realise.'

'Or the Commissioner might realise?'

'Yes.'

This was the gist of the conversation I had with the Minister, Emmerson Mnangagwa. My first meeting with him had been several weeks previously, in March, when I and the Armed Forces Commanders had gone to offer our services to the newly elected Prime Minister of Zimbabwe, Robert Mugabe. In a somewhat aloof though perfectly correct manner, Mnangagwa had said that I should continue in the post I had occupied for seventeen years, Director-General of the Central Intelligence Organisation (CIO), to ensure that it was controlled professionally. He had added that he would provide the political link between the organisation and the government.

I knew little about Mnangagwa, save that in 1963 he had switched from the Zimbabwe African People's Union (ZAPU) to the Zimbabwe African National Union (ZANU) and had led the first group of Zimbabwe African National Liberation Army (ZANLA) revolutionaries to China to be trained in sabotage. On returning to Rhodesia he had blown up a railway locomotive and had been captured; he would have been sentenced to death but for his age, erroneously assessed as under sixteen although subsequent checks indicated that he must have been about twenty-one.

Mnangagwa's statement that it was not necessary for me to discuss the Commissioner's allegations with the Prime Minister were repeated by Mugabe himself when I called on him. Instead, the Prime Minister talked of his wish to get to know me better and suggested that we should meet regularly for a tête-à-tête. Such meetings, he said, would give him the opportunity of discussing any issue he might wish to raise with me in private and would allow me to pass on Intelligence which was too delicate to be conveyed through any other channel.

My first tête-à-tête with the Prime Minister, within a week of the unsettling conversation with Mnangagwa, quickly dispelled any false image I might have had of him. He had no wish to talk of the allegations against me, dismissing the Commissioner as just another police informer and he laughed when I showed readiness to confirm some of our attempts to kill him.

'Yes, but they all failed, otherwise we would not be here together,' he remarked. 'And do not expect me to applaud your failures.'

He paused for a moment, and then continued: 'As far as I have realised the position, we were trying to kill each other; that's what the war was about. What I'm concerned with now is that my public statements should be believed when I say that I have drawn a line through the past. From now on we must trust each other if we are to work together for the benefit of the majority. I want people to believe in my policy of reconciliation and to respond accordingly.'

Walking back to my office in the hot sunshine, I felt as if a great burden had been lifted from my shoulders. Perhaps, at long last, the government servant and the politician could establish a worthwhile rapport. During the ten minutes or so that I walked, I reflected upon the various aspects of service with the four Prime Ministers with whom I had been closely associated and upon the man I was now serving. Robert Mugabe was emerging as someone with a greater capacity and determination to shape the country's destiny for the benefit of all its people than any of his four predecessors. Even Field, who remains in my memory as a perceptive and knowledgeable man, honest beyond most expectations held of politicians, had given up the fight when trying to steer an even course in the national interest.

My thoughts went back to the day in April 1964 when Field had summoned me to remove 'Top Secret' papers from his safe on his last day in the office in which I had just seen Mugabe. The papers represented many months of work by the Service Chiefs and Heads of Ministries on the possible consequences of UDI and were overwhelmingly against such action. Field had handed the papers to me, saying: 'My political friends will misrepresent the matter, but I want you to know – and to advise your colleagues – that I will not take the responsibility as Prime Minister of this country to declare UDI against all this weight of professional advice.'

There followed seventeen turbulent years, from Field to Mugabe – UDI; the break with Britain; the silent war in which men and women disappeared without trace; the bloody war in which thousands died; the economic war in which so many countries became involved through the enforcement or violation of sanctions: seventeen years during which our Intelligence expanded to establish worldwide links, allowing us to follow guerrillas in training from Algeria to Cuba, from Russia to China.

The fact that I was there at the beginning of it all, and still there at the end, suggests that there must have been some thread of mutual confidence which linked me to these Prime Ministers – although 'survival' in the world of Intelligence has an unfortunate connotation to do with 'moles' and suchlike. But my acceptance by the disparate leaders whom I served should speak for itself, and I believe I have no greater need to defend myself before any alien critic than I had before Mugabe.

The story I tell in this book is one which I believe passionately must be told, to put the record straight, to sustain the historical perspective, to preserve the reputations of those who deserve well of their country and to elucidate such lessons as others may wish to learn from our mistakes. And I must do it now, for any septuagenarian is entitled to take heed of the Bible's warning that one's allotted lifespan is three score years and ten. In telling this story I like to think I have uncovered something of the real cause and effect of events and thrown light on some of the mysteries previously hidden in the murk of politics and war. But I realise only too well that no one person could have known everything and that I was as prone to mistakes as the next person. I can merely claim that I ought to have known what was happening through personal involvement and that it was expected of my profession as an Intelligence Officer to forecast something of the future or, at least, to advise politicians of the trends to be followed.

In order to protect those who need protection, the full story may not be told for many years – if ever. And having lived anonymously for almost two decades I have no wish to betray the mutual trust and confidence that preserves anonymity.

Some of my story can be authenticated by extracts from my personal diary – notes jotted down and comments made in the heat of the moment; but long gaps appear in it, particularly when I was depressed with the futility of affairs. There was an official record, mostly destroyed, although some of it has survived through my refusal to allow its destruction or removal to South Africa when such action appeared unconstitutional. These papers (a few representative samples of which are reproduced in the Appendix) provide the documentary background to my personal account. In addition, I managed to keep some semi-official and other notes taken soon after certain events and I was trained to remember 'detail in depth' throughout long discussions when no artificial aid to memory could be used. From this detail – recorded, recovered and remembered – and from such depth of perception as I could acquire, emerges this account of white revolt, black revolt, the death of Rhodesia and the birth of Zimbabwe.

CHAPTER I

Birth of An Intelligence Service

They used to say of Cornishmen that you would find them in almost any part of the world except Cornwall. Most of them are born there, of course, and a few go home to die, but for centuries smuggling and piracy led many of them overseas, while others took up their miners' picks and went to Malaya, Canada, Australia and Southern Africa.

With little prospect of employment in Cornwall in the deep recession of the 1930s, I too looked across the seas. Things seemed as gloomy there as they did at home. My one hope – a job as a trapper in the Arctic wastes with the Hudson's Bay Company – fell through the ice, as it were, when Canada stopped all immigration. In desperation I responded to an advertisement offering a post with the English Customs. The chairman of the selection board queried the motives behind my application; no Cornishman had applied for a job with the English Customs for five hundred years, he said, and presumably it was my intention to pass on inside knowledge of how the Customs worked to my smuggling acquaintances in Cornwall. I offered the right assurances, and for the following three years boarded and searched ships of every flag as an employee of the London Waterguard, or succoured sea-sick passengers off the Irish ferry at Holyhead in north Wales.

But my feet were restless, and when my eye caught this advertisement on the back page of the *Daily Telegraph* early in 1937 I was immediately attracted:

> Sons of gentlemen who can ride and shoot required
> for service in the British South Africa Police,
> Southern Rhodesia.*

I could neither ride nor shoot but my father was a parson so presumably I qualified as the son of a gentleman. My reply to the advertisement

---

* The name 'Rhodesia' was in common use as early as 1896. Thereafter the country became known as 'Southern Rhodesia' to differentiate it from 'Northern Rhodesia', later Zambia. After the dissolution of the Federation of Rhodesia and Nyasaland in 1963 'Rhodesia' again came into common usage. In the late 1970s the Muzorewa government renamed the country 'Zimbabwe-Rhodesia'; at Lancaster House the name 'Rhodesia' was used and in 1980, with the achievement of Independence, the name 'Zimbabwe' was officially adopted.

brought a summons to attend for interview at Rhodesia House in London. There I learnt that there were two thousand men on the waiting list and my heart began to sink – until my interviewer asked if I would be ready to board the ship sailing from Southampton the following week. He dismissed the waiting list as being of lesser consequence than the fact that the British South Africa Police (BSAP) Rugby team needed a replacement full back and it had been noted that I had been playing in that position in Cornwall. I borrowed the fare from my eldest sister and sailed for Africa in March 1937 to start service as a Mounted Trooper in the BSAP, a force in which young gentlemen were literally hammered into the ground for the privilege of earning £150 a year.

The recession had hit Southern Rhodesia but the Prime Minister, Dr Godfrey Huggins (later Lord Malvern), refused to shut shop. He sought to encourage immigration through the BSAP and the Nursing Services, and in this way supplemented the white population and sustained the economy at virtually no cost to the Exchequer. Police recruits signed on for a compulsory three years. They were taught an African language and the rudiments of African law and customs; this stood them in good stead if they decided to stay on in the country, which more than 80 per cent of them did on completion of their initial service.

Within my first year in Southern Rhodesia I was patrolling remote areas on horseback or, where the presence of tsetse fly prevented the use of animals, by bicycle or on foot. The relationship then between the policeman and the public was good and one made friends easily, on or off duty. I was encouraged to sit the Civil Service Law examinations as a step towards obtaining a commission in the BSAP and spent many nights studying in the solitude of my hut, breaking out from time to time to participate in the relatively riotous lifestyle pursued by the wilder characters among the prospectors, small workers (gold miners working on their own) and remittance men. During my second year I was transferred to Gokwe, the administrative headquarters of one of the least developed parts of the country, to share life with a Native Commissioner who had indicated that he needed a chess-playing companion. The remoteness appealed to me. I spent the days criss-crossing an area larger than Belgium to seek out lawbreakers and hold court, or drifting down the great Zambesi River on month-long tax-collecting patrols; at night I studied, or played chess by gaslight under a mosquito net. Before dawn I was out hunting for the pot.

This 'Sanders of the River' existence came to an end with the outbreak of the Second World War, and in June 1941 I found myself among a small group of Rhodesians sailing to Berbera in the Gulf of Aden to take part in the re-occupation of British Somaliland following the Italian invasion of August 1940. There followed seven years of varied experience in the Horn of Africa where, as part of the British Military Administration, we hung on precariously to the 'Reserved Areas of Ethiopia' (predominantly Somali areas, including parts of the Haud and the Ogaden).

In the Ogaden we tried to disarm the nomadic Somali tribesmen who lived or died by the gun. Then they fell prey to their traditional enemies raiding across the boundaries dividing Arabia-in-Africa from the old Christian Empire of Ethiopia. So we attempted to correct our mistake – with two men and a dog. We protected the Somalis from Ethiopian depredations and struggled to unite the Somali nation, previously dismembered by the British, the French, the Italians and the Ethiopians. To do this we trained the young men as 'Illaloes' (irregulars) to defend their kinsmen, and after our departure they became 'Shifta' (bandits), the scourge of the Ethiopians.

Most of our military liaison duties were comparatively straightforward, but sometimes we had to contend with the unexpected, like providing six hundred girls for the 11th East African Division to try to reduce the incidence of VD (running at 40 per cent amongst blacks and 60 per cent among whites) to make the men fighting fit for Burma. There was no shortage of female volunteers but most of them were infected. We had to confine them to a camp from which they could not escape and to which the men had no access until the girls had been treated by Italian doctors. It meant a lot of work, done unofficially, and it attracted considerable criticism, but we were vindicated insofar as the overall VD rate was reduced to 5 per cent. The War Office sent an Anglican Bishop out from England to help silence the moralists in the argument as to whether prostitution increased or decreased the incidence of VD. At the end of our experiment I received my only Commendation from the GOC-in-C, East Africa Command, worded euphemistically: 'For Good Service and Devotion to Duty'.

We did what we could to repair the ravages of war in the Horn of Africa, working closely with the Duke of Harar, Emperor Haile Selassie's second son, but in the end Clement Attlee's government decided that Britain must abandon the Somali cause. We prepared to return the 'Reserved Areas' to Ethiopia and I said goodbye to the Emperor, leaving him with the bitter comment that his intransigence would create a running sore across the Horn of Africa that would fester throughout our lifetime. I started out on the overland journey to Southern Rhodesia, through Kenya and the Belgian Congo where the rumblings of discontent were growing louder, but before I reached home I was recalled to Mogadishu. The Resident Magistrate there had died and I was to replace him during the visit of the Allied Commission (Russian, French and British) enquiring into the future of Italian territories in Africa. But the Italian Empire was finished, and that message was starkly conveyed to the visitors by the Somali Youth League one Sunday morning in January 1948, when fifty Italian men, women and children were butchered in the streets of Mogadishu. The youths were aided and abetted by the Somalia Gendarmerie, and as Magistrate I sentenced dozens of gendarmes for their complicity in murder.

By April 1948, I was back in Rhodesia. I relinquished the rank of Lieutenant-Colonel in His Majesty's African Colonial Services and re-verted to Corporal in the Mounted Branch of the BSAP, a levelling process shared by most ex-servicemen joining or rejoining the BSAP from the various theatres of war. To start the climb upwards again it was necessary to compete in whatever I could. I entered the Civil Service Language examinations with little hope of success, for my ability to write and speak Shona had suffered badly during my long absence. When I had completed the oral examination the chairman of the ex-aminers called me back into the room.

'Will you promise me something?' he asked.

'Of course,' I replied, expectantly.

'It is this: if we are crazy enough to pass you, will you please do your damndest to learn the language!'

I left, chastened, and was awarded 50½ per cent. The examiners were able to report a 100 per cent success rate that year, for I was the only entrant from the BSA Police which probably accounted for their charity.

I then competed in the new Police promotion examinations under a British Police system. This system had been recommended by the Mundy Commission of 1946, which had been set up to examine the dissatisfac-tion with the old military system. Amongst other things, the Commis-sion condemned the influence of Roman Catholicism in the BSAP during the preceding half-century, when few non-Catholics had been commis-sioned; so prevalent was this influence that some members of the Force had gone so far as to become Roman Catholics to improve their pros-pects for promotion to commissioned rank. The Irish Roman Catholic influence had been paramount amongst several Police Forces in the English-speaking world, including the United States, but it had declined in Southern Rhodesia during the Second World War.

I was re-commissioned Lieutenant in 1949 and, as a Captain, in Au-gust 1953 was given command of the Southern Rhodesian contingent sent to 'pacify' Nyasaland. On 1 August that year the Federation of Rhodesia and Nyasaland had been born; it was a laboured birth and within a few days complications set in. The unwelcome imposition of Federation was the spark that set fire to a train of anti-government activity in Nyasaland and the country became the scene of the most serious manifestation of African nationalism in the Central African region up to that time.

In comparison with the disorders that subsequently plagued the Federation, however, the Nyasaland 'Emergency' was a mild affair. In the only serious riot with which we had to contend, at Domasi, I moved ahead to speak to the ringleaders of the approaching mob and was cut off from my detachment. This was against all tenets of counter-insurgency drill. Six of the African constables accompanying me fled and I had to use my revolver to regain command. By this time, however, the senior Warrant Officer of the detachment was already firing and between us we broke the proud record of the BSAP of not having fired a shot in anger since the turn of the century. The riot was quelled in a matter of minutes; two of the ringleaders had been killed and a few others injured. The District Commissioner emerged from his courthouse and a chair was found for him to stand on and issue the appropriate warnings. Surprisingly little damage had been done considering that some of the assailants were armed with spears, axes, bows and arrows. The injured were treated at the local clinic; I was among them, for I had been winged by a spear and my left ear needed a stitch or two.

At the time of the Nyasaland 'Emergency', Garfield Todd was taking over as Prime Minister of Southern Rhodesia from Sir Godfrey Huggins, who was about to become the first Prime Minister of the Federation. Both Todd and Huggins showed an interest in my report on the occurrences in Nyasaland, for it boded ill for the success of the Federation. The report outlined the difficult task facing the Nyasaland authorities in trying to maintain law and order; it illustrated the differences in tactics and principles of the Police contingents from Northern Rhodesia, Southern Rhodesia and Nyasaland, holding out little prospect for a common approach to internal security, let alone the possibility of acceptable 'Joint Operations' within the three Federal territories; and it portrayed the precarious position of a handful of whites who favoured the concept of Federation but who formed an insignificant part of one of the densest masses of population in Africa south of the equator.

The stirrings of African nationalism which had begun further to the north of us led Police GHQ to instruct me to go to Kenya to study the Mau Mau insurrection, something which was causing great concern to

white governments throughout Africa. The blacks, in their pursuit of
freedom through the arcane Mau Mau organisation (the very name
'Mau Mau' had a hidden meaning), were poles apart from the whites
who communicated with their fellow countrymen – if they communicated at all – through a bastard Swahili rather than Kikuyu or English.
My brother, a farmer in Kenya, had fallen victim to this lack of communication and was doing time in Nyeri gaol for shooting and wound-
ing two of his labourers 'to make them talk' about their association with
Mau Mau guerrillas.

Everything that could be learnt about the causes, consequences and
handling of the Mau Mau insurgency was recorded, and a series of
lectures and training demonstrations was prepared for delivery throughout Southern Rhodesia. A new Police (Field) Reserve was formed to
operate in the rural areas, together with a Police Reserve Air Wing
comprising farmers who could fly at will from their own backyards and
report on anything untoward happening around them. Counter-
insurgency training for all Rhodesian Security Forces was adapted
according to the lessons learnt in Kenya. For example, the Royal Rhodesian Air Force was more appropriately equipped and trained in counter-
insurgency than had been the case with the Royal Air Force in Kenya
which, through its use of 'pattern-bombing' in the Aberdare Mountains,
had wounded more rhinoceros than members of Mau Mau.

By this time I was fully committed to a role in counter-insurgency,
serving first as Chief Staff Officer to the Police Reserve and, subsequently, as Officer Commanding, Manicaland Province and then OC Salisbury. An entry in my diary on 9 January 1961, two months before my
appointment as Deputy Commissioner of the BSAP, gives a taste of the
stirrings of nationalism we were now facing inside our own borders.

In February 1959 we put 500 leading nationalists in the bag in 'Op Spider' – the
biggest operation of its kind to date, and as near as dammit 100 per cent
successful, allowing for the fact that Nkomo was out of the country at the time
so that his 'Youth' could cause mayhem 'to create a crisis in Southern Rhodesia'
to accord with Nkomo's allegations at the United Nations!

Police work in Salisbury had its excitements: it certainly had its responsibilities, as for instance when we saved Sir Edgar [Whitehead] from being lynched
by arranging his undignified exit through a kitchen window in Highfields: and
when we stopped 'The March of 7000 on Salisbury' in July 1960 peacefully, and
when I could be proud of my officers who could still make a mob laugh rather
than allow it to go on the rampage [Mugabe appeared on the local scene for the
first time, making a reasoned address to the 7000 under difficult circumstances].
But the BSA Police lost its unique record of not firing a shot in anger in
Rhodesia this century [I had lost it for them in Nyasaland!]. One riot succeeded
another. Week by week we stood by with a growing sense of futility … I'm full

of foreboding, all we seem to be doing is trying vainly to stem the tide of black nationalism ... Then, sadness: Olga's mother died when we were about to move into our new home and our own occupation of it was frustrated by my transfer to 'Commandant, Depot' where I had to live-in. A strange Germanic title – putting me in charge of recruitment, training and ceremonial – but giving me my last serious exercise in horsemanship when I commanded three Royal Escorts for the Queen Mother when she came to open Kariba Dam.

Sir Edgar Whitehead had succeeded Todd as Prime Minister in 1958 and was showing great interest in all aspects of Security and Intelligence. Until the formation of the Federation, Security and Intelligence in Southern Rhodesia had been the sole responsibility of the BSAP. Intelligence was a responsibility acquired through practice or simply because no one else could handle the subject, whereas the responsibility for Internal Security was derived from the Police Act, although the recently formed Army took over that responsibility if a situation developed to a point where it was beyond the power of the BSAP to keep it under control.

The establishment of the Federation saw the formation of the Federal Intelligence and Security Bureau (FISB), headed by Bob de Quehen. De Quehen had served as an officer in the BSAP but, more recently, had been employed by the British MI5, under Sir Percy Sillitoe, also ex-BSAP. De Quehen's appointment as Director of FISB made it clear that liaison between the BSAP and MI5 was an essential part of his functioning. But his task was complicated because the Police Force in each of the three territories retained responsibility for Intelligence and Internal Security within its own territory. FISB was not empowered to collect Intelligence in its own right and was thus dependent on the three Police Forces; its principle function was to co-ordinate Intelligence and to serve as a 'Bureau'.

This state of affairs did not appeal to Whitehead. The increase in African nationalist activity after the Nyasaland 'Emergency' and the consequent deterioration in internal security prompted him to seek advice on how to establish an organisation which would serve the Prime Minister directly with Intelligence and with advice on all aspects of internal security, both in the territorial and Federal spheres. He discussed the subject with local officials, myself included, and then decided to enlist the services of British experts. As a result, Sir Roger Hollis, then Director of MI5, visited Southern Rhodesia in 1961, and in 1962 General Sir Douglas Packard was invited to conduct a survey of the BSAP and of related Internal Security matters.

In May 1962 I returned from three months' leave overseas to find the run-up to the December general election well under way. Packard's survey was also under way, but things were not going as smoothly as the Commissioner of Police, B. G. Spurling, would have wished. Against the advice of myself and the other Deputy Commissioner, F. E. 'Slash' Barfoot, Spurling had agreed to the survey in the belief that it would show him up in a favourable light, not realising that a military man from overseas would find much to criticise in the way a Police Force was run in Africa.

Spurling was due to retire and, following tradition, was paying farewell visits to all the Police Stations. What was not traditional, and what brought him considerable criticism, was that he attempted to use these visits for political purposes. I wrote in my diary at the time:

Sunday 6th May 1962: [Spurling] has been using his farewell visits to Police Stations throughout the country to address our now considerable Police Reserve [30,000 whites with an influence over all their families] – warning them that if Sir Edgar Whitehead's government is returned to power this will be the end of Rhodesia . . .

By taking advantage of such a large captive audience to preach politics and using the authority of his position on the subject of Internal Security, it is my belief that Spurling was as responsible as any other single Southern Rhodesian for getting the Rhodesian Front (RF) into power in December 1962. The African nationalist leader, Joshua Nkomo, was another decisive influence. By persuading the African voters on the 'B' Roll to boycott the elections he virtually ensured Whitehead's defeat, for it swung the balance of political power from moderate-white to the extremism of the RF.

Spurling's successor had not yet been named. Packard, just prior to his departure, advised me that he had submitted a secret report to Whitehead recommending that I should take over the Force as soon as possible. But the election was then only a few weeks away and the recommendation was put into cold storage. On the night of 14 December 1962 I was at the Government Information Centre in the Ambassador Hotel, Salisbury. My companion was the Army Commander, Major-General 'Jock' Anderson. The election results were coming in and when the outcome became apparent – victory for the newly formed RF – we commiserated with each other in the belief that Southern Rhodesia, as we knew it, had ended. The RF had introduced two new features into Southern Rhodesian politics: a 'cowboy element', from which many of their candidates were drawn; and blatant intimidation of political opponents.

It now seemed unlikely that Packard's recommendation would be implemented. Within days of the election victory I was advised by Jack Pithey, the Secretary for Justice, that Clifford Dupont would hold the dual portfolios of Law and Order (responsible for Police affairs) and Justice and that he would almost certainly appoint Barfoot, the senior Deputy, to the position of Commissioner of Police.

The RF government took several months to settle in. As one of their Cabinet Ministers put it: 'Only Winston Field and Ian Smith have been active in politics, and no one in our party has ever held public office.' Field, the new Prime Minister, studied Whitehead's plans for a State Intelligence and Security Organisation and then instructed the Armed Forces, Police and selected Heads of Ministries (Internal Affairs, Law and Order, Justice, Defence and External Affairs) to form a working party to prepare for such an organisation. I, as the Police representative, and the other members of the working party considered the British recommendations and looked at local requirements. It soon became apparent how difficult it is to get a group of otherwise friendly officials to agree on the subject of Intelligence, something none of us knew much about and yet all of us needed. The Army was adamant that the control of Intelligence should be removed from the Police; Law and Order wanted control for themselves; Internal Affairs insisted that they should have a vital part in it; External Affairs tended to be good on theory but poor on the practical applications of their theories; the Air Force displayed a wider and more practical grasp of the subject than most of the others; and the basic attitude of Police Headquarters was to leave things as they were. My belief was that an organisation could be formed which would satisfy the requirements of all interested parties provided that Police Special Branch, as. the primary internal intelligence-gathering agency, was an integral part of it.

The working party reached some measure of agreement after three or four months of deliberations and submitted its recommendations. While they went through the labyrinthine channels of separate Ministries to the Prime Minister, I settled down to life as Deputy Commissioner and noted in my diary: '24th May 1963: Spurling has gone to South Africa. Life under "Slash" is much improved, and he has accorded me special status as the unquestioned second-in-command of the Force.'

My respite was shortlived. In mid-August I received a peremptory command to report to the Prime Minister at his official residence. Without preliminaries, Field put the proposition to me that I should head a new Security and Intelligence organisation to be established upon the dissolution of the Federation on 31 December 1963 and that I should begin work immediately on setting it up. I was given forty-eight hours to make up my mind. My acceptance of the offer was greeted with some dismay by my wife and the few friends who realised that as Head of a Secret Service I would become a non-person. But none of us had foreseen that I would disappear into almost total obscurity for the following eighteen years.

I knew next to nothing about Intelligence. I had said as much to Winston Field when he offered me the job and he had replied: 'Nor does anyone else, but it's time we learnt.' A personal contract of service was drawn up between the Prime Minister and myself, to run for five years in the first instance. The most vital clause of the contract was that I should be responsible directly to the Prime Minister and, to facilitate this, the new organisation, entitled the Central Intelligence Organisation (CIO), was to be 'hidden' as 'The Department of the Prime Minister'. Its finances were to be controlled by the Secretary to the Prime Minister, the Secretary to the Treasury and myself as Director; parliamentary sanction for expenditure was to be obtained through a 'one-line-entry' on the Prime Minister's vote. In effect, then, we were following the British rather than the American system in that the name, function and head of the organisation were to be kept secret as far as possible.

Before committing CIO to any particular direction, I considered it essential to study Intelligence systems elsewhere in the world, starting with Britain. Field did not take the suggestion kindly. 'What can you learn from others that we cannot do better ourselves?' he asked. Like the bulk of his party he had developed an antipathy towards anything British, but when I outlined the reasons why I should go to Britain first – that they probably had the best Intelligence system in the world, that through FISB and other liaisons they were pre-eminent in our region and that I believed they would be willing to offer assistance – he assented, saying that I could 'learn from their mistakes'.

My diary recounts a little of my first sortie, under British patronage, into the world of Intelligence:

22.9.63 I flew to London to get an insight into the workings of British Intelligence, Scotland Yard and Special Branch. It was a fascinating three weeks, and I was fortunate that Sir Joseph Simpson, Commissioner of the Metropolitan Police, invited me to his home so that I could chat to the Commissioner of the Royal Canadian Mounted Police as well, concerning their set-up which operates through a national Police Force (which the British lack but which would appear to be closer to what we need in Rhodesia). The Head of M16 thought we should aim at something like the Canadian system.

I learnt a tremendous amount on this trip and met some fascinating characters who helped me to get an insight into how the gamekeepers (M15) and the poachers (M16) work [the main function of M15, the Security Service, is to preserve the nation's secrets and concentrate on Counter-Intelligence; M16, the Secret Intelligence Service, operates abroad to acquire Intelligence by any means, particularly from hostile nations] ... The senior British officers I met impressed tremendously, as did the Commissioner of the RCMP; and I was lucky enough to bump into Sir Ivor Stourton, Inspector-General of the Colonial Police.... Discussing our new organisation, the British remain convinced that we would be wrong in trying to integrate Special Branch into CIO, as the Head of SB could not be expected to 'wear two hats', one to the Commissioner of Police and one to myself.

The British insistence that Special Branch should be kept separate from other arms of Intelligence was based upon their experience of the suspicions and rivalries that can develop between one service and another. The British Special Branch, for example, appeared to trust no one; M16 personnel in particular, because of their role as 'poachers', had to avoid Special Branch. I later unearthed something of the same suspicions at home between the BSAP, Special Branch and other or-ganisations. The lack of liaison between our Special Branch and FISB extended almost to the point of sabotaging each other's efforts, while the distrust of the Police by the Army, FISB and certain Ministries amounted to the strongest antipathy against any form of 'police' control of the new organisation.

In the event, fitting Special Branch into CIO was made easier by my retention on the Police seniority roll, as 'Deputy Commissioner', for the following six years and by the ability of Bill Crabtree, OC Special Branch, to wear two hats – not least because of his ebullient character and his extravagant mop of hair. Although it was the government's wish that Special Branch be removed from the Police and incorporated *in toto* within CIO, the Commissioner of Police and I considered that we would be better served if Special Branch retained its Internal Security function within the Police and transferred its Intelligence function to CIO.

The practical application of this compromise was that Special Branch Headquarters were incorporated within CIO but all Provincial, District and Station units continued to work jointly with Police, which meant that Police would still benefit from Special Branch functioning but Spe-cial Branch Intelligence would be readily available to CIO. Generally speaking, this arrangement, which lasted until 1980 and was unique in the Intelligence world, worked like a charm.

Before returning home from London, I had a brief look at the French and Portuguese systems. Whatever prestige they had seemed to depend upon the personality, even the charisma, of the head of their organisa-tions, while their effectiveness depended upon the head's personal relationship with the political ruler of the country. In time, I became better acquainted with Continental systems but at that stage I learnt enough to see that those systems were not particularly suited to our requirements because of the dominance of the military and the very different role performed by their police.

I realised that in my report to Field I would have to mention something of British 'mistakes'. The most compelling fact that I could put down was that British Intelligence works in spite of mistakes and relies to some extent on the Briton's well-known flair for improvisation. The British have acquired expertise through being first in the field; they insist upon quality, not quantity, in their personnel; they provide a thorough training; and they demand an exceptionally high standard of integrity and dedication to duty from those who serve them. In short, the British are still the best in the world at the Intelligence game, but so much of it must remain a closed book, or it is no longer 'Intelligence'.

Certainly, there are aspects of the British system which detract from efficiency, such as the fact that MI5 are kept separate from MI6 (similarly, in the United States of America the CIA as an organisation is kept separate from the FBI, DIA and all the ramifications of the military system). But efficiency is not everything. In some respects the KGB is the most efficient Intelligence organisation in the world, but a secret service modelled on KGB lines – that is, dominated by State apparatus and used entirely by and for the State as an instrument of power – lacks the fluidity of more democratic systems, and we did not wish to spawn that sort of monster in Rhodesia. We needed an organisation that would best serve the *national* interest and be beyond the narrow reach of politicians.

Field's response to the report was, in essence, that we should get on with setting up the new organisation. With the wealth of information and advice now at my disposal I prepared a 'Top Secret Mandate' for CIO. The composition and functions of the organisation were to be based upon British expertise, American adaptation and the observance of local requirements; CIO would attempt to emulate or improve upon the inter-service functioning seen in London and Washington and would try to avoid building as monolithic a structure as the USSR's KGB. In discussion with government law officers and Gerald Clarke, the Secretary to the Prime Minister, it was considered preferable for CIO to operate under a Prime Minister's Mandate rather than seek legislation in Parliament. The Mandate was signed by Field in October 1963 and issued to Ministers and Heads of Ministries. Its salient points were:

CIO should be known as 'The Department of the Prime Minister' whose first responsibility was safeguarding the security of the State.

CIO, and only CIO, should co-ordinate all Intelligence acquired from internal, external and liaison sources. No body other than CIO should engage specifically in the collection of Intelligence, and any Intelligence acquired by other Services or Ministries during the course of their functioning, or otherwise, should be passed forthwith to CIO.

CIO was to consist of eleven Branches, the important ones being:

Branch I (Internal) – the name given to Special Branch of the BSAP – was to be responsible for the acquisition and co-ordination of all internal Intelligence but should cease all external operations; it was also to be responsible for counter-subversion and counter-intelligence.

Branch II (External) was to be responsible for acquiring Intelligence in the international sphere, for liaison with foreign Services and for the operation of specialist Divisions, such as 'Evaluation', 'Collection', 'Economics' and 'Communications'.

Branch III was to be responsible for Military Intelligence (the headquarters of the Director of Military Intelligence and the Director of Air Plans were later incorporated into CIO and the title of Head of CIO was advanced to Director-General to encompass the various Directors in the organisation).

Branch IV (Government Telecommunications Agency) was to be responsible for encyphering and decyphering.

Branch V (Close Security) was to be responsible for the protection of VIP's.

Branch VI (Government Protective Security) was to be responsible for the protection of key points.

Although the Mandate required that Special Branch divest itself of all external functioning, we soon found this to be a retrogressive step and I granted Special Branch permission to continue its external activity, rather than allow an otherwise systematic investigation to be halted at an international border and passed into other hands, resulting in a loss of efficiency. Other than mentioning to the Prime Minister what I had done, no Ministry or Service was consulted, an indication of the freedom of action I was given by Winston Field.

With the structure and responsibilities of Special Branch settled, I found that there was no need for FISB as a separate 'Bureau'. At the specific request of Field and Sir Roy Welensky, who had succeeded Huggins as Federal Prime Minister in 1957, all serving personnel in FISB were given the option of service within CIO or transfer to British,

South African or other Intelligence agencies; however, De Quehen, the Director of FISB, was expressly excluded from re-employment by both Prime Ministers, presumably because of his links with British Intelligence. Most FISB personnel elected to join CIO, but four of them, without reference to us, chose to continue their careers in Military Intelligence in South Africa; they later suffered ignominious discharge when the South African authorities realised that these four had ignored the gentleman's agreement between our services to accept only inter-service recommendations. This incident, and the exclusion of de Quehen from the offer to join CIO, illustrates the extreme sensitivity and suspicion with which any Intelligence Officer will be treated by any other government or service, whether friendly or not.

During the earliest stages of establishing CIO we sought advice not only from abroad but also from internal sources, including Prime Ministers past and present. Such a course was encouraged by Winston Field. From the outset he had made it clear that his first objective was to achieve national unity. His tolerance of opinions that differed from his own extended across political and racial lines. Autocratic and right-wing though he was, he displayed a rare knowledge of African nationalism and was personally acquainted with many of its leaders. I had noticed this some months prior to my appointment when, accompanying him to his farm near Marandellas, he talked of certain nationalists living in the area over which we were flying. Describing Josiah Chinamano as a 'worthy man', he ventured the opinion that both Chinamano and Nathan Shamuyarira would be 'Government Ministers in this country one day'. Such a prophecy was far removed from the comprehension of most of his RF colleagues. And it was Field, alone, who struck up a lasting friendship with Dr Hastings Banda while the latter was detained in Gwelo gaol. I remember clearly an occasion in later years when Banda exclaimed: 'As far as Sir Roy Welensky was concerned my reaction was "To Hell with Federation!" But my dear friend Winston laid the foundations of Rhodesia's link with Malawi. Without him there would have been nothing between our two countries and you, Ken Flower, would not have been speaking to me now if it had not been for Winston Field!'

Field displayed a tolerance towards non-RF whites that would cost him dear. For instance, early in his premiership he appointed Evan Campbell (whom he had personally defeated in the Marandellas constituency in the 1962 elections) as High Commissioner in London; and Jack Quinton, a Minister in Whitehead's government, was given the appointment supervising development in the south-eastern Lowveld. Field made it clear to me that he wished me to cultivate the acquaintance

of earlier Prime Ministers so that I could learn from them. From time to time he sent me to see Lord Malvern, Sir Roy Welensky and Sir Edgar Whitehead. In contrast, his party colleagues showed no inclination to have anything to do with men they considered to be 'failed politicians' and probably thought Field's attitude showed that he was living more in the past than was good for him.

In Malvern's case I was dealing with a man who for a quarter of a century had kept the country on an even keel whilst holding the British at bay – a man who must surely have known most of the answers. Unlike his successors, Malvern knew how to handle British governments; a doctor by profession, he was as much at home in Harley Street, London as he was in North Avenue, Salisbury and he treated successive British governments with the same patronage with which he treated his patients.

Welensky, during my visits to him, behaved true to form. As Prime Minister of the Federation he had not visited Nyasaland because the British Governor in Zomba was not to his liking and because he would have felt ill-at-ease in a 'black' state. But he did offer some useful advice, particularly on the shortcomings of FISB. I remember him saying: 'In the early days of Federation, I felt I must rely on my Intelligence advisers ... but I learnt as time went by that their reports were cotton wool without substance, so hedged about with "ifs" and "buts" that I found it impossible to form any conclusions, let alone make a policy decision on them. What is the use of Intelligence unless a government can rely on it for the formulation of policy?' He implored me not to follow the same path of 'make-believe' but to be positive always, saying: 'For surely, if you are wrong some of the time you'll be right the rest of the time and it is much better to provide a positive service with mistakes than no service at all.'

In those days I could not offer any opinion but subsequent experience showed that Welensky's comments might apply only to a government that wished to use Intelligence as a positive asset; too many politicians prefer to have facts that please and are unlikely to concern themselves with anything unpalatable.

Unlike Malvern, Welensky had never been in tune with London; nor had London been in tune with Welensky. The same had applied to Whitehead and Todd. Whitehead was seen in London as having fascist tendencies and yet was perhaps the most liberal of all Rhodesian Prime Ministers, while Todd, subsequently considered 'liberal' by London when he became a victim of the Rhodesian Law and Order Maintenance Act, had evinced a surprising readiness to use 'maximum' rather than 'minimum' force when quelling African disturbances. But both Todd and Whitehead were undermined by obstructive officialdom within Rhodesia and a misunderstanding in London of the true nature of Rhodesian politics. And no serious effort was made in London to settle Rhodesia's future until Ian Smith, the most right-wing Prime Minister of all, threatened UDI.

My visits to Whitehead were on the explicit instructions that the Leader of the Opposition should receive regular Intelligence briefings, a courtesy which had been extended to Field himself while in Opposition. I saw Whitehead on several occasions in his office in Parliament Building. We would go through a routine of no great consequence: I would outline the impending threat of African nationalism while he would regale me with accounts of how he had been undermined in his 'Build a Nation' campaign. (The multiracial motivation essential in that campaign had been crudely represented by enthusiastic amateurs and was premature in its concept. Certainly, Whitehead had meant well but his timing was wrong and he was a poor judge of men, which resulted in a bad choice of lieutenants; moreover, his habit of conducting government business late at night at his home, with the beer flowing freely among his bachelor cronies, left his political supporters nonplussed and antagonised the more rigid disciplinarians among the officials who were frequently summoned for discussion in the small hours when the Prime Minister was less coherent than he should have been.)

Although my visits to Whitehead ended usually in sad and sorry recriminations, they were valuable in terms of Field's search for national unity. But they were not to last. Shortly after Field's dismissal, stories were passed by parliamentarians and others that I was 'consorting with the Opposition' and that Whitehead was using the information I passed to him for political purposes. In no time at all the convention was broken, never to be renewed.

From August 1963 until the dissolution of the Federation at the end of that year our new Intelligence organisation began to take shape. It was fortunate in being able to start from scratch with full government backing, thus ensuring maximum co-operation from all arms of government. And it was fortunate in its personnel in that they had acquired a wide enough experience of the ways of the world to get their perspectives and priorities right, to know how to sort out the wheat from the chaff without having to report to government just for the sake of it. They worked hard to produce an independent, self-reliant organisation within which we could concentrate on the true nature of Intelligence, rather than one which was over-concerned with the fictional world of spies, defectors and the fanciful use of 'cloak and dagger'.

In January 1964, just a few weeks after CIO's official birth, Field put before it a little test to see how well it was faring. He had listened to my accounts of Welensky's poor opinion of the service he had received from FISB and had asked what percentage of success the British expected in Intelligence assessments. To my reply that a 60 per cent success rate was considered satisfactory he had retorted: 'You'll be no good to me unless you're right at least 80 per cent of the time.' He was about to visit Britain and demanded that I give him something of consequence to lay before the British Prime Minister. We racked our brains but could think of nothing the British would not know better than ourselves. Field would not take this for an answer, so in desperation I showed him a report from an untried source of ours in Dar-es-Salaam. The report indicated that the Tanzanian Armed Forces were about to mutiny. I suggested to Field that he try this out on the British, tentatively, but to my horror he went considerably further and tendered the report as an authoritative assessment. On reaching London he cabled me, seeking confirmation of the report, for the British had told him they had no knowledge of such an eventuality although they were better placed in Dar-es-Salaam than we were. I cabled back: 'Confirmed as far as we are able.'

The mutiny in Tanzania occurred before Field left London and he set off back to Africa tickled pink that his fledglings had shown the British up in British Africa. He chose the long route home, travelling by sea to the Cape, perhaps because he was despondent about his failure to get the British government to agree to work towards a settlement that would guarantee independence for Rhodesia. The extra time spent away from home may have contributed to his downfall. He arrived back in Salisbury to find the rug pulled from under his feet.

CHAPTER 2

The Fall of Field and the Advent of Smith

I handed the letter to Ian Smith. He read it and then, to give himself more time, he read it again. He looked up from the letter and said quietly: 'Do you think I would stab my leader in the back when he has trusted me to hold the fort for him?'

It was early 1964. Field had not yet returned from London and Smith was Acting Prime Minister. The letter in question had been sent to CIO, and its author, who chose to remain anonymous, wrote that the RF caucus would take advantage of Field's absence to have him replaced by Smith. It seemed advisable to show Smith the letter and get his reaction; he might have been able to identify the author who, judging from the letter's contents, was privy to political secrets which were kept from officials such as myself.

This was my first official meeting with Ian Smith. In answer to his question, which left me somewhat nonplussed, I replied: 'Prime Minister, I know nothing at all about this. I just presumed you would know whether the allegation is truthful or not. You are privy to party politics, I am not. You have said publicly that your party keeps its own secrets and I am not probing for secrets. It is just that my colleagues in CIO are worried about the implications of the letter and have urged me to discuss it with you.'

This sort of unconvincing conversation went on for a while, and then we dropped the subject. But Smith offered no denial, and I left his office convinced that he was going to do just what he himself had put to me – stab his leader in the back.

This was not exactly the best way for us to start our political, let alone personal, relationship, but politics is a dirty game and I realised later that I should not have shown my concern or naivety as I did.

A few days after this meeting with Smith I received a visit from two Deputy Ministers, Lance Smith and Andrew Dunlop. The purpose of their mission was to persuade me that their party was taking the right course in replacing Winston Field by Ian Smith. Lance Smith and I had matured together as Mounted Corporals in the BSAP and no doubt it was because of this friendship that he had been deputed to see me; Andrew Dunlop, an officer and a gentleman, always honourable though sometimes misguided, believed passionately that Field should go in favour of Smith, whom he subsequently revered as the 'saviour of Rhodesia'. My visitors hoped that, should they win me over, I would in turn satisfy the Commanders and the Heads of Ministries that a change in leadership would be in the national interest. I was not convinced, and told them so. Their party had come to power under the umbrella of Winston Field and, in the opinion of CIO, most of the electorate who had favoured the RF had voted for the leader rather than the party. Smith and Dunlop did not dispute this. What they did dispute was my suggestion that a change in leadership might split the white electorate at a time when unity was needed. However, I had to concede that the decision was essentially a political one and that people like myself should not try to influence it one way or the other. The real reason why Field had to go, as subsequent events showed, was to clear the way for UDI, a subject not even mentioned by my visitors.

Outside the RF caucus, no man in Rhodesia knew more about what was going on within the RF at that time than the South African Diplomatic Representative in Salisbury, Daantjie Olivier. Since the RF had come to power there was hardly a government Minister who did not frequent Olivier's home in Salisbury; his popularity rested partly on the fact that he had the ear of the South African Prime Minister at a time when Rhodesia was shifting her political association from Britain to South Africa. Prior to Field's trip to Britain, Olivier had commented to me that the Prime Minister 'sticks out like a sore thumb in his own Cabinet'. During Field's absence he advised me that the Prime Minister would return to find his Cabinet 'hell bent on UDI' and suggested that perhaps 'this is why he is keeping out of the way'.

In March, shortly after Field's return, I reported to the Governor, Sir Humphrey Gibbs, what I understood to be happening. Gibbs already knew, and said he had tried to persuade Field to resist dismissal or go to the country to seek a new mandate from the electorate, which we agreed he would almost certainly obtain. But Field seemed to have lost heart and would do neither.

On the weekend of 11/12 April I flew with Gibbs to the bombing range at Kabanga, near Thornhill Air Station, to watch an Air Force demonstration of fire power. Also on board was Jack Howman, Minister of Internal Affairs. Field should have attended in his capacity as Minister of Defence but he withdrew at the last moment. The news was out. During the trip Howman made no secret of his intention to resign in sympathy with Field, whose dismissal now appeared more imminent than I had realised.

Early on the morning of Monday 13 April I received a call from the Prime Minister's Secretary, asking me to go to the Prime Minister's office immediately. Field explained forthwith that this was his last day in office, that he had already packed to go and that all that remained was to hand over to me the 'Top Secret' papers in his safe. I told him of the approach made to me by Lance Smith and Andrew Dunlop, and he commented tartly that Lance Smith had been one of the ringleaders agitating for his removal. I asked why he had not resisted dismissal or gone to the country. He replied that he could never do another Garfield Todd. The memory of that was so fresh in everyone's mind that he could not be seen to be fighting his own party as Todd tried to do. (In 1957 Todd's Cabinet had sought his dismissal, whereupon Todd had sought their resignations, which were not offered; the dispute went to the party caucus and to Congress where, after much in-fighting, Whitehead was chosen as the new party leader.)

Field thanked me for my services and handed over the papers, saying that they were mostly the memoranda, including my own, prepared by Heads of Ministries and others on the probable consequences of taking UDI. I would see for myself that the consensus of opinion was over-whelmingly against UDI, and he had made it clear to his colleagues that he would not take the responsibility as Prime Minister to declare UDI against all the weight of professional advice in the papers. Other reasons might be given for his dismissal but he wanted me to know that this was the real reason why he was going. Admittedly, it must be a political decision in the end, but what he was saying was that he was not pre-pared to take that decision against official advice on a subject as impor-tant as UDI.

Many other reasons, such as Field's state of health and the loss of confidence in his leadership, were subsequently produced to explain his departure. Obviously, the truth of the matter could not be aired because UDI was not at that stage a declared issue. Like the gentleman he was, Field merely made a brief statement to the Press that 'serious disagree-ments' had arisen between himself and his party. Through his refusal to fight and his decision to remain in Parliament as a backbencher, thereby stilling any speculation that he no longer supported party policies, his departure was made to look more like a resignation than a dismissal.

As far as the majority of the RF were concerned, Field was an estab-lishment figure and they were opposed to what the old establishment stood for; he had failed in July 1963 and again in January 1964 to advance the cause of independence during his visits to Britain and when they became aware that he would not support UDI it was too much for them. He had served his purpose in getting them into power. Now he was expendable.

In private discussion with various R F Ministers, I learnt that another grievance they harboured against Field was his decision to attend the 1963 conference at Victoria Falls convened by the British to discuss the dissolution of the Federation. They considered that Field had acted against party principles by agreeing to attend without insisting on a prior guarantee of independence for Rhodesia in the aftermath of the break up of the Federation, and they were among the sources of the many lies subsequently spread on this subject. Field, however, as I knew only too well from my discussions with him, had been under no illusions concerning British intentions. He knew, as did his Ministers, that no British government would guarantee Rhodesia's independence without some significant constitutional changes. He had been informed by R. A. Butler and other prominent members of the British government that they would proceed with the dissolution of the Federation and the granting of independence to Malawi and Zambia, the other two territories of the Federation, whether or not Field attended, though they would prefer it if he were there. Field believed he must attend in order to get the best deal he could for Rhodesia – a fair division of the Armed Forces, the railways, Air Rhodesia and the Central African Power Corporation – which, in the event, he managed to achieve.

If one sought other reasons for Field's dismissal they might be found in his character. His quick temper and his intolerance of 'fools' made him an unsuitable leader of the R F. His tendency to ignore his colleagues when making appointments such as Evan Campbell's and Jack Quinton's and his 'new approach' to racial matters, such as ordering the release of African nationalists from detention, had upset the party.

But, as Field himself said during my meeting with him on his last day in office, the only significant reason for his dismissal was his objection to U D I. At the end of that meeting we shook hands and parted sadly. I, at least, was a wiser man when I returned to the same office later that week to pay my respects to the new Prime Minister, Ian Smith.

My continuity in office as the Prime Minister's Intelligence and Security adviser seemed assured, for by this time it was known that I had no political axe to grind. Much of C I O's time was now devoted to studying the constitutional causes and political justification for U D I. As to the consequences, the same prognosis continued to be made: that U D I would be unlikely to succeed and that it was an unnecessary risk to take, when to negotiate constitutionally or to do nothing at all involved much lesser risks. Field's dismissal, then, had not improved Government's chances of making UDI a success; it had served only to harden their determination to take it despite all risks.

The main motivation for UDI was, of course, the preservation and entrenchment of white rule and, to this end, British 'interference' had to be removed. The politicians sought to persuade the electorate that Britain had reneged on a promise of independence and would continue to interfere in Rhodesia's internal affairs unless the country became independent. In doing so, they misrepresented the true nature of that 'interference'.

The legislative powers reserved by Britain in the 1923 Constitution had largely fallen into disuse; an inter-government convention had developed whereby the Southern Rhodesian government tested acceptance in London before submitting 'reserved' legislation for British government approval and, according to any objections raised, the legislation was then amended or withdrawn. As a result of this convention, confrontation on constitutional issues had been avoided and no British government had considered it appropriate to legislate for Southern Rhodesia. A further reduction in British power had been agreed in the 1961 Constitution, on the condition that the franchise was extended, thus bringing the prospect of black rule nearer. According to Whitehead, this extension of the franchise would produce the first black Prime Minister by about 1979, but this was a mathematician's solution to a political problem and no one could be quite sure when such parliamentary advancement would be reached.

Since 1961, Britain had insisted that there should be a built-in guarantee that an independence Constitution for Rhodesia could not be tampered with after independence. The Rhodesian politicians' response to this was that they would not be seen to have achieved genuine independence if there were to be constraints after independence. Subsequently, the British had introduced a requirement that the proposed amendments to the 1961 Constitution would have to be 'acceptable to the people of Rhodesia as a whole' but no Rhodesian government was prepared to grant the African majority a veto on such a vital issue as the country's Constitution. As far as most of the electorate were concerned, Whitehead had gone far enough in 1961 by providing for universal education and the removal of some racial discrimination (repeal of the Industrial Conciliation Act and declaring public swimming baths multiracial); and he had gone too far in his concept of 'partnership' and the creation of an African middle class when he declared his intention to repeal the Land Apportionment Act, the cornerstone of white rule in Rhodesia.

While the response of the R F government to British proposals was to
dig its heels in, the response of the African nationalists, who had seen
their counterparts in Zambia and Malawi achieve independence on far
more favourable terms than Rhodesia's whites were likely to come up
with, was to coerce the British government through violence or the
threat of violence. Black resistance to white rule in Rhodesia had grown
since 1959, leading to widespread disorders in urban areas and convincing the white electorate that the country was not far removed from a
state of anarchy. It was the prospect of anarchy – such as that which
reigned in the Belgian Congo after the precipitate granting of independence in 1961 had caused many whites there to seek refuge in Rhodesia –
that had frightened many Rhodesians into voting for the R F in 1962.

The R F politicians showed themselves to be adept at exploiting the
fears of white Rhodesians, thus providing the emotional cause from
which grew the euphoria for U D I. It is my belief that the politicians
realised that there was no honest cause for U D I. Significantly, they never
fought an election or by-election with U D I as an issue. On the contrary,
from Ian Smith down, the R F asserted time and again on public platforms that 'in all honesty' they had no intention of taking U D I. And they
could not ventilate what was undoubtedly their unavowed purpose – to
move towards apartheid, for which U D I was an essential prerequisite.
So they fabricated a cause, and thereafter it grew as an exercise in
deception. They played particularly on the fear that to leave Rhodesia's
future in the hands of 'Once Great Britain' would precipitate black rule,
adding that one had only to look at the countries to the north to see
what black rule meant. They reminded Rhodesians of their proud record
of service in support of the Empire and Commonwealth in two World
Wars, for which Britain now showed her gratitude by turning against
them. They exploited the white electorate's sense of grievance that
Rhodesia, which had been self-governing for forty years and which had
probably made a better job of government than any other British colony,
was less well treated at the break-up of Federation than the less advanced northern territories.

But they omitted to mention the obvious contradictions that arose
from this complaint: if Rhodesia was genuinely self-governing and had
made a good job of it – an efficient and incorruptible Civil Service, a
buoyant economy and so on – what need was there for independence?
And if there was a need, why had it not been satisfied during all those
decades of self-government? In the light of such contradictions, many
experts have attempted to explain the R F's drive for and eventual gaining of U D I. My belief is that U D I grew out of frustration which burst

like a boil on the body politic; but, as indicated above, the cause of that frustration was not genuine. Dr Huggins probably came nearest to the truth when he offered this diagnosis: 'UDI becomes a piece of madness, a sort of collective rush of blood to the head, which cannot be explained by rational means at all.' (Quoted in Robert Blake's *History of Rhodesia*, London 1977.)

To understand a little of the 'madness' which led to UDI, one must look at the men who made UDI happen. Before the Second World War many white Rhodesians, including Field, fitted into that category so well described by Harold Macmillan as resembling the planter aristocracy in the Southern States before the American Civil War. In the decade after the war, however, the nature of Rhodesian white society changed dramatically with the influx of immigrants from Kenya, India and Britain. The white population almost doubled; the old spirit of adventure and discovery and the sense of guardianship over the indigenous people was replaced by a desire to seek a more privileged life than that in Britain in the aftermath of war and a determination to avoid the fate of whites in Kenya and India.

Whereas most whites in pre-war Rhodesia had been content to leave politics to 'Good Old Huggie' for a quarter of a century of uneventful government, many of the new immigrants tended to be much more politically conscious. They took the parliamentary system by the scruff of the neck and introduced an edge to Rhodesian politics which had never been there before. They had no real pretensions to the 'Rhodesia' we knew and they shared a suspicion of all things British and a disdain for all things black.

In the RF caucus they were represented by Clifford Dupont, a lawyer from London; Bill Harper, known as a 'Bengal Chancer'; Andrew Dunlop, of the Argylls; and P. K. van der Byl, a scion of one of South Africa's oldest families, from Her Majesty's 7th Hussars and with a reputation for dalliance with aristocratic ladies. There were others, but they tended to be less motivated and were easily led by Dupont, Harper, Dunlop and van der Byl. Among the few members of the caucus who were 'real' Rhodesians were Jack Howman, from one of the country's most respected families (but he resigned with Winston Field); Ian Smith, who was born in the country (but he was thoroughly orientated towards white South Africa); Desmond Lardner-Burke, a South African who had been in the country for thirty years (but his anti-black sentiments outraged even the South Africans); Lance Smith, ex-BSAP (but now a hardline farmer); and Lord Angus Graham, one of Kipling's 'White Men' if ever there was one.

The RF out-politicked their opponents, and their dismissal of Field out-manoeuvred those in positions of authority, such as the Commanders and the Heads of the Civil Service. Although the attitudes of these officials helped defer UDI for over two years, and even after UDI helped maintain Sir Humphrey Gibbs in the position of 'British' Governor, there was no one in Britain to take advantage of this except Harold Wilson. And he reacted quite differently to what had been expected of him.

Throughout 1964 CIO continued to make the same assessment – that the case for UDI was unsustainable – and the same prognosis – that it would fail. On the basis of reports we collated from military, economic and other sources, which were still overwhelmingly against UDI, we advised that the best course of action was to do nothing because Rhodesia already enjoyed self-government and that status would be damaged irretrievably if change was forced through UDI. It occurred to me in about June that year that CIO's role in collating the reports might appear gratuitous, for it had been Field's government, not Smith's, that had asked us to perform this task. I decided to take the first opportunity to raise the subject with Ian Smith and to use the occasion to avert a possible loss of confidence between us by attempting to clear some doubts over our respective attitudes. The conversation proceeded along these lines:

'I realise that many of our reports might embarrass you with your party, Prime Minister. They may even cause you some personal distress. Or you might draw the conclusion that there is a developing loss of confidence between us; in which event it would be better for me to return to my position in the Police as arranged with Winston Field, or to retire from the Civil Service.'

'I don't see why you need to do this.'

'Perhaps the point is this, Prime Minister. Too many of our reports may appear disparaging of your government's intentions and I would not like you to get the impression that we are deliberately going out of our way to undermine what you are trying to achieve.'

'I have not thought of it, specifically.'

'It would seem to me important that we should work together as a team, provided that you understand that we are reporting officially – and in good faith – not politically. In which event you might agree that we can continue our association. On the other hand, your predecessor selected me for the job, and I'm sure we could find a convention that would entitle you to make your own selection and not continue with someone such as myself whom you have inherited from an earlier regime.'

'Yes, I get your point.'

'In other words, Prime Minister, it might make things easier for you – it would certainly make life more tolerable – to have as adviser someone more in tune with your aspirations, or someone in political support.'

The Prime Minister pondered for so long that I thought he would take up my offer of resignation. Then he said he would like to think the matter over and would let me know his answer within a few days. When we next met, he said: 'I've been thinking about what you said and have decided that it should be no concern of mine whether you are or are not a supporter of my government. I'm surrounded by well-meaning people who give me all the political advice I need but I can see a decided advantage in having someone like yourself in office to counter the "wishful thinkers" and to present the other side of the story.'

So it was that I continued in office as one of Smith's principal advisers, and during the turbulent years that followed I never had cause to doubt his sincerity towards me personally. However, it was an uneasy relationship, as illustrated by the difference in his attitude towards me and towards my wife, Olga. He had known Olga since childhood and would chat happily with her on Christian name terms about their early days in Gwelo and Selukwe, but not once in seventeen years of the closest association could he bring himself to address me by my Christian name. But it is to Smith's credit that he continued the association, renewing my five-year contract on two subsequent occasions knowing that I was neutral in attitude or opposed to his government's policies, and rarely in support. It is also to his credit that he did not cavil at our reports during the months preceding U D I, though they continued to oppose that course of action.

While our internal analysis of the justification and consequences of U D I continued, we also tried to assess the external support for U D I and to forecast something of the likely external reaction to such a move.

The real confrontation over U D I was with Britain and the squabble was essentially domestic – whether we continued as kith and kin or whether we became enemies. It was in this context that the links C I O had forged with British Intelligence turned out to be of great value. It now suited the British to apprise C I O of every possible consequence of taking U D I and the wealth of information conveyed via British Intelligence from British military, political and economic sources helped me to compile as complete a picture of the Anglo-Rhodesia jigsaw as if I was getting direct access to the sources. In Salisbury, senior C I O staff had ready access to the British High Commissioner and his staff. To add to this, there was no shortage of British visitors to Rhodesia, journalists and others who were prepared to exchange views with us; and Rhodesian visitors to Britain moved in all levels of society. In short, there was no excuse for CIO not knowing as much as it needed to know about all aspects of the British attitude to UDI.

British Intelligence was as troubled by 'wishful thinkers' as we were, and from time to time we would receive reports of British support for UDI, even in Whitehall. Such support gave Ian Smith considerable encouragement and I felt it necessary to warn him on several occasions not to give these reports too much credence. Smith's own 'wishful thinkers' attempted to sway opinion towards UDI by saying that no British government would dare act against their own kith and kin in Rhodesia for fear of alienating British public opinion.

Our understanding of Britain's attitude to UDI was not matched by Britain's understanding of the motivation for UDI. Those in power in London misunderstood much of what was happening in Rhodesia and from this stemmed their inability to cope effectively with Rhodesia's leaders; this, as much as any other single factor, accounted for UDI.

Similarly, it was the RF's misunderstanding of South African attitudes that would eventually contribute to the demise of the RF. Rhodesia's political, economic and military links with South Africa were vital but to understand the nature of these links it was essential to be aware of the fundamental differences between the two countries. Few of the RF, in their unavowed pursuit of apartheid, realised that as far as the South Africans were concerned Rhodesia had chosen a different course in 1922 by rejecting South Africa's offer of integration into the Union of South Africa. Ian Smith and Desmond Lardner-Burke, for example, believed that full South African support would be forthcoming in time of crisis. But John Vorster, South Africa's Minister of Justice and subsequently Prime Minister, and General Hendrik van den Bergh, Head of the South African Security Branch and subsequently my counterpart as Head of the Bureau of State Security (BOSS), saw the Rhodesian-South African link in quite a different light. They were proud of the years they had spent in detention in Koffiefontein during the Second World War rather than fight for the British (and Rhodesian) cause against Germans who had befriended the Boers in the Anglo-Boer War. And many South Africans reminded me that it was a group of Rhodesians, led by Dr Leander Starr Jameson, that had precipitated that war by their foolhardy and deliberately provocative raid into the Transvaal in 1895. The true relationship between South Africa and Rhodesia in the early 1960s was well expressed by Daantjie Olivier in Salisbury, using his Prime Minister's words: 'I have offered advice to three Rhodesian Premiers. The first two were wise enough to take it.'

Dr Verwoerd's government was friendly but cool. South African politicians kept their distance and, as far as we could see, their officials ignored the euphoria for U D I. They did what they could to dispel the R F belief that any South African government would have to react to popular fervour among its electorate for the preservation of white rule in Rhodesia. In Pretoria, Rhodesia's Diplomatic Representative, John Gaunt, was summoned to Union Buildings and admonished for trying to appeal to the South African public over the government's head. At no stage did those in power in South Africa encourage U D I; behind the scenes they did what they could to dissuade Ian Smith from such a rash course. They remained absolutely correct in all their dealings with Rhodesia and when asked to commit themselves in writing would go no further than to say that although they would not break existing links or support any punitive action against Rhodesia (an obvious reference to their non-participation in economic sanctions if applied), there would be no diplomatic recognition of U D I.

In the numerous discussions I had with South African Intelligence personnel, in their Police and Military headquarters and in their Foreign Ministry, I was left in no doubt whatsoever that the South Africans looked askance at the prospect of U D I. Any support they might offer would come reluctantly and only because of the accident of geography. None of those who advised me believed in an expansion of the South African laager to include Rhodesia and they were all strongly critical of what they knew of the R F's pretensions towards apartheid.

In contrast to Rhodesia's links with South Africa, a relationship between Rhodesia and Portugal hardly existed at this time. The liaison conducted between the government and successive Portuguese Consuls in Salisbury was friendly but at a low level. The first hint of change in this relationship came in July 1964 when the then Portuguese Consul, Dr Pereira Bastos, informed 'Barney' Benoy, the Secretary for Foreign Affairs and Defence, that:[1]

Portugal is fully prepared to recognise any government in Southern Rhodesia whether based on U D I or not. If, as a result of unilateral action, we (Rhodesia) became the subject of a trade boycott or certain embargos, Portugal would wish to replace such losses in trade as she could. Portugal is anxious to achieve much closer collaboration than at present and would readily agree to our use of military bases and facilities in Mozambique if circumstances rendered this desirable.

To confirm this, I sent one of my senior officers to see Dr Bastos. He reported back to me on the same day. The salient points of his report were:[2]

Dr Bastos ... confirmed Portugal's desire to achieve a much closer link with Southern Rhodesia than at the present time. He also confirmed that Portugal is fully prepared to recognise any Government in Southern Rhodesia based on a unilateral declaration or not ... He stated that this initial approach and advice was more in the nature of a political move, and that once high level agreement had been reached between the two governments then this would clear the way for a working body to be set up to work out the mechanics for any assistance between the two countries in order to replace trade boycotts, etc. As an example he mentioned that if Southern Rhodesia was cut off from fuel supplies it would need a team of experts to work out all the details for the supply of fuel from Portugal.... I gained the impression that this new direct approach by the Portuguese is a result of present recent trends in Southern Africa, in particular the growing external threat to Mozambique.... This would clearly indicate that Portugal realises that she could not hold Mozambique if there was any serious deterioration in the situation in Southern Rhodesia.... (Dr Bastos) indicated that his personal position in passing his Government's sentiments on to Mr Benoy had been purely as an intermediary and that if the Southern Rhodesia Government wanted to seek confirmation or elaboration of his Government's desires he suggested that there should be no delay in either a Government Representative, or someone nominated by the Prime Minister, or even the Prime Minister himself, paying a visit to Lisbon in the immediate future, when complete details of what the Portuguese Government envisaged could be obtained.

(This paper and the one quoted above are typical CIO products of these early years; they illustrate a low-level liaison, as indicated in the text; later papers illustrate the higher level of liaison which CIO developed.)

Even allowing for the fact that this was an over-enthusiastic approach at a low level, it seemed that the Portuguese were keen to make the running before rather than after UDI. This was confirmed within a matter of days when the Salisbury Consular post was upgraded to 'Minister' and the man chosen to fill the post was Joao de Freitas Cruz, who had been Dr Salazar's personal secretary for many years and must have known Salazar's thinking as well as anyone.

De Freitas Cruz became a firm favourite with many Rhodesians and greatly enhanced understanding between Salisbury and Lisbon. However, considerable apprehension remained as to whether or not the Portuguese would be forced into making a choice between the British, their partners in the 'Ancient Alliance', and the Rhodesians, their new-found friends in Africa. All the Intelligence that CIO received from Britain indicated that the Portuguese would favour their older and more powerful ally, a view known to be supported by Lord Woolston and other

British government emissaries in Lisbon. But should Portugal come down on Rhodesia's side, the British feeling, as expressed by their Intelligence Liaison Officer in Salisbury, was:

> You Rhodesians must face a fact of life. You are stuck with the Portuguese as your neighbours, but you should know their record of 'support' for their allies in two World Wars. They were more of a liability than an asset in the First World War and their alleged neutrality in the Second World War worked as much in favour of the Germans as it worked for us. I would remind you what Winston Churchill said when placed in a similar position between Mussolini and Hitler (and he did try to win over the Italians): 'Whichever side is unfortunate enough to have Italy as an ally will lose the war.'

In their assessment of Portugal's stance, the British seemed to have overlooked one vital issue. I well remember De Freitas Cruz telling me what emotional fervour had been generated in Portugal against Britain because of her 'betrayal' of her oldest ally when Britain favoured India's annexation of Portugal's colony, Goa, in 1961. De Freitas Cruz said that this sense of betrayal would outweigh any other consideration because it was more recent than, for example, Wellington's support for Portugal in the Peninsular War and because it had led Portugal to fear that Britain would adopt the same 'save yourself' attitude if faced with a similar problem over Mozambique and Rhodesia.

Benoy and I began preparing for the Prime Minister's visit to Lisbon, scheduled for September 1964. By this time, whenever Benoy travelled abroad he asked that I accompany him, which was useful in that it allowed me to move freely in the highest circles of Foreign Affairs and Defence. We flew to Portugal to pave the way for Smith and for the first few days moved among the military in Lisbon. We got to know, in particular, General Deslandes, Chief of the newly appointed Joint Defence Staff and until recently Governor-General of Angola. In the years ahead, Deslandes was to become one of my most valuable friends and counsellors in Portugal.

For our benefit, he assembled all his senior officers to discuss the military implications of UDI; most of them had seen service in Guinea, Angola or Mozambique, unlike Salazar who during his thirty-three years as Portugal's ruler had never set foot in Portugal's overseas empire. We admired their frankness in discussion, particularly when they spoke of the defects of their near-feudal society and the restraints of Salazar's dictatorship; no ministry or individual was allowed to acquire too strong a position and the degree of control exercised by heads of departments was determined by the degree of access they had to Salazar and their acceptability to him. From this meeting it emerged that the Army and the Air Force were generally supportive of Rhodesia's position but the Navy were opposed or, at best, luke-warm.

When Ian Smith arrived in Lisbon he was taken to see Salazar alone – 'where, and only where', we were advised, 'the true position will be found.' While the two premiers were talking, Benoy and I called on the Portuguese Foreign Minister, Dr Franco Nogueira. Our intention was to brief him on the causes and likely consequences of UDI, as we saw them, but he cut us short with a monologue about how Portugal had survived world pressure in holding onto her overseas possessions, how inevitable UDI was and how, by working together, we could negate any punitive action taken by Britain.

The following morning, over breakfast coffee at the Ritz, Smith said to me:

'Oh, by the way, Dr Nogueira told me yesterday evening that I had two traitors in my midst – you and Benoy – and his advice to me was to get rid of you as soon as possible.' Smith did not query our motivation in attempting to argue the case against UDI; instead, he seemed to accept that we were better placed to put the case against UDI than any Portuguese could put the case for it.

Although we were not informed about what was said at the meeting between Salazar and Smith, there is little doubt that Smith was given every encouragement to proceed with UDI and that Salazar acted as midwife in helping Smith abort the independence talks about to start in London; these talks failed more quickly than any previous Anglo-Rhodesian discussion on independence. Ian Smith must have seen, however, that Portuguese support for UDI was artificially based in that it was anti-British rather than pro-Rhodesian.

This was my first encounter with the Portuguese at high level and I was impressed with the capability of their senior representatives and the charm of the upper strata of their restricted society (one member from it informed me that 'there are only twelve families that really count in Portugal'). At an official lunch given by Dr Nogueira for Ian Smith, I was seated next to Sra Nogueira. Charmingly Chinese, she skipped from English to French to Portuguese and when I asked her how many more languages she had to her credit she replied: 'Naturally, I speak Mandarin and Cantonese, also some Russian, some German ...' And so on, until I lost count.

I was less impressed with their Intelligence Service. My visits to Portugal's strongholds in Africa earlier in the year to try to establish a working liaison for the efficient exchange of vital Intelligence and my

current visit to Lisbon prompted me to write the following in an office
note:[3]

It soon became apparent that there is less co-ordination in Lisbon than in
Lourenco Marques and certainly less co-ordination than in Luanda. Dr Salazar's unique position is the prime factor accounting for this. No Ministry or
individual is allowed to acquire too strong a position.... The position of PIDE
is all-powerful, but they are detested so strongly in certain quarters that any
attempt to achieve co-ordination through PIDE, e.g., by having a PIDE representative in Salisbury looking after the interests of others, would be doomed to
failure from the start.... All in all, it seems that the best prospect so far as we
are concerned is to concentrate on our liaison with SCCI, who are keen to have
someone posted to Salisbury ... (but) there remains the problem of PIDE, and it
seems that we would be best advised to continue liaison as we do at present,
primarily through Police channels. For our part, I said we would agree to the
posting of a liaison officer if we were to receive through him the co-ordinated
Intelligence reports produced in Lisbon that are not made available to us at
present.
    The problem has been set. It was discussed at length in our presence in
Portugal and, quite obviously, had been debated before our arrival. Someone
should give us the answer. At this stage it is not even known who this would be,
but I presume the answer will come in due course through the Consul-General in
Salisbury.

    It was ingenuous of me to think that I could change any part of a
Portuguese system that had evolved over the centuries. There was no
ready solution offered by the Portuguese, merely a tendency for them to
imagine that they had solved a problem once they had identified it.
There was also a tendency for their Military to take over everything they
possibly could, as emerged during a subsequent visit to Lourenco Marques in July 1965. On this visit I came face to face with inter-service
jealousies and the resultant problem of ineffective liaison, as indicated in
my report to the Prime Minister at the time.
    In order to further our association with the Portuguese I had tried to
learn their language and to find out what made them tick. This included
a visit to Tete, Mozambique's north-western province, where my host
was Sr Antonio Craviero Lopes, the Governor of Tete province and
brother of the then President of Portugal. We lunched at his palatial
residence on the banks of the Zambezi River and then moved to the
verandah to watch the first attempts by Portuguese engineers to fling a
bridge across the river. Craviero Lopes began to speak with pride of
Portugal's history in Mozambique and then moved on to talk of the
prevailing situation in his province:

You will have seen that there are no soldiers in Tete, and as long as I am Governor there never will be. Portugal has survived in Africa through freedom of association – not force of arms. Portuguese men and women were fathers and mothers of these people and we can live in peace with each other. I am even reluctant to allow Police into my area – though I suppose they are necessary to deal with the occasional criminal. But who are the soldiers going to fight? Terrorists? There is much talk of terrorism in the north and now you have them in Rhodesia, but there are none here. As long as I can continue to govern on traditional Portuguese lines there will be no terrorists, but if we let the Army in they will create terrorists!

FRELIMO, the Front for the Liberation of Mozambique, had been active since 1962 and, even as we talked, were launching their armed struggle in northern Mozambique. Within the year Craviero Lopes had been removed to vegetate elsewhere in Mozambique and the military were firmly entrenched in Tete province.

I found the Portuguese relationship to be essentially personal – one either struck up a rapport or not – and I travelled as widely as I could to establish that rapport. The Portuguese had suffered a bitter revolt in Angola in 1961 and I witnessed something of its repression. Then in Guinea in 1963 and in Mozambique in 1964 there occurred revolt after revolt, until the Portuguese Army was committed to counter-insurgency campaigns over the length and breadth of Africa. What was the reason for it all, other than nationalistic pride? It seemed to us who saw it happening that they would bleed to death in foetid Guinea rather than relinquish a foot of territory that had never been 'colonised' in the true sense of the word.

The Portuguese metropolitan soldiers were adrift in Africa, as I saw when visiting Cazombo on the headwaters of the Zambezi in Angola and heard them lament their fate 'ao fim do mundo' (at the end of the world) as they called it. None of their forbears had been expected to survive so far from the sea. I recalled a meeting I had had with Admiral Sarmento Rodrigues, the Governor-General of Mozambique, which illustrated something of the inspiration he and his nation drew from the sea. He questioned me on my scant knowledge of Lord Nelson and I had to explain that where I came from we were more familiar with the history of the Elizabethan sea-dogs such as Drake, Raleigh and the Grenvilles. He cut me short with the brusque comment: 'But they were all pirates. I'm asking you about a famous British Admiral.' I was advised too late by his Naval Attaché that the Governor-General had just written a 'Life of Nelson' in English. The Portuguese should have abandoned the sea if they were to survive in Africa. As one of their soldiers, Brigadier Dos Santos, exclaimed: 'We are not facing reality discussing our war here in Lourenco Marques, when the nearest scene of action is over a thousand miles away in the African bush.'

In order to discover what made the Portuguese tick and find out for myself how they were coping with wars on three fronts in Africa, I explored the other side of Lourenco Marques and Luanda with their world-wide reputations for night-life across the colour bar, and would soon be set at ease by girls and their consorts who appreciated what they saw as an untypically British approach. If nothing else, I experienced something of the spirit of 'Fado' (Fate or Kismet) derived from centuries of Moorish domination which has been their personal strength in adversity but their communal weakness when badly governed.

The deception of the Rhodesian public, through a Goebbels-type prop-aganda campaign, was by now well under way. The chief architect of this campaign was the Minister of Justice and of Law and Order, Clif-ford Dupont, ably assisted by propagandists recruited by the Ministry of Information. Sometimes it suited the government to pretend that there were no plans for UDI, particularly if they felt that the electorate was not yet prepared for such an event. For example, Ian Smith said in London after his visit to Lisbon: 'We have thrown UDI out of the window for the time being'; this statement was calculated to cut the ground from under Sir Roy Welensky's feet when he was standing in the by-election in October 1964 specifically to oppose UDI. At other times, when the government was trying to orchestrate support for UDI, they would issue statements calculated to persuade a gullible public that it was *British* double-dealing that might force a reluctant Rhodesian gov-ernment into UDI.

The duplicity and emotionalism that characterised the campaign be-gan to widen the rift in European opinion. In September 1964 I wrote in my diary:

Since the departure from office of Winston Field, the government under Ian Smith has hardened its intention towards the all-pervading issue of UDI ... to the extent that the cleavage of opinion amongst the Europeans – not to mention the opposition of the Africans – has been sharpened throughout the government service. The Governor stands on one side of the rift, and the Prime Minister on the other, which places persons such as myself in a very delicate position as we serve both of them.

Typical of the effect that the campaign was having on those who felt caught in the middle was a comment made by Sir Ian Wilson, retiring Speaker of the House of Assembly, when he intruded politics for the first and last time at one of our after-hours sessions at the Salisbury Club: 'I'm leaving politics for good and going home to squat on the Mozambique border, disillusioned and dismayed, for there is no longer any sincerity in politics.'

The prospect of UDI was hardly ever discussed in official circles. The pre-planning which had begun under Field never developed into planning for the event. CIO ceased issuing specific warnings towards the end of 1964, for, unlike Goebbels-type propaganda which grows through repetition, an Intelligence assessment loses impact if it is bandied about. Only occasionally thereafter did I make reference to the case for or against UDI in my monthly briefings to the Cabinet. These monthly briefings had begun in the concluding months of 1963, at Field's insistence, and became a regular feature in 1964. Field had asked that during the briefings I should concentrate on the subject of African nationalism so that he could persuade his colleagues that a new approach was needed towards 'Nationalism' as a threat to Internal Security. But after his departure, and indeed for the following fifteen years, rarely did any Minister show any interest in that subject.

Field's dismissal had coincided with the decision taken in a secret session by the ZANU Congress in Gwelo to renounce all further negotiation with the whites and to pursue the armed struggle with all means at their disposal. I remember only too well studying with grave foreboding the Special Branch reports coming into CIO from Gwelo during May 1964, giving details of the resolutions of that fateful meeting and of a similar decision taken by the leadership of the People's Caretaker Council (PCC), formerly ZAPU. But my warnings then and later as to the possible effects of the nationalists' change in strategy were heeded only to the extent that the government decided to ban the nationalist parties and detain their leaders.

The government concentrated instead on furthering its attempts to unite the white electorate on the independence issue and on pursuing its efforts to clear the decks for action by placing officials sympathetic to UDI in key positions. In an attempt to impress the British with a demonstration of white unity, the government held a referendum in November 1964 and asked the electorate: 'Do you want independence under the 1961 Constitution?' – adding that 'Yes means unity, not UDI'. Of the 64,000 people who voted, over 58,000 answered 'Yes' to the ambiguous question.

As for clearing the decks, the government believed that the removal of a few anti-UDI officials would sound a warning note to others. They dismissed the prevailing anti-UDI attitude among businessmen and industrialists (the 'business barons', whom they considered pro-British and part of the old establishment) on the grounds that they would have to commit themselves to UDI eventually or lose any chance of economic survival. Anti-UDI attitudes in official circles, however, could not be ignored. Until the RF winds of change began to blow through the Services there was only one senior official, as far as CIO was aware, who was pro-UDI – 'Slash' Barfoot, the Commissioner of Police.

The first serious casualty was Stan Morris, who was in the powerful position of Secretary for African Affairs (subsequently renamed 'Internal Affairs'). Morris was highly regarded throughout the Civil Service; his handling of 'African Affairs' was paternalistic but pragmatic. But he began to show a reluctance to do the government's bidding. In October 1964 he was given the task of staging an *indaba* which would produce pro-government resolutions and thus show the British Prime Minister that RF policies had African support. The *indaba* was held at Domboshawa, north of Salisbury, and was attended by over 600 Chiefs and Headmen; the outcome was a unanimous verdict in favour of independence for Rhodesia under the 1961 Constitution. I remember Morris saying shortly after the *indaba* that it had been 'a risky thing to arrange; it would have needed only one, or at the most two, Ndebele Chiefs to have come out in opposition and the verdict would have gone the other way.' Such honesty, and a growing reluctance to carry out the government's wishes, resulted in his being quietly removed from his executive position and kicked upstairs to the purely administrative post of Chairman of the Public Services Board.

He was replaced by Hostes Nicolle, an advocate of apartheid whose actions and attitude epitomised the RF's intentions to 'keep the native in his place'. Nicolle charged into the political arena by announcing publicly that he was withdrawing his account from the Standard Bank because its new chairman and former Rhodesian High Commissioner to London, Evan Campbell, had stated that 'England is still Rhodesia's best friend' and that UDI would result in political and economic disaster. Within a short time Nicolle had turned the Department of African Affairs into a political weapon for the government's use.

Next to go was the Commander of the Army, Major-General 'Jock' Anderson. Shortly after my return from Lisbon in September 1964, the Prime Minister questioned me on Anderson's conduct and subsequently CIO produced a few reports of no greater significance than that he had been somewhat indiscreet in some of his utterances in Army messes; at most, these indiscretions could be seen as challenging the government to test his and his officers' loyalty to the Queen. The government could not respond to this challenge publicly, nor could it be alleged that Anderson's 'indiscretions' had attracted unwanted publicity. Nevertheless, enough was made of the affair to force Anderson's resignation, offering no explanation other than the bogus statement that he had reached retirement age. When Anderson asked for an interview with Smith so that he could be told why government wished to get rid of him, his request was turned down.

Anderson was every inch a soldier, with a distinguished record of service in two famous regiments, the Black Watch and the Blues (The Royal Horse Guards), and he would not have allowed any politician to override what he knew to be his duty. CIO's enquiries indicated that the stories passed to the government criticising Anderson, which prompted Ian Smith to question me, emanated from a few political activists serving as territorial Army officers. This was perhaps the saddest aspect of the affair in that it precipitated a tendency among government Ministers to accept criticism of military officers from territorials junior in rank and status, a tendency which in the years ahead was to have more damaging effects.

The Ministers mainly responsible for Anderson's resignation, Ian Smith and Clifford Dupont, believed that their path to UDI would be made easier by Anderson's departure. In this they were mistaken. Anderson's replacement, Sam Putterill, was no more politically pliable than his predecessor. He did not accept the appointment until Anderson had persuaded him to do so 'to save the Army from disintegration' and had satisfied himself through consultation with the Governor and the Chief Justice that his assumption of command met with their approval and was constitutionally correct. The only difference between Anderson and Putterill was one of style (not of attitude, as was popularly assumed): Putterill preferred to make his points directly to the Governor or the government, whereas Anderson tended to wear his heart on his sleeve and talk more freely among his officers than he should have done.

Putterill took the first opportunity to advise the Prime Minister that under no circumstances would he carry out any unconstitutional or illegal order, which in effect meant that he would not order his Army to oppose British forces or to break their oaths of allegiance to the Crown. All Putterill's subsequent actions were in line with the stance he took at the time of his appointment and when retirement freed him from political restraint in 1969 he opposed the RF government with considerable vigour as a leading member of the Centre Party.

The government gained little satisfaction from the Anderson affair, save that it might be construed as a warning shot to other senior officers (the majority of whom were opposed to UDI) and that it contributed to the sudden resignation of 'Barney' Benoy, Secretary for Defence and Foreign Affairs. The warning did not prevent the Commander of the Rhodesian Air Force, Air Vice-Marshal Harold Hawkins, from advising the Prime Minister that, like Putterill, he would not issue illegal or unconstitutional orders to his Force. As to Benoy's action, I was as surprised by it as anyone else for, during the many months that we had worked closely together, he had frequently insisted that unless top officials stood together on constitutional issues the government would knock us down like nine-pins, one by one.

I had first got wind that Benoy was in trouble when we returned from Lisbon. Whilst still at the airport, Benoy's Deputy in Foreign Affairs advised him that his safe had been removed from his office while we were in flight. As we were speaking, attempts were being made to have the safe forcibly opened in a search for incriminating papers. Apparently, Dupont, now Minister of Foreign Affairs, had ordered Benoy's staff to open the safe that morning but they had denied that they knew the combination, whereupon the safe was locked in Benoy's office until demolition officers arrived. Two members of his staff had then risked their careers – and their necks – by climbing along the outside parapet of the second floor, entering the office through the window, opening the safe and removing all papers that might have appeared incriminating.

Benoy went straight from the airport to confront Dupont, saying no more to me than that he might have left secret plans in his safe that could be construed as a manoeuvre to prevent the government from taking UDI. From his meeting with Dupont he learned that one of his aides had told the Minister that Benoy was plotting some nefarious action against the government. Within a few days Benoy had offered his resignation, which was readily accepted. During the long and earnest discussions I had with him at the time, reminding him of his oft-repeated exhortation that none of us should resign unless forced to do so, all he would say on the subject was that he was resigning in sympathy with Anderson. However, I am convinced that the prospect of UDI, with its undermining of loyalties, was too much for Benoy to stomach and that he preferred to become a casualty rather than continue to serve a regime he now clearly detested. Benoy's resignation provided the government with the opportunity to reorganise the two Ministries, Defence and Foreign Affairs, that Benoy had represented. Each Ministry was now to be represented by a different set of officials, giving the government the added advantage of appointing a new Minister of Defence (allowing the Prime Minister to relinquish that portfolio) and creating a new post of Secretary for Defence which was filled by an RF-supporter, Eldon Trollip.

As a result of what appeared to be the forced resignations of Anderson and Benoy, the warnings issued by the British government against UDI now became more insistent, and in September 1964 speculation that UDI was imminent was rife among British journalists. But nothing happened then because the Rhodesian government knew it could not command the loyalty of the Armed Forces in an enterprise such as UDI.

Talks about talks between Rhodesian and British politicians continued in an apparent attempt to negotiate a settlement. In January 1965, during a visit to London to attend the funeral of Sir Winston Churchill, Smith talked to the British Prime Minister, Harold Wilson. The outcome of the meeting was an agreement that Arthur Bottomley, the Commonwealth Secretary, and Lord Gardiner, the Lord Chancellor, should visit Salisbury for more talks. The visit took place in February, and I accompanied the small group of officials deputed to brief them on the facts of Rhodesian life. I remember Bruce-Brand (Secretary for Law and Order) trying to convince Bottomley and Gardiner that successive Rhodesian governments had always adhered to the Rule of Law and Bottomley arguing forcefully with me as I tried to compare the evils of 'Mau Mau' in Kenya with what we were beginning to experience in Rhodesia. When Hostes Nicolle (Secretary for Internal Affairs) started his peroration, he made the dramatic statement that all of us around the table were putting too fine a gloss on things. According to Nicolle the facts were indisputable: Rhodesia had been conquered by force of arms, the natives had been defeated and should be treated ever after as subject people. Bottomley was incensed. Lord Gardiner, sitting next to me, puffed on his pipe, saying nothing throughout these proceedings, but when we concluded with a drink-and-talk session he said quietly to me, 'Your Government is well served with able civil servants, but interpretations must differ on The Rule of Law, and in Nicolle you have a firebrand impossible to control.'

In May Smith called a general election, during which the RF continued to deny that they were seeking a mandate for UDI; they won all the 'A' Roll (white) seats, an indication of the success of Dupont's propaganda campaign. In July Cledwyn Hughes, Minister of State for Commonwealth Affairs, visited Salisbury for more talks and reported back to Bottomley.

In September a considerable amount of Intelligence on British and American attitudes to a declaration of independence began to be fed into CIO from British sources. Some of it was deliberately planted, which now made our task of assessing the British government's likely reaction to UDI a difficult one. Our assessment was contained in a 'Top Secret' paper,[4] the significant points of which were: there would be strong pressures on Britain to use force; the possibility of a secret agreement between Rhodesia and Britain (suspected by African members of the Commonwealth) was unlikely; in some quarters it was felt that Britain had gone far enough in her attempts to settle and should let UDI happen; although Britain would probably not intervene immediately, alleged Rhodesian 'interference' in Zambia might force her to do so; British official reaction would be sharp and immediate; mandatory resolutions on Rhodesia would be passed in the United Nations; there would be a tobacco boycott; there would probably be an embargo on the supply of oil to Rhodesia; UDI would not endear Rhodesia to her friends, Portugal and South Africa; and there would be strong reaction to UDI from the Americans.

Both the British and the Americans seemed to accept that UDI was imminent. This accorded with CIO's view; to us it was no longer a question of whether or not there would be a unilateral declaration of independence but of whether or not the British government would use force to prevent or abort such a declaration. The more CIO studied this issue, the more likely it seemed that it would eventually be decided not by the actual use of force but by bluff. The question now was: who would call the other's bluff first? The answer came in October 1965.

The Unilateral Declaration of Independence

In the first week of October 1965 Ian Smith flew to London with the avowed intention of trying, once again, to get the British to grant Rhodesia independence on the basis of the 1961 Constitution. He carried up his sleeve a new suggestion of an Anglo-Rhodesian treaty to guarantee against amendments to the constitution after independence had been granted.

I had my doubts as to whether there was any serious intent or genuine expectation of success in Smith's mission. My doubts were confirmed to some extent by Dupont, the Acting Prime Minister, who sent for me a few days after Smith's departure. Obviously, he wanted to use his temporary authority as my Minister to check our Intelligence on UDI; for my part, I believed I would get a clearer indication of where Rhodesia was going from Dupont than from any other member of the government, for he seemed as much in charge of affairs as Smith. He was known as the keenest gambler in the Cabinet and was perhaps the greatest protagonist of UDI; according to the way the cards were dealt, he might show his hand or continue the game of bluff.

Dupont had always shown a far greater interest in Intelligence than any of his colleagues. He knew I had been in touch with the Head of MI6, with whom he had been at school, and probably guessed that his old schoolmate would have warned me against him – which he had. In turn, Dupont often warned me against certain people among my staff whom he believed were 'working for the British'. He may or may not have known that I had picked up an intriguing snippet of information from other Intelligence sources indicating that someone very close to him had been connected with British Intelligence (this was categorically denied by my British contacts but it left us guessing).

I recorded my visit to Dupont on 9 October at some length so that it might be useful to those members of my staff who were responsible for interpreting Anglo-Rhodesian relations and assessing the build-up to UDI.[1]

We talked for nearly two hours on a very friendly basis, and it was perhaps significant that when seeing me off he mentioned that he had had some difficulty in sleeping recently because he was turning over the various problems in his mind, and he had greatly appreciated the opportunity of 'talking to someone' about them.

At one stage we talked about the desirability of implementing UDI – if it is to be implemented – at this particular juncture. I gave it as my view that we must expect a sharper reaction right now because of the considerable heat that had been generated all over the world. Commenting on this Mr Dupont said that the subject itself generated heat and that this would occur at any time. In the event they would have to commit the entire white population to UDI in the same way that Hitler and Goebbels got the German nation dedicated to their war effort by a process of commitment, leaving no alternative but complete support.

Mr Dupont explained why government could not just go on and on ... the Prime Minister had taken the electorate to the brink on several occasions and it was then necessary to withdraw; but on this occasion, as he put it, 'he has got the electorate virtually with their legs dangling over the brink', and he was clearly worried over the political repercussions of appearing to withdraw yet again....

At no stage was there acrimony. Mr Dupont was genuinely anxious to use me as a sounding-board for whatever doubts he might have. He is obviously well informed, but he did make a rather surprising observation, that 85–90% of the Europeans were behind Mr Smith, with the implied suggestion that they would support him in any steps he took to get independence.

I told him of a definite uneasiness that had made itself apparent, particularly in business circles in the past week or so, which indicated that there would not be support for UDI in some circles. Mr Dupont said it was inevitable that in certain circles individuals would suffer....

He seemed not to be blaming the British Government as much as the American Government, who, he thought, were really dictating to the British; but I would disagree here. He didn't seem to think that Britain was actuated so much by the need to maintain the Commonwealth as in her own self-interest.

Mr Dupont was inclined to discredit what we knew of South African uncertainties, but he did say that Mr Gaunt (Rhodesian Accredited Diplomatic Representative in Pretoria) had really put his foot in it and had made Dr Verwoerd 'terribly cross'....

On the question of sanctions, Mr Dupont mentioned the vitally important fact that the United Nations are in session at the moment, that we must expect a Security Council resolution on the subject, and he asked me what we thought of the prospects of a French veto, clearly believing that no other major power would veto sanctions. He thought that as the French had always opposed the principle of sanctions, there was a prospect France would veto and he asked me if we could get something specific on this through our sources....

Talking of the possibility of the Prime Minister staying longer in London, Mr Dupont inferred that he might be having further private talks with the British Prime Minister and that he hoped that if nothing else they could come to some secret agreement. We have tried to disabuse Government on this score before, because this is exactly what other members of the Commonwealth suspect might occur – therefore Britain will not lend herself to it, but Mr Dupont still seemed to think it possible.

Towards the end of our discussion I asked him what the prospects were of neither taking UDI, nor just staying as we were, but of 'chipping away' at the Constitution and achieving de facto independence this way. Mr Dupont said they had considered various ways of doing this, one of which would be to persuade the Governor not to forward to London legislation subject to the reserved clauses, but Mr Dupont said the Governor seemed to have scant respect for their Government and I got the impression that he may have sounded out the Governor in this respect and had received no satisfaction.

I could now be reasonably sure that Dupont was firmly committed to UDI and would jump with Smith into the abyss, on the brink of which sat the electorate 'with their legs dangling'. But there was still nothing clear-cut about the issues involved and CIO was not given any direction in planning for the event. We could get no further indication from South African sources as to which way their government was likely to move. Portuguese Intelligence continued to be misleading. And British Intelligence seemed to be following the official government line, as indicated by the reports that had reached CIO in September.

When Smith returned from London, however, there was a feeling of movement. He reacted to some of my representations of British threats with the significant comment that 'It's not practical politics'. It was the first time I heard him use a phrase he was often to repeat, and it indicated that he had assessed Harold Wilson much more accurately than Wilson had understood Smith or what Smith stood for.

The fateful decision to go for UDI was taken at a planning session of our Security Council on 19 October 1965, less than a month before the event. Ian Smith was in the Chair, supported by five Ministers, with thirteen officials present; this was considerably more than the usual complement of Security Council, whose function was normally confined to matters affecting the Security of the State. The established procedure at these meetings was for me to deliver my Intelligence brief first, followed by a general discussion before any other matters of Security interest were raised.

As the Minutes of this meeting show (partially reproduced in the Appendix), my Intelligence appreciation of the implications of UDI was concentrated on the position of Zambia (for this factor posed the greatest military threat to Rhodesia) and on the timing of an independence declaration.

Military action should not be discounted in circumstances of (a) internal disorders on a scale justifying direct intervention, (b) the destruction of Zambia's lifelines to and from Rhodesia and (c) a failure of sanctions.... The use of force was not likely unless Zambia was threatened. The threat from the Organisation of African Unity or from individual African states could be discounted. It was believed that the United States of America would not act independently against

Rhodesia. Internal strife was not likely and what did develop could be handled by the Police....

On the general question of timing, doubt was expressed as to the wisdom of early action to declare independence. It was suspected that the country was not psychologically prepared to move onto a 'war' footing at short notice and morale would suffer if setbacks were experienced without previous conditioning.... Early action would compel Britain to retaliate, where a delay would force them to take the initiative which might suit Rhodesia. The United Nations was at present in session. In all the circumstances, a delay might be to Rhodesia's advantage.

My Intelligence brief was cut short at this point by a statement from the Prime Minister who effectively ignored much of what I had been saying.

The Prime Minister intervened to bring the Security Council up to date on certain factors which were contributing towards the general consideration of a unilateral declaration of independence. There was no doubt at all that circumstances were favourable for a early decision and, with every day's delay, the prospects deteriorated. Massive support for Rhodesia existed in the United Kingdom which would be the target for erosion from now onwards. Support on the Continent, and particularly in France, was growing, whilst in the United States of America the Rhodesian 'problem' had now reached the table of the President, and some criticism over its past handling had been directed at Mr Mennen Williams and the State Department. The American Service Chiefs were sympathetic. It was quite clear that a campaign of intimidation and fear had been mounted against Rhodesia with the object of steering the people away from UDI. In regard to the position of South Africa and Portugal, their backing was assured but for obvious political reasons, they could not come out in the open for the present. The Government was convinced that unless a decision was taken soon, Rhodesia would 'lose out'. Even under the worst conditions, a UDI would be worthwhile in the long run.

At the conclusion of the Prime Minister's statement, the Commissioner of Police, Chief of Air Staff and Chief of General Staff made their reports, after which there was a general discussion. The outcome of this discussion was that the government, having weighed up the pros and cons, had accepted that the official view was opposed to UDI, but decided that a political decision had to be taken without further delay. That decision was to go for UDI at the first favourable opportunity.

The Minutes of Security Council meetings were the official record of a consensus and in my experience they had always been as honestly recorded as human frailty allowed. Prior to circulation, they would be taken to the Chairman for approval, allowing him to intrude his own emphasis. On this occasion, the Prime Minister's emphasis was marked. For example, the Intelligence assessment given at the meeting that 'under the most favourable circumstances the chances of UDI succeeding may be no more than even' were entirely omitted from the Minutes, whereas Smith's statement that 'even under the worst conditions, a UDI would be worthwhile in the long run' was not. In the general discussion the Minutes record that 'all three services in the United Kingdom had confirmed that there would be no military intervention' whereas the actual point made was that 'there was no plan for intervention at present'.

There is no doubt that much of the reasoning behind the conclusions the Prime Minister and his colleagues were reaching at this time was directly influenced by the assessments they were receiving from Rhodesia's High Commissioner in London, Brigadier Andrew Skeen.

Skeen had been chosen to succeed Evan Campbell in this vital post at a time when there was a real prospect of military intervention. His background enabled him to work through the 'old boy' network formed by men who had been his contemporaries at Sandhurst and who were now in Britain's highest military echelons. Skeen was an amateur when it came to making Intelligence assessments, although his prediction that there would be no British military intervention happened to be correct. But it was difficult for CIO to establish whether or not force was to be used without asking our British colleagues to cross-examine their military commanders, which was too much to expect. The most CIO could say was that Skeen's reporting was politically motivated – it was certainly diametrically opposite in theme and substance to that of his immediate predecessor. But it had a marked effect on the Cabinet and, through Smith and Dupont, on the Security Council. To illustrate the level of his observations I recorded some of his reporting on his return to Salisbury in the final week of October:[2]

Brigadier Skeen called on 28.10.65 for what I expected to be a discussion on affairs of mutual interest – in fact, he gave his personal account of the Independence issue as seen in London.

He referred to his own efforts as 'Skeen's ninety days', and, rather jocularly, to his period of 'restriction in London'.

He said he had adopted the line, immediately on arrival in London, that he must do everything in his power to influence public opinion in Britain.... He took credit for being able to influence opinion quite considerably before the Prime Minister arrived in London for the Independence Talks, when, according to Brigadier Skeen, the stage was set and the Prime Minister successfully ignited the mass opinion which was already warmed in our favour....

He made it fairly clear that he does not expect to go back to Britain. As a Regular soldier in the British Army, he said, and recently retired to the Reserve of Officers, he could in any event be hanged as a traitor, and nobody else at Rhodesia House is in that same category.... He was quite sure that the British Government would have no option but to take over Rhodesia House in the

event of UDI, and he said he had explained to the senior Civil Servants there
that if they were wise they would not fall prey to any blandishments of the
British Government to try and take them over, as 'the British will always betray
you'....
     From numerous comments made it is quite clear that Brigadier Skeen has a
very low opinion of the morality of British politicians – most of them, apparently, would kill their own grandmothers to get votes – and seems to think that he
has managed so to work the Rhodesian cause that it is now the deciding issue
which will make or break Wilson's government. Brigadier Skeen was quite
confident that there would be an election in Britain by next Spring in any event.
He mentioned that several Labour MPs will die this winter (I queried whether
some Conservatives might not also die but he said the Conservative Party members were much fitter!)....
     Referring specifically to the possibilities of British military intervention, he
said that he had it categorically from (General) Sir Richard Hull and others who
were personal friends of his, that there was only the normal contingency plan in
existence – and they even had one to 'evacuate Eskimos from the North Pole if
the Russians cracked the ice there'.... He said that the control of the British
Army was vested in its hereditary leaders ... that most of the Commanders
would refuse to fight against Rhodesia and that some of them had told him they
would 'lead their troops on to Rhodesia's side'....
     I tried to draw Brigadier Skeen on the complications that might arise out of
our relationship with Zambia following UDI, but he was inclined to dismiss
these as being of no consequence – it is merely a question of 'knowing the munt
mentality' – 'we all know they respect firmness' – 'if you can show firmness at
the start, they'll toe the line.'

     In essence, Skeen's assessments were based upon his opinion that the
bonds of 'kith and kin' would bind Rhodesia and Britain closer than any
politician realised. Experience had taught me, however, that no matter
how many elderly ladies of Croydon decorated their car windows with
'Support Rhodesia' and 'I Hate Harold' stickers, national interest would
prevail over 'kith and kin' sentiments. This point was aptly illustrated by
Private Eye on a cover of a current issue: Ian Smith was portrayed
pushing an African's face into his nether regions, under the caption 'Kith
My Arse!'
     I doubted Skeen's claim that most British Commanders would refuse
to fight against Rhodesia; on the contrary, CIO knew for certain that
some of the senior Commanders would willingly use force against
Rhodesia. British military tradition – loyalty to the Sovereign and a high
sense of military discipline and national pride – would override any
other considerations. I remembered Admiral Lord Louis Mountbatten
making it clear, during the brief chat I had had with him when he visited
Salisbury in 1961, that he, for one, would not be averse to the use of

force against recalcitrant officers who might be diverted from their oath of allegiance to the Crown.

By the last week of October it was still a question of who would call whose bluff first. Wilson knew the situation in Rhodesia was charged for UDI unless he could persuade Smith to take avoiding action. He flew to Salisbury on 25 October to make a last attempt at settlement, but he got nowhere other than to reach agreement in principle on a Royal Commission being appointed to recommend the constitutional arrangements by which Rhodesia could move towards independence. However, Smith was holding fewer cards at that stage, knowing that neither his Army nor his Air Force would oppose force with force. Wilson, although he might have had some political worries over reaction in Britain to the use of force, must surely have known from his advisers that the British Commanders would obey his government's orders even if this meant the use of force against Rhodesia.

Why, then, did Wilson throw away what little advantage he had by broadcasting on the BBC to the whole world on 30 October: 'If there are those in this country who are thinking in terms of a thunderbolt, hurtling through the sky and destroying their enemy, a thunderbolt in the shape of the Royal Air Force, let me say that this thunderbolt will not be coming.'

By making this statement Wilson had removed any immediate prospect of a negotiated settlement and had cleared the way for the RF government to take matters into its own hands. Inevitably, the African nationalists would have to fight for their rights to the bitter end.

Of what use, then, had Rhodesian and British Intelligence been? It seemed now that neither the Rhodesian government nor the British government wished to use the Intelligence they possessed. The British Intelligence Service knew that senior Rhodesian military officers would not fight against British forces; CIO was certain that British Commanders would do what was required of them even if some of their number were reluctant to use force against Rhodesia. Therefore, both sides knew it was a game of bluff, waiting to be called, or to be abandoned according to political dictates. Certainly, this is how Dennis Healey, Wilson's Minister of Defence, saw it. On the Granada Television series 'End of Empire' screened a decade later he said: 'I think it was insane (for Wilson to make his statement). I simply cannot understand the Prime Minister letting Ian Smith know that we wouldn't intervene by force, because in the situation where you've so few cards in your hand, you mustn't tell the other side that you have no cards.'

I remember Air Vice-Marshal Bentley, Rhodesia's Diplomatic Representative in Washington, saying during consultations in October that anyone familiar with the relative capability of the Royal Air Force and the Rhodesian Air Force, as he was, knew that the Royal Air Force could neutralise the Rhodesian Air Force without a shot being fired in anger. One way of doing this would have been for the Royal Air Force to have their Vulcan bombers (then based in Nairobi, but which could be moved to Lusaka) keeping a permanent watch in the skies over New Sarum and Thornhill, the two Rhodesian Air Force bases, with the threat issued in advance that if any Rhodesian aeroplane tried to get airborne the runways and the planes on the ground would be bombed.

The reality of UDI was taken a stage further within forty-eight hours of Wilson's broadcast, at a Cabinet meeting on 1 November. A copy of Item 1 of the Minutes of this meeting (reproduced in the Appendix) was sent to me so that I could advise the Commanders and other colleagues what to expect by way of Cabinet decisions affecting their preparations for UDI. One significant passage read:

The Prime Minister declared that in his opinion nothing had been achieved by Mr Wilson in leaving Mr Bottomley and Sir Elwyn Jones behind in Salisbury because they had been unable to reach decisions and it was evident that they had no authority to decide anything. In an attempt to close the gap the discussions had been a failure.... The Prime Minister said that he felt that Rhodesia's position was today stronger than it had been before Mr Wilson's arrival.

Of further significance in the Minutes was Cabinet's decision to proclaim a general state of emergency as a prelude to UDI, relying on the constitutional requirement imposed on the Governor to sign such a proclamation, even if it was to be represented to him as a declaration of a state of emergency and *not* for UDI.

The Prime Minister informed Cabinet that he had received advice from several sources, including the Rhodesian High Commissioner in London, that it would be the right tactics, in the event of the Rhodesian Government having to take the extreme step, first to introduce a general state of emergency and thereafter let the impact recede before taking the next step. The advantage of this course would be that while most people would appreciate that a general state of emergency was but a prelude to a declaration of independence, it was still a legal proceeding and when the actual declaration did come people generally would have been resigned to it.... In discussion it was felt that the gradual assumption of independence after a declaration of a state of emergency was likely to minimise the impact overseas. It would have the additional advantage of not disclosing until the last minute Rhodesia's hand. The declaration of independence would then be chosen at a time to suit the Rhodesian government.

Meanwhile, preparations for UDI were going on in other spheres. The

Commissioner of Police had already drafted instructions for the Police in the event of UDI. The Army Commander's instructions were carefully worded so as to avoid any reference to the possibility of the Army having to take action against British troops.[3]

At the next meeting of the Security Council, held on 5 November, the Prime Minister took over the discussion from the start with a statement of government's intentions to declare a country-wide state of emergency with the least possible delay. The Minutes (reproduced in the Appendix) record that:

He emphasised that the reasons for this action were quite unconnected with a unilateral declaration of independence, a decision on which had not yet been taken.... Government's hope was that the state of emergency could be handled as quietly and calmly as possible so as to avoid any panic reactions and certainly to prevent any misconceptions as to the reason for its declaration.

So much for the decision in principle in the same forum on 19 October and for the discussion on a state of emergency in the Cabinet meeting of 1 November!

The rest of the discussion in the Security Council meeting of 5 November revolved around the justification of a state of emergency based on security, not political, considerations. However, once again, the Minutes of this meeting are not a true reflection of the proceedings. Firstly, they did not make any mention of the statement by A. M. Bruce-Brand, the Secretary for Law and Order, that had it not been for political considerations neither he nor his colleagues in the Ministry (he was referring to the Minister of Law and Order and the Commissioner of Police) would have been likely to make representations for a state of emergency.

I noted this omission on my record of the Minutes at the time. I also noted an even more serious omission – that the Minutes included nothing of the Attorney-General's comments. My note reads: 'No mention made of the AG's strong attack on Government (Ministry of L & O?) for trying to keep the proclamation "on ice" after the Governor had signed it. The AG's objections were the main reasons for rushing through the proclamation that same day.'

The Attorney-General, T. A. T. Bosman, QC, was in charge of the legal draughtsmen who would have been responsible for the preparation of a proclamation declaring a state of emergency. He rarely spoke at Security Council meetings, but when he did he was always forthright and what he said was unarguable. On this occasion, however, none of the officials present, including myself, grasped the implications of what he was saying. The reason was simple. We did not know that the proclamation in question was intended to be used for more than a declaration of a state of emergency – it was to be used to secure the emergency powers Smith needed to declare independence. Smith had taken the proclamation to the Governor for signature, and Gibbs had signed it after he had been assured by Smith that it was to be used only for the declaration of a state of emergency.

From my earlier discussions with the British Intelligence Officer, on 3 November, and with John (later Sir John) Pestell, the Secretary and Comptroller to the Governor, on the morning of 4 November, I had learnt that a proclamation had been signed and that it had been *signed undated*. Pestell said: 'The proclamation was undated. It was brought to H. E. by the Prime Minister for signature and it was only subsequently when I wanted a file copy that I found it undated and therefore inoperative.'

The non-dating of the proclamation, as I realised after UDI had taken place, was deliberate, so that it could be put 'on ice', as alleged by the Attorney-General, and used for purposes other than those represented to Sir Humphrey Gibbs. At the time, however, both Pestell and I presumed the proclamation was for a state of emergency and that it would have to be signed again and then dated before it could be used. I remember telling Gibbs later on the morning of 4 November that I saw no reason to question Smith's representations that the proclamation was 'not for UDI', for Smith had said the same thing to CIO and other officials. Moreover, I was aware that, according to the Minutes of the Cabinet meeting four days previously, the government's intention was 'first to introduce a general state of emergency and thereafter let the impact recede before taking the next step.' I told the Governor that he could presume that the government would bring another proclamation, appropriately dated, for his signature if they wished him to 'legalise' UDI.

Later, of course, the RF strongly denied any suggestion that they had tricked the Governor into signing the UDI proclamation. In the House of Commons on 27 March 1968, Harold Wilson said:

During my talks with him on HMS *Tiger*, as the House knows, Mr Smith admitted to me that he had lied to the Governor a day or two before UDI in order to obtain a grant of emergency powers, when conditions under the law which had to exist to justify emergency powers did not exist, and when ... his purpose was to secure those powers for UDI, a purpose he had denied when the Governor challenged him on this point.

In reply to this statement, the Rhodesian Minister of Law and Order, Desmond Lardner-Burke, defended his government's action by putting the blame on the Commissioner of Police. He told the Rhodesia Parliament on 19 April that:

An affidavit had to be sworn by the Commissioner of Police and this, together with a recommendation from the government, was presented to the Governor. I prepared the documents in connection with this matter and I am perfectly satisfied that on the affidavit which was submitted there was no need to lie, as suggested by Mr Wilson, and I can categorically say that Mr Wilson is deliberately falsifying the facts when he alleges that the Prime Minister made this admission to him.

In those last few days before UDI while most of us holding senior jobs in the Civil Service found ourselves between the devil and the deep blue sea, Sir Humphrey Gibbs was in the worst position. If independence could have been negotiated with some semblance of legality, he would have been happy to resign and slip away to his farm. Indeed, when I saw him at his request on 10 November that was exactly what he had in mind. But he was considering an alternative.

'What would be the position,' he asked me, 'if I now say to Ian Smith that I will oppose UDI and as Governor will declare his government illegal and appeal to the Chiefs of Staff to support me as their Commander-in-Chief?'

Although I considered that the loyalty of the Chiefs of Staff, Putterill and Hawkins, was not in doubt and that many of their senior officers would follow their lead, I advised Gibbs that an appeal for their support would put them in an almost impossible position, between the government that paid them and an overseas Queen to whom they owed allegiance. Gibbs insisted on knowing whether I thought his suggested course of action would lead to bloodshed. My reply was that it could not be guaranteed that there would be no bloodshed, for many of the middle and lower ranks of the Rhodesian Light Infantry (RLI), an all-white regular battalion, would willingly 'jump into the Makabusi' (a muddy river on the outskirts of the city) for Smith, even if this meant going against their seniors.

This discussion was one of several oft-interrupted sessions I had with Gibbs during the twenty-four hours preceding the declaration of independence. My notes written at the time reflect the anxiety and confusion of those hours:

2 pm 10th November. Advised by GC (Gerald Clarke, Secretary to the Prime Minister) of Harold Wilson's eleventh-hour phone call to PM to try and avert UDI – but it failed. I let H.E. (His Excellency, Sir Humphrey Gibbs) know through Pestell.

3 pm 10th. Caught up in discussion with L R (Leo Ross, Secretary for Information) on timing of declaration. P. K. van der Byl and advisers believe will only be weekend wonder if catches world media at weekend, but most say, as does PM, 'seven or nine day wonder'. We all wonder!

8 pm 10th. John Pestell phones for discussion. I go to him. H.E. worried and frustrated – decide to go together to see him. H.E. tackles me re 'shift in opinion resulting in more opposition to UDI' – refers to my assessments, Gwebi constituency etc, but I say this amounts to relief at prospect of UDI being 'off' and this is not necessarily opposition to government. Agreed that many senior officials have grave misgivings and there appears to be opposition even in Cabinet because of inordinately long time taken to reach decision.

H.E. suggests he will tell PM he will oppose – will declare government illegal and appeal to Chiefs of Staff for support. I advise this will place them in impossible – even dangerous – position.... H.E. looks to future after UDI – sanctions failing or running down, then appeal to Smith to start all over again. Would it not be better therefore to make last effort now to stop? – and he feels the mere threat of opposition as outlined might stop PM – I say 'OK, but if it does not stop him the Chiefs of Staff would have no option but to resign'.

H.E.'s other fear is that he will be frustrated from making his appeal to the country and that failure to do this would aggravate the position – agree no hope of RBC* carrying message but Press will, if not censored – and BBC will carry and be heard by many.

Agree to talk to Chiefs of Staff. Putterill says 'Yes' would support H.E. and considers he has a right to call on him as Commander-in-Chief, and knows that most of his seniors will agree; but RLI already deployed on 'government business'. Hawkins says no sign of split in government. No prospect of taking majority of his force. His previous instructions from Chief Justice were to carry out orders of government. He is fully in support of H.E. but is the present suggestion practicable?

8.15 am 11th. Tell H.E. above and also that vital third Commander (Commissioner of Police) would consider suggestion 'political' and would not support. In any event he is completely in pocket of Ministers Dupont and Lardner-Burke. H.E. appears to accept. Says he will call editors to him after PM has seen him. Hawkins mentions that Dupont queried with him whether helicopter allegedly flown in to G.H. (Government House, Official residence of Governor) yesterday was to remove Governor? H.E. unaware and laughs!

And on that day, 11 November, at the eleventh hour, it happened – the rebellion that was made to appear as though it was not a rebellion. The declaration was phrased in such a way as to give the impression that the 'rebels' were still loyal to the Queen; and it ended with the words 'God Save the Queen'. An added touch was that it was signed beneath the official portrait of the Queen.

---

* At the time all senior staff of the RBC (Rhodesian Broadcasting Corporation) were supporters of the government. Staff known to be of different persuasion had been forced to resign before UDI.

I was informed at the time of the declaration that the members of the Operations Co-ordinating Committee (OCC) were to call on the Prime Minister that afternoon. Set up in October 1964, the OCC was responsible for combined operations and comprised the Commissioner of Police, the Commanders of the Army and Air Force, and myself. When Putterill enquired of Mrs Smith whether her husband was ready to see us, however, she said he had gone to bed. The strain of publicly announcing UDI appeared to have been too much for Smith; this was the first sign of weakness that the OCC noted in him.

As Wilson had promised, no 'thunderbolt' appeared from the skies. The nearest thing to an immediate confrontation occurred on the banks of the Zambezi River. Putterill described it to me thus:

I spoke to all the troops in the Salisbury area on the afternoon of 11 November. I told them to stay at their posts and continue to function in the maintenance of law and order. I assured them that they would receive no unlawful orders from me.

The following day I visited the RLI at Kariba (deployed there as a gesture of defiance against the prospect of a British invasion) and found their morale sky-high. I subsequently got a message from Major-General John Willoughby, British Army GOC, Aden, who had given me and my wife lunch some six weeks previously when on our way to the British Chief of Defence Staff's exercise, and who had obviously been watching my inspection from the north bank of the Zambezi: 'Tell Sam Putterill I would much rather be drinking a beer with him in some pub than observing him from this distance through a pair of binoculars.'

That same day I visited the RAR (Rhodesian African Rifles, a predominantly black battalion) at Wankie. The African troops were understandably jittery, and there was some tension at the airfield when an African RSM told some troops: 'Hurry up and get your slit trenches dug for the British may be here soon!' The troops queried this: 'Are we fighting the British?'

The Company at Victoria Falls was very nervous. But the opposite side was manned by my old regiment from Federal days (Northern Rhodesia Regiment, with red flash on hat and red hose-tops) and I recalled the occasion when my old RSM, Lameck Mbewe, had said to Peter Walls (subsequently Rhodesian Army Commander) and me: 'Don't worry, Sirs, if we ever have a confrontation across the Zambezi just wave your old scarlet hose-tops and we will know not to open fire.' My hose-tops were not handy, so I withdrew the Company to an observation point at 'Spray View' airstrip and covered the bridge with 3″ mortars.

On the day following UDI the British High Commissioner, Jack Johnston, left Salisbury. This symbolic gesture had obviously been prepared well in advance and was designed to show that the British were pulling out with, it seemed, no thought for the Governor who had decided to stay at his post. I went to the airport to wish Johnston farewell, and found that I was the only Rhodesian official extending that courtesy. As Johnston boarded the aircraft he said: 'Don't worry, Ken, we'll be back inside three months. Sanctions will have worked and legality be restored.'

'You must be joking!' I replied, directing my glance more at the British Intelligence Officer present than at Johnston himself. 'If you really believe that, we've been wasting our time in liaison all these years.'

Later that day I was back at Government House to find out whether Gibbs intended to stay at his post or not. Clearly, the government were counting on him resigning in order to cut the final link with Britain and thus overcome the serious problem of split loyalties. Dupont claimed that Gibbs had promised to go; this may well have been the case, but neither Dupont nor his colleagues realised with what abhorrence Gibbs would regard them once he discovered that he had been tricked into signing the proclamation which 'legalised' UDI. My visit to the Governor had been preceded by visits by Smith, Dupont and Lardner-Burke who were trying, one after the other, to persuade him to resign. In my notes on the events of that day I recorded this:

12th Nov. 65. Pestell advised that PM visited H.E. to persuade him to resign. Then PM, Dupont and Lardner-Burke together accused him of being a traitor! He retaliated – 'Do you want constitutional government?' – 'Yes, but had been forced into UDI' – 'Then think out some means of restoring constitutionality.'

On several occasions over the next few days Smith and his colleagues asked if I could help in persuading the Governor to go but from my contacts with him and from other sources I was left in no doubt that he considered that he was doing the right thing by staying and he still had a function to perform as the only constitutional link with Britain.

It seemed to us on the terraces that Sir Humphrey Gibbs was emerging as a knight in shining armour surrounded by guileful gnomes. He soon began to attract friends and supporters. Among the first was the Chief Justice, Sir Hugh Beadle, who decided to stay at Government House to act as Gibbs's Constitutional adviser. He declared that he would not change his oath of allegiance in favour of an unconstitutional (UDI) government and added that all the other Judges supported him; moreover, he would refuse to be discharged and would have to be physically removed from office if necessary. Even Judge Hector Macdonald, who was more inclined towards the RF than the others, had, in Gibbs's words, 'stumped up to Government House on his wooden leg demanding that I lock up the entire Cabinet – as if I could!'

As to the support for Gibbs as Commander-in-Chief, these notes in my diary give an idea of what was happening at the time:

20th November 65. I relay report to H.E. that several senior Army officers have disclosed strong opposition on principle to government. CGS (Chief of General Staff) mentioned he had told PM before UDI at least 20 per cent of Army were opposed. Now he had told him probably 10 per cent opposed, as some had decided to go along with UDI, some had resigned, and a more acceptable attitude had prevailed when known that PM more conciliatory and that no Regent would be appointed to clash with Governor.

CAS (Chief of Air Staff) tells Governor happy to have his head counted with others and try to take Air Force with him. Would like H.E. to declare new elections to prove that country wants UDI. Alternative is to let country go to ruin first before trying to recover. CGS and I say climate not right; there would have to be real deterioration first.

By this time the RF, having failed to persuade Gibbs to resign, had begun to make use of his position as the only constitutional link with Britain. My diary notes for 20 November:

The wrangle continues. PM and Co submitted proposals to H.E. to negotiate on Rhodesian terms for a Royal Commission – committed to one sheet of paper and carried to UK last night, containing proposals for Constitutional Council; African MPs; Chiefs and African Nationalists to be included.

In spite of PM's assurance that everything going well, he seems anxious to re-open negotiations (eight days after UDI – the 'nine-day-wonder'!) rescind UDI and revert to constitutional government. Appeared not to have believed that Wilson would, in fact, implement sanctions. Obvious that suits PM – but probably not the others – for H.E. to remain and provide the link with UK.

All our reports on the likelihood of sanctions being imposed in the event of UDI had, it seemed, been ignored. This was underlined in a conversation I had with Lord Graham, Minister of Agriculture at the time. We were in a lift in Coghlan Building, on our way to the first post-UDI Cabinet meeting, which I had been asked to attend. Very affably, Graham said:

'Ken, I've got a couple of questions. Let's stand outside in the sunshine and chat awhile.'

We went outside.

'First of all, do you really believe that the British will impose sanctions on tobacco?'

I was flabbergasted. 'But in all our briefs we have made that point time and again, and your own officials in the Ministry have confirmed this. Tobacco is the most vulnerable of all commodities – it will be the first and most certain sanction.'

Graham shook his head, not believing that any British government would take such dastardly action. Then he put his second question to me:

'Do you know whether my colleagues intend to use force to remove Sir Humphrey Gibbs from Government House?'

'You must know, better than me, what your colleagues intend to do!'

'Yes,' he replied, 'but I would like you to know that it would be over my dead body that they would put a hand on the representative of the Queen!'

Graham's ancestor, the first Marquess of Montrose, was executed in 1650 for fighting for his King against an English government only partially supported by the Scots. The present Duke believed he was fighting for his Queen against a British government utterly unable to determine Rhodesia's destiny. I went on my way wondering how many Rhodesians saw UDI in the same way as Graham did.

The RF realised that it was now more important than ever to commit the population in support of UDI. This they did by assuring the waverers that UDI was not rebellion; it was merely a quarrel with a despicable Labour government in Britain and most British people were on Rhodesia's side. It was poorly played propaganda but it had its effect, just as any propaganda has an effect if it says what people want to hear. And the Rhodesian man-in-the-street was not alone in his gullibility. During my daily visits to Ian Smith's office in the weeks following UDI, I saw that he was virtually inundated by tens of thousands of congratulatory letters from all over the world, mostly from Britain. From being the relatively unknown son of a Scottish butcher in the village of Selukwe in central Rhodesia, Smith had become a world figure overnight and a hero to millions. Propaganda saw to it that the image of a 'strong, honest, simple man' was created; that his war-time experiences as an RAF pilot were made into a legend; and that he was portrayed as the 'saviour' of western civilisation in central Africa.

CHAPTER 4

The Economic War
1965–72

In the wake of the unilateral declaration of independence the politicians, the officials and the man-in-the-street waited to learn what reaction there would be from Britain. The British High Commissioner had been recalled, a political response which was to be followed by other ineffective political manoeuvres in the remaining months of 1965. The use of military force had been eschewed, though from time to time during those months CIO was fed with reports of imminent British invasion. Rhodesians therefore focused their concern on British reaction in the economic sphere.

As far back as October 1964 Harold Wilson had warned that 'UDI would inflict disastrous economic damage on Rhodesia'. The reports from British sources on which CIO had based its assessments of likely British reaction to UDI indicated strongly that the British were serious in their expressed intention of imposing economic sanctions. On the day UDI was declared Wilson had told the House of Commons: 'Our purpose is not punitive: it is to restore a situation in Rhodesia in which there can be untrammelled loyalty and allegiance to the Crown and in which there can be, within whatever rules the House lays down, a free government of Rhodesia acting in the interests of the people as a whole.' These noble sentiments were probably forced on him by the stand Sir Humphrey Gibbs had taken in declaring his allegiance to the Queen, rather than because of any sudden conversion of the British Labour government from Socialists to Royalists. In CIO we still believed that Wilson considered the economic lever, as opposed to the military and political levers, would force Smith's surrender, and this belief was underlined by his statement in January 1966 at the Commonwealth Conference in Lagos that 'the accumulative effect of economic and financial sanctions might well bring the rebellion to an end within a matter of weeks rather than months'. In contrast, Clifford Dupont had predicted that economic sanctions would fail, largely because the Rhodesian business community would have no option but to close ranks to fight for economic survival.

Wilson was wrong; Dupont was right. Many white Rhodesians, including those who had not supported UDI or the RF, became committed to using every ounce of resourcefulness, courage and cunning they had in order to outwit Britain in the economic war.

A major factor accounting for Rhodesia's initial success in the economic war was Britain's staggered rather than immediate and comprehensive imposition of sanctions; Rhodesia had time to adjust to the new situation and to work out ways of by-passing economic barriers as they were raised, bit by bit. The first measures struck Rhodesians as a damp squib. Rhodesia was expelled from the sterling area, Commonwealth preferences on Rhodesian goods were withdrawn, selective exchange controls were imposed and Rhodesia was excluded from the London market. This was followed in early December by Britain's seizure of the Rhodesian Reserve Bank's assets in London, which had the effect of convincing the RF Cabinet that they could now default on British and World Bank loans under British guarantee; this outweighed the losses incurred by the seizure. The balance in Rhodesia's favour increased when the Rhodesian government blocked all payments of dividends and interest to Britain. The money thus saved was swelled still further by locally floated loans which soaked up the liquid reserves trapped within the country by exchange controls and the discontinuance of external investment.

By mid-December 1965 Rhodesia was swimming in liquidity. It was easy to balance the national budget and to defray the cost of economic sanctions with no great risk of inflation. Little material change was discernible, a factor which encouraged and consolidated support for the RF. As Dupont had forecast, some small enterprises went under and the shortage of foreign currency hampered those in the import/export trade. But to many, the only serious effects of Britain's early economic measures were that imported wines became scarce, whisky was unobtainable and the Salisbury Club, that relic of the old establishment, ran out of port for the first time since its foundation in 1893.

Things took a slightly more serious turn on 17 December. Britain placed a ban on British oil and petroleum products destined for Rhodesia and prohibited the importation of Rhodesian tobacco and sugar; as Rhodesian minerals and meat had already been banned from Britain, the theoretical embargo on Rhodesia's exports to Britain now amounted to 90 per cent of the total. Later that day Harold Wilson sent a message to Sir Humphrey Gibbs which began:

Following my talks in the United Nations and my discussion with President Johnson I must tell you that events are moving rapidly to a climax so far as Rhodesia is concerned. While our decision to announce an oil embargo and a Zambian air lift may temporarily stabilise the United Nations position, we shall be lucky to avoid a mandatory resolution under Chapter 7 of the UN Charter binding on all states to apply full economic and oil sanctions.

The message went on to outline the military threat should the United Nations become involved but the economic threat contained in the above excerpt was seen by the RF as something which would have more serious repercussions in the House of Commons than in Rhodesia. Hitherto, Wilson's actions had been designed to accommodate both Labour and Conservative opinion, his slender majority in the House making such an all-party approach necessary. Now, however, it appeared that Britain no longer considered Rhodesia her sole responsibility and would turn to the United Nations for help. Such a move meant that the divisions in the House of Commons would inevitably reappear.

Smith remained perfectly calm under the threat and waited for the split. The first signs came when Reginald Maudling said in the House that Britain would lose control if mandatory sanctions were imposed, that mandatory sanctions would not work unless all other countries (including South Africa) joined in, and that the effect of such action would further consolidate opinion in Rhodesia behind the die-hards in the government and render impossible any chance of moderate Rhodesian opinion changing the course of events.

Selective mandatory sanctions were imposed by the United Nations at the end of 1966, but by that time the all-party approach had long since fallen by the wayside as a result of Wilson's action, in April 1966, to establish a naval blockade to make the oil embargo effective.

Wilson's belief that the decisive factor in ending the rebellion would be an effective oil embargo – by naval blockade, by closure of the Beira–Umtali pipeline and by stopping oil reaching Rhodesia from South Africa – led to a series of wrong moves by Britain, based on incorrect assumptions about Portuguese and South African attitudes. CIO was aware, for example, that Britain had been deliberately misadvised that the closure of the pipeline would prove effective and that Portugal would not challenge United Nations action. We knew that the Portuguese simply intended to ignore such action. We were also aware that Britain had misunderstood South Africa's statement that it would treat Rhodesia on the basis of 'business as usual'. Somewhat surprisingly, London had interpreted this to mean that there would be no increase in the volume of trade between the two countries, whereas it clearly meant that South Africa would not impede normal trade, which is usually expected to find its own level.

Britain's wrong assumptions led to this sort of statement, made by the

British Ambassador to South Africa and reported in the South African Press on 18 February 1966: 'We are keeping a close watch on this situation with the movement of petroleum products and will continue to keep a close watch on it. It is our aim to ensure that the oil embargo should be 100 per cent effective.'

How could it be effective so long as normal trade continued between South Africa and Rhodesia? Why were British diplomats making such patently meaningless statements? Was the British Prime Minister using British Intelligence assessments, or did he prefer his own advice? From our checks and cross-checks with British Intelligence we knew that they had all the right answers, but it seemed that their views were subordinated within a system that did not permit them direct access to the Prime Minister.

The Beira–Umtali pipeline had been operative before UDI, with the principal objective of guaranteeing petroleum supplies to Zambia through the Rhodesian refinery, thus keeping Zambia in pawn. But a strong note of warning was sounded shortly after UDI when the Rhodesian government formed a consortium to take over the pipeline management from the Mozambique–Rhodesia Pipeline Company (CPMR) because Lonrho as the major shareholder was seen to be subject to British control. 'Tiny' Rowland cried 'Foul!' because he was deprived of ownership, but this deprivation was temporary. He made much of his opposition to Ian Smith and his government. But despite this opposition Lonrho retained its many interests in the country such as gold and copper mines and a million acres of cattle ranches and forestry.

In March 1966 the new consortium announced that they would commence pumping oil to the refinery when two Greek tankers *Ionna V* and *Manuela* appeared on the horizon. This announcement produced a flurry of diplomatic activity. The Portuguese, under pressure, put the tank farm linking the quayside to the pipeline 'out of bounds to Rhodesian oil'. But our Ministry of Transport had been tipped off that this would happen and a local Portuguese-Greek, Souglides, was engaged to take ownership of the land between the quayside and the pipeline. Here, land storage tanks were installed at great speed, to connect directly with any arriving tanker.

The owner of *Ionna V* had had his vessel deprived of Greek registration and had switched to Panamanian registration. On 10 April the British representative at the United Nations persuaded the Security Council that Rhodesia's actions were 'a threat to world peace' and a British naval force in the Mozambique channel started enforcing a blockade of the port of Beira (this became known as the 'Beira Patrol').

This frightened Panama into threatening to cancel the ship-owner's registration, which, in turn, frightened the ship-owner and a few days later the tanker sailed away without discharging her cargo. On the surface, it appeared as though Wilson had won the 'battle of Beira' and won it easily. But behind the scenes there had been moves and counter-moves which had far more bearing on the reason for *Ionna V*'s departure than the stance taken by Britain, Greece or Panama.

Two days after the 'threat to world peace' statement in the United Nations, Smith received a visit from Joao de Freitas Cruz and Jorge Jardim. Jardim, who as Salazar's youngest and most vigorous Minister, had saved Angola for Portugal virtually single-handed when the revolt erupted there in 1961 and who had become a legend in his own lifetime, was currently amassing a fortune in Mozambique and wielding unbridled power. The Secretary to the Cabinet, Gerald Clarke, in his record of the visit, wrote:[1]

It indicated that the Portuguese Government now believed that they were the focus of Britain's attention and attack because Britain found herself unable to deal with the Rhodesian situation without first undermining the Portuguese position ... The Portuguese claimed that they had evidence of Britain's decision to concentrate on Mozambique and Beira and land military forces if necessary. They had been told by their own legal advisers that the UN resolution provided the British with the legal right to land troops at Beira if required to enforce the observation of the United Nations' mandate. The Portuguese, therefore, queried the wisdom of Rhodesia's proceeding to pump 18,000 gallons of crude oil ashore from *Ionna V*.

Jardim went on to say that it seemed unnecessary to provoke military action over this small quantity of oil; that Portuguese advice was that pumping should not commence; and that if Rhodesia took this advice Portugal was prepared to increase its supply of petrol to Rhodesia.

Before giving an official reply, Smith sent for Albers, the Acting South African Diplomatic Representative, to establish whether, in view of Portugal's apparent change of attitude, South Africa would continue with and consolidate her assistance. The situation was then put before Cabinet where it was agreed in discussion to seek confirmation of the Portuguese and South African governments' attitudes if oil supplies through Beira were stopped:

The major principle involved was Rhodesia's entitlement to make full use of the Beira port in the future. This might now be the time to ask the Portuguese and the South Africans to declare themselves. To allow the ship to leave Beira without unloading would be publicising the fact that Beira was no longer a source of oil for Rhodesia and this might turn world attention on South Africa to that country's embarrassment.

If pumping from the *Ionna V* was abandoned, the Cabinet would issue a statement deploring Britain's 'immoral behaviour' in dragging other countries into what was a domestic dispute. The decision to follow Portuguese advice and stop pumping would, however, depend upon South Africa's response to Rhodesia's request for increased assistance and upon what guarantees the Portuguese could give on an increase in oil supplies through Lourenco Marques.

By the time of the next Cabinet meeting on 19 April, the Minister of External Affairs had received an ambiguous assurance from the Portuguese that they would 'resist any request for the passage of troops through Portuguese territories in Africa, although the terms of the United Nations Charter might oblige a country to allow passage of troops under certain Security Council mandatory sanctions.'[2] And the Prime Minister had learned from the South Africans that 'they were not looking for trouble and although they would give every support to Rhodesia on normal commercial and industrial levels, they could not be expected to court danger unnecessarily nor become openly committed or take sides.'

At the same Cabinet meeting on 19 April counter-measures were considered against copper consignments from Zambia and Zaire passing through Rhodesia to Beira and Lourenco Marques. The convoluted reasoning which appeared then would be developed to considerable effect, ensuring that Rhodesian counter-action became at least as effective as Britain's application of sanctions:[3]

... the question was simply whether it was opportune to stop copper shipments or not. It seemed to be immaterial for the objective – which was to show to the world what British oil sanctions might lead to – to be particular about the mechanics of stopping consignments or about their destination. A threat of interruption of railings should be sufficient to bring home to Britain and other copper consumers the likely results of the sanctions now being pursued. There seemed to be no need to make any public statements nor to leak information to the press...

CABINET agreed:

(a) that consignments of copper on the railways through Rhodesia should be interrupted and delayed on a selective basis for the present on the grounds that fuel supplies were being cut off by British oil embargoes;

(b) that the mechanics and administrative arrangements of how this should be achieved be left to the Minister of Transport and Power to determine...

In the meantime, however, CIO had been pursuing its own course in the *Ionna V* issue. Gerald Clarke had informed me of the meeting between Smith and Jardim, bemoaning the fact that he had been excluded from what appeared to have been a vital discussion. He had tried to persuade Smith that some other representative, such as myself, should be called into the discussion, but reported that Jardim had said to Smith, in Clarke's presence, that 'we cannot trust any Rhodesian official in a matter such as this – particularly Mr Flower'. As a result, Smith had continued the meeting with Jardim and de Freitas Cruz alone.

I had already learned from the Minister of Transport, Brigadier Dunlop, that on his recent visit to Beira he had been told that the Portuguese did not trust CIO; they had also indicated their reluctance to deal with certain other Rhodesian officials.[4] I decided to tackle De Freitas Cruz and found that he was embarrassed by Jardim's effrontery. I then saw Smith to try to discover his reaction to Jardim's statement about my 'untrustworthiness'. I said that if he accepted the statement, then I must resign; if he did not accept it, then I should be allowed to attempt to verify Jardim's story. Smith said that he had been suspicious of Jardim's story until he had heard that the Portuguese Air Force were now flying interceptor aircraft from Luanda in Angola across to Beira and strengthening their ground forces there. My conversation with Smith then proceeded along these lines:

'Prime Minister, if there is, in fact, a British invasion force in the Mozambique channel, all our liaison sources have failed us, including the Portuguese, the South Africans, the French and the British themselves. Please give me time to get the right answer.'

'How long will you need?'

'I don't know, but with a bit of luck I can clear this up one way or another later today.'

And I was lucky. I managed to get General Deslandes, the Portuguese Commander-in-Chief, on the telephone in Lisbon. When I told him of the reason for the call he asked if I was joking, adding that he knew nothing of a British invasion force in the Mozambique channel nor that Portuguese Air Force planes were flying from Luanda to Beira. He returned my call within an hour, having received assurances from the British that there was no such force, either destined to overfly Mozambique or to attack Rhodesia.

With this information at hand CIO then sought explanations from contacts in Lourenco Marques. But neither they nor the Governor-General in Lourenco Marques knew anything of Jardim's visit or of his allegations; they could only presume that he was a special emissary direct from Salazar and that any disposition of air or ground forces in Beira would have been under his direct instruction. I went back to Smith with the news that he had been hoodwinked. He took it well, but said: 'What option had I other than to comply with something requested by

Salazar? We could not survive without their co-operation and if they want us to send *Ionna V* away and are prepared to let us have petrol from other sources, this is what we must do.'

Still feeling resentful that he had preferred to listen to a Portuguese chancer rather than his own Security and Intelligence Adviser, I agreed we were in a rather helpless position but told him that I had just returned from Beira, where Rhodesian morale was sky high at the imminent prospect of oil sanctions being broken. I went on:

'If that ship leaves port with its cargo of oil, morale will take a nasty knock. All the good work of Brigadier Dunlop, Colonel Leslie and Commander Trethowan in building the new tank farm at Beira will be wasted – not to mention the loss of money, and poor Souglides destroyed – for no other ship dare come again. Rhodesians will believe the British have won. But only Jardim will win. And we cannot ever be certain that Jardim came from Salazar. He may have been acting entirely on his own.'

Smith queried this: 'But surely De Freitas Cruz would not have represented Portuguese interests except in an official capacity?'

'I just don't know, Prime Minister. They do not function as we do, and I fear that even De Freitas Cruz could have been subordinated to Jardim's personal interests.'

We did not know then that Jardim was already well advanced in his plans to build a petrol station immediately across the Mozambican/ Rhodesian border, only five miles from Umtali, and to ensure that it would be his oil refinery, Sonarep, in Lourenco Marques that would cater for much of Rhodesia's oil needs during the economic war. Twelve years later Jardim published a book justifying his role in that war. The title he chose says it all – *Sanctions Double-Cross*.

With their control over sanctions slipping away from them, the British authorities continued to classify the Beira Patrol as 'effective' although only Lonrho's pipeline had been put out of commission and all petroleum products necessary for Rhodesia's survival were coming directly from Lourenco Marques or indirectly from South Africa. By the middle of 1966 fuel shortages in Rhodesia were manageable, and by 1971 fuel rationing could be abandoned – with the Beira Patrol playing to an international audience like something out of Gilbert and Sullivan.

In December 1966 the London *Daily Telegraph* featured a front-page exposure by their ace reporter, Ian Colvin, of an outfit which had all the hallmarks of a British or American Intelligence operation:

SECRET FUND TO BACK SANCTIONS

A powerful organisation in Zurich, working with funds from a large American foundation and several African States, has launched a secret political and propaganda campaign to create 'liberal opinion' against the Smith régime in Rhodesia and make mandatory sanctions effective.

This pressure consortium, named the 'Interform Organisation' estimates that at least £225,000 in secret funds must be spent to close gaps in sanctions and condition public opinion ... It consists of independent companies operating in New York, Washington, Paris, Rome, London, Frankfurt and Brussels. But the credibility of its campaign is likely to be much compromised by the removal of a number of key documents from the registry of an African diplomatic mission in London. [Dare one say it ... compromised by good counter-intelligence.]

The key document upon which Interform policy is based is a circular written after the Commonwealth Prime Ministers' Conference in September when the central planning committee considered that an agreement between Mr Wilson and Mr Smith was no longer possible. Another document defines Interform methods as 'firmly based on the principle that all techniques used must be unobtrusive and that results achieved must appear to stem naturally from a consensus of informed opinion which cannot easily be identified with any direct source of propaganda.'

Nor could the London company be 'easily identified' from its stated address in Dover Street; Colvin, when calling there, discovered that 'it is a postal forwarding address with a firm of chartered accountants'. He concluded: 'Interform Great Britain Ltd is not a member of the Institute of Public Relations, whose members are required to disclose the interest for whom they are working.'

The imposition of comprehensive mandatory sanctions in May 1968 made very little difference to the overall situation. Certainly, imports continued to be expensive and exporting through devious routes at cut prices presented difficulties, but most countries continued to ignore United Nations sanctions. Only Britain and some Scandinavian countries appeared to be trying to enforce sanctions, but even Britain did not always seem to take sanctions seriously. For example, when the British authorities were advised by 'Tiny' Rowland in 1968 that British and British-linked oil companies were the main defaulters in the oil embargo, no action was taken. Similarly, CIO was aware from its part in a sanctions spy scandal, if from nothing else, that the British and American authorities had a mass of evidence about sanctions evasion – but they used it either defensively or not at all.

The sanctions spy scandal began to come to light towards the end of 1969. The 'spies' concerned were Roger Nicholson, financial editor of the *Rhodesia Herald* and confidant of Treasury officials and top businessmen, and Trevor Gallagher, a lawyer who used his New

Zealand Air Force background to provide him with access to RF circles, in which he propounded eccentric theories on the application of constitutional law. Gallagher came to notice because of that little something that raises suspicion in the mind of a policeman. He professed liberalism in lawyers' company but associated with the die-hards in the RF, which included the party chairman, Colonel Mac Knox. I mentioned this to Smith, advising him that Knox was just the sort of gullible person who would be taken in by Gallagher. Smith listened, and then warned Knox off.

The warning, however, seemed to have little effect. A few days later I was in 'La Fontaine' restaurant with my CIA colleague, Irl Smith, when I observed Knox and Gallagher at a nearby table in earnest conversation. With no ulterior motive in mind, I asked Irl Smith what he thought of Gallagher's association with Knox. He replied that he did not know either man. Why he lied to me I do not know. Knox was a public figure who would surely have been the subject of some CIA reports; and only a few hours previously I had seen a Special Branch report in which mention was made of a visit by Gallagher to Irl Smith's home the previous evening. Immediately after lunch I discussed the matter with OC Special Branch and we moved into action. Irl Smith was placed under closer surveillance than we normally reserved for colleagues in the world of Intelligence, and in no time at all he was caught collecting reports from Gallagher and Nicholson in dead and not-so-dead letter-boxes.

The politicians were suddenly proud of CIO, but they were less impressed with the plan we concocted to exchange Nicholson and Gallagher as surety for American goodwill. I had worked out the deal with CIA emissaries visiting Pretoria and had secured Ian Smith's support for it. Then Lardner-Burke, Minister of Justice, stepped in. Supported by none other than Knox, he seemed determined that the 'traitors' should pay for their deeds by rotting in gaol; he introduced tougher legislation to deal with spies and traitors and made it retrospective to include Gallagher and Nicholson.

This put me in a dilemma. I knew by now that the information sold by the two agents to CIA, and previously to MI6, was worthless compared to the real Intelligence exchanged between our services. And I did not wish to expose Irl Smith or the fact that CIA, and MI6 before them, had broken a gentleman's agreement not to run agents in each other's territories. After many bitter arguments I won the day by threatening to resign on a point of honour: I had assured the British and the Americans that Ian Smith would agree to the release of the agents and that the 'swop' would go through.[5] The result was that the debate on the Official

Secrets Bill was adjourned; Gallagher and Nicholson were released and deported; and although the American State Department later countermanded what CIA had agreed by closing the American Consulate in Salisbury, CIO had gained an *entrée* into Washington that would stand the Rhodesian government in good stead later on.

Far more damaging than the intensification of sanctions in May 1968 was the drought of that year, which had depressed farming activities and killed off thousands of cattle. However, by the time the HMS *Fearless* talks commenced in October 1968 the agricultural outlook had improved. Simultaneously, there had been new discoveries of chromite and nickel deposits. Both these factors contributed substantially to the feeling of economic well-being in Rhodesia, which in turn largely accounted for Smith's rejection of the favourable terms offered by the British on *Fearless*.

Sanctions-busting by this time had become a highly intricate and successful game in which players from many countries were participating. Many South Africans felt that, rather than stand idly by and watch sanctions become effective (thereby risking having sanctions imposed on South Africa), they should do what they could to help Rhodesian businessmen defeat them. A South African, Noel Bruce, in his capacity as Governor of the Reserve Bank of Rhodesia, worked wonders with the Rhodesian economy. The Portuguese, of course, had both an ideological and a commercial interest in flouting sanctions. Zambia, whether she liked it or not, had to flout sanctions or perish; the country could not survive without power from the hydro-electricity installations on the south bank of the Zambezi at Kariba, and attempts to alleviate shortages and transport problems by expensive air lifts and the construction of the TANZAM railway failed to wean Zambia from her dependency on Rhodesia and South Africa. Goods trains continued to cross the Victoria Falls bridge at the height of sanctions enforcement, carrying copper from Zambia and Zaire and returning with food, coke and explosives absolutely vital to their mining operations. How often some of our wild boys contemplated arranging what might have been a disastrous explosion! But it was decided at higher level to sustain Zambia's and Zaire's lifeline rather than have them heading for economic ruin, particularly after their only viable alternative, the Benguela Railway line through Angola, was closed, never to be opened again.

The government showed considerable skill in managing the economy and fighting sanctions. In this it received great assistance from both the Civil Service and parastatals such as the Grain Marketing Board and the

Cold Storage Commission. It also established new parastatals specifically tasked with evading sanctions by planning the diversification of
commerce and industry. The operations of these parastatals were master-
minded by professionals in government and a few business barons, and
diversification took place on a large scale. Rhodesia became self-
sufficient in many crops which had been grown only marginally before
UDI, and from an almost total dependence on the importation of manu-
factured goods was soon manufacturing a host of goods required for
domestic consumption.

Some of those engaged in sanctions-busting abided too literally by the
dictum that one must 'set a crook to catch a crook'. The government's
own sanctions-busting department, headed by Charles Cook, who was
given the title of 'The Prime Minister's Customs and Special Adviser',
included a few people whom CIO had warned government against and
who took advantage of a situation in which they could make a considerable amount of money. I remember Jim Samuels, Chairman of Rhodesian Breweries, saying: 'Regrettably, all of this – now routine – activity
is producing a new and crooked generation of businessmen within
Rhodesia smart enough to deal with the widest of wide boys.'

The government had to save the major industries, such as tobacco, by
buying successive crops and stockpiling them in aircraft hangars until
their clandestine sale or barter could be arranged elsewhere in the world.
There was no shortage of customers. Indeed, in the opening years of
UDI Rhodesia enjoyed more affinity in economic terms around the
world than opposition. Those who worked behind the scenes in the
evasion of sanctions were legion: Senators and Congressmen from the
United States of America; representatives of British and French companies who concealed their origins by dealing through South Africa or
elsewhere; Swiss, Italian and Japanese businessmen who came and went
without any qualms; West Germans who, amongst other things,
arranged to send an expensive printing press in a disguised Rhodesian
Air Force plane so that Rhodesian bank notes could be printed locally,
not in Britain; Greeks and Jews who were more than ready to set up
dummy companies and disguise the Rhodesian origins or destination of
certain goods; and Russians who plied their ships in and out of Mozambican ports to load Rhodesian chromite.

There is no better example of the international cynicism which helped
Rhodesians defeat sanctions than the competition between the two
super-powers to acquire Rhodesia's high-grade chromite, despite the
fact that both Russia and America had voted in the United Nations for
mandatory sanctions against Rhodesia. Because the chromite began to

find its way to Russia by various routes, the United States Senate amended their Strategic Minerals Acts in January 1972 to legalise the purchase of chromite from Rhodesia rather than have to buy it at a high price from the Russians or take an inferior Russian product. And when the Mozambican border closure in 1976 finally stopped the export of chromite through Lourenco Marques, the considerable stockpile of Rhodesian chromite was promptly paid for by Russian agents and clandestinely removed in Russian bottoms.

Because it suited most sanctions-busters to keep their business secret, CIO's role was vital, and we spent much time seeking entrepreneurs, trying to assess the relative reliability of inherently unreliable dealers (particularly those who would satisfy the Armed Forces' ever-increasing demand for weapons of war) and engaging in numerous other projects. We watched the strangest of developments and helped where it served Rhodesia's interests to do so, and we hindered British and other efforts to expose sanctions-busting activities. Our Intelligence liaisons developed to such a point that the problem became not one of seeking new friends but of keeping liaisons within the practical limits of reciprocity.

All this merely confirmed the fact that business is business and international politics a sham. My fund of anecdotal material to illustrate this point grew rapidly. To take but one example, Rhodesia was visited by a number of powerful Americans, mainly Southerners, who believed that little old Rhodesia had to be helped to 'put the niggers right back where they belonged'. Among them was Senator Jim Eastland, a Democrat and the Chairman of the Senate Judicial Committee; he was accompanied by some Texan oil men seeking to engage in a touch of dirty 'Dallas' business. During my conversation with Eastland at a business promotion dinner, it became clear that a Southern 'Democrat' was worlds apart from Western 'Democracy'. He declaimed loudly and offensively about our choice of venue, the multiracial Ambassador Hotel: 'You've inserted the thin end of the wedge by allowing stinking niggers into such a fine hotel.'

Diplomatic and other international links which had been severed by UDI continued underground through CIO channels where we could obtain some reciprocity. Only South Africa and Portugal maintained the facade of 'Accredited Diplomatic Representatives' through their Ministries of Foreign Affairs, but the restricted functioning of these establishments meant that even they became reliant on the economic, political and military Intelligence which CIO could provide. Elsewhere, the world became our oyster, sometimes reluctant to be opened by Intelligence probes but eventually responding if commercial needs prevailed; our

Intelligence liaison services expanded tenfold in Europe, Africa and the Middle East and increased significantly in Asia and the Americas.

And there went I, frequently bemused but rarely rebuffed, either as an unaccredited (and therefore 'deniable') emissary of Ian Smith or as the anonymous head of the Rhodesian Secret Service seeking something to exchange in the grey world of Intelligence. Some Chiefs of Intelligence led me directly to their Heads of State; others led to valuable political and commercial connections; and a few led straight into an Army rut.

France provided the *entrée* into much of Europe, the Middle East and Africa. De Gaulle and Pompidou were only too ready to snub their noses at the British and ignore the United Nations, and thus I found that my opposite number in Paris, the head of SDECE (Service de Documentation Exterieure et de Contre-Espionnage) was always anxious to help; the fact that he had once worked on a Rhodesian farm and had thus developed a warm affection for the country may have had a little to do with it. His influence led us into Belgium, Italy, Greece and several countries in North and West Africa.

The Italians were as uninhibited by United Nations sanctions as Mussolini had been when faced with similar League of Nations action over Abyssinia in 1935. Amongst our most valuable connections in Italy were those in the Holy See itself. And in the Italian Intelligence we found a firm friend in the Head of the organisation, General Michelli. Michelli would draw on his pipe and recount his experiences in Africa when vast tracts of the continent were ruled by Italy, or he would talk affectionately of Ian Smith, the RAF pilot who had been on the run in northern Italy until taken into the homes of partisans. Italian vehicles appeared on Rhodesian roads and Italian aircraft patrolled our skies in the colours of the Rhodesian Air Force. When Michelli went to prison (nothing to do with Rhodesian matters) all at first seemed lost, but the connections we had established survived through commercial channels.

The Greek connection was based on the fact that thousands of Greeks lived in Rhodesia and most of them had retained their Greek nationality. The politicians in Athens responded favourably to the influence of these Greeks. Rhodesian beef, for example, appeared in Athenian restaurants (just as it improved the menu in Paris, Brussels and Rome) and when the rule of Greek Colonels was shattered commercial interests sustained the links which had already been formed.

The Portuguese connection was based on contiguity in Africa and Salazar's determination to help Rhodesia against the British. The Head of PIDE/DGS did all he could to establish the commercial links that our sanction-busters needed, making valuable introductions with international arms-dealers and assisting our entry into Spain.

In Africa we went where the spirit moved, easily attracting mercenary rulers, such as Mobutu of Zaire, or the leaders of Biafra, Togo and Chad who could use our services in fighting their own wars. One of the few countries in Africa to spurn us was Somalia, when we offered assistance in their war with Ethiopia.

We found friends in South America, particularly in Brazil, and in such unlikely places as the Yemen and Mauritius. We got as far afield as Taiwan, whose merchant fleet could be put to good use. And our two-way trade with the Eastern bloc involved many more countries than the number of those with whom we dealt in the West.

A vital aspect of our dealings with the rest of the world in the sanctions game was the air link established by the legendary Jack Malloch. Rhodesian-born flying companion of Ian Smith in the RAF during the Second World War, the intrepid Malloch literally covered the globe to ensure Rhodesia's survival. There was no job too small, too remote or too difficult that Malloch would not lend himself to in whatever aircraft could be found in his specially formed 'Rhodesia Air Service', 'Air Trans Africa', 'Affretair' or 'Air Gabon Cargo'. There were many other titles but they all had the same objective – to tear sanctions apart and fly the tatters sky high.

For most of the time a CIO officer served with Malloch to try to keep his numerous activities integrated with Rhodesian government requirements and to satisfy the Treasury that government funds were not being wasted, for finance was not Malloch's strong point; he got on with the job and left it to others to provide the cash that was needed to keep his activities at full stretch, such as spending a couple of million dollars here and there on buying an extra Boeing or DC8. The purchase of such aircraft was, in itself, a considerable victory over sanctions and involved the need to overcome certain minor problems, such as trying to keep large aeroplanes 'invisible' to Air Traffic Controllers or explaining to the Captain of a routine South African Airways flight to London, flying around the 'Bulge of Africa', that there was no need for panic when he saw one, then two, then three unidentifiable aeroplanes coming from the opposite direction on a route no one else used.

Many of Malloch's exploits must remain shrouded in mystery. He was a modest, unassuming character who rarely spoke of himself, and his death in March 1982 in one of his beloved Spitfires, which he had recovered from the Rhodesian Air Force base and completely refur-

bished, finally put paid to the likelihood that he might one day reveal
more. But CIO was aware that he spent much time carrying out dangerous and almost impossible tasks: landing on disused airfields elsewhere
in Africa without aids of any sort amidst one shooting affair after
another; carrying arms and ammunition, food and contraband; and
evacuating starving or wounded refugees while evading fighter aircraft
in foul weather. He would go back time and again to areas where
natural or man-made dangers convinced those who needed his assistance that only he could provide it.

Some of Malloch's sorties were fairly sedate, such as flying top-grade
Rhodesian meat to Amsterdam; others were less so, such as conveying
arms into and out of Arabia for British or Rhodesian purposes. Sedate or
not, such activities were a full-time occupation, but Malloch still found
time to assist the French in Central/West Africa, the Portuguese on the
borders of Angola, the Belgians in the Congo and the British in the
Sudan. He participated in CIO's operations in aid of Biafra during the
secessionist war; in one of these operations, which included flying newly
printed Biafran money from Rome to Togo, he was double-crossed and
spent five months in a Togolese gaol. Malloch flew for African potentates such as Mobutu or Bongo for no other reason than to keep them in
power. He knew, as we did, that the benefits we might derive from some
of his operations in Africa were negligible, but Rhodesia benefited considerably from other operations in which he was involved, until a situation prevailed in which many leaders in Africa knew they could call on
aid from Rhodesia when they were unlikely to find it anywhere else.
There is no doubt that by bringing the world to Rhodesia's doorstep,
Malloch and his aeroplanes contributed more than any other single
factor to the defeat of economic sanctions.

Without Malloch and without the resourcefulness displayed by
Rhodesian entrepreneurs, sanctions might have succeeded. In theory,
they should have worked. Rhodesia was a small landlocked country
dependent on imported oil and foreign trade to sustain her economy.
Many of her vital exports, such as chromite, tobacco and asbestos, were
easily identifiable throughout the world. The tobacco crop alone
accounted for one third of all exports and 40 per cent of Rhodesian
tobacco had normally gone to Britain, who was now applying sanctions.
But theory is of less consequence than practice in the competitive world
of commerce.

Rhodesia survived the economic pressures because most whites and a
great number of blacks were committed to help defeat sanctions. The
material condition of the blacks did not worsen; if anything, it im-

proved. Years later I was with a prominent black lawyer and staunch supporter of Robert Mugabe when he said to the American Ambassador: 'You whites had it all wrong. UDI was a benevolent act which gave Africans their chance politically and otherwise. Sanctions helped in that they led to great diversification and much development which was of material benefit to the Africans.'

White emigration increased shortly after UDI but it was still less than had occurred at the dissolution of the Federation three years earlier. Even when the outcome of sanctions may have hung in the balance, there was no public reaction against the Rhodesian government. This disproves the theory that sanctions are a corrective measure. The dividing line between 'correction' and 'punishment' is wafer-thin, and those subjected to sanctions in Rhodesia responded to what they saw as collective punishment by joining forces to oppose the 'punisher', not by 'correcting' their behaviour. Ian Smith became more – not less – intransigent, contrary to Harold Wilson's belief that sanctions would force Smith into a negotiated settlement.

But Wilson alone should not be blamed for the failure of sanctions. Rhodesia had won the economic war long before 1972 through high endeavour, resourcefulness and great pride in national achievement. No one could have foreseen that a few thousand Rhodesians would hold out against a world which appeared determined to eradicate white power in Africa. This raises a final and interesting point. Rhodesia found new friends whilst defeating sanctions; many of them were commercially motivated, but one must ask oneself whether they would have helped defeat sanctions unless there was widespread acceptance of what Rhodesia stood for.

CHAPTER 5

The Political War
1965–72

On the day after the unilateral declaration of independence I received a
message from the Governor's Comptroller, John Pestell, with the request
that I read it and pass it on to Gerald Clarke, the Secretary to the
Cabinet. I read the message with utter disbelief.

STATEMENT ISSUED BY HIS EXCELLENCY
THE GOVERNOR OF RHODESIA
AFTER THE DECLARATION OF INDEPENDENCE

The Government have made an unconstitutional declaration of independence.
I have received the following message from Her Majesty's Secretary of State for
Commonwealth Relations:–
Message begins:
   'I have it in command from Her Majesty to inform you that it is Her Majesty's
pleasure that, in the event of an unconstitutional declaration of independence,
Mr Ian Smith and the other persons holding office as Ministers of the Govern-
ment of Southern Rhodesia or as Deputy Ministers cease to hold office.
   I am commanded by Her Majesty to instruct you in that event to convey Her
Majesty's pleasure in this matter to Mr Smith and otherwise to publish it in such
manner as you may deem fit.'

Message ends.

In accordance with these instructions I have informed Mr Smith and his colleagues that they no longer hold office. I call on the citizens of Rhodesia to
refrain from all acts which would further the objectives of the illegal authorities.
Subject to that it is the duty of all citizens to maintain law and order in the
country and to carry on with their normal tasks. This applies equally to the
judiciary, the armed services, the police and the public service.

How could the British government and supporting officials have got so
out of touch in such a short time? Surely they realised that the Governor,
alone and powerless, was in no better position than they were to dismiss
Ian Smith or his Ministers? The only consolation in the message was the
appeal to the Judiciary, the Armed Services, the Police and the Civil
Service 'to carry on with their normal tasks'.

My task as adviser to both the Prime Minister and the Governor now
included regular nightly meetings at Government House. I would meet
the Commanders, Putterill and Hawkins, at one or other of their homes
and we would set off to collect Pestell and enter the grounds of Govern-

ment House through his premises after all the staff had left for the evening. Although no risk was involved in our meetings, it suited us to follow a somewhat conspiratorial pattern so as not to involve others who might not wish to be involved and to avoid embarrassment to the Governor and the Prime Minister, who had their own reasons for keeping this strange arrangement to themselves. These nightly rendezvous occasioned Hawkins' children to refer to us as the 'three wise men passing like ships in the night'.

Gibbs dare not leave Government House for fear of being denied re-entry; nor could he contact officials or friends by telephone for the government had indulged in the petty action of cutting off his telephone, as well as removing his official car and withdrawing his salary. Consequently, a part of our meetings was usually taken up with discussing farming matters or giving him news of his many friends, over a game of snooker. Sometimes we were joined by Sir Hugh Beadle, the mercurial Chief Justice who would describe with asperity his most recent confrontation with Lardner-Burke, Minister of Law and Order, or tell us how he had refused to resign or take a new oath, advising us to do the same because the issues were quite straightforward: refuse to be sacked by an illegal regime and put its actions to the test in the High Court when his Bench of Judges would decide in our favour!

Gibbs wished to put his case across to the people – that he was holding the constitutional fort, hoping that the worst effects of UDI could be avoided – but complete censorship of all local media was imposed immediately at UDI. The Governor was barred from the broadcasting services and the national newspapers were appearing with sometimes more blank spaces than print (new regulations were promulgated in February 1966 making it an offence in law to publish any newsprint with blank spaces). Views expressed by Gibbs's supporters were similarly suppressed. Malvern's attempt to publicise his opinions was censored out of local newspapers, radio and television, but his statement did appear in *The Times* (London) on 15 November, making the point that UDI had precipitated the chances of a direct clash between blacks and whites in Rhodesia: 'Surely they (the RF) have the wit to learn – if they can learn anything – that what a revolting minority can do a revolting majority can do so much better.' On the censorship issue he drew an analogy with the suppression of freedom of speech in Germany at the time of Munich, and went on to say that: 'I am particularly concerned with the position of Sir Humphrey Gibbs but delighted with the stand he has taken. This may swing against them, because Sir Humphrey is so very popular with the farmers. I have discussed his position with him and we agree that nothing much could be done within the country to oppose Mr Smith because he has the police in his pocket.'

Gibbs could have been removed forcibly from Government House without a shot being fired – his ADC, Captain Owen, and Pestell would have been powerless to prevent it for they had no influence with the government – but it was the silent stand taken by the Commanders that deterred the government from taking such action. The Commanders' stand could not, of course, be publicised, nor could information be released about the growing number of prominent Rhodesians who were in support of Gibbs and who contributed to a fund to maintain him and his staff at Government House. Among them were Malvern, Welensky, all the judges, Campbell (Chairman of Standard Bank), Alec Hampshire (Chairman of Meikles Trust) and hundreds more. (The demonstration of sympathy for Gibbs, organised by Malvern on the first anniversary of UDI, led to what became known as the 'Battle of the Books'; Gibbs's supporters were encouraged to sign the Visitors' Book at Government House, in response to which Dupont encouraged government supporters to sign the book he had opened at Parliament Buildings, as 'Officer Administering the Government'.)

After the telephone at Government House had been disconnected, I suggested to British Intelligence that their radio communication network, then being dismantled, should be moved to Government House under CIO's protection. My suggestion was not taken up. The greatest 'risk' the British appeared to be willing to take was to leave a Deputy High Commissioner, Stanley Fingland, in Salisbury to maintain diplomatic links without resuming constitutional responsibility. I did what I could through my British contacts to get the decision to remove the High Commissioner reversed, arguing that the rupture was political and that official and constitutional links should therefore be preserved – but without success.

Through no fault of Fingland's, the British High Commission quickly became more out of touch than ever with local affairs. To some extent the British staff found it more comfortable to associate only with those who welcomed their company (intellectuals and Rhodesians with pro-British sentiments). It became a function of Special Branch to keep members of the High Commission under surveillance, partly because there were many Rhodesians who would have relished the opportunity to stage an open confrontation with the British.

The High Commission's degree of isolation from affairs in Rhodesia stemmed also from the weakening of the Intelligence liaison between Rhodesia and Britain. Among those who had departed with the High

Commissioner was the M I 5 representative. The French and most other foreign liaison services had also been withdrawn, obviously under British pressure; all that remained were the C I A representative (who, until his departure in 1970, was helpful to us and, no doubt, to the British as well) and, for a short period, the M 16 representative.

M 16 was, of course, the appropriate service for dealing with a hostile or potentially hostile situation, and it is very much to their credit that they kept themselves closer to the Rhodesian problem than their colleagues in the Ministries of Foreign Affairs and Commonwealth Relations. I saw no need to let the politicians' squabble affect the liaison between British Intelligence and C I O, or turn erstwhile friends into enemies, and argued forcibly that Wilson and Smith had presented us with a golden opportunity to divert all Anglo-Rhodesian communication through Intelligence channels. The immediate predecessor of the British Intelligence man now in Salisbury would have agreed with me; he had often quoted the Suez affair of 1956 as an example of Intelligence services providing the essential link between countries whose diplomatic and other links had been ruptured. But it seemed that my new friend from British Intelligence was under instructions to reduce liaison to the remotest contact and offer only minimal assistance. Had the British accepted my arguments in favour of maintaining links, or at least confirmed the British connection with the Governor by installing radio communications at Government House, this might have provided the positive commitment needed to reverse the anti-British drift in the country. However, it now appeared to be all a question of 'face'; the position taken in advance of U D I (to break diplomatic relations and impose sanctions) had to be pursued to some sort of finality.

Some officials in Whitehall continued to be helpful despite the rupture. Others lent themselves to 'spoilers' intended to persuade Smith that unless he retracted U D I force would be used to impose a government to Britain's liking. But Gibbs had already expressed the strongest disapproval of any attempt by the British to impose a solution which might result in bloodshed. 'If they try that, I'm off,' he said to me, quite simply. And we knew by now that he would not even allow his commitment to the British Crown to interfere with his duty to Rhodesia or in any way encourage an attitude that might lead to a conflict in loyalties. Obviously, this made life even more complicated for those of us trying to keep the peace between Salisbury and London.

The B B C coverage of events in Rhodesia had been fair and accurate until U D I, but its image was then marred through the propaganda beamed out of the hurriedly erected station in Francistown, Botswana.

Because this broadcasting service was described initially as 'clandestine', CIO sought correction of it through British Intelligence, only to be told that they were not involved in the enterprise. Our criticism reverted to the BBC, but the bias was not corrected. We found that senior British Intelligence officers had retained a nostalgic belief in the BBC as the voice of truth that had sustained them during perilous days in the occupied Europe of the Second World War. CIO arranged with postal engineers to have the Francistown station jammed; they did this so effectively that no one on the British side would admit to such an ignominious failure and the station disappeared off the air.

The bizarre relationship between officials and politicians continued, with the Commanders and myself continuing to report to both the Rhodesian Prime Minister and the Governor. However, it did have its lighter moments, as the following incident illustrates. The government had asked Putterill, but not Gibbs, to officiate at the first ceremonial 'Opening of Parliament' after UDI. When Putterill queried the appropriateness of his involvement, Gibbs said: 'Sam, you had better open Parliament, for not to do so would be a confrontation. But don't appear as if you are enjoying it!'

In due course, the official photographs depicted an unhappy general standing amongst bewildered politicians – bewildered because they had taken UDI in the name of the Queen, had then excluded the Queen's representative from taking part in the ceremony and now found themselves in the company of an unhappy general who, on the instructions of the Queen's representative, decreed that there would be no Royal salute (with which Parliament was traditionally 'opened') and no Queen's Colours on parade.

Gibbs continued to insist with Ian Smith that the government renegotiate independence and restore constitutionality. CIO helped by arranging an exchange of views through MI6 and CIA channels and by April 1966 'talks about talks' were well under way. CIO staff prepared an emotionally worded paper showing their deep concern to assist towards a settlement on the theme that quick action would be needed to coincide with the return to power after general elections of Wilson in Britain and Verwoerd in South Africa.[1]

We, in the meantime, are concerned that:
(a) After nearly five months of rule, not a single country has yet recognised the Rhodesian government...
(b) HMG cannot conceivably allow the Rhodesian UDI to succeed by default
(c) Rhodesia's present financial buoyancy and currency strengths are the result of abnormal and largely temporary benefits...

We believe that the following aspects should be fundamental to the re-opening and conduct of the negotiations:

(i)   There is really only one basic issue in the Rhodesian problem − the protection of the inescapable human and citizenship rights of all Rhodesians, both black and white...

(iii) For there to be any possibility that negotiations can be re-opened, low-level and unpublicised discussions must have taken place to ensure that the top-level negotiations themselves are predestined to a settlement.

Through CIA channels I learnt that the American Ambassador in London had had discussions with Wilson and was anxious to use his influence to try to get negotiations started:[2]

During the evening of 25th April, I saw Mr Pestell, who put me in the picture concerning the 'feelers' being put out both from Mr Smith's side and from Mr Wilson through Mr Oliver Wright, who has now made a third visit to Salisbury in less than a week. Mainly from information passed down by the Chief Justice, Mr Pestell understands that there is definitely a willingness on both sides to get talks going and Sir Hugh Beadle believes that Mr Smith would accept the British-sponsored 'six principles' as the basis for talks, provided there were no other pre-conditions and provided Rhodesia's independence was a 'built in' principle.

Gibbs expressed concern as to his position should these talks fail. My advice to him was that he should stay as long as he could, for there would be little relevance in subsequent attempts at rapprochement if he did not. However, by the end of 1966 his continuing presence at Government House was beginning to appear like 'all things to all men'. CIO produced a document analysing his position and the effect it was having within Rhodesia and on Anglo-Rhodesian relations.[3]

There seem to be at least four different attitudes towards the stand that Sir Humphrey Gibbs has taken:

(i)   It is believed in some circles that by remaining in his position as Governor he has merely served to divide the loyalties of Rhodesians. This seems to be the view of many back-benchers and other supporters of Government, and it coincides with the view expressed to me some time ago by Brigadier Skeen, who also argued that Rhodesia should have cut every existing tie with Britain at the time of UDI. This same gentleman has made several public expressions to the effect that Sir Humphrey is a tool for Mr Wilson.

(ii)   Another school maintains that, by remaining, Sir Humphrey has provided a rallying point for those who have confidence in Britain's ability to resolve the confrontation. To this extent these people are basically loyal to Britain (not necessarily HMG) but they would claim that loyalty to Britain is not inconsistent with loyalty to Rhodesia. They are not necessarily anti-Government, but most of them would appear to have been anti-UDI and some of them are opponents of Government.

(iii)   The third school represents all political persuasions, and Mr Pestell has told me that it includes a number of strong Government supporters who have mentioned to him, or have indicated to Sir Humphrey, how disastrous it would be if Sir Humphrey were to leave his present position. They seem to appreciate that Sir Humphrey is a man of the highest integrity who has the true interests of Rhodesia at heart, and that he is providing the only real insurance against the possibility of extreme action being taken by the British Government. His presence is the best shield against the use of force; it prevents the British imposing direct rule through a British Governor; it keeps control within Rhodesian hands; and, whilst he remains, there is less possibility of Britain referring the Rhodesian issue to the United Nations and disclaiming responsibility for Rhodesia.

(iv)   Insofar as it is possible to assess 'moderate African opinion', it appears that there is a substantial number of 'moderate Africans' who are particularly interested in the stand taken by Sir Humphrey, and that as long as he remains this 'opinion' is likely to remain 'moderate'. Should Sir Humphrey go, it is possible that they would think this has removed their sole hope for a just settlement.

The 'talks about talks' culminated in the Anglo-Rhodesian negotiations aboard HMS *Tiger* in November/December 1966. The Rhodesian delegation consisted of Ian Smith, Jack Howman (Minister of Foreign Affairs) and three officials, Sir Cornelius Greenfield (Chief Economic Adviser), Stan Morris (Chairman, Public Services Board), and Gerald Clarke (Secretary to the Prime Minister); Sir Humphrey Gibbs and Sir Hugh Beadle also attended. The British put forward proposals based on a modified 1961 Constitution; these proposals would have had the effect of creating more African seats in the House of Assembly, leading eventually to an African majority in the House as more Africans became enfranchised through improved educational and income-earning opportunities.

On Sunday 4 December, Smith and his delegation flew back to Salisbury to put the proposals before Cabinet. There is little doubt that Smith was in favour of accepting them. I recorded a comment by Gerald Clarke:

He (Clarke) said that when they were in flight coming back from HMS *Tiger*, the Prime Minister had checked individually with the three officials on the 'plane – Greenfield, Morris and Clarke – seeking their advice, and that all three separately had advised the Prime Minister that they considered the British proposals were acceptable, although they had some doubts concerning the mechanics of the return to legality. Mr Clarke believed that the Prime Minister held similar views.

From my discussions with Clarke, and from my position as a linesman who was occasionally asked to throw the ball to the players, I was able to get some idea of how the game had gone. The Cabinet gathered for a private meeting at Smith's home immediately upon his return. On Monday morning the Cabinet meeting began early and the Prime Minister opened play by stating that the members of Cabinet must make up their own minds about the proposals, without any influence from him. Significantly, he added that he wanted a unanimous decision, to the extent that if any one felt he could not go along with the proposals he was entitled to say so – in which case Cabinet would have failed to achieve the necessary unanimity.

Initially, according to Clarke (who attended the meeting until mid-morning tea but, contrary to normal practice, was not invited back into the Cabinet Room until the end of the day), it seemed that the majority were in favour of accepting the proposals. Then two Ministers, probably Harper (Minister of Internal Affairs) and Graham (Minister of Agriculture), began to make their opposition felt; this incipient opposition was bolstered by Dupont, whose obsession against any sort of settlement was well known in Cabinet and who insisted on his right as Officer Administering the Government to address Cabinet.

The British had requested a decision by noon on Monday but, at the Rhodesians' request, extended the deadline a few hours, allowing Cabinet to adjourn for lunch and resume discussions in the afternoon. At 6 pm the British were told that the answer was 'No'.

Historians and other analysts have offered numerous explanations as to why this attempt at settlement, and the subsequent one aboard HMS *Fearless* in 1968, failed. There was speculation in the case of the *Tiger* talks, for example, that the rejection of the proposals had something to do with the nature of the advice Cabinet members had received over the lunch table from their wives! But the best answer is perhaps the simplest one: that on each occasion the inherent strengths and weaknesses of Ian Smith's character decided the issue. He appeared strongest when saying 'No'; and he would say 'No' not because he was convinced it was the right answer but because he feared being wrong by saying 'Yes'. He would delay decisions until there was absolutely no alternative but to make up his mind, at which point he would usually accept a minority decision in Cabinet rather than allow the majority to override the minority. Added to this, his concept of negotiation was 'not-to-negotiate' but to leave it entirely to the other side to make all the concessions.

The possibility of a division in Cabinet, the fear of which underlay Smith's insistence on a unanimous decision, was something the British may have begun to exploit by this time in the mistaken belief that a split would work to their advantage. In 1967 CIO began to have fairly clear

indications that a Civil Service secretary was a British agent, planted to
help exploit the split. Later that year Harper became the subject of what
appeared to be a breach of Cabinet security. My 'Top Secret' note of 16
February referred to above includes the following:

What Mr Harper was letting loose was that the Prime Minister had returned
from the 'Tiger Talks' fully prepared to accept the British proposals, and that
this had been his first approach to Cabinet, which might have won them over,
but that one or two of them 'saw the light', and, in consequence, swayed
Cabinet to the extent that the terms were rejected.

It seemed fairly certain that Mr Harper's motivation was to discredit the
Prime Minister, one way or another; where the right-wing were concerned, they
would be appalled to think that it was the Prime Minister who wished to 'sell
them down the river'; where the moderates or left-wing were concerned, they
would lose confidence in the Prime Minister if they believed he had been so
weak as to allow the Cabinet to be swayed by just one or two extremists...

Throughout 1967 moves were being made towards more 'talks about
talks'. Smith's initial approach was to the Governor about these talks.[5]
Smith had just returned from holiday in South Africa, where he had had
discussions with Vorster, the South African Prime Minister, and his
attempt to persuade Gibbs to pressurise Britain into further talks was, in
fact, a reaction to the first instance of the arm twisting by South Africa
that was to become so painful later on. Of equal significance was the
change by the end of that year in Smith's attitude towards Gibbs. In
March 1968 I made a note of this in an addendum:[6]

The Prime Minister spoke more frankly with me on this subject than he has ever
done before, making it quite clear that he wishes Sir Humphrey to remain at
Government House. In the course of what he told me, he said that Sir Humphrey, having stayed now as long as he had done, would be well advised to stay
a little longer, because it was appreciated that he was only interested in trying to
help towards a negotiated settlement, and he had a useful role to play in this
regard.

Discussions dragged on for many months until, in September 1968, a
message was received at Government House stating that:[7]

Mr Wilson will agree to meet Mr Smith in the near future to try and negotiate a
settlement.... Mr Pestell says he personally conveyed this message to Mr Stall-
wood for Mr Smith at mid-day Saturday, 28.9.68 ... no reply or acknowledge-
ment had been received by 1.10.68.... Mr Pestell said it was obvious from the
terms of the message that the British Government were anxious to get a settlement ... the meeting should be arranged in Gibraltar, with Smith being given
such facilities as he requested, e.g. if he wished something better than on Tiger,
they could provide a separate ship, or, if he was not satisfied with communications these could be improved...

On 1 October the Cabinet agreed to a meeting between Smith and Wilson, but Smith indicated that rather than another *Tiger*-type exercise he would suggest as possible venues Salisbury, London or Zomba, in that order of preference.

My memorandum from which the extract above is taken includes comments which show that even at this late stage – a mere week before the commencement of talks – the British, Gibbs and others were indulging in wishful thinking if they really believed Smith was prepared to settle. Mention is made of recent statements by Smith to Cabinet, the Party Executive and the Divisional Chairman indicating that he considered *Fearless* had less chance of success than *Tiger*, that 'Government was not undertaking any deviation or weakening of its approach' and that 'the right course for Rhodesia now was to continue steadily along the path they had set for themselves and not be lured into action which might cause them to be deviated.'

On the day that the Rhodesian delegation departed for Gibraltar, Jimmy Spink, who had succeeded Barfoot as Commissioner of Police, commented in conversation with me that the talks were 'merely a matter of form' to tie up officially what had already been agreed behind the scenes. This opinion seemed to be fairly widespread. Dupont, however, who questioned me on public feeling about *Fearless* while the talks were in progress, considered that such optimism was prevalent only in Salisbury; he said that elsewhere in the country 'there was strong suspicion against trying to get any sort of settlement'.[8]

The results of the *Fearless* talks, before Rhodesia's outright rejection of the British proposals, were still being discussed in Salisbury by Ian Smith and George Thompson (Wilson's Minister with Special Responsibility for Rhodesia) when the third anniversary of UDI loomed up, and Thompson had to leave Salisbury to avoid the embarrassment of being in the country during the anniversary celebrations. Smith invited a few people, including past and present members of the OCC, to dine with him at his official residence. At one point in the evening General Putterill asked the Prime Minister how the discussions were going, to which Smith replied: 'Sam, we've had our fun. We intend to settle this time.'

What fun? What 'settlement' intentions? Everything about *Fearless* was already fizzling out like the soda in our drinks.

Hostes Nicolle, who had accompanied Smith to the talks, was busy steering the government in the way it should go. CIO learnt through its MI6 links that the British believed Nicolle had been set up to knock the settlement down. He had made no secret of his intention to create 'Bantustans' in Rhodesia. And to encourage the acceptance of his views – or to salve his conscience – Nicolle had advised all and sundry why the *Fearless* proposals had to be jettisoned. His 'Confidential Circular' to District Officers throughout the country dated 5 December 1968 was so extravagant in its wording and attracted such notoriety when some District Officers went public in pursuance of Nicolle's views that it was removed from the record. All trace of it disappeared and it only came to hand again eighteen years after its compilation.*

A few attempts were made to implicate the Royal Family in the Anglo-Rhodesian dispute, mainly through the Queen Mother (Honorary Colonel of the BSAP) whom Rhodesian politicians believed to be particularly sympathetic, but without response. The only time the Queen was advised to exercise her constitutional rights it misfired, as a diary entry of mine shows:

10th March 1968: I have just been to see the PM in his home before the emergency meeting of Cabinet summoned for tomorrow morning on a matter that is world news – whether the six Africans condemned to death for 'terrorist acts' should hang in the morning or not – following the Government's rejection of the Queen's reprieve for three Africans executed last week.

As I understood it from Gerald Clarke he wanted me to say something about the internal/external security situation and how it might be affected by the hangings – perhaps also the Pope's plea for clemency, because Gerald as a good Catholic, would prefer an 'unbeliever' such as myself to make the points required! . . . . Leo Ross (Secretary for Information) had interrupted my gardening to solicit support for the reprieves . . . but the PM greeted me as if I was an intruder, with 'I understand *you* want to see *me*' and I was put in the position of being the only official advising Government – the rest not wanting to be involved. . . . I had no option but to tell the PM what I thought – that the Queen's reprieve should be upheld – and I like to think it will have a bearing on the decisions to be made.

My advice was ignored. The Queen's reprieve was rejected and the 'terrorists' were hanged at dawn.

Official feeling in Rhodesia was that Britain either had to deal with UDI as a rebellion or ignore it. Any rebellion must produce acts of treason and if no action is taken against the 'traitors' it is no longer a rebellion. And for the British to do nothing against their own citizens merely exposed the British case as devoid of substance. Had Britain been consistent in highlighting instances of traitorous behaviour by prominent white Britons this would have encouraged the loyalists and discouraged those who would otherwise lead Rhodesia into a ruinous war against the blacks. With no lead coming out of London other than the

* See Appendix for an extract from this Circular.

ambivalent request to remain at our posts, Rhodesian government servants had little option but to continue 'in rebellion'.

An instance of inconsistent and half-hearted action by Britain concerned Sir Frederick Crawford, an ex-Colonial Governor and British pensioner living in Rhodesia. Crawford was deprived of his British passport. Two other ex-Colonial Governors living in similar circumstances had expressed their support for Gibbs and the principle of constitutionality, but Crawford was known by British Intelligence to have given support to the 'illegal regime' and his wife, Lady Cleo, who had a Greek passport, was the epitome of a 'Greek offering gifts', whether flowers for Mrs Smith or oil in tankers bound for Beira. In a similar display of inconsistency in a confused relationship, the British denied Lord Graham entry to Britain because he was named in an Order-in-Council as having signed the Unilateral Declaration of Independence, but as a Peer of the Realm he was commanded in the name of the Queen to attend opening sessions of the House of Lords. Fortunately for the British government, Graham was too gentlemanly to cause embarrassment by trying to enter Britain.

Another story of British inconsistency found its way into the British Press, with a little help from CIO. For a few days in May 1968 several British newspapers made much of the fact that while Rhodesian Africans were being given passports which enabled them to travel to Russia, China, Cuba or Algeria for guerrilla training, Rhodesian whites, such as Crawford, were having their British passports impounded or were being denied the right of renewal. The dominant issues of citizenship and national loyalty were expanded upon under such headlines as 'Freedom in Peril' and 'Dignity and Value of the British Passport'. Harold Wilson promised a 'rigorous enquiry', but it never saw the light of day, presumably because the ill-conceived action of issuing passports to blacks without proof of nationality would undermine British immigration policy for decades to come.

Half-hearted action such as that taken against Crawford failed to dissuade 'Friends of Rhodesia' in Britain from supporting the campaign. Several British Members of Parliament travelled openly to Rhodesia in support of Smith. Others came to see for themselves and were impressed. I well remember Evelyn King, MP for Bournemouth and a friend of the family, saying:

'It seems ludicrous; but with an effective population smaller than Bournemouth you run a country over twice the size of Britain, man an Army and Air Force, and now defy Britain, the Commonwealth and the rest of the world!'

Many British businessmen appeared only too willing to defy the various Orders-in-Council, believing they could carry on business with impunity. Then, like nuts in May, came the way-out supporters of the Rhodesian government, most of them having some link with Lord Graham, the Duke of Montrose, with whom they shared an almost obsessive concern over communist encroachment and a belief in Caucasian superiority. Graham's attitudes stemmed in part from his visits to Germany to attend Hitler Youth rallies in the 1930s; there he and his boyhood companion, the Duke of Hamilton, had become acquainted with Rudolf Hess. When Hess fled Germany in his attempt to see Winston Churchill, he set course for the estates of the two Scottish Dukes, hoping they would make the necessary introductions for him. He landed on the Duke of Hamilton's estate, a few minutes' flight from the Montrose estate.

Among those whom Lord Graham introduced to Rhodesia were The Gayre of Gayre and Nigg (who, according to *Who's Who*, bore a host of other titles – Falkland Pursuivant Extraordinary, Chamberlain to the Prince of Lippe, Grand Bailiff and Commissioner General of the English Tongue and so on). He came with offers of knighthoods in the medieval orders of the Mediterranean and was always ready to expound racial theories which were in line with RF thinking. His book *The Zimbabwean Culture of Rhodesia*, published in 1972, on Great Zimbabwe, the impressive stone ruins which are the remains of a fourteenth or fifteenth-century city in the south-east of the country, sought to prove that Great Zimbabwe could not have been African in origin because Africans had not the ability to organise a society or construct buildings on such a large scale.

Another visitor of this ilk was Knupfer, who introduced himself as a modern-day Keynes with a Soviet connection and tried unsuccessfully to sell his theories of a new (isolationist) economic order for Rhodesia; to enable Knupfer to get a hearing where it counted, I persuaded Ian Smith to let me take him to John Wrathall, Minister of Finance, but neither Wrathall nor his senior official, David Young, could be moved from the strictly orthodox.

Then there were Captain Henry Kerby, used by Harold Wilson as an interpreter in the Russian language and political adviser on the Russian scene, and Ron Hubbard, leader of the esoteric 'Scientology' cult, who was befriended by Dupont and his wife. Hubbard was about to ingratiate himself with Mrs Ian Smith when I advised the Prime Minister of Intelligence reports which we had received from Australia, and Smith responded well enough for us to have Hubbard deported without caus-

ing too much embarrassment to Mrs Smith and Mrs Dupont. This move
was helped by the fact that Australia, ahead of the rest of the world, was
preparing to ban Hubbard and his cult from the country, and Smith, like
most Rhodesians, considered that Australians had the lead when it came
to knowing how to treat undesirable aliens.

Most of these exotic characters had Intelligence links with the outside
world. Some of them may have been sent to us as spoilers, a subject we
raised with British Intelligence colleagues. British Intelligence declined to
discuss Knupfer with us. As to Kerby, he was subsequently fingered by
British journalists as an agent of the KGB.

Many people on both sides continued to work for a settlement after the
failure of the *Fearless* talks. Among them were well-intentioned do-
gooders, such as Sir Max Aitken, and stout personages, such as Lord
Goodman.

Aitken, a comrade-in-arms of Ian Smith during the Second World
War, hoped to cement the loose wartime liaison by informal encounters
with the government and officials; he would meet me in places where we
could talk unobserved, such as in the bar of my Deputy's house. Goodman's many cheering visits, in his capacity as solicitor-adviser to Harold
Wilson, were much appreciated by officials. We would arrange to meet
him secretly at Beit Bridge because he preferred to travel by road rather
than attempt to squeeze his large frame into the small seats available on
the aircraft then flying between Salisbury and Johannesburg. As a solici-
tor extraordinary, he displayed great dexterity in unravelling the intrica-
cies of the Anglo-Rhodesian dispute; and as a patron of the culinary
arts he was well able to judge the effects of sanctions on diners in
'La Fontaine', a restaurant in the hotel, Meikles, at which he usually
stayed.

By the time of the *Fearless* talks the entire basis of the connection with
British Intelligence had changed to one bedevilled by numerous obstacles, rendering the relationship unfriendly, even antagonistic. The last
British Intelligence representation in Salisbury had been withdrawn in
1966, but not before the ground had been prepared covertly for CIA to
continue with joint undercover operations. I persisted in trying to resume the old relationship, for the new situation was a handicap that
inevitably led to a distortion of the picture we and the British were trying
to paint for our respective political masters.

I had some success in meeting British Intelligence representatives on
neutral ground and sometimes in Rhodesia. These were usually retired
officers. They all looked askance at my open way of living (my name in

the telephone directory and on the gatepost of my home, where we
sometimes met) until I explained that in the small community in which I
lived I would draw more attention to them and to myself if I tried to
'disappear'.

When Sir Denis Greenhill, Permanent Under-Secretary to the British
Foreign Office, visited Salisbury, I implored him to strengthen my links
with British Intelligence. But there was no improvement. Eventually I
contrived to visit relatives in UK several times a year from 1968 to 1980
and was then able to restore some contact.

These visits gave me the opportunity to assess the attitude of the 'man
in the street'. During the earlier visits it became clear to me that Smith
was a more popular leader at home and in Britain than Wilson in either
context. Some of Smith's popularity could be explained by traditional
British sympathy for the underdog or by the strange inversion at the time
whereby the British public seemed to champion any leader who attempted to resist black encroachment. In pubs and taxicabs I often had to
listen to such strong professions of support for Rhodesia's cause that I
sometimes wondered whether I was correct in advising Smith not to
count on the support of the British public should the Anglo-Rhodesian
problem develop into open confrontation. As to assessing the attitudes
of the British government, the discussions I had with British Intelligence
officers made such a task simple, for I was always given a clear indication of what these attitudes were.

I made no attempt to indulge in clandestine activity while in Britain. I
considered there would be little value in doing so since whatever Intelligence I might obtain covertly would less accurately reflect the real position of the British government than what I learned from official sources.
It no doubt suited the British that I could return to Rhodesia with a true
understanding of their position and thus offer Smith a coldly realistic
appraisal of how things stood.

Most spy stories are crammed with references to Intelligence services
and their cloak-and-dagger agents; the KGB, GRU, SDECE, CIA, MI5
and MI6 are emblazoned on almost every page, while blood, sex and
daring escapades ooze liberally from between the pages. The pursuit of
'real life' Intelligence is much more prosaic and rarely fast and furious.
However, it does have its little moments. On one of my visits to Britain, I
stayed at the East India and Sports Club where one evening I was entertained to drinks by two characters from British Intelligence. Before I left
the Club to have dinner elsewhere, they handed over the keys of a car
put at my disposal for the weekend, with the guarded warning that
before retiring for the night I should move the car from the Club

entrance into a proper parking bay, for it would be embarrassing if I came to the notice of the police.

I returned to the Club, well wined and dined, at about 3 am. After much fumbling with the car keys I found the right one, opened the door and lowered myself into the driving seat. I located the light switch, found the gear lever and started the car, only to realise that there was a brick wall immediately in front of me and the gear I had chosen was moving me forwards, not backwards. Just as I managed to correct this, the door was wrenched open, a torch shone in my face and a voice said: 'Gotcha!'

The ensuing conversation went something like this:

'Is this your car?'

'No.'

'Whose car is it?'

'I don't know.'

'What's the registration number?'

'I don't know.'

'Where do you live?'

'I'm staying here, at the Club.'

'Why are you driving away then?'

'I'm not driving anywhere; I'm just going to park the car.'

'But it's already parked.'

'Yes, but in the wrong place.'

'Why move it at 3 o'clock in the morning? Strikes us you're in the wrong place! Get out!'

I climbed out, and tried another tack.

'The car was loaned to me by a friend, which is why I've got the keys. If you come to the Club you'll find that I'm booked in as a reciprocal member.'

But the front door was locked and no one answered the bell. One of my inquisitors murmured: 'That Paki doorman is asleep as usual.'

'How do I get in then?'

'You ring number ... from the call box on the corner. The telephone will ring in his ear and wake him up.'

There was a pause, and then he exclaimed:

'But why are we telling you this?'

After another pause his colleague said:

'We're from Scotland Yard. There've been scores of car thefts from this Square at night. We thought we had a firm suspect at last.'

'Sorry to disappoint you,' I replied, affably, 'but thanks for the tip about the doorman. Goodnight!'

For almost ten years of discreet visits to Britain I went unnoticed. My 'exposure' in July 1976 was brought about by Edward du Cann, an MP and a director of Lonrho who asked a question in the House of Commons about my visits and hence promoted publicity in the Press. His interest seemed to stem from Lonrho's activities in Rhodesia. But Rowland had no success in stopping my visits to Britain.

The incipient movement towards the declaration of a Republic in Rhodesia gained momentum after the failure of the *Fearless* talks. Government propaganda sought to convince the electorate that if Rhodesia could afford to reject the best terms Britain could offer, then why not sever all links. It went on to maintain that no friendly country dare recognise Rhodesia as independent so long as she was tied to Britain.

The Commanders of the Armed Forces were as opposed to the declaration of an 'illegal Republic' as they had been to UDI, and exercised their right to express their views directly to the Prime Minister. The following extract from a 'Top Secret' paper signed by Putterill and Hawkins shows the strength of this opposition:[9]

UDI was taken in the name of the Queen, Christianity and civilisation. The Union Jack was to continue to fly and the National Anthem to be retained. The principles of the 1961 Constitution were to be enshrined in the 1968 Constitution. The abandonment of these things may not seem much to some politicians but they mean a great deal to servicemen, particularly long-serving members....

The issue of an illegal Republic raises a completely new set of circumstances; some of them are:–
a) Traditional Symbols...
b) Oath of Allegiance...
c) Pensions...
d) Conditions of Service...

Acceptance of Republican status could imply condonement of an illegal state of affairs to which we would commit our Forces, thus laying them open possibly to charges of treason...

There is also the worthy tradition of keeping our Forces non-political. A Republic declared in existing circumstances would be a political act, and our acceptance of it would commit our Forces politically...

Our strong links with the British forces ... have militated strongly against any threat of intervention by force from the UK – or the UN; a Republic would forfeit much of this sympathy in Britain, in the older Commonwealth, and in the West, with consequently increased dangers...

Our personal position, about which there must be no doubt, is that we believe firmly that the long-term interests of Rhodesia would be harmed by the illegal declaration of a Republic under present conditions and in no foreseeable circumstances would we personally align ourselves with such a move.

The Commanders followed this up by directing that a Joint Committee of Enquiry comprising Army and Air Force officers should examine the implications. Most of the senior CIO staff held similar views and had taken the unprecedented step of preparing an unsolicited paper 'representing the considered views of all the sections of CIO', which I was happy enough to forward to the Prime Minister. I did this not as an act of collusion but as an indication of the deep disappointment felt in official circles over the failure of the British and Rhodesian politicians to negotiate an independence settlement. Part of the CIO paper reads:[10]

Only in terms of political theory does Republican status add to the stature of a country. In hard economic terms – and it is these that matter – dependence and inter-dependence are a necessary modus vivendi for almost any country.... There is no evidence yet available to substantiate the thinking that republican status would, at this point in time, induce recognition of Rhodesia by the governments of other countries – and, if the argument were valid, such evidence could be acquired simply by asking the Governments concerned whether they would or would not recognise a Republic of Rhodesia. [CIO had asked through Intelligence channels and got the answer 'No'; the Rhodesian government preferred to hope that the answer would be 'Yes' once the deed was done.] ... there is within Rhodesia itself, so far as the European element is concerned, a considerable emotional appeal for a Republic and this emotion can easily be exploited by propaganda ... but emotion is seldom a wise counsellor and many of the people who express pro-Republic sentiments are unaware of the real issues involved.

The issue of a declaration of a Republic *was* an emotional one. My staff were emotionally committed, which was wrong in an Intelligence organisation, just as the discursiveness of their paper was faulty. But what is significant is that although Smith never referred in subsequent discussions to either the CIO or the Commanders' papers, some of the points must have struck home for the movement towards a Republic slipped into low gear for the following two years. By the end of that time Smith had more pliant Commanders to deal with: Keith Coster, who had come to Rhodesia from the South African Forces and succeeded Putterill in 1968; and Archie Wilson, one of Ian Smith's flying companions, who succeeded Hawkins in 1969.

The difference between the old and the new Commanders was not so much one of experience as of personalities. Putterill and Hawkins were unquestionably the most professional, independent and a-political representatives of the Armed Services in the OCC during the fifteen years that that body functioned. Wilson, on the other hand, was devoted to Smith both as a friend and as the 'saviour' of Rhodesia; and Coster, a man with a charming personality, was always happy to let Wilson take the lead in our discussions in OCC. While still serving, Wilson managed

to get his and Coster's appointments upgraded to Air Marshal and
Lieutenant-General yet their command responsibilities were in no way
increased. (Shortly after his retirement in 1973, Wilson accepted a Ministerial post in Smith's government.)

During the years between the first moves towards a Republic and its
implementation in 1970, Rhodesia's political development continued
along its chequered way. In March 1967 the government had appointed
the Rhodesian Constitutional Commission under the chairmanship of
W. R. 'Sam' Whaley 'to advise on the constitutional framework which is
best suited to the sovereign independent status of Rhodesia'. Other
members of the Commission were Stan Morris; H. H. Cole, Secretary
for Education in the Federal era ; Charles Mzingeli, a trade unionist; and
S. M. Sigola, a Ndebele chief. Those of us who discussed matters with
the members of the Commission during the many months of their deliberations saw their mission as a sop to placate international opinion or
to impress upon Harold Wilson that if he did not come up with something better Ian Smith would have no recourse but to find a locally
produced solution. On 5 April 1968 the Commission published its recommendations – that while there should never be majority rule there
should ultimately be racial parity in government – but the response by
the RF caucus was cool and almost immediately the party began to draft
alternative proposals.

The Commission had had to contend with right-wing propaganda and
counter-proposals from political sources that grew more outrageous
with every move. A break-away group from the RF, led by Len Idensohn
and Commander Chris Phillips, formed the Rhodesian National Party
(RNP), which called for immediate Republican status, permanent white
rule and separate development. The RNP described the Whaley Commission proposals as 'dangerously extreme' and went so far as to label
Ian Smith a 'white kaffir'.

In the meantime a joint committee of the RF caucus and party chairmen had produced its own draft constitution in a 'Yellow Paper'; the
committee proposed that there should be two stages of parliamentary
development, the second of which would produce a National Parliament, with representation based on income tax qualifications (and
therefore mainly white), and three separate Provincial Councils for
whites, Ndebele and Shona (thus keeping the races separated for all
time). These proposals were sponsored by two of Smith's Ministers,
Harper and Graham, and, as noted in my record of the discussion between myself and Stan Morris, received 'far more prominence, and
perhaps support, than they deserved because they were advertised as

being representative of the expert views of senior officers in the Ministry of Internal Affairs.'[11]

Few people expected the Whaley Commission to produce an answer to the problem it had been set. Even within the Commission itself there were doubts, as the file note referred to above indicates:

Mr Morris said that his two European colleagues on the Whaley Commission, Mr Whaley and Mr Cole, saw Cabinet on 27.8.68 to explain the reasons why they had arrived at certain conclusions, and to voice objections to certain changes that were now contemplated in their findings by Government, R.F. Caucus and others.... (Mr Morris then) addressed Cabinet specifically on the subject of the vital need to maintain African support ... (and said that) if Government adopted the so-called 'second stage' of the principles now being contemplated, this would mean the end of African co-operation....

Concluding his account of their confrontation with Cabinet, Mr Morris told me that his European colleagues – and himself to a lesser extent – received a most sympathetic hearing, but they got the impression that the Prime Minister was no longer in control to the extent that he could dictate to his Cabinet colleagues – let alone the Party Caucus – what was best in the national interest.

Morris and his colleagues may have underestimated Smith's degree of control. The Prime Minister, having led Harper and Graham on and allowed them to produce a draft constitution altering the essence of the Whaley Commission proposals, now dropped them; he forced Harper into resignation, allegedly as a 'security risk', and although Graham was retained as a Cabinet Minister his advice was increasingly ignored by Smith and the inner Cabinet. Whether or not Smith was in control at this time, he had emerged as a moderate in comparison to most of his party. And it was this 'moderation' and his apparent control which had encouraged Wilson to go ahead with the *Fearless* talks in the belief that Smith's actions in ridding himself of extremists indicated a genuine desire to explore again the possibility of a negotiated settlement.

Smith's actions were not directed at settlement, however, but at the consolidation of his party and the electorate behind the moves towards republican status. None of his or his party's proposals went anywhere near Britain's demand for 'unimpeded progress towards (black) majority rule'; his inclinations were quite the opposite – the enshrinement of permanent (white) minority rule. Government propaganda on the issue of a Republic was now stepped up and concentrated on the advantages of assuming republican status. A new 'Republican Constitution', which included those parts of the Whaley Commission proposals which appealed to the RF, was produced and put to the electorate in a referendum in June 1969. A handsome two-to-one majority voted in favour of this constitution. The government then capitalised on the renewed euphoria, last seen during the build-up to UDI, by asking the electorate in June 1969 to vote in favour of a Republic, which 55,000 did, compared with 20,000 doubters. As to black opinion on the republican issue, government showed little interest in what CIO or other officials had to say about it.

After Rhodesia became a Republic in March 1970 there was no further purpose in Sir Humphrey Gibbs remaining in residence at Government House. He gave way to Clifford Dupont, who was proclaimed the first President of the Republic of Rhodesia. This was followed immediately by a general election in which the RF won all fifty white seats, proving once again what Dupont had told me so often – all that was necessary was to commit people to a certain course of action and they would adhere to it.

In no time at all CIO was again involved in arranging secret visits by British intermediaries. Following the Conservative victory in the British general election in June 1970 Edward Heath had given the Rhodesian problem to the thoughtful care of his Foreign Secretary, Sir Alec Douglas-Home. The Anglo-Rhodesian relationship improved and during the remainder of 1970 and throughout 1971 there was renewed hope on both sides, leading to high level settlement negotiations. (An example of one of the messages between Douglas-Home and Smith will be found in the Appendix. These passed via the British Embassy and the Rhodesian Diplomatic mission in Cape Town.)

In May 1971 my staff came up with yet another analysis of the Anglo-Rhodesian dispute.[12] But when I handed the paper to Jack Gaylard, Secretary to the Prime Minister, I was told politely that our views would be of considerable value to the negotiating team but that the two Heads of Ministries most responsible for safeguarding the nation's economy, David Young, the Secretary to the Treasury, and Jim Baker, the Secretary for Commerce and Industry, considered that there was 'merely a marginal need for settlement' and were 'confident that our economic position will improve regardless of a settlement.' Such attitudes gave me little hope of success in convincing Ian Smith of the need for settlement. I instructed CIO staff to be advised of the reaction to their analysis and the paper was filed away.

I made three visits to Britain in 1971. The British still preferred to deal with CIO through retired officers who usually acted as intermediaries but occasionally provided official contact. After my third visit I conveyed the following message to my London contacts on 9 November: 'You will know before this reaches you that our political problem with

Britain is as near solution as it ever can be; and we have hopes that all might be resolved within the next few days. This being so, dare I say we are as anxious as I hope you are to pick up the reins of accredited liaison – sooner rather than later.' London's reply on 24 November read: 'It looks as though settlement will at last be achieved. We all have our fingers crossed here!' Later that day the Smith/Home agreement was signed, prompting London to add a 'Stop Press' to their earlier message: 'All is settled.'

The significant political development leading to the Smith/Home agreement was that Smith had at last agreed to amend the retrogressive 1969 Constitution and replace the RF concept of parity with the principle of majority rule. Once again, however, Smith had conceded little, where-as the Conservatives had conceded something on all the five principles which had previously governed negotiations. Overall, the terms were, for the RF, more favourable than those offered on HMS *Tiger* and HMS *Fearless* or those contained in the 1961 Constitution they had inherited in 1962.

Yet the RF were unhappy about the terms. Within the party they maintained that there was no need for a settlement. Sanctions were not biting and the 'terrorist' war was not making serious inroads into what counted most of all – the Rhodesian way of life. They were unimpressed by the fact that the British government's terms were better than ever before or that they halted the retrogressive course the RF had set for itself.

Within days of the agreement being signed it became obvious to the officials that we would be hard put to attempt to ensure its enforcement. Then, to confirm our suspicions about the RF's duplicity in signing an agreement they had little intention of trying to make work, we were advised that it was no part of our responsibilities to assist in the crucial feature of the agreement, the so-called 'test of acceptability'. We were told that the British, unaided, must carry out the task.

The British had underestimated Smith's capacity for evasion; already he was looking for a way out, and he was afforded an early excuse to blame the British for the failure of the agreement when it became known that Lord Pearce and his team would not be arriving until early in the new year. Smith said the British were thus deliberately using delaying tactics to give the Africans time to organise a rejection of the proposals. CIO asked that if this was so, why did the government not also use this time to organise an acceptance of the proposals. At this stage we finally got the truth of the matter. Hostes Nicolle, who had played such a prominent part in aborting the *Fearless* talks, wanted nothing to do with this or any other settlement that might give the Africans a greater say in the government of Rhodesia.

Nevertheless, under the guidance of Leo Ross, the Secretary for Information, I and a few other officials met to discuss what could be done to encourage acceptance. We confronted Smith, who gave a little ground by agreeing to our suggestion that we organise a working party to prepare the public for the acceptability test, but when we sought the co-operation of officials in various Ministries we found that they had been instructed not to get involved. The reason they gave was that such involvement might be seen by Lord Pearce's Commission as an attempt to pre-empt the Commission's task or to influence Africans against their better judgement. The field was open, therefore, for Bishop Muzorewa, as leader of the ANC, to organise the anti-settlement movement on the theme: 'Reject this settlement. We will get better terms later on.'

Our efforts to introduce a positive attitude into Rhodesia's view of the agreement terms came too late; they were rendered ineffective by Nicolle's actions and by the attitude of Smith who long before the test got under way was seen in official circles as having washed his hands of the whole affair. One of the few things we did manage was to get Smith's approval for Stan Morris's expert services and advice on local issues to be made available to the Pearce Commission. However, this came to nothing; what had started as an independent commission of inquiry was put into the hands of Foreign and Commonwealth Office officials, most of whom were persistent critics of all things Rhodesian and were unwilling to use the services of any local experts, particularly an expert in African affairs.[13]

Clearly, there were faults on both sides, making it easy for Bishop Muzorewa to get a massive 'No' to the Smith/Home agreement; but it was to the credit of the Rhodesian Forces that peace was maintained whilst the agreement was debated. The continuing frustration over yet another failure to settle the Anglo-Rhodesian dispute is reflected in a secret report submitted by Rhodesia's Diplomatic Representative in South Africa.[14]

I had a long conversation with Sir Arthur Snelling (British Ambassador to South Africa) and found him friendly and eager to talk ... we both felt that since we had tried so hard to bring about the meeting between the Foreign Secretary and our Prime Minister which led to the Anglo-Rhodesian accord last year we should keep this line of communication open.

We had to agree to differ on the Pearce Report. He thought it was a pretty fair thing: I told him it was shocking ... inaccurate, biased, contradictory, naive and barren. I was in no doubt that it had been written largely by the Secretariat and merely signed by the Commissioners. I said many Rhodesians believed that the

British Government had yielded in the face of the antagonistic pre-emptive Press campaign allied to pressures mainly from Nigeria, Zambia and Canada. He did not rebut this very convincingly.

Snelling agreed that Sir Alec's speech in presenting the Report to the House of Commons, exhorting Rhodesians to think again, was pitched principally towards the Africans. But he thought the 'pause for reflection' phrase indicated that Home did not have the vaguest idea how to proceed from here. Snelling had been encouraged by the restrained manner in which both sides had acted since Pearce. He was pleased to see no severe White backlash in Rhodesia and noted the peaceful internal security situation.

The last attempt at settling the Anglo-Rhodesia dispute through peaceful negotiation had been deliberately rendered ineffective and the last opportunity for a genuinely multiracial effort in Rhodesia thrown away. Thereafter, the need to settle took second place to the need to satisfy Smith's objective – 'no majority rule in a thousand years' – which became the dominant theme during the following eight years of monolithic RF rule.

CHAPTER 6

Counter-Insurgency
1964–72

The decisions made by Rhodesia's white leaders in April 1964 and by her black leaders just a few weeks later were perhaps the most crucial in the story that began with the RF victory in 1962 and ended with the ZANU(PF) victory eighteen years later. The whites ousted Winston Field and took a sharp turn to the right, from which course they never deviated until the country had almost bled to death; the blacks, frustrated by repeated detentions of their leaders and the bannings of nationalist parties, realised that their aspirations would not be achieved through peaceful negotiation and turned down the road which led to guerrilla war.

The nationalists' formal decision to pursue the 'Armed Struggle' had been preceded by growing militancy (which started in the late 1950s, mainly as faction fights and riots in the black areas) and by the formation of the Zimbabwe Liberation Army in 1962. Special Branch was aware that in that year small numbers of activists had begun to leave Rhodesia to undergo training abroad in sabotage and guerrilla tactics, but several years were to elapse before enough recruits could be trained to make an impact in the country.

The declaration of UDI itself passed without incident as far as militant nationalism was concerned. CIO's involvement with anything of a military nature in the months after UDI was confined to investigating reports that the British might be preparing to invade Rhodesia and with reports of disaffection in the Rhodesian Armed Forces.[1]

Harold Wilson's 'Top Secret' signal to Sir Humphrey Gibbs on 17 December 1965, if acted upon, would have changed the whole course of UDI. Couched in the strongest terms available to a British Prime Minister threatening another Prime Minister, Wilson, after his discussions with President Johnson and at the UN, had apparently formed the opinion that:[2]

... it is doubtful whether a mandatory military resolution can be delayed more than a few weeks if that.... Smith should realise that it is most unlikely that international military action including inevitably certain big powers can be delayed for more than a very short period and the likelihood of Russian or Eastern European participation is very grave.... In my view you should send for Smith now and give him the full substance of this message and underline the grave responsibility lying on him if Rhodesia is going to become the cockpit of the gravest type of military intervention.

The message was passed through Pestell and myself to Ian Smith. Reading between the lines we could not help thinking that 'Harold Wilson doth protest too much' and were unsure as to what advice to give the Governor and the Prime Minister. In the event, Gibbs did nothing to support the threats contained in the message for he would not lend himself to being dubbed 'Wilson's man', and Smith quickly decided to ignore the message. He even declined to pass it on to any of his colleagues and would not have it discussed in Security Council.

More reports of possible invasion came in to CIO, emanating from British, American, South African and other sources. Presumably these reports were orchestrated in an attempt to put some semblance of verisimilitude into Wilson's message. However, the reports were so lacking in subtlety that we exonerated British Intelligence as a likely source and assumed instead that the likely origin was 10 Downing Street, the Foreign Office or the Commonwealth Relations Office in Whitehall.

The first of this batch of reports, relayed to CIO on 25 December by the South African Diplomatic Representative in Salisbury, contained the 'categoric but extremely sensitive' information that a British brigade of troops, including parachutists, was standing by in England to be flown to Kariba.[3] This proved to be false. Then CIO was fed information that British troops were being flown into Francistown, Botswana. We disposed of this ourselves by a quick reconnaissance. A few days later we got a 'confirmed' report from South African Military Intelligence of a pending invasion by British troops who had been flown into Swaziland from Nairobi and from aircraft carriers in the Mozambique Channel. We asked the South African Security Police to check the report on the ground and were advised that the landing field in question was empty of aircraft and could not possibly have accommodated the type and numbers described in the report. These findings embarrassed South African Military Intelligence who should not have confirmed a report so palpably false.

Meanwhile, we learnt from friends of friends in Britain that there was a threatening build-up of British troops on Malta. My Deputy flew to the island to check personally on the British paratroopers being trained at Luqa airport and found that they were engaged in simulated practice for dropping on Salisbury airport. Naturally, British Intelligence did what they could to inhibit our enquiries, but we took a leaf out of their book and exposed the story to Ian Colvin, who was visiting Salisbury at the time and was a master of interpretive journalism. Without qualms he introduced the following into an editorial entitled 'What next in Rhodesia?' in the London *Daily Telegraph* on 30 March 1966:

... the Rhodesian authorities believe Mr Wilson considers using military force against them even without the excuse of internal disorders or an invitation from the Governor. As neither of these latter contingencies remain likely, Mr Wilson should re-word his pledge and say that we will not send British troops into Rhodesia if sanctions fail to achieve their object. This is the real issue, and he should make his position plain in seeking re-election.

That did the trick. We suffered no further 'spoilers', no further 'threats' of invasion.

The failure of Britain or other Western powers to intervene militarily dashed the hopes of the nationalist leaders for support in toppling Smith's government. It caused a major delay in their pursuance of the guerrilla war both while they waited in vain for action and then while they built up an extended range of contacts for the training of recruits and the supply of arms, starting with Ghana, Uganda and Tanzania and moving on to Algeria, Egypt, Cuba, North Korea, China and the Soviet Union. Because of these factors, militant nationalism in Rhodesia would have little impact on whites for at least a decade after it started, unlike Mau Mau in Kenya, an essentially domestic movement centred in the heart of the country which at no stage depended on external recruitment, training or provisioning.

The split that had occurred in the nationalist movement in 1963, leading to the formation of ZANU in opposition to Nkomo's ZAPU, was perpetuated by CIO. Our means of doing this and of penetrating ZAPU and ZANU were made easier by the tribalism and nepotism with which both organisations were afflicted at that stage. This applied also to the two main nationalist guerrilla forces, the Zimbabwe People's Revolutionary Army (ZIPRA) and the Zimbabwe National Liberation Army (ZANLA).

In order to preserve our advantageous position within the nationalist forces, CIO conducted the first stage of the conflict as a 'silent war'. We resisted publicity or any reference to the successes that sustained our operations; the tighter the secrecy, the greater the successes, although there were occasions when it suited us to go public. The secrecy made it difficult for the armed groups of nationalists operating clandestinely in Rhodesia to be aware of the true overall picture; instead they had to rely on the grossly exaggerated reports from the Front Line States which, if taken literally, would have accounted for more helicopters than had ever flown in Rhodesia and more casualties than the number of men in the Rhodesian Security Forces. The advantage, therefore, remained with CIO as long as nothing needed to be said. And when it suited us we would let the nationalists know that they had traitors in their midst; then we would leave them guessing, for the ultimate line between white and black had yet to be drawn.

CIO's penetration of the guerrilla organisations from pre-UDI days until the early 1970s was as complete as it could have been. There was virtually nothing we did not know of their inner workings at all levels, for our informers served us no less faithfully than they served their nationalist leaders. We knew who had been recruited, where they came from, where they went for training and when they were likely to return.

In their last staging posts in Zambia the guerrillas were at a disadvantage in that they were in an alien land and, if they belonged to ZANLA, among unfriendly hosts; on re-entry into Rhodesia they had to travel through a no-man's land well patrolled by Game Rangers or Security Forces and devoid of a resident population apart from small groups of Batonka tribesmen who tended to be more kindly disposed towards the Security Forces than the guerrillas. Any local knowledge and expertise we needed was provided by the civilian Police Reserve and the Army Territorial battalions. An additional and overwhelming factor in CIO's favour was that we had our own men in most of the guerrilla groups. With such advantages, CIO was able to account for virtually every guerrilla coming into Rhodesia across the Zambezi in the early stages of the war. And the few who escaped death or capture were not necessarily luckier than their companions in arms. (OCC communiqués listing 'kills' were always accurate; the numbers 'captured', however, were often doctored to keep the nationalists guessing as to how many we had 'turned' and sent back to Zambia as survivors or kept in Rhodesia in a pseudo role.)

The fact that Rhodesian Security Forces kept on top of the situation for seven long years went unheralded, leading military and other observers to be inclined to dismiss this stage of the campaign as being of little consequence. The same observers criticised the nationalists for their ineptitude, their poor morale and their lack of motivation. I saw it differently in that I never failed to respect the nationalist leadership for their ability to develop the campaign in spite of early losses, nor could I help admiring the persistence with which the guerrillas continued to come, in the knowledge that most of those who had preceded them had been killed or captured.

Among the early ZANLA groups was one group of seven who were

killed in April 1966 in what has since become known as the 'Battle of
Chinoyi'. This incident would have been a 'non-event', like all other
ZANLA incursions at that time, had it not been for a rare disagreement
within OCC. The issue was whether to wrap up the incursion as a
'police' action (through arrests and publicity in the Courts) or to allow
Special Branch to continue to accompany the group to determine what
contacts they might have at their ultimate destination.

Three of the four of us in OCC believed it would be better not to make
martyrs of the seven men who, since crossing the Zambezi, had tried
ineffectively to blow up an electricity pylon, had made a half-hearted
attack on a police station and were now dependent on CIO agents for
food and succour. But the Commissioner of Police disagreed. At that
stage he had an advantage over me in that Special Branch came more
directly under him than under CIO, and he was anxious to prove that
the Police acting on their own were best able to handle any aspect of
subversion. He was also keen to satisfy the government's demand for
'the toughest possible action against terrorists', to which the rest of OCC
did not subscribe.

In the event, the Commissioner acted on his own authority and
obtained the use of helicopters from the Air Force, ostensibly for a
'Police Operation', but used them militarily and not in a 'law-and-order'
role. The entire group was wiped out from the air shortly afterwards.
Apart from anything else this cost us the services of some very valuable
agents. This sorry incident attracted publicity at the time because some
of the townspeople who knew of the attack on the police station heard
the helicopters firing weapons in the vicinity of the police station and
presumed that a 'battle' was on. Subsequently, the 'battle' assumed
national significance because a British journalist wishing to prove to the
new rulers of Zimbabwe that ZANLA were ahead of ZIPRA in their
guerrilla campaign produced such evidence as he could find (fourteen
years after the event) to prove that ZANLA started the Second Chimurenga* War at Chinoyi; he did so against CIO advice, for we knew
that the facts did not support his theme. In one respect, however, we are
now all agreed: the men who died in the 'Battle of Chinoyi' have become
martyrs in a cause.

The meeting of the OCC immediately after the Chinoyi incident was
traumatic. Accusations and counter-accusations of bad faith hurtled
around the room. Eventually, we decided that, in spite of all, we would
continue to adhere to the principle of 'Minimum Force' when dealing

---

* Shona word for 'rebellion'. The 'First Chimurenga' was the Mashona revolt against white
rule in 1896.

with subversion; to adopt drastic measures so early in the campaign would not only produce martyrs and prolong the campaign but would eventually turn the entire population against the Security Forces. Air Vice-Marshal Hawkins left us in no doubt that he would not in future permit his aircraft to be used in a killing role where the alternative use of ground forces could be equally effective and result in less loss of life; and he ruled out bombing or strafing of civilians from the air.

The incident also taught us a lesson in co-ordination and general strategy. Henceforth, incidents which passed beyond the control of any single Service would be dealt with by the combined operation of all arms of the Security Forces; the tactical approach would be decided by consensus between the four of us in OCC or, should a stalemate arise, we would defer to the Prime Minister. Another outcome was that my military colleagues in OCC insisted that all Intelligence should be controlled by CIO (not as in the Chinoyi incident, divided between Police and CIO) and that Special Branch should come directly under my control for all operational purposes.

Because of the essentially clandestine nature of the guerrilla war between 1964 and 1966 OCC issued a minimum of communiqués. During this period, over a hundred ZANLA and ZIPRA guerrillas were known to have been killed; the Rhodesian Security Forces suffered no losses but CIO lost a number of men. Several of our black operators disappeared and for a time we had no means of knowing whether they were dead or alive. Three of our best white operators were killed one dark night on the banks of the Zambezi when the explosives they were loading into a canoe for a sabotage operation in Zambia exploded, through over-exposure to the heat of the Zambezi valley; this accident taught us some valuable lessons both in the use of operators and of equipment for such operations. I subsequently found employment in CIO for two of the widows.

In August 1967 the Security Forces had their first real opportunity for combined military action. A force of eighty ZIPRA and South African National Congress (SAANC) guerrillas sought a southwards route through the Hwange Game Reserve; they had waded across the crocodile-infested Zambezi River upstream from the Victoria Falls and had thus evaded attention, although their presence in the nearby Livingstone area of Zambia had been reported over a period of several weeks.

In a series of engagements code-named 'Operation Nickel' the Security Forces had suffered twenty casualties (including seven dead), killed thirty guerrillas and captured twenty. Their commanders in the field reported that the guerrillas' morale and standard of training was much higher than anything yet encountered in Rhodesia; the guerrillas had fought a military action face to face, with no civilians involved, and were defeated only by the Security Forces' air power, mobility and much greater effectiveness in communications and medical services.

The significant result of the ZIPRA/SAANC incursion was that it brought South African forces into Rhodesia's guerrilla war. Within hours of the exchange of Intelligence between CIO and South Africa concerning the SAANC presence, General van den Bergh, Head of BOSS, telephoned me from Pretoria to say that he had arranged through the South African Prime Minister for a detachment of South African 'Riot Police' and helicopters to be sent to share in our defence of the Zambian border. I reported this to Ian Smith and he accepted with alacrity. When I saw the Commanders, however, they rejected the offer of South African aid as unnecessary. I returned to Smith to report this. He stated flatly that it was not for the Commanders to query what he saw as a most promising political development, adding that he could understand Vorster's reasons for agreeing to 'police' rather than 'military' aid. I then advised the Commanders that it would be better to comply, which they did.

South African aid, whether 'police' or 'military' proved to be a mixed blessing, politically and militarily. On the political front it gave Vorster the advantage because his offer had been unsolicited, and he later used this advantage when twisting Smith's arm over settlement by threatening to withdraw South African contingents after they had become part of Rhodesia's joint defence system. On the military front, the South African units were a liability initially. The Riot Police had received their training in an urban context and were thus totally inexperienced in the hazards of bush warfare; the Rhodesian Forces had to operate as 'long stop' to the South Africans in order to plug a gap in the overall defences. This was necessary despite the efforts of the South Africans' outstanding Commander, Major-General Pat Dillon who, with his own vast experience in Africa, realised only too well that it would take some time to get his men trained and experienced in counter-insurgency. Ultimately, the involvement of South African units in Rhodesia's war was of more use to South Africa than Rhodesia in that South Africa used Rhodesia as a training ground, withdrawing units as they became trained and replacing them with untrained ones.

In the last few days of 1967 ZAPU/SAANC tried a new tactic. Using a supply line across the Zambezi River and forming a chain of well-stocked bases across the inhospitable valley floor during the rainy sea-son in the remote Chewore area, they hoped to escape detection until they could climb into the escarpment area and find refuge among tribesmen who would be better disposed to their cause than the people of the valley, the nomadic Vadoma who were feared (wrongly) as cannibals. But the temptation to supplement their rations by shooting for the pot after three months of porterage led to their discovery by a perceptive Game Ranger who noticed a change in the pattern of animal movements and, on investigation, found human tracks where none would have been expected. The Security Forces plunged into 'Operation Cauldron' during March and April and fought a running battle with 125 guerrillas, killing sixty-nine, capturing fifty and losing six of their own forces.

CIO had failed to provide the Security Forces with Intelligence that might have pre-empted 'Operation Cauldron'. This was partly because our penetration of ZAPU was less complete than in ZANU and partly because of the difficulties of relaying messages across a flooded Zambezi. Thereafter we employed scouts well within Zambia to watch developments further back along the line of approach by guerrillas, and special measures were taken to keep suspected crossing places under permanent observation.

In the ensuing discussions within OCC, other weaknesses of 'Operation Cauldron' emerged. The Air Commodore at Tactical Headquarters had hesitated in making a decision as to which type of aircraft should be sent into action to relieve forward troops pinned down by guerrilla gunfire. Although he would never have hesitated in combat himself, his hesitancy in command led my colleagues in OCC to query his suitability as next in line to command the Air Force. (Throughout the war, Commanders were automatically retired after four years; some of us argued, however, that they should not be axed just for the sake of it and that where there was some doubt about their successor they should be retained. Graham, as Minister of Defence, supported this argument but Smith preferred to change Commanders, particularly when the replacements were politically attuned to RF thinking.)

In spite of faults, the efficiency of the Security Forces continued to improve with each encounter. The difference between them and the guerrillas was exposed starkly in subsequent ZAPU/SAANC incursions in 1968. In one such incursion, three groups of guerrillas, totalling ninety men, were sent simultaneously to cross the Zambezi as far apart as could possibly be managed, presumably to test the Rhodesian defences over a wide front. In the ensuing widespread engagements code-named 'Operation Griffin', Security Forces killed thirty-nine guerrillas and captured forty-one. The Forces fighting the middle group of twenty-eight who crossed between Kariba and Chirundu included fast-moving tracker units who hung on to the guerrillas' trail over the most difficult terrain and were able to gauge their speed and direction so accurately that other units could leap-frog ahead to lay a series of ambushes; of this guerrilla group twenty-four were killed, three were captured and one was allowed to escape.

By the end of 1968 the Rhodesian Commanders, had they been inclined to boast, could have said with justification that they had been outstandingly successful. Although CIO did not fully appreciate it at the time, the nationalists' morale had been shattered by the Security Forces' successes; the extent of this defeat was such that the war virtually stopped for four years. There were no clashes with guerrillas in 1969. In 1970 James Chikerema, Acting Chairman of ZAPU, announced a change in tactics whereby ZIPRA would use both conventional and guerrilla methods of warfare. This was easier said than done. ZIPRA was still beholden to the Russians, whose emphasis on conventional warfare meant that Russian-trained ZIPRA members would continue to be outmatched by Rhodesia's Security Forces. Chikerema was also faced with leadership problems and with a slowing down of recruiting as a result of ZIPRA's defeat and Rhodesia's increasing control of the Zambian border.

In desperation, ZAPU resorted to press-ganging Zimbabweans living in Zambia. Many of those who were press-ganged escaped at the first opportunity; a number proved unreliable in other respects. Reports of faction fighting between Shona and Ndebele groups in Zambia began to reach CIO and then, to our great surprise, we were notified by the Zambian authorities that they had deported some 'dissidents' from Zambia and wished to send sixty of them to Rhodesia; they implied that some of these men might be part of our espionage network, which was not necessarily the case. Kaunda's concept of dissidence differed from ours. He was referring to those involved in the faction fighting which was troubling his country and, rightly or wrongly, we encouraged this form of dissidence because it weakened the nationalists' cause. We arranged for the handover of the sixty 'dissidents' at a point between Victoria Falls and Kazangula. We noted that most of them were Shona-speaking, an indication of Kaunda's continuing pro-ZAPU bias. The men were detained as 'terrorists'; some were subsequently convicted and sentenced to death, while a few entered our service.

The disarray of ZANU and ZAPU in Zambia continued, and CIO continued to foment it. We also kept an eye on training camps in Tanzania and were aware that, following the arrival of Chinese instructors at the Itumbi camp in 1969, ZANLA too was undergoing a change of tactics along the lines of Mao Zedong's teaching − to politicise the masses before preparing to strike. However, we considered that as neither ZANU nor ZAPU had managed to mobilise support in areas adjacent to the Zambian border between 1964 and 1969 there was no reason why they should manage to do so now. The point we missed was that ZANU, in particular, would have a much better chance of mobilising support in the north-eastern area bordering Mozambique because the area was far more densely populated and most of the population were Shona-speaking.

Inside Rhodesia, as far as the members of the government were concerned there did not appear to be any need to change course. They were riding on the crest of a wave, having won the economic war and apparently having won the guerrilla war. However, there was growing concern among officials that such 'victories' were meaningless unless the closer co-operation of the African population was sought.

In 1967 and 1968, after several discussions with Ian Smith, I realised that to argue the need for African advancement from a political angle would have little impact; I therefore prepared a paper which looked at the issue from a security angle: what would happen to the country if the whites lost the trust and confidence of the Africans. I outlined the essence of the paper thus:[4]

The subject with which we are concerned is the developing trend towards separation of the races in Rhodesia and all that this implies: the exploitation of differences rather than similarities; the growth of fear − the African's fear of apartheid and the European's fear of the black masses through loss of contact; the eclipse of goodwill and the upsurge of hate. If unchecked, these trends will destroy the Africans' confidence in Europeans and could result in the estrangement of the races, leading to a security situation where Black and White become opposed in physical conflict.

In a direct reference to the moves towards a republic based on a retrogressive constitution, I wrote:

From their side of the house it was the African Nationalists who started pushing − even hammering − on the door to European co-operation and occasioned the adverse reactions which we know of; but it is the European who is now trying to slam the door tight.

The concluding paragraph summed up my fears concerning the inevitable outcome of current RF policies:

I cannot say how long the erosion [of goodwill between the races] would take, nor how serious it might be − much will depend on the final political solution −

but I must sound a note of warning here and now that cracks are beginning to appear in the edifice and that if we lose the confidence, trust and mutual support of the African, there can be only one result: sooner or later the building will collapse.

I submitted the paper formally in August 1968. Smith declined to have it circulated in Cabinet or the Security Council but gave me authority to discuss it with Lance Smith, Minister of Internal Affairs. I explained the theme of the paper to the Minister and invited the comments of his senior officials. Ten months later I still had had no reply. By that time the Republican Constitution had been accepted and I wrote on my copy of the paper that: 'I can only presume that such views as are outlined in this memorandum, and the notes of warning included in it, have been ignored by the Minister and his senior officials, in view of their whole-hearted support of the new Constitution, the main purpose of which is to separate the races.'

When I raised the issue with Lance Smith he said, in essence, that although he had taken my views into account and even supported some of them, he and his colleagues in government had to adopt certain attitudes in furtherance of their political struggle and had no option but to proceed along the course they had set for themselves.[5] By implication, Lance Smith indicated that he considered some aspects of government policy unworkable; from his specific statement that apartheid could never be introduced into Rhodesia I deduced that at least he would be working towards a softening of the government's declared policies.[6]

On several occasions in the following years the CIO paper was taken out and aired, with polite interest shown in it, but each time I felt as I had done in my early days in the African bush when I was so inexperienced as to pee into a strong wind – not relieved, just dampened and depressed. My frustration was shared by the Commanders, who at that time were trying to advance their campaign to 'win the hearts and minds of the people'. They saw that they had not the slightest hope of success as long as it remained implicit in RF policies that no African could possibly have the sort of 'heart or mind' that would entitle him to participate in the affairs of state.

During the lull which followed the Security Forces' victories in 1968 it took a brave man to speak out against government policies. One such man was General Putterill. When he had completed his stint as Army Commander in 1969 he attacked the government for producing a constitution which would deny the Africans any political future and force them into more militant action. Smith described his comments as 'despicable' and castigated him for his 'extremist leftist views'. When Putterill said in public meetings that the war could not be won by force alone and that 'the ingredient that is missing is a positive dynamic programme designed to win the loyalty of all people', he was howled down by RF thugs. And when he criticised government for failing to take advantage of the lull in the fighting by 'building up African support through an imaginative policy [instead of introducing] a racist constitution with leanings to apartheid and white supremacy', he was denounced as a 'communist' and a 'traitor to Rhodesia'.

Another brave man subjected to the same treatment was Allan Savory, who left the RF to speak publicly on the theme that the war was political, and therefore required political, not military, solutions: 'The guerrillas only require the mass of the population to be passive. We, to win, require the mass of the population to be actively in support of us and not passive. We are at a severe disadvantage here.' This was the first time the word 'guerrilla', instead of 'terrorist', had been used by a Rhodesian MP in Parliament. It caused a stir. But when Savory went on to suggest that guerrilla leaders should be invited to a constitutional conference, this was altogether too much for the RF, and Smith described the suggestion as 'the most irresponsible and evil I have ever heard'.

Men such as Putterill and Savory, who publicly declared their opposition to the political trend and its impact upon the war, and those of us in official circles who privately expressed our views in favour of liberalisation were faced time and time again with total intransigence on the part of the RF and their followers. Before his retirement, Putterill had fought his own battle for African advancement to commissioned rank but, after much argument with the Minister of Defence, he lost.[7] Even Lance Smith, a comparatively enlightened Minister, together with Hostes Nicolle as the Secretary of his Ministry, had answered a subsequent proposition in Security Council that African Militia should be armed with modern weapons for their own defence and the defence of the government with the statement that, 'only over our dead bodies will we agree to firearms being passed to Africans'.

The growing intransigence of the RF began to make itself felt within the OCC. When the OCC had first been formed in 1964 (comprising Major-General Anderson, Air Vice-Marshal Bentley, Commissioner of Police Barfoot, and myself) we seldom had trouble reaching a consensus. The second OCC (Major-General Putterill, Air-Vice Marshal Hawkins and myself, with Deputy Commissioner Mervyn Harries standing in for Barfoot over most of the period) provided an even stronger consensus. Our conduct of the war was never queried by the Prime Minister or the Cabinet and the strength of our position was derived from political detachment. Without doubt, it was the consensus view of OCC that delayed UDI by eighteen months and the declaration of a Republic by two years.

But from 1969 onwards OCC rarely achieved consensus on any subject that might conflict with government policy. Throughout the last decade of the war there were always at least two members of OCC who were politically activated in favour of the RF. Despite this, however, OCC remained, for most of the time, an effective body when it came to the conduct of the war and confirmed the value of joint control of operations, where national strategy would not be dominated by a single Service or the whims of a politically minded Commander-in-Chief.

A few minor incursions occurred during the lull in fighting. CIO was never fully certain at this time what ZAPU and ZANU were up to – regrouping, licking their wounds or just lying low. We were enlightened to some extent by captured ZANU and ZAPU Intelligence officers sent into Rhodesia by the nationalist hierarchy on probing missions; these Intelligence probes helped our counter-intelligence more than they could possibly have helped the nationalists, for the men in these groups seemed surprisingly ignorant of Rhodesia's northern regions and obviously had no affinity of purpose with the inhabitants in the areas through which they passed.

CIO now had more time to develop its 'special operations' and we continued to seek whatever advice and assistance was available in this sphere. From outside our borders we attracted a number of experts who had served in other theatres of conflict, including Ian Henderson from Kenya who worked with us for years, unobserved in the Prime Minister's Office. Others offered their services and were accepted because they possessed some special flair or expertise; there were those, too, who were double agents or turned mercenaries, useful but untrustworthy characters whom we took on in small numbers. But the best recruits came from within our borders; the usefulness of their local knowledge and dedication far outweighed the usefulness of foreigners. It was an unending source of amazement to us that we never lacked local recruits for any murky or perilous calling.

'Special operations' is a game that must proceed silently; public applause spells failure. We had proceeded quietly and in a small way in the early years of CIO by probing the weaknesses in the structure of the African nationalist organisations within the country. Later, we went with nationalist movements into Zambia, Botswana, Mozambique, Tanzania and further still.

As the pressures of war developed, we found ourselves having to play in the more open field of counter-action against the countries concerned, starting with Zambia. We kept our counter-action in low key for as long as possible, providing disinformation (or 'grey propaganda') which led, for example, to ZIPRA taking most of the blame for the deaths of Zambian civilians or for accidents involving their colleagues in ZANU. It also became necessary to bring some of our agents in the nationalist movements under the operational control of Special Branch or under men in the Services with specialist knowledge. This led to the formation in 1966 of the first 'pseudo-terrorist' groups, which included turned guerrillas as they became available. From these groups evolved the Selous Scouts at a later date.

The original 'pseudos' worked, fought and died alone. If there were any citations (and this was rare, even posthumously), they were one-line entries which gave little away: 'For brave and gallant conduct over and above the call of duty'. Sometimes a slight elaboration was permissible, at the risk of raising an eyebrow: 'Killed in the operational area whilst undertaking assignments which demanded of him brave and gallant conduct over and above the normal call of duty.' For nearly seven years after their formation, the activities of the 'pseudos' remained unknown to the nationalists and throughout this period they were therefore extremely effective. Small groups of six to ten guerrillas disappeared time and again without trace. Regrettably, some of our 'handlers' within these groups also 'disappeared' in the violence of the encounter, with no quarter asked or given.

The lull in the war showed signs of being over in the latter half of 1971 when Intelligence reports coming from the north-eastern districts indicated a guerrilla presence in the border regions and fleeting contact was made with columns of porters passing southwards through the Mazarabani and surrounding areas. The guerrilla presence and activity were not defined clearly enough for the Security Forces to react militarily, but the consistency of the reports was such that it seemed that guerrillas were now living among the population.

More and more frequently the words 'Chaminuka' and 'Nehanda' appeared in the reports. Initially, we identified these words as being the names given to the ZANLA military zones which overlapped into Rhodesia from Mozambique. Then we realised that ZANLA had moved ahead of us in the spirit world by invoking the national spirit of 'Chaminuka' (the greatest Shona prophet at the time of the First Chimurenga in the 1890s) and by taking into Mozambique the spirit medium Mbuya Nehanda, the 'reincarnation' of Nehanda (the powerful regional medium who had been executed during the First Chimurenga).

There was little one could do to counteract this development. Black guerrillas could invoke the spirits; white administrators could not. Some of us gave encouragement to young officers in the north-east who appreciated the tenacity with which the people of the area adhered to their spiritual past and who tried to get local spirit mediums 'on side', but these officers were given scant support from whites in the top levels of government who would not lend themselves to what they called the 'mumbo jumbo of witchcraft', or who failed to appreciate the significance of the simple fact that the war had now taken us into the heart of the former Munhumutapa empire, the spiritual home of the Shona peoples and their allies across the border in Mozambique.

My concern with the situation in the north-east was heightened by the knowledge that the Portuguese were losing ground to FRELIMO in the adjacent Tete province. FRELIMO had switched from their prime objective of sabotaging the Cabora Bassa dam on the Zambezi River (planned as a major source of hydro-electric power for both Mozambique and South Africa) to politicising the population and they were systematically eliminating all the tribal chiefs north of the Zambezi. From being confined to the Makonde people, their campaign had now spread throughout the provinces of Cabo Delgado and Niassa and into Zambezia, and the 40,000 conscript troops sent from Portugal were proving unable to prevent the ever-increasing FRELIMO incursions out of Zambia into Tete. The situation convinced CIO of the need to carry out our own Intelligence pursuits in Tete province for which we had the blessing of DGS; our probing led to the discovery of a significant ZANLA presence in Tete.

By September 1971 the situation had deteriorated to such an extent that I suggested to Ian Smith that I fly to Lisbon to discuss the problem with the Portuguese Prime Minister, Dr Marcello Caetano, in an attempt to stop the rot. I believed I was well enough accepted in Lisbon to persuade my friends there to clear the way for me, but it was essential that I get the blessing of General Deslandes, Chief of the Joint Defence Staff. In my interview with Deslandes on 23 September I thought it desirable to deviate occasionally to talk of things other than what he knew was the underlying purpose of my visit – to try to convince Caetano that the Portuguese Armed forces in Mozambique, for whom Deslandes was ultimately responsible, would lose the war unless they changed direction. We talked, for instance, of Portugal's secret plan, developed in 1969 by Jorge Jardim and Dr Nogueira, to invade Malawi should Dr

Banda seem in danger of being overthrown and Mozambique's security be further threatened.[8]

Deslandes proved to be as helpful as I could have wished, as did Major Silva Pais, Director General of the DGS, with whom I also discussed the situation, and I was duly received by Caetano in Queluz Palace, Portugal's 'miniature Versailles' near Lisbon.[9] The theme I tried to develop in my interview with Caetano was that his peripatetic, posturing Generals in Mozambique would lose the war for him there unless more reliance was placed on the indigenous population and the Police were afforded more appropriate responsibility. Caetano queried whether a highly intelligent General such as Kaulza de Arriaga would not have studied the appropriate military lessons, which forced me into a criticism of de Arriaga that I would rather have avoided. The atmosphere in which we talked was uneasy. And I did nothing to improve it when, to emphasise a point, I brought my hand down rather heavily on the maps spread across the ornate table between us, which resulted in a sharp clatter of decorative gilt as the table collapsed onto the marble floor. In the ensuing silence I felt the gloom of decaying empires envelop us.

On leaving, I implored Caetano not to take any of his Generals to task for failures that were not necessarily of their making, or to let it be known that criticism of the Generals had come from Rhodesian sources. Within an hour, however, Caetano had sent for General Costa Gomes to instruct him to have Kaulza de Arriaga recalled because the Rhodesians, and Mr Ken Flower in particular, thought he was a 'bum General'.

Now I would have to stand my chances with Kaulza de Arriaga, who remained Commander-in-Chief in Mozambique. Hopefully, Rhodesia's case would have been represented fairly to Caetano by my friend Costa Gomes (with whom I shared an 'aniversario' – born on the same day – something which means a lot to the Portuguese). I recalled how, in January 1969, he had seen for himself how our soldiers lived rough and tough in the worst of the Zambezi valley for weeks on end, in contrast to the metropolitan Portuguese soldiers in Mozambique who rarely moved from their base or transport and remained dependent on supplies of bread and wine. I had heard Costa Gomes say to his Military Attaché: 'But do the Rhodesians really expect us to follow their example, living like animals in the African bush merely to confront guerrillas?'

The Attaché replied: 'No, Senhor. It is the example that is quite magnificent, and it suits the Rhodesians who are Anglo-Saxons, but they don't really expect that sort of behaviour from us Latins!'

To reassure myself that I was more in touch than Caetano or de Arriaga, I went alone that evening to various places of assignment in

Lisbon where one could listen to girls eating their hearts out whilst husbands or boyfriends were dying overseas and learn from them that the mass of the population no longer supported Portugal's 'civilising mission' in Africa.

On my return to Salisbury, and frequently throughout the following year, I tried to outline something of CIO's apprehensions on the Mozambican situation to the Cabinet and the Security Council. The government was being regaled with comforting reports from Rhodesia's Accredited Diplomatic Representative in Lisbon, who preferred to believe his friends among the Portuguese Generals.

In a further attempt to bring home the significance of developments in Mozambique to Rhodesian Ministers, I chose as the subject of my monthly Cabinet briefing in July 1972 the only known episode in Portuguese history that had a direct bearing on our affairs – the failure of their attempt in July 1572 to conquer the kingdom of Munhumutapa, which had encompassed much of what was now the Tete district and Rhodesia's north-eastern region. I quoted extensively from accounts of the first known action of whites against blacks in the area which was to become our main battleground, suggesting that it was but a historical prelude to the black/white confrontation now looming over us.

This attempt to warn Cabinet of the dangers of too close an association with Mozambique had been preceded by scores of others, during the seven long years since UDI, but only two Ministers showed any appreciation of the causes of my concern. David Smith, on several occasions, spoke in encouraging terms, while P. K. van der Byl said: 'Keep it up, Ken. Only by constant repetition will you drive the message into the thick heads of some of my colleagues.'

Something of my concern over Mozambique did get through, however. Part of my brief during a visit in August 1972 to Lisbon (one of my many stopping-off points during a tour of Europe where I discussed the Mozambiquan issue, amongst other things, with the Germans, the French and the British[10]) was to give Caetano a letter from Smith expressing his desire for a meeting between the two Prime Ministers.[11] Caetano agreed to such a meeting, which took place in September. Smith stayed in the once elegant Seteais Palais Hotel, on the edge of the Sintra Woods. During his morning and evening walks through these woods the relatively unfit DGS security guards accompanying him had to resort to working in relays to try to keep up with him.

Smith used as his brief for the meeting with Caetano a paper prepared by CIO in June that year. Entitled 'Mozambique: Threat to Rhodesia', it was carefully balanced (or so we hoped) so as not to give the impression that CIO was the only authority on the issue. The following comments appeared in the paper:

Most of what is now apparent in Tete has been predicted for several years; but any real attempt to resolve the problem has been bedevilled by diverse apprecia- tions of what it is all about.

Far be it from us to propose solutions ... (but) it seems increasingly certain that the current Portuguese approach of dealing with the developing situation in Tete as an essentially military problem is wrong....

The paper stressed the need for a re-think of the Portuguese approach and then went on to outline the threat to Rhodesia should the possible Portuguese abandonment of Mozambique now being hinted at by senior officials in Lisbon become a reality:

... we should not ignore the possibility of a Portuguese withdrawal (or the granting of premature independence) in the foreseeable future. The point to make here is that Rhodesia's interests could not be served adequately *after* such a withdrawal: it is imperative for us to keep sufficiently close to the developing situation to try and guarantee appropriate aid or political adjustment *before* it becomes too late.

The paper quoted the contradictory assessments being made of the situa- tion in Tete by General de Arriaga, by the Governor-General of Mozam- bique, by the DGS and by CIO.

Caetano and Smith met with only interpreters present. We never got the full story of the meeting, although we gathered from the de-briefing that Smith had represented matters with both fairness and strength. The only public comment Caetano offered indicated that he was not impress- ed with Smith's representations: 'Our timorous neighbours (the Rhode- sians) were more concerned over the situation in Mozambique than the Portuguese themselves who are well used to such a state of affairs and perfectly capable of coping with it.'

CIO's apprehensions about ZANLA activities in Mozambique and in north-eastern Rhodesia were confirmed in December 1972. An unde- fended homestead on Altena Farm in the Centenary area was attacked by a small group of guerrillas firing rockets and other weapons from a safe distance; a week later two military vehicles going to the relief of farmers in the same area were blown up by landmines; and more attacks and landmine explosions quickly followed. The guerrilla war had moved into its second stage. From a winning position between 1964 and 1972, Rhodesian Forces were entering the stage of the 'no-win' war, which lasted from December 1972 to 1976; after that, they were fighting a losing war.

CHAPTER 7

The Internal Situation
1972–76

In 1972 Ian Smith was riding on the crest of a wave. The verdict of the Pearce Commission, made public in May that year, had caused him neither disappointment nor defeat. Government propaganda had long since prevailed over fact and no one in authority was prepared to encourage disillusionment or mention the possibility of defeat in a game which had taken a new and serious turn. Most of the electorate by this time were unable to discriminate between fact and fancy, or were so confused as to have lost all powers of discrimination, and their leader appeared as one who had assumed a cloak of infallibility.

The mood of the electorate was reflected to some extent among the incoming Commanders of the Rhodesian Security Forces. Although they were as competent professionally as their predecessors, they were over-committed politically to the RF. This, and the fact that they were itching to prove themselves in a game they had just started playing, made them less amenable to suggestions within the OCC that Rhodesia was now engaged in a 'no-win war' and that they should therefore insist that the government find a political solution to Rhodesia's problem.

The difference of opinion in OCC on whether or not the war could be won militarily had, of course, to be kept within OCC or the Cabinet or the Security Council. Morale in the Security Forces was high; for most of the soldiery, the real war had just begun and they were imbued with a strong belief in the cause for which they were fighting. It was easy, even for doubters, to be caught up in the new enthusiasm and all-pervading willingness to face any hardship, even death, to preserve the Rhodesian way of life. Perhaps I was guilty at this stage of absorbing some of this enthusiasm and guilty, therefore, of failing to exert the necessary pressure on the Commanders to influence the Prime Minister on the vital need for a political settlement. Certainly, I developed a tendency to confine some of my doubts to my diary rather than air them in the appropriate forum.

14th February 1973: Shortly after the last entry (18th November 1972) things started to go wrong with internal security: penetration by ZANU out of Mozambique through the Mazarabani and other areas into the Centenary and adjacent farming districts ... the Africans in these areas going 'dead' on us – no Intelligence being volunteered although scores of locals had been recruited for training as terrorists and many more enlisted as porters to carry war matériel into Rhodesia.... A dismal failure of our much vaunted 'ground coverage' and our previously successful techniques of counter-insurgency – tracking, etc – and generally the realisation that we have become terribly vulnerable in many border and adjacent areas.... The PM and other Ministers talking publicly of a 'breakdown of security'. My vindicatory session with the PM, pointing out that much of the 'breakdown' was Government's failure to provide anything approaching an adequate presence in the border areas.... RF policies, moving towards apartheid, have embittered the Africans, or at best, turned them into neutrals waiting to see whether the terrorists are 'Freedom Fighters' or whether Security Forces emerge victorious ... but what can be done unless there are to be radical changes of attitude amongst the politicians?

The problem we all faced now was that of coping with widespread subversion in the north-eastern areas, from Sipolilo in the west to Mutoko in the east. Guerrillas were living among disaffected tribespeople, fed and sheltered by them and easily re-supplied with war matériel from across the Mozambique border. The Rhodesian Security Forces' response to this situation was to establish the first permanent Joint Operations Command (JOC) in December 1972 to co-ordinate the activities of Police, Army, Air Force, Special Branch and Internal Affairs in an area stretching from Sipolilo to Mount Darwin. The initial Army deployment in the area, which was designated 'Operation Hurricane', was one company of troops; within a year this had been increased to twenty, plus the requisite air support.

At the beginning of 1973 the members of OCC flew to Mount Darwin on a tour of inspection, and we found ourselves in the centre of action. Guerrillas had carried out their first night attack on a government target, firing on the Police Station and nearby buildings but causing no casualties. We were briefed by the members of the JOC – Brigadier Sandy Maclean (Army), Pat McCulloch and Mike Edden (Police) and representatives of the Air Force and Internal Affairs – and were impressed both by their overall efficiency and by their prompt reaction to the attack.

But efficiency in the conduct of the war, as few of us realised then, was not enough. Military confrontation was to become a thing of the past and in its place came a much more difficult problem – the new ZANLA tactic of mobilising the masses. Guerrillas were beginning to avoid contact with the Security Forces and to concentrate on 'politicisation', which led inevitably to intimidation and in its worst forms became terrorism – murder, rape and other brutalities. Civilian deaths mounted and were publicised by the government to add weight to its propaganda. The government later published a dossier entitled 'Anatomy of Terror' designed to portray African nationalists solely as terrorists bent on the destruction of law and order for the benefit of their communist masters in Russia and China. In this way the war could be represented as black anarchy without reference to white injustice, and such a representation could therefore justify the government's cure – a more punitive dose of law and order 'because this is what the African really understands'.

The Counter-Insurgency (COIN) operations in which the Commanders and senior officials in government Ministries were engaged were based increasingly on the government's belief that there had to be less 'carrot' and more 'stick'. The Army, for example, would demonstrate its strength by 'sweeps' through tribal areas and the Air Force struck the right note of awe through displays of fire power. But I and several other officials believed that demonstrations of Army and Air Force strength would be less effective in countering subversion than Police and Internal Affairs action. The people in the rural areas would soon realise that such demonstrations could not be sustained and that a transient military presence could not enforce government policy, whereas the Police and Internal Affairs personnel, based permanently among the people, could provide continuity in counter-subversive action. The differences of opinion on the strategy to be followed in COIN operations boiled down to this: on the one hand, the government wished to keep the Africans 'in their place' and to deal with subversion accordingly; on the other, most officials believed it was important to keep the Africans 'on side' and discourage them from joining the guerrillas. Already there was a mounting spiral of violence: guerrillas against tribesmen to force their allegiance; Security Forces against tribesmen suspected of supporting guerrillas. As one victim put it: 'If we report to the Police, the terrorists kill us. If we do not report, the Police suspect us of harbouring terrorists. We just do not know what to do.' And, of course, it was much easier for the guerrillas, who could threaten death, to recruit more guerrillas, than it was for government officials to prevent recruitment by promises of political advancement that might not be fulfilled.

In February 1973 the Chiweshe Tribal Trust Land, wedged between the white farming areas of Centenary, Mount Darwin, Umvukwes and Bindura, became something of a testing ground for the government's policies. All facilities – schools, shops, clinics and churches – were closed, under the negative threat of 'tell us what you know about the guerrillas or these facilities remain closed'. The entire population of Chiweshe (about 50,000) was resettled in 'Protected Villages' (PVs) to keep them apart from the guerrillas. The Army supported the PV concept enthusiastically because of its undoubted success in COIN operations in Malaya. But the essential ingredient of the Malayan operation had been an effective policy of 'winning hearts and minds' whereas those affected by the PV system in Rhodesia saw it solely as collective punishment of the innocent with the guilty and they thus became alienated to the point where they had nothing to lose by joining the guerrillas.

The essentially military operation of erecting a 'cordon sanitaire' along the Mozambique border, coupled with a 'no go' area where trespassers would be blown up or shot on sight, had practical as well as psychological advantages and was applied in Rhodesia much less ruthlessly than in many other parts of the world. As time progressed our military forces developed an extremely effective tactic against guerrillas when their position had been exposed, using a concentrated Fire Force carried in helicopter gunships. This all contributed to the fact that during the first three years of 'Operation Hurricane' the Rhodesian Forces were definitely on the ascendancy.

The first Police Anti-Terrorist Units (PATU) employed on operations were knocked into shape by my ex-Police friend, Bill Bailey, who had served with Rhodesians in Stirling's Long Range Desert Group in North Africa and Southern Europe during the Second World War. PATU personnel were drawn from the Rural Police Reserve, which had been remodelled in the 1950s as one of the lessons learnt from the Mau Mau insurrection, and they appeared as a motley crew of farmers, Game Rangers and others with high professionalism in a tracker-combat role not often matched by the regular forces. Their successes in the early stages of the war were outstanding, accounting at times for more kills than the rest of the Services put together.

But efficiency in COIN is incidental. The whole nature of the war in Rhodesia was changing to terrorism perpetrated by guerrillas indistinguishable from the African population all around us. It was merely a measure of the renewed conflict that the guerrillas were forced to terrorise in order to control the population, and that the Rhodesian Security Forces could not turn this to their advantage because the government they served could offer only 'liberation' from guerrillas. And the more successful we were in winning the war, the less pressure there was on Ian Smith to end the war. Indeed, the militants in the RF used the Security Force successes of 1973/74 to agitate against Smith, on the theme: 'Forget all about settlement. Just get on with governing the country.'

In 1973 CIO's pseudo-operations began to run into trouble because of the spread of the war and the loss of some of our key operators. Among them was a close friend of my family, whose death I recorded in my diary:

26 March 1974 Our family have not been short of tragedy.... Robin Hughes, ever young, ever happy, killed when leading a pseudo-terrorist gang. I can't remember when I felt so devastated. Robin and Grettl had only been married a few weeks, and with such fresh memories of their wedding and our visit to stay with them on the banks of the Zambezi at Mana Pools – and the sound of his laughter still in my ears – it was like losing a cherished son!

It seemed appropriate now to incorporate a military component and I put this suggestion to General Walls. It was not until November that year, however, after Ian Smith's enthusiastic support had overridden the military reluctance to embark upon anything irregular, that military participation became a reality. But as it happened, my insistence upon the militarisation of pseudo-operations and the consequent formation of the Selous Scouts proved to be the worst mistake I made in the conduct of the war.

The Selous Scouts' contribution as originally envisaged would have complemented that of Special Branch and should have enlarged the scope of pseudo-operations. But instead of fulfilling that role the Scouts abandoned all pretensions to secrecy, attracting attention rather than deflecting it (for example, by growing beards, which few Africans wear) and emerging as the glamour boys of the Army. Certainly, the unit contained individuals who performed heroic feats and fought with the greatest honour and distinction, such as 'Schulie' who was the first recipient of Rhodesia's Grand Cross of Valour (equivalent of the vc). But it also attracted vainglorious extroverts and a few psychopathic killers.

Perhaps I was expecting too much in trying to develop a complex unit owing allegiance to various Services, but some of the fault lay in the choice of the commander of the unit, Lieutenant-Colonel Reid Daly, who had been a highly efficient RSM in the RLI but who lacked those exceptional qualities that made men such as Orde Wingate and David Stirling great, albeit eccentric, leaders of irregular forces. Moreover, by allowing the unit to expand, thereby sacrificing quality for quantity, we overlooked one of the first lessons we should have learnt in our study of counter-insurgency – that the more it becomes necessary to extend a pseudo-operation, the less effective it is likely to be.

Having initiated the unit, I was committed to it, but I soon ran into problems. The Commissioner of Police complained that the Selous Scouts had neutralised the role of Special Branch and I had to agree reluctantly that the Special Branch component should be separated from

Selous Scouts Headquarters at Inkomo and moved to Bindura. Before long, I was being pressurised to withold Intelligence from the Scouts because of its misuse. I could hardly blame the Scouts for subsequently acquiring their own Intelligence, although they broke one of the basic rules of Intelligence by acting upon unprocessed information. Reid Daly also took it upon himself to report Scouts' Intelligence directly to General Walls, frequently over a glass of beer in Walls's home, and this caused disruption of normal Intelligence links. Later, when the unit was allowed to encroach upon the Special Air Service (SAS) role in external operations CIO was forced to maintain separate links with the SAS and the rest of the Rhodesian Army.

In contrast to so much in the conduct of the war which was well co-ordinated, the Scouts frequently operated without authority or beyond recall, and in the latter stages of the war their activities became so questionable that they were the only Rhodesian unit to be disbanded with obloquy.

Adverse developments in the military sphere reinforced the government's tendency to handle other internal threats in a heavy handed manner, and hence contributed to the erosion of Smith's control of the situation. This led ultimately to the weakness in the government which Kissinger was able to exploit so ably in 1976.

Journalists reporting for foreign media became a focus of the government's attention. The case which precipitated the deportation of several journalists during this period was that of Peter Niesewand, a domiciled Rhodesian who reported mainly for the BBC and *The Guardian*. My role in the Niesewand affair was that of devil's advocate, unlike my stance in the controversial deportation two years previously of Guy Clutton-Brock, a founder member of Cold Comfort Farm and one of the first white nationalists in the country.[1] In Clutton-Brock's case I had personally argued in favour of deportation on the grounds that he was 'a threat to the security of the State' but in Niesewand's case I felt there were no grounds for deportation.

During November 1972 Niesewand had reported that a number of Mozambican women and children had been killed in an ambush set by an RLI unit operating beyond our borders in Tete province. At that stage, the government was firmly denying that it had extended the war into Mozambique and Niesewand was tried 'in camera' for divulging Official Secrets. CIO's opposition to the action taken against Niesewand was based on several factors. We knew that he had special access to the nationalists and we believed his reporting to be factual; therefore, it had

Intelligence value. Also, we viewed Lardner-Burke's desire to deport Niesewand – a desire he had been expressing for some time – as part of his vendetta against members of the Niesewand family; the family lived in Gwelo, the Minister's constituency, and had long been outspoken in their opposition to the RF. But the main reason for our support of Niesewand was that his Tete report was accurate – women and children *had* been shot, albeit by accident, when an RLI unit was on the track of guerrillas – and I believed that it was high time the Rhodesian public was made aware of the extension of the war across our borders.

CIO's views were disregarded. Niesewand was convicted and then given the unusual option of remaining in gaol for several years or accepting deportation. Not surprisingly, he chose deportation and left the country in May 1973. Even after deportation, he continued to report both sides of Rhodesia's case. His report in *The Guardian* on 27 September 1973 on Eddison Zvobgo's fall-out with Bishop Muzorewa contained a quotation which stuck in the minds of whites:

Zvobgo: I believe the Bishop is a man of great courage and sincerity ... but remember that he is not being schooled in the crucible of real nationalist politics. He is not able to speak with more than one voice. He is sincere in what he says.
  Whites must be led down the garden path to the place of slaughter. Morality does not come into it.

The grounds for the subsequent deportations of a number of journalists were, in most cases, just as symptomatic of a government which had begun to believe the myths it had created to delude its electorate. When asked in later years why so many journalists had been deported during this period, P. K. van der Byl, then Minister of Information, replied:[2]

You should have asked why more journalists were not deported; there were too few deportations. I don't believe you can defend Western Christian civilisation against Soviet expansionism with liberal, laissez-faire policies. We were actually far too tolerant and acquiescent about the whole thing.

Shortly after the Niesewand affair Smith began making ill-defined moves towards settlement with internally based nationalist leaders. He started by negotiating with Bishop Muzorewa, in July 1973. The talks went on intermittently until May 1974. Smith was insisting on the Bishop's acceptance of the Pearce proposals – proposals which Smith had been happy to cast into limbo in 1972 and which the Bishop had rejected more positively than anything he had ever done in the political arena. Smith then sought to initiate talks with Nkomo and Sithole, who for a while appeared to offer alternative prospects for settlement. This time Smith's theme was parity or power sharing, whereas Sithole was rapidly losing what little power he could have shared and Nkomo talked only of majority rule.

For over a year I moved between Smith, Muzorewa, Nkomo and Sithole, arranging meetings and carrying messages, sensing something akin to fear among all parties that they might actually be caught settling. And yet, against all logic and against all our experience of Smith's capacity to negotiate-but-not-to-negotiate, CIO's hopes were raised. Perhaps our optimism was based on desperation out of despair, something of which showed through in my diary:

Sunday 1st December 1974: Things are on the decline in Rhodesia. In spite of increased Security Force successes we are not keeping pace with terrorist recruiting. Indeed, we have lost the goodwill of the Africans in the forward areas and over much of the rest of Rhodesia as well . . . but strangely there appears to be a better prospect of settlement now than ever before; although how can the whites in Rhodesia reverse the trends of the past decade or more? Or if they are going to be forced into change will there be sufficient goodwill, and enough sincerity, to reach a lasting accommodation?

Sam Putterill lunched with me (and other guests) today and I couldn't help feeling something of the despair that affected us at UDI. Also the disillusion of *Tiger*, *Fearless* and the Pearce Commission. But I have given it as an assessment of mine that – unlike earlier occasions – Smithy cannot just do nothing now, or try to get away with a negative approach.

Perhaps I've been too long in the game. Perhaps I'm too weary, mentally and physically, to stand another failure? . . . . More than anything, I believe it is the deep-seated duplicity of it all that riles me.

Three months passed before I wrote again:

Sunday 2nd March 1975: How often have I had to eat my words; or check back on my last recital before putting pen to paper again?

On the last page: 'Smithy cannot just do nothing now. . . .' After months of anxious endeavour working towards a settlement as part of 'detente', that is exactly what is happening!

Tomorrow or the next day I expect a stark confrontation between the PM and Ministers on one side and we officials [OCC and the Secretaries of the Ministry of Defence and Ministry of Law and Order] on the other, who have not been consulted recently – as at the time of UDI – because our advice would obviously run counter to political trends. Indeed, there is much of the UDI saga repeating itself – full circle after ten years! The difference now is that some of the officials realise that we are in a 'no-win' position and that it is up to the politicians to find a political solution if Rhodesia is to survive. But with all the goodwill in the world, and all the promise of 'detente', it seems just too much for the governing politicians to advance sufficiently to a point where they can accept any African as an equal; for as P. K. van der Byl said to me some time ago: 'It will be over my dead body before any kaffir would be invited into this [Cabinet] room.'

The confrontation occurred but we achieved nothing by it. Smith and his Ministers showed no inclination to discuss the need for political solutions with us and were content simply to accept our successes and ignore anything less encouraging. The Army Commander reined back from actually insisting that there had to be a political settlement or Rhodesia would lose the war. The Air Force Commander was won over by Smith fairly easily, and agreed that he should get on with fighting the war and not concern himself with politics. The Commissioner of Police and the Secretaries accepted Smith's argument that their principal function was to maintain law and order. And the Ministers agreed readily with Smith that he was under no political pressure to settle; in fact, they said that the reverse applied, for strong sentiments were now being expressed publicly by many whites to the effect that settlement would be seen as surrender.

The government was basing too much of its ostrich-like stance on its belief that the economy was flourishing. It also derived a measure of satisfaction from the fact that Kaunda, despite his insistence in public that the Zambian border would remain closed, had been forced into a secret agreement whereby Zambia's copper was once again being exported through Rhodesia and certain essentials, such as explosives for his country's mines, were again passing northwards across the Victoria Falls bridge. The complacency was further entrenched by the slowing down in the rate of white emigration.

While Rhodesia's politicians were taking a step backwards, ZANLA was penetrating further south along Rhodesia's eastern border into the zones which became known as 'Operation Thrasher' and 'Operation Repulse'. The spread of the war despite Security Force successes made the control of guerrilla recruitment more vital than ever, and as Rhodesia's 'no-win' position began to deteriorate into a 'losing' position towards the end of 1975 CIO felt it imperative once again to bring this issue to the fore. In September 1975 we prepared a paper with the following theme:[3]

Every Black man fighting on our side is committed in our favour. If he is for us, he is not against.
Every Black man fighting with us is one man and his family not committed to the terrorists.
One of the greatest dangers facing us is a continuation of terrorist recruiting on anything like the scale that has developed over the last six months....
For more than a decade we could number terrorist strengths in scores – never totalling more than 300 – but now we must number them in thousands – all Black....
With a limited White population and a White/Black ratio now in excess of 1:21

it seems utterly illogical to leave the defence of Rhodesia in White hands ... why not pave the way for greater African participation now?

The paper went on to suggest that extensive recruitment of Africans into all sections of the Armed Forces and promotion of some of them to commissioned rank might ease the situation. It was sent to various Ministries and circulated among members of OCC. The reaction from the government was discouraging, to say the least. The only positive response was a proposal to encourage recruitment of labour for South Africa's gold mines, so that African males would be moved southwards to employment rather than northwards to swell guerrilla ranks.

The talks between Smith and Nkomo dragged on until March 1976, when they eventually and inevitably broke down on the issue of majority rule. Smith's explanation of the breakdown was this: 'I have said we are prepared to bring black people into our government.... But I don't believe in majority rule, black majority rule, not in a thousand years. If it is white one day and black the next, then we have failed.' Nkomo said: 'After months of evasiveness and prevarication by the regime, it has become clear that we live in different worlds and speak different languages.'

Smith now tried the new tack of bringing 'moderate' blacks into the government to give it a multiracial veneer. Van der Byl, among others, lent his support to this move, having changed his mind over allowing blacks to enter the Cabinet Room. He influenced Smith towards the French colonial system whereby blacks were put into key positions but whites stood behind them, pulling the strings (what he overlooked was that for generations blacks in French colonies had enjoyed universal acceptance as 'Black Frenchmen'). A few 'moderates', including Chief Jeremiah Chirau, representing the Shona, and Chief Kayisa Ndiweni, representing the Ndebele, were brought in. But this move had no effect, and Rhodesia's position continued to deteriorate. In June 1976 I wrote in my diary:

Sunday 10th June: ... we go from crisis to crisis – as if twelve years of constant tension and pressure had not been enough!

Our terrorist threat has developed to the greatest we could possibly have expected, with incursions building up since January to a presence of about 1600 within Rhodesia, 2000 under training, and many more – possibly 10,000 – waiting in the wings for training.... The increased call-up (for whites) has affected the economy but we seem no worse off than most of the rest of the world; and infinitely better off than our hostile neighbours, Mozambique and Zambia.

One would still wish to see an end to it all....

And the unexpected – at a recent meeting of OCC our staff interrupted proceedings to produce a birthday cake with five candles, and champagne for a toast. The occasion was the 500th meeting of OCC, which struck a nostalgic chord when they read from the first Minutes, to find that I was the only survivor from that meeting in October 1964.

The seeds of yet another crisis, sown in the 1960s, began to germinate in mid-1976 – the conflict between State and Church, in this case the Roman Catholic Church. The Catholics, mainly through their mission schools, held sway over a million or more blacks in Rhodesia, and many leading nationalists had been educated at Catholic mission schools. While the whites' attitude towards such leftist bodies as the World Council of Churches had become extremely hostile, their attitude towards the Catholic Justice and Peace Commission (CJCP) was generally favourable. It began to change in the early 1970s, however, and things came to a head when a fiery Irish Bishop, Donal Lamont, took over the chairmanship of the Commission. (It is interesting to note that the CJCP, which was the bane of Smith's government, has become the bane of Mugabe's government through highlighting 'atrocities' committed by government forces in Matabeleland.)

As Bishop of Manicaland, Lamont had been immersed in the problems facing the numerous missions in the eastern border area caught between the demands of the guerrillas and the retributive measures of the Security Forces. From his pulpit and through the Commission he castigated the government for the brutality of the Security Forces against civilians, until the alienation of Church from State was virtually complete. In August 1976 he published an open letter to Smith:

Conscience compels me to state that your Administration by its clearly racist and oppressive policies and by its stubborn refusal to change is largely responsible for the injustices which have provoked the present disorder.... In a state which claims to be democratic, people are restricted and imprisoned without trial, tortured or tried 'in camera', and put to death by secret hanging; and justification for all this barbarity is sought by you in the name of Christianity and of Western civilisation and for what you call the 'maintaining of Rhodesian standards.' Surely this is the final absurdity.

There were enough home truths in this homily that needed saying, without adding the imputation that trials 'in camera' meant torture or the falsity that there had been deaths 'by secret hanging'. The home truths were ignored and Lamont was sentenced and deported in March 1977 for failing to report the presence of guerrillas. Under interrogation he admitted a one-sidedness in his attacks but excused himself on the grounds that the government agencies had fully publicised guerrilla atrocities and he was merely putting the record straight.

The government's reaction to 'threats' by the Church or the Press was generally swift and unequivocal, but the major threat – guerrilla recruitment – continued to be ignored. In a general review of the Security situation which I delivered to selected government employees in Salisbury and Bulawayo in July 1976 I divulged the following information:[4]

During the quarter ending 30th June, 152 terrorists were killed and 33 captured in Operation Hurricane.... Security Force casualties during the quarter in question were 11 killed and 124 injured.... In Operation Thrasher 96 terrorists were killed and 16 captured.... Security Force casualties have been 10 killed and 72 injured.... Since commencement of Operation Repulse 24 terrorists were killed and 11 captured. Security Forces lost 9 members killed and 8 others injured.... In Malaya it took something like 350 servicemen to kill one terrorist a year. We are doing infinitely better than that, but unless terrorist casualties exceed their present rate of infiltration, no amount of continuous call-up will, of itself, provide a military solution. Indeed, it is doubtful whether any purely military solution is possible.

I lacked the courage of my convictions to say to the audience what I was saying within the confines of OCC or top levels of government: that we were fighting the wrong war at the wrong time. However, my brief did include this comment:

It is nearly four years since Operation Hurricane started, and although Rhodesia has faced serious incursions before, this is the most sustained threat we have had to face since the 1896/7 rebellions and now with the recurrence of incursions across the Zambezi out of Zambia and the spread of terrorism into southern Matabeleland we must accept that virtually the whole of Rhodesia is under threat.

At question time I gave away enough for my listeners to appreciate that, whatever the politicians said, the official assessment was that Rhodesia was beginning to lose the war. And, from the response to my brief, it was evident that the middle ranks of the Ministry of Internal Affairs clearly knew the score.

As the situation deteriorated in the latter half of 1976 my colleagues in OCC began to lend the full weight of their support to CIO's Intelligence assessments. The specific opportunity to do so arose in August/September, when we produced a quarterly assessment of the overall Security situation. As with our previous assessments, this paper was utilised by the Joint Planning Staff (JPS) in preparing their appreciation of the military/police implications of the threat. The CIO paper painted a sombre picture of a country suffering severe strain in every limb, for which the only remedy was immediate political action.[5] The JPS's paper endorsed our views by painting an equally disturbing picture, although it lent more weight to military remedies than CIO considered appropriate.

The theme of CIO's assessment was that 'Rhodesia is being increasingly subjected to various forms of external and internal pressure which are seriously affecting the country's security, politico/economic and social structure.' It then outlined the nature of these pressures:

The threat from terrorism lies in the capacity of the terrorist organisations to recruit, and in consequence train large numbers of terrorists to attack Rhodesia. It is known that their intention is to infiltrate and infest border areas, with the ultimate objective of isolating the white settlements on the periphery, cutting lines of communication and eventually, applying a stranglehold on the capital....

The Security Force's 'kill' rate is not keeping pace with the increased number of terrorists being infiltrated into Rhodesia.... The growing number of terrorists operating in Rhodesia will lead to more Security Force casualties in men and vehicles. Rhodesia cannot afford to suffer increased casualties to either....

We delude ourselves ... if we ignore the mood of the blacks which makes nationalism attractive....

Unless positive steps are taken to guarantee a secure existence for whites for the foreseeable future, emigration will continue at a steady rate and immigration will practically cease....

Britain's European partners, and more recently the USA, have now unmistakably joined her to bring about majority rule in Rhodesia in the shortest possible time....

Rhodesia is wholly dependent upon South Africa for military and economic survival ... the Republic is currently being subjected to formidable international pressure to coerce the Rhodesian Government to accept the principle of early majority rule ... it is considered that the former level of assistance is likely to be materially and progressively reduced.

Zambia ... has recommitted herself to facilitate insurrection and terrorism inside Rhodesia....

The Mozambique Government is committed to providing full support to Rhodesian terrorists. Indeed it now assumes a command and control mantle over terrorist activities....

Tanzania's military forces have built up during the past four years and its training establishments for FRELIMO have been assigned to Rhodesian terrorists....

Botswana ... endeavours to align its attitude towards Rhodesia with the tenets of the OAU.... The Botswana Government has been subjected to increasing pressure to close its border and deny Rhodesia use of the railway line....

Soviet exploitation of African nationalist aspirations has been escalated....

The conclusion read, in part: 'It is vital and urgent that new political decisions should be taken if the security situation within the country is not to become untenable and if we are to attain the capacity to turn the terrorists' threat.'

The suggested military response to the threat, as outlined in the J P S paper – 'that a more bold and aggressive strategic policy must be adopted now [by] attacking Rhodesian terrorists' bases in adjacent territories, thus eliminating the enemy at source' – led inevitably to arguments within O C C. Not only was it an appeal to the government to sanction external operations, but it also implied that immediate action in the military sphere should take precedence over the need for civil and political action.

Equally disturbing was the fact that C I O's quarterly assessments (previously circularised on a need-to-know basis) had become increasingly restricted by the Prime Minister in his apparent attempt to protect politicians, including some members of his own Cabinet, from the facts. This occasioned a 'Top Secret' letter to him on 1 September, worded as carefully as I could to register the mildest of protests against a development which appeared to be likely to be further entrenched if officials lined up against the politicians:[6] 'It is implicit in my mandate that I should analyse and report any threat to the Security of the State.... I believe that the dangers which now confront us should be brought to wider notice than before and accordingly request the Prime Minister's authority for circulation, at least, to Security Council or its equivalent.' When I enquired after due lapse of time whether I could expect an answer, the Prime Minister's Secretary replied: 'Yes, but not in writing. The Prime Minister expects you to continue to function as before – that is, by submitting reports to him – and he will decide whether they should have any wider circulation.'

Simultaneously, the Prime Minister was devising another method of restricting information. He decided to convert the Security Council into a smaller body to be known as the War Council.[7] Part of his reason for doing this, although it was not fully appreciated at the time, was to keep the conduct of the war exclusively in white hands now that there were black Ministers and Deputy Ministers in the 'Security' Ministries who might be untrustworthy or too inquisitive. At the first meeting of the War Council, held in the Prime Minister's office on 7 September, the politicians were represented by only two Ministers and a Deputy Minister.[8] The issue of terrorist recruiting and counter measures to reduce it, such as the extension of the P V system, dominated the discussion; it was also noted that, in the context of support from South Africa, a 'dangerous situation had been reached in respect of stocks of fuel and ammunition'.

The meeting was adjourned until the following day, when we considered a memorandum on the introduction of a policy of surrender (or 'safe return') but the Minister of Internal Affairs had serious misgivings about implementing such a measure, as the following extract from the Minutes indicates:[9]

National Surrender Policy: The Director-General CIO drew attention to the conclusions of the memorandum and advised that OCC supported them. It was, however, important to have the view of the Minister of Internal Affairs and the Secretary for Internal Affairs.

The Minister of Internal Affairs [said] his Ministry had certain reservations and could foresee problems. The agreement of the Chiefs was essential....

The Secretary for Internal Affairs said that he believed that surrender terms offered to terrorists should be limited in time. He also believed that it was not possible to protect the families of those who surrendered. If the terms were followed ultimately by an amnesty, this would exacerbate the position....

The Minister of Law and Order said there was no need to alter the law as it was inconceivable that the death sentence would be passed on terrorists who surrendered voluntarily....

PSYAC wished to introduce a system where terrorists would be encouraged to report to certain designated centres....

There must be no indication whatever of an amnesty....

Thought should be given to directing the campaign towards terrorists in Mozambique by means of leaflets and radio broadcasts....

The Chiefs should be told that a plan was being put forward to encourage terrorists to give themselves up on the basis that their lives would be spared, but they would not go free....

The policy of safe return was so ill-defined that, despite attempts by the Commanders to make it work, no one surrendered. Similarly, the belated and half-hearted attempts now being made through the Psychological Action unit (PSYAC) to 'win the hearts and minds' of the blacks were getting nowhere and soon became the source of derision, as exemplified by the oft-quoted saying: 'Why bother about the munt's heart or mind? If you've got him by the balls, the heart and mind will follow.'

This unit had been formed as part of COIN operations (and in December 1976 came under the CIO umbrella) but although the Commanders, their staff and the rest of us spent hours trying to boost Psyac's limited chances of success, we were thwarted at every turn. There was nothing we could offer the blacks, in the name of the government, which was as attractive as the promises now being held out to them by the guerrillas.

CHAPTER 8

External Escalation
1972–76

For seven years, from the declaration of independence in November 1965 to the burst of guerrilla activity in the Centenary area in December 1972, the Rhodesian public was given little reason to doubt the government's control over the external threat to its chosen course. The public's first indication that this control was waning came in a radio broadcast by Ian Smith on 4 December 1972: 'The security situation is far more serious than it appears on the surface, and if the man in the street could have access to the security information which I and my colleagues in government have, then I think he would be a lot more worried than he is today.'

This was underlined almost immediately by the government's closure of the Zambian border, in January 1973. The Intelligence on which the government's manoeuvre was based suggested only a fifty-fifty chance of achieving the overall objective: to remove from the Zambezi valley the ZIPRA bases from which incursions were being launched so that more attention could be paid to the new ZANLA threat out of Mozambique.

CIO was advised by British Intelligence, acting as the 'honest broker', that a promise could be obtained from Kaunda that, as a result of the closure, Zambia would see to the removal of ZIPRA bases if that was the price for moving essential supplies across the border. I realised that the promise could be revoked as soon as it was made, but with the security situation deteriorating through the opening of a second front in Mozambique I believed a stage had been reached when firm action must be taken or Rhodesia, as the defender against aggression, would lose all initiative. My argument in favour of the closure of the border went against the advice of my most trusted colleague in CIO, Ken Leaver, my Director 'External', and as Smith's closest adviser in the matter I must take some responsibility for the fact that the manoeuvre rebounded on Rhodesia.

Knowing that Leaver felt strongly that any attempt by Smith to manipulate Kaunda would fail, I took him with me to participate in the final discussion with the Prime Minister. I was also accompanied by Derrick Robinson, my Director 'Internal'. Smith was more than half committed to closure before we began our discussion, which made it very easy for him to accept my arguments; Robinson seldom committed himself in opposition to the Prime Minister; and thus Leaver was left to battle on his own. He spoke on the theme that no black ruler dare become politically beholden to Smith, and Kaunda was no exception. He said the President of Zambia would rather let his people starve, if that was to be the effect of the closure, than succumb to a white man's pressure in order to have the border re-opened.

Leaver stated his case too strongly for Smith's liking and was silenced unceremoniously before his argument had run its course. The only comfort I could offer him as we left the Prime Minister's office was that he had been provided an opportunity to personally represent the views of most of his staff.

As Leaver had predicted, Kaunda did not respond to Smith's 're-opening' when the closure had failed to elicit the right response, and so it remained closed, with the consequent loss of some political support abroad. South Africa's leaders were chagrined because they had not been consulted prior to the act, and the Vorster/Smith relationship deteriorated. Portugal was critical of the manoeuvre insofar as a border closure violated an important principle the Portuguese had sustained in Mozambique and Angola – never to transgress an international frontier. Nevertheless, the manoeuvre did produce some positive results, as indicated in the brief from the Secretary, Jack Gaylard, to the Prime Minister on 5 February.

Our prime objective was to save lives by discouraging direct incursions from Zambia at a time when our forces were committed in the Centenary area. Since the border was closed there have been no incursions from Zambia by ZAPU or FROLIZI, although these had been planned – this despite the successes gained by ZANU which would have been expected to spur the other groups on ... Despite propaganda to the contrary, we have shown clearly the extent of Zambia's dependence on its rail and road communications through Rhodesia and the impracticability of the alternate routes. The longer Zambia keeps the border closed, the more apparent this will become.

The advantage we gained was that the action perpetuated the split between the nationalists and ZIPRA bases on the Zambian side of the border were closed temporarily. In the new direction in which the war was progressing, any advantage was vital.

The new direction had been hinted at in 1971 by Herbert Chitepo, the Lusaka-based chairman of ZANU, when he said: 'It is useless to engage in conventional warfare with well-equipped Rhodesian and South African troops along the Zambezi.' By 1973 Chitepo was saying that too much emphasis had been placed on 'military activity' at the expense of 'political matters' and that:[1] 'We have since tried to correct this tragic error by politicising and mobilising the people before mounting any attacks against the enemy. After politicising our people it became easier for them to co-operate with us and to identify with our programme.'

The conflict by this time bore little resemblance to 'war' in the conventional sense. The guerrillas were avoiding contact with the Rhodesian Security Forces, striking instead at 'soft' targets – unprotected men, women and children – to be burnt, maimed or slaughtered in the process of 'politicisation'. CIO changed tack accordingly and tried to match the guerrilla tactics by using 'pseudos' and paid agents to operate against similarly chosen 'soft' targets. To this extent we participated in the deadly campaign of terror now being waged in the remote rural areas: but our victims were those who had chosen a course of violence for themselves, to kill or be killed, and most of the perpetrators were their own kind.

Among the paid agents was the Reverend Arthur Kanodareka, who in 1976 was to accompany Bishop Muzorewa to the Geneva Conference as Treasurer-General of the UANC. Just as any war will inspire the noblest deeds of courage and self-sacrifice, so at the other end of the spectrum one finds the basest of motivation which an Intelligence officer can exploit. For more years than I would like to tell, young men were recruited for the guerrilla cause under the aegis of CIO and with the willing co-operation of Kanodareka and his helpers who supplied them with poisoned uniforms. The men would be sent on their way to the guerrilla training camps, but before reaching their destination would die a slow death in the African bush. Many hundreds of recruits became victims of this operation. It became so diabolically successful that exposure seemed inevitable and so the principal perpetrators had to be eliminated – rather as a hunter will finish off a wounded animal to stop further suffering.

This is not to excuse ourselves from the means or the end. But so it was that the bullet-riddled body of Kanodareka was found in a motor vehicle in the Salisbury area in 1978, assumed to have been the victim of the nationalist struggle-within-the-struggle but in fact the villain in a most sordid tale of treachery and betrayal. And no matter what passed through the minds of other perpetrators, I realised then that no terrorist can ever wipe the slate clean. My own thoughts kept going back to the bitter experience of forced disarmament and tribe fighting tribe, in the Ogaden in 1942, when a proud Somali said to me: 'We can kill each other. We are fighting men. We can loot our enemies' stock and abduct their women, for this is war. But whatever we do, we must never poison the wells.'

In developing our plans for clandestine counter-action in Zambia and Mozambique it was necessary to get the South Africans 'on side'. I took advantage of a visit to Rhodesia in November 1973 by P. W. Botha, then South African Minister of Defence, to exchange vital Intelligence and deliver a personal address to the Defence Ministers and Joint Chiefs of Staff of both countries. My address opened with:[2] 'Communism as such does not constitute as great a threat to our respective governments, to the white man in southern Africa, as say, African nationalism.' It was necessary to make this point yet again for the politicians were still promoting the belief that communism was the greatest threat, whereas the professionals maintained that the 'white order' was threatened by 'black nationalism' and that communist countries were no more likely to interfere in the Rhodesian issue than Britain or other Western countries who wielded far greater influence. I then outlined something of the 'threat':

Although there are essential differences between the territories in question, the threat to Mozambique, Angola, Rhodesia and South Africa remains one of subversion, insurgency or terrorism ... subversive influences know no political boundary, nor do native populations with trans-border ethnic affiliations. Whether we like it or not we are all in this thing together; over the past year – and in spite of considerable losses inflicted by Rhodesian Security Forces – the number of terrorists aligned against us has increased. From the initial deployment of one military company within Rhodesia in 'Operation Hurricane' in December 1972, we now have the equivalent of twenty companies deployed with increased air and other effort; Rhodesian terrorist organisations are more united than they were. ZANU in particular have profited from their union with FRELIMO.... The deteriorating security situation in Mozambique has already rendered our north-eastern districts much more vulnerable. Further deterioration affecting our eastern borders and South Africa's north eastern borders will occur.... Although Botswana continues to retain a reasonable neutrality, the terrorist threat to Rhodesia and South Africa from or through that country must increase.... Zambia will continue as a hostile base and spring-board for all our and your terrorist organisations....

My final remarks included the following:

With every year that has passed our enemies have become more united and in some respects more efficient, whilst the component parts of Southern Africa have become more vulnerable and in some respects more disunited.

The steady increase of terrorism and terrorist recruiting during recent years will continue....

Our enemies, who receive open and world-wide support, are in no way inhibited, whilst our efforts to achieve greater co-ordination are seriously inhibited by outdated foreign policy....

1 & 2 Ken Flower in 1940, as a Trooper in the British South Africa Police, and on his last day as Deputy Commissioner in 1963, before becoming head of the Secret Service.

The Royal Escort of the BSAP, led by Ken Flower, is reviewed by the Queen Mother outside Government House, on her visit for the opening of Kariba Dam in 1960.

4 Sir Humphrey Gibbs, last Governor of Southern Rhodesia.

5 Major-General R. R. (Sam) Putterill, Commander of the Rhodesian Army, at the first opening of Parliament after UDI in June 1966. Humphrey Gibbs had told him: 'Sam, you had better open Parliament, for not to do so would be a confrontation. But don't appear as if you are enjoying it!' President Dupont is in the middle and Lieut. Col. N. Jardine of the Rhodesia Regiment, beyond.

6 The signing of UDI, 11 November 1965. Seated (*left to right*): Lardner-Burke, Dupont, Ian Smith, Harper, Lord Graham; (*second row*) Howman, Van Heerden, Musset, Wrathall, Rudland; (*back row*) Phillip Smith, Dillon, Lance Smith, Maclean, Van der Byl, Dunlop.

Harold Wilson and Ian Smith walk towards the conference room aboard HMS *Fearless*, Gibraltar 1968.

8 Rejecting the Pearce Proposals for an Anglo-Rhodesian settlement, 1972.

9 Celebrating the 500th meeting of OCC, the Operations Co-ordinating Committee, in June 1976, complete with birthday cake. Seated (*left to right*): Walls (Army), Sherren (Police), Mussell and McLaren (Air force), Flower (Intelligence).

10 Jason Ziyapaya Moyo, Vice-President ZAPU, killed by a parcel bomb in Lusaka, 22 January 1977.

11 Herbert Wiltshire Chitepo, National Chairman ZANU, killed by car bomb, 18 March 1975.

12 Josiah Magama Tongogara, C-in-C ZANLA, Chief of Defence in the Dare re Chimurenga (ZANU War Council), died in motor accident in Mozambique, December 1979.

13 Ndabaningi Sithole on his return from
exile, July 1977.

14 The 3 March Agreement (1978). Seated (*left to right*): Muzorewa, Smith, Chirau, Sithole.
Behind Muzorewa and on his left: Mundawarara. Behind Smith: David Smith. Behind Chirau:
Ndiweni. Gaylard, the Cabinet Secretary, leafs through papers.

5 OCC on tour with President Dupont, (*left to right*): McLaren, Flower, Walls, Sherren, Dupont.

Army and Air Force padres hold a service at the remains of the second Viscount airliner shot down by ZIPRA, February 1979.

17 Ken Flower leaves the Carlton Tower Hotel during the Lancaster House Conference. British Intelligence stopped the publication of this picture, at his request.

8 A session at Lancaster House, Autumn 1979. Bishop Muzorewa's delegation on the left, Lord Carrington and the British in the centre, and the Patriotic Front on the right.

British Police and Paras sent to supervise the 1980 elections.

20 Lord Soames and Robert Mugabe shortly after the election results, March 1980.

21 Joshua Nkomo, Minister of Home Affairs, January 1981.

2 Mugabe in 1981, the winner.

23 The loser: Bishop Muzorewa (*right*) has a chance meeting with Kenyan politician Oginga Odinga at Harare Airport, January 1981.

24 'You have inherited a jewel in Africa, don't tarnish it': President Nyerere's words to Mugabe on his first visit to Zimbabwe in March 1981. President Banana of Zimbabwe is in the middle.

There may be those in South Africa who would favour a retreat into the laager but most South Africans with experience of subversion and insurgency will realise the advantage of dealing with these problems across South Africa's borders and as far away from their homeland as possible – certainly as far as the Zambezi River.

There was more political content in this brief than I would have liked, but I was speaking to politicians as well as to officials. Six months later, as indicated in my brief to the Prime Minister prior to his meeting with his South African counterpart, I was still stressing the need for co-ordinated Southern African action in the face of the threat of African nationalism, and in particular the need to 'control our joint destiny by effective clandestine action'.[3]

In the meantime, however, the political and military map of Southern Africa was being radically altered by events in Portugal.

The unfortunate introduction of General de Arriaga as a subject of discussion during my meeting with Dr Caetano in Lisbon in September 1971 had affected relations between Mozambique and Rhodesia to such an extent that I considered it necessary to fly to Nampula in northern Mozambique to make my peace with him. The visit took place in January 1973 and thereafter our inter-territorial and inter-service relations did improve, but my own opinion of the General did not. During our discussion in his 'Ops Room' he stood beneath flashing lights as he surveyed the wall maps, liberally decorated with coloured pins. Carried away with his own enthusiasm, obsessed with pretentious plans, the deployment of troops and the portrayal of tactics, he then faced me, reluctantly turning his back on his playthings, and exclaimed:

'Is this not magnificent!'

And I thought: 'What has his "magnificent" battlefield got to do with the men who are dying out there in the African bush?'

But at least we were talking to each other.

In the following July, OCC gave the General a farewell dinner in Salisbury shortly before his return to Portugal. After dinner he distributed copies of his latest book, *Coragem, Tenacidade e Fé* ('Courage, Tenacity and Faith'), and drew our attention to his inscription on the fly leaf, asking my military colleagues whose signature it resembled. They had no idea, and the General was crestfallen when he found he had to explain what he considered should have been obvious to any student of military history – that his signature was almost identical to that of Napoleon!

With time running out for Portugal in Mozambique, it became even more urgent to attempt to co-ordinate the available Intelligence between

Portugal, South Africa and Rhodesia. The military leaders had been holding tripartite discussions and had agreed in principle that there should be a common strategy of 'Joint Defence of the Zambezi River Line', but there seemed little prospect of translating theory into practice. In the dying months of 1973 I flew like an aimless shuttlecock between the Portuguese and South Africans trying to promote greater co-ordination in anything affecting national security. By March 1974 I was beginning to feel dejected by the lack of progress (Diary):

26 March 1974: My colleagues and I in OCC have endured months of frustration, prevarication and downright resistance when trying to set the scene right.

I travelled to Pretoria before Xmas '73.... I've been to Lourenco Marques and managed to get agreement from the DGS to form 'Flechas' for trans-border operations in Mozambique where the security situation continues to deteriorate....* Thence to Pretoria again, this time to see their PM, Mr Vorster, and others, to try and get South African support for our efforts with the Portuguese in Mozambique. On return now the PM wishes me to go to Lisbon to try and sell his concept of 'Joint Defence of the Zambezi River Line'.... I've never felt so tired: sometimes dispirited: as in the past few months.

Four days earlier I had submitted a report to Ian Smith, entitled 'Security Situation in Mozambique: Approach to the Portuguese and South Africans', in which I wrote:[4]

Although all the South Africans seen on my visit displayed a commendable interest and some keenness in trying to counter the increasing threat to South Africa by tripartite effort between themselves, the Portuguese and ourselves, I regret to say they are still disorientated in many ways; or they are fatalistic to the extent that they have either written off the Portuguese in advance, or are unnecessarily pessimistic over our own chances of survival ... one is left with the impression that they still have a long way to go before really committing themselves to the concept of 'joint defence of Southern Africa'.

The 'aide memoire' of my meetings with Vorster, van den Bergh and Kruger, the Deputy Minister of Police (which was attached to the above report) contained the following:

Mr Vorster said that they had already spent millions of Rands in helping the Portuguese. He agreed that 'Flecha' type operations could provide the most practicable answer and that the development of such operations could be discussed with General van den Bergh, whom Mr Flower was due to meet the following morning.... Mr Vorster said it seemed imperative to act with speed as some reports indicated that terrorism was now encroaching very far southwards in Mozambique.... Mr Flower said the Rhodesian Prime Minister supported the concept of joint defence ... but he wondered whether there was now less chance than ever of a military type solution following General Spinola's assertions that

* Top Secret Note on 'Flechas and the formation of the Mozambique National Resistance', April 1974; reproduced in the Appendix.

Portugal cannot provide a military solution to her terrorist wars in Africa.... Mr Vorster queried the ease with which terrorists could cross the Zambezi; and the relative merits and de-merits of working to a natural barrier of this sort were explained by Air Vice-Marshal Hawkins. Mr Flower mentioned that the Portuguese planned to put naval patrols on Lake Cabora Bassa, therefore, to some extent they had accepted the Zambezi River line as the defence line for Southern Africa.

From my meeting with General van den Bergh on the following morning I got the impression that:

General van den Bergh accepts the necessity for 'Flecha' type operations ... but he said that the South African Cabinet is now faced with making a vital decision concerning their involvement in Mozambique based on these considerations:
    (1) whether to defend the White colonialist landowners in Lisbon;
    (2) whether to prepare for a Black take-over in Mozambique, in which event they must not continue to antagonise the Blacks and should withdraw now;
    (3) whether to prepare for a UDI in Mozambique and Angola when they would have the advantage of dealing with a local (perhaps European dominated) government.
    I posed the question as to which solution he believed the South African Cabinet would prefer, and General van den Bergh said he believed they would prefer to seek solution No. 1. I then asked whether the same approach applied to Rhodesia. He laughed and said that in the same way as South Africa had kicked out the British colonialists, Rhodesia had, in effect, done the same! In other words, we had already provided solution No. 3.

Kruger's attitude reflected a slightly different approach and, with hindsight, was much nearer the mark than CIO assessments at that stage:

From some of his comments it appeared he had already written off Mozambique (even saying that the Portuguese would have abandoned the territory within six months!) By adding Mr Kruger's apprehensions to the sort of comment made by Mr Vorster and General van den Bergh on the same subject, I could not help feeling that General van den Bergh's 'Bureau' had produced an unnecessarily pessimistic – even alarmist – picture of the situation in Mozambique and I was at some pains to try and correct it.

As requested by Ian Smith, I soon found myself flying once again to Lisbon, seeking Portuguese acquiescence in becoming involved in a joint defence strategy. I made a little headway and prepared to return to Salisbury to submit my report to Ian Smith.[5] My plane was scheduled to leave at midnight on 24 April and, a few hours before my departure, I called at the office of Silva Pais. Most offices surrounding his were deserted and he must have known that the coup was imminent. He greeted me with:

'It's always a pleasure to see you. I only hope you have not come to discuss business?'

I reassured him that I had come merely to thank him and to say goodbye. We sat quietly for a few minutes, and then he said: 'Thank you for not talking. But I know you like *Vinho do Porto*; can we drink a glass together – still saying nothing? It's vintage port from my own *quinta*.'

We savoured the precious port in silence (the bottle was as old as we were) and then, after an affectionate *abraco*, I left to catch my plane. It was the last plane to leave before the airport was closed later that night. By dawn General Spinola, General Costa Gomes and others of the Portuguese military hierarchy had replaced Caetano and his government as the rulers of Portugal.

Silva Pais was one of the very few officials who made themselves available that morning to be detained and he was bundled into gaol (where he later died, having consistently refused release unless brought to trial or until all his colleagues were exonerated). The heavy brocade curtains in his office were flung aside and a photograph taken and published with the caption that this was the office of '*um dos principais responsaveis pela repressao politica*' ('one of the principals responsible for political repression'). And there, in the picture, were the two port glasses, one with my fingerprints on it.

The sin that cost Silva Pais dear was that he loved his country and its people too much ever to believe that they could be guilty of treachery. Although he had been warned by his subordinates that a coup was coming, he would have none of it. When they told him that the real cancer of communism lay in the heart of the Portuguese Navy, he ignored them in the belief that Portuguese tradition would prove more powerful than the communists and that the Navy was the guardian of that tradition.

On my arrival at Salisbury airport that morning I was greeted by my Deputy, Ken Leaver, with: 'What a dark horse you are! We had no idea you were starting a coup. But of course you were always so close to Costa Gomes.'

Perhaps I was close, but not so close as General Spinola who had written his book *Portugal e o Futuro* while second-in-command to Costa Gomes at Defence Headquarters in Lisbon, implying the consent of Costa Gomes and probably of Caetano himself. It was this book that had ignited dissension amongst the Armed Forces in Portugal and spelt the end of the Portuguese Empire. I remember first seeing the book a few days after its publication, while having breakfast on the terrace of the Polana Hotel in Lourenco Marques. It was brought to the table by Sao Jose Lopes, Head of DGS in Angola, who, with tears in his eyes, said: 'I am sorry to intrude myself when I feel so terrible. I have been unable to sleep throughout the night – reading and re-reading this book – for it is the end of us. It is the end of the Portugal we have known and loved.'

Within a matter of weeks after the coup Costa Gomes ordered Lopes' transfer to remote Timor, ostensibly to protect him from the retributive action of whites and blacks. Lopes fell ill passing through Johannesburg and died in hospital there, with no prognosis offered other than that he had 'died of a broken heart'.

The situation in Mozambique did not alter dramatically in the immediate aftermath of the coup. The Portuguese presence there had been ineffective in stopping the advance of FRELIMO or the entrenchment of ZANLA in the Tete province. Portuguese forces were withdrawn from the border areas but the Rhodesian Commanders had been prepared for this.

In Lisbon, Spinola might do the bidding of the junior officers of the 'Movimento des Forcas Armadas' (Armed Forces Movement) who had staged the coup – for as long as it suited them. He could protest in public that the Portuguese Army in Africa had not been defeated, but those who served there in the lower ranks had a different view: they demanded as end to the war, even if it meant peace at any price. Costa Gomes flew to Lourenco Marques to make his own assessment of how the war had progressed in Mozambique since he had left to serve in Angola and in Lisbon, and to estimate the cost of peace. Following a brief exchange of signals, I flew alone to meet him in Lourenco Marques, to try to convince him of our continuing need for co-existence in Africa. He insisted that we talk without interpreters, giving the impression that he could not trust the junior officers who surrounded him on any subject affecting the future of Rhodesia or Mozambique. He led in Portuguese and I replied in English. After an hour or so there was mutual acceptance that neither of us had anything to offer the other and we went our separate ways, Costa Gomes to Lisbon and I to Salisbury, holding but a slight advantage – two bottles of vintage port as a gift for that *aniversario*.

Then, out of the blue, came an invitation to Ian Smith to send a senior Minister and an official to Lisbon to be advised of Portugal's intentions regarding Mozambique. In September P. K. van der Byl and I flew to Portugal. During our discussions in Lisbon it was explained to us by Dr Costa Almeida, Minister for Overseas (formerly a lawyer in Lourenco Marques), why the Portuguese considered their position in Mozambique untenable and why, therefore, they must make the best deal they could with FRELIMO. He expected that most white Portuguese would remain in Mozambique and that inter-territorial relations between Rhodesia and Mozambique would remain friendly. In our subsequent meeting with Dr Mario Soares, Minister of Foreign Affairs, little was added.

I then held discussions with senior officials in the new Military Intelligence Directorate (MID). They considered Almeida's expectations unrealistically optimistic and implied that the Minister had misled us into believing that Portugal would hang on to Mozambique whereas we should be preparing to deal with FRELIMO in Lourenco Marques and not with the regime in Lisbon. During these discussions it emerged that the MID would have preferred to plan the dismemberment of Mozambique in such a way as to ensure that the territory to the south of the Zambezi River was retained under white control and linked with Rhodesia and South Africa; but it was too late for that now.

We flew back to Rhodesia, and I later wrote briefly about the trip in my diary:

1st December 1974: Went back to Lisbon in the first week of September with P. K. van der Byl – for what it is worth, recently appointed as Minister of Foreign Affairs and Defence – to be told by the new-look Portuguese Ministers why they are giving away Mozambique and with such rapidity. Some of the trip was personally instructive: P K rejecting four successive bottles of South African wine served during dinner on a SAA plane, for being 'corked – just undrinkable – try it yourself, old man!' ... and the South African representatives on the same mission, General van den Bergh and Brand Fourie, happily drinking the same stuff; although the Chief Steward confirmed with P K that it should have been condemned....

I got mixed up with a bunch of conspirators – leading all the way to General Spinola himself – plotting to reverse the march of events in Mozambique. Then came two abortive counter-coup attempts in Lourenco Marques; the ousting of Spinola; and General Costa Gomes made President of Portugal! Still very friendly disposed ... critical only because I presumed to take P K with me when making a courtesy call....

But P K at his mercurial best, putting Mario Soares' effete young secretary right when he queried whether his ancestry was 'Hollandaise' – 'Dutch, young man – not a sauce – but my ancestors shook the grime of Holland off their shoes three and a half centuries ago for Africa and have never been back since.' And, on departure, asking me to slip a pornographic book into 'Boss Hendrik's' pocket in the hope it would be fished out involuntarily – and to everyone's consternation – when arriving at Johannesburg.

The tale of the conspirators may never be told, but something of the aims and the inadequacy of the conspiracy can be gauged from the following extract of my earlier report to Smith dated 16 September 1974:

The immediate and direct causes of the 'conspiracy' were the growing realisation that the Central Government had settled with FRELIMO in indecent haste, and on an agreement which gave virtually everything to them, ignoring the just claims of other tribal groups and the whites in Mozambique.

In simplified form the conspirators plan to:–

(i) Reject the Lusaka agreement;
(ii) Mobilise the whites and supportive Africans in Mozambique;
(iii) Revert to the original intentions (provisional government, elections and a transitional period during which power would be transferred to a more representative government);
(iv) Insist on representatives additional to FRELIMO being included;
(v) Appeal to South Africa and Rhodesia;
(vi) Inevitably, some officers in key positions would have to declare their loyalties and others might have to be eliminated.

The conspirators are opposing what they believe to be unnecessary appeasement – and appeasement has never paid, in Africa or elsewhere.

Unfortunately, in the short space of time I was travelling from Lisbon to Salisbury the position of the conspirators had slipped, and now it must be expected to slip further. One observer described the 'rebel' activity so far as a 'Brazilian carnival'! And the Portuguese know all about Brazilian carnivals.

We must not forget, either, that here we have a case of 'rebels' trying to act against 'rebels' who have just staged a successful coup in Portugal. However, we have the advantage of being in with the conspiracy and should be able to provide practical assistance if and when the next stage occurs.

A year after the coup I was in Lisbon again, to experience something of the changes. Several of the former DGS personnel were awaiting trial for the murder of General Delgado some years previously; and the control of Portugal had moved from a few privileged families to a few military ones. My friends in Lisbon were sure the pendulum would swing once again, though they conceded that the Portuguese empire had gone forever. For after Portugal had handed over the reins of power in Mozambique to FRELIMO in September 1974, full independence followed in June 1975.

The issue of joint clandestine action between Rhodesia and South Africa had continued to occupy much of CIO's time during the period of our liaison with Portugal over the fate of Mozambique. In August 1974 I submitted a brief to Ian Smith which I suggested he use in his forthcoming off-the-record discussion with Vorster; my brief was based on the belief that 'it should suit the South Africans to put more effort into joint clandestine effort, within and outside Rhodesia'.[6] I pointed out that most of Rhodesia's recent successes in the guerrilla war had been based on 'pseudo' action and Intelligence gained by the Selous Scouts, adding:

With the shutters coming down along our border with Mozambique we need to project these activities into Mozambique, and possibly into Zambia. This needs money and materiel: and it should be to South Africa's advantage to participate, particularly as their SAANC will be using the same facilities as ZANU.... Subversion and insurgency can only be countered by well co-ordinated jointery of *all* Services, and it would be invaluable experience for the SADF to be working with the SAP in actual operations now.

By this time, CIO was in possession of Intelligence of vital significance concerning the numbers and deployment of ZANLA guerrillas operating within Rhodesia, their tactics and the availability of supplies. Acting upon this Intelligence, we had met some of ZANLA's junior commanders in the field. From these meetings it was clear that there was dissension within their ranks which we could turn to our advantage.

Among those contacted were Thomas Nhari, ZANLA commander of the Nehanda Sector, and Dakari Badza, commander of the Chaminuka Sector. At a meeting with them at Mukumbura on the Mozambique border our Special Branch representatives learnt that the guerrillas were suffering the effects of indifferent command and serious shortages of supplies caused by the lengthening of their lines of communication. In the light of such disaffection, it was easy for us to convince them of the injustice of their fight for survival in the bush while their leaders 'relaxed in comparative luxury' in Zambia and Tanzania. We were offering substantial rewards at the time for surrender of 'Terrorist Leaders', or for their collaboration, and had something to bargain with. We could even talk of negotiating an end to the war.

The opportunity to exploit this situation came in November 1974 when, with the release of nationalist leaders from Rhodesian gaols, CIO became aware for the first time of even greater dissension within the political ranks of ZANU. A group of detainees had replaced Sithole with Mugabe as their leader, a development which was not accepted by Nyerere, who was then chairing a meeting of the Front Line Presidents in Lusaka. At the time, Vorster's detente policy was making progress with Kaunda and it seemed likely that the Presidents would try to enforce unity between ZAPU and ZANU. But now that we knew the depth of the rift within ZANU, and were convinced that neither ZANU nor ZAPU would accept each other's leadership, it seemed that the only course open to the Presidents in their pursuit of guerrilla unity was to turn to the 'moderates' of the ANC.

To sow further dissension we had ready tools in Nhari and his companions, who became willing conspirators. Nhari seized command of ZANLA's Chifombo base on the Mozambique/Zambia border, indulging in random killings as he did so. His followers then planned to kidnap Josiah Tongogara, the Lusaka-based Commander of ZANLA since 1972, but he was out of the country at the time. Apparently aided by the

Zambian Police and Army, they kidnapped his wife and children instead, together with about twenty members of the ZANU hierarchy. On his return, Tongogara appealed to Sithole, who in his weakened position thought it politic not to interfere.

With every day that passed, CIO was gaining ground within ZANLA. But Tongogara then began to recover something of his command and re-entered Chifombo with the co-operation of FRELIMO. Nhari, his principals and some fifty of his followers were executed, and in the ensuing purge within ZANLA forces in Zambia about 150 more guerrillas were killed.

We learnt that Herbert Chitepo had presided over some aspects of the purge, which could only exacerbate the fast deteriorating relations between him and Kaunda. Kaunda's bias towards ZAPU, his annoyance with ZANU for allowing Zambia to become a battleground for ZANLA in-fighting and his impatience with the ZANU leadership's opposition to unity and detente indicated that some sort of showdown was likely. CIO continued to feed disinformation to the Zambian Special Branch, and we soon learnt from our contacts in that organisation that they were ready to take action against ZANU.

For CIO and many other interested parties, Chitepo now became the prime target. As ZANU's most dedicated protagonist, CIO considered him the biggest obstacle to ending the war and, in the circumstance then prevailing in Zambia, it became clear to us that if Chitepo were to be eliminated the blame could be laid at any number of doors. Accordingly, CIO gave the 'green light' to a carefully prepared physical and psychological operation. In March 1975 Chitepo returned to Lusaka from Malawi, where he had been detained briefly on evidence produced by ZANLA's Head of Security, Cletus Chigowe (evidence that was almost certainly false). On 13 March Chitepo had a meeting with Kaunda during which he told the Zambian President that the situation in ZANU was out of control and that his own life was imperilled. Five days later, in the early hours of the morning, a bomb placed in Chitepo's car detonated as he started the engine. He was killed outright.

The extent of the reaction in Zambia to the death of Herbert Chitepo astounded even CIO. Zambian authorities rounded up some seventy prominent ZANU figures and increased that number as time went on; ZANU's office in Lusaka was closed; and both of ZANLA's guerrilla holding camps in Zambia were put under armed guard. During the following nine months at least 1300 ZANLA guerrillas were put out of action, and twenty months after the assassination those of Chitepo's comrades who had not managed to flee from Zambia were still being held in Zambian gaols.

Lonrho intruded itself upon the scene once again. Their representative in South Africa, Marquard de Villiers, had been working hard behind the scenes to help promote Vorster's detente. The Zambian government's official newspaper, *The Times of Zambia*, owned by Lonrho, demanded that the 'Special International Commission on the Assassination of Herbert Wiltshire Chitepo' which Kaunda had established must 'not only discover who killed Chitepo but must sort out the Zimbabwean Liberation Movements'. Cornelius Sanyanga, Lonrho's Secretary in Lusaka, emerged as principal witness for the prosecution.

The Commission comprised thirteen representatives from disinterested African states and from the OAU Liberation Committee. It was a farce from start to finish. The evidence was led by Mainza Chona, Zambian Minister of Legal Affairs and Attorney-General, and on occasions it seemed as if the Commission was using the attempt to clear Zambia's name and to implicate anyone who had offended Kaunda. The Zambian Minister of Home Affairs, Aaron Milner, played a decisive role behind the scenes, and supported ZAPU at the expense of ZANU. The Zambian Special Branch who investigated the assassination were not interested in ZANU's version of events; they prepared their own statements and tortured those in detention to obtain false confessions. Tongogara, in particular, was handled with the utmost brutality. At one stage it was reported that his back had been broken under interrogation, which persuaded me to take the unusal step of sending a personal message to the Head of Zambian Special Branch, expressing regret and suggesting that our disinformation had gone far enough. There was no reply, indicating that he was unaware of the convention between Intelligence Services that on the rare occasions when one Head speaks to another on an issue such as this it is most likely to be the truth, no matter what one's juniors are required to do when practising deception. In the circumstances, Mugabe could not be blamed for later labelling Chitepo's death as 'an act done through or by direct participation of the Zambian government'.

ZANLA's war was brought to a standstill. The detention and flight of the leaders had a serious effect on morale and ZANLA's casualty rate grew catastrophically as less experienced commanders and their men fell victim to Rhodesian Security Forces. By December 1975 only a handful were still operating within Rhodesia. Superficially, it appeared that Rhodesia was once again on top of the situation, which encouraged Ian Smith to begin his talks with Nkomo. I went to Lusaka to prepare the ground for the talks and by coincidence was waiting in the ante-room of State House, prior to a meeting with Kaunda, when his lawyer walked in. Under his arm he carried the findings of the Chitepo Commission. He was bubbling over with information: 'As a Rhodesian you might like to know that we have resolved all the confusion over Chitepo's death!'

'I am tremendously interested. Does this mean that you have found the guilty party? If so, I would be fascinated to know.'

'Yes.'

He then read out something to the effect that the decision to kill Chitepo had been taken by the ZANLA High Command, under the chairmanship of Tongogara. He continued: 'The members of the DARE [literally a "war council", referring in this case to ZANU's Supreme Council] and the High Command could *all* be indicted as principals to the murder because, jointly or severally, they actively desired to bring this about.'

'But how many principals does this implicate?'

'Over twenty in all.'

'I had not realised that it was part of your function to determine who was guilty of the crime. I had thought you were a "Commission of Enquiry"?'

'Yes, but in completing our enquiry it has become absolutely clear who the guilty ones are. We are advising the President accordingly and recommending that the accused should be tried in court for Chitepo's murder.'

All sorts of thoughts raced through my head. Should I divulge what I knew? If so, how would that help Rhodesia? Would there really be a trial? Suddenly, I got the hell in me – Chitepo was dead and Tongogara had suffered enough, so surely Rhodesia could afford to be magnanimous. I said:

'What would you say if I were to tell you that your precious findings are not worth the paper they are printed on? Tongogara had nothing whatsoever to do with Chitepo's death.'

'How can you possibly say that! You were not a witness. You have not given evidence!'

'You could call me a witness against self-interest and as a lawyer you should appreciate the value of that. You might even call me an expert witness.'

'But that still doesn't entitle you to condemn our findings ... unless, of course, you killed Chitepo yourself, or you have evidence as to who did!'

'We'd better leave it at that. If you care to check, you will find that I have already divulged certain information to your Head of Special

Branch. And if you genuinely wish to resolve this matter you could tell him I'm available in Lusaka overnight and could explain to him why I'm speaking to you as I am, saying that your Commission has made the wrong finding.'

And that is where the matter ended. No Zambian sought to contact me then or subsequently. Much later I learned that my 'confession' had merely added to the general derangement in Lusaka and that no one there wished to be further confused by the facts.

Shortly after Chitepo's death, Dr Edson Sithole declared in Salisbury that the incident had 'shattered irreparably any hope of negotiated settlement'. Sithole, the Secretary for Information in the UANC and legal adviser to Muzorewa during the Smith/Muzorewa negotiations in 1974, had been detained briefly in June that year because of the effect his obstructive tactics were having on the progress of the negotiations. After Chitepo's death he expressed the fear that the Rhodesian authorities would move against him too, while in turn the Rhodesian authorities became increasingly convinced that his militancy was the main obstacle to settlement. In October 1975 he and his girlfriend were bundled into a vehicle outside the Ambassador Hotel in Salisbury and were not seen again. An eye-witness, Brother Arthur of the Catholic Justice and Peace Commission, said the deed had been perpetrated by Special Branch. The subsequent investigation was inconclusive, leading to widespread speculation that the bodies had been disposed of in a disused mine shaft.

The popular clamour amongst the whites to extend the war across our boundaries increased as the length of the eastern border came under attack and during 1975 Rhodesia struck further and further into Mozambique. By the end of that year the pressure on OCC to execute large-scale external raids had begun to grow. Hitherto, I had been able to convince the Prime Minister and my fellow officials that the adverse political effect of such raids outweighed whatever military advantage we might gain, adding that we should not ignore the reasons why the Portuguese had never transgressed their boundaries in Mozambique and Angola and why the South Africans were strongly opposed to any sort of excursion into neighbouring countries.

Now, however, we began to give way to the clamour for cross-border action and it was at this point that the Selous Scouts began to assume the role for which they later became notorious. General Walls favoured the use of the Scouts in external operations, although this was contrary to the role envisaged for them when the unit was formed. The responsibility for operations outside Rhodesia lay originally with CIO and the SAS, a unit trained specifically for an external commando role. However, the Selous Scouts had already encroached upon CIO and SAS territory and, as they came under Walls' command, none of the rest of us in OCC could query his decision. I was aware, however, through Intelligence reports from my staff, Special Branch and Military Intelligence that most Army officers would have preferred to use the SAS in an external role.

Reid Daly was raring to go and in August 1976 his unit was given the go-ahead to reconnoitre a suspected guerrilla base at Nyadzonia, in Mozambique. In his book, Reid Daly gives a highly dramatised account of the manner in which he persuaded Walls and Hickman to agree to a Selous Scouts raid on Nyadzonia, implying that decisions on details of the raid were made casually over a glass of beer or relayed by telephone.[7] The raid went in on 9 August. The Scouts arrived in the camp dressed in FRELIMO uniforms and riding in trucks with Mozambican number plates. The men, women and children of the camp were preparing to continue with celebrations begun the previous day to mark a public holiday. By the end of the day over 1000 of them lay dead, killed by the hail of bullets, burned to death or drowned while trying to escape by crossing the Nyadzonia River. Reid Daly took the credit where he could:

The raid on the Nyadzonia/Pungwe base was, to my mind, the classic operation of the whole war ... carried out by only seventy-two soldiers ... without air support ... and without reserve of any kind....
    The risk factors were staggering ... but so were the rewards...
    The terse communiqué which was issued by the Rhodesians did not cover the method of attack, nor did it say who mounted it.

OCC's communiqué was 'terse' because we were not prepared to take responsibility for lying about the nature of the raid and we could not devise a formula which would account for the death of such large numbers of unarmed, untrained people. Hitherto, OCC had confined itself to facts when issuing communiqués on enemy casualties, recording as 'kills' only the deaths of trained guerrillas, armed or identified and with the 'kill' confirmed. From the time of the Nyadzonia raid onwards, however, we had to cook the books.

The unease in official circles caused by the Nyadzonia incident was reflected among some of my own staff, who were not impressed with the perpetrators of the raid. They had been working on a CIO paper, 'Threat to Rhodesia', in which it was stated that 'the effort to counter subversive activities was in the proportion of 20 per cent military and 80 per cent political'. In their note to me on 9 September 1976 they wrote:[8]

If this statement is true then it must be accepted that any major clandestine operation such as the Pungwe attack produced its full quota of 20 per cent military success, but an almost minus quantity of political dividends. Surely, if attacks of this nature are to be carried out in future a correct balance of military and political dividends should be studied, with particular regard to propaganda and psychological effect?

As far as OCC were concerned, things were never quite the same again. Most of us saw the Nyadzonia mission as one which had failed in its main objective – to confirm or refute that Nyadzonia/Pungwe was an operational base from which attacks were being launched into Rhodesia. No prisoners were brought back and no real evidence was produced by the Selous Scouts to suggest that the base was anything more than a staging camp in which some low-level training took place.

Within a very short time Rhodesia began to feel the adverse political effects of its escalation of the war. Vorster was seriously embarrassed by the raid and encouraged Henry Kissinger to make much play of the issues arising from it when the American Secretary of State began forcing Smith into a corner during their crucial meeting in Pretoria in September 1976.

CHAPTER 9

South Africa and Kissinger

On Monday 20 September 1976 I wrote optimistically, in my diary: 'This could go down in history as the week that changed Rhodesia!'

A week earlier I had flown to Pretoria with the Prime Minister's delegation to discuss the Kissinger proposals with Vorster. The talks had culminated in the dramatic meeting between Smith and Kissinger on 19 September. And five days later Smith turned the world upside down for most Rhodesians by announcing that he had accepted the principle of majority rule. The South African political, economic and military arm-twisting, which had been growing steadily more painful, had finally proved too much for Smith, his government and his country to bear.

To understand the nature of this arm-twisting, which had begun imperceptibly a decade earlier, it is necessary to backtrack a little to outline something of the Rhodesia–South African Intelligence connection and the political factors which led to the final showdown between Smith and Vorster.

CIO had established a working relationship with South African Intelligence which was based on a gentleman's agreement that we would not operate against each other. With the appointment in 1968 of Hendrik van den Bergh as head of the newly co-ordinated South African Intelligence service, BOSS, there followed a brief period during which the agreement was ignored, for no other reason than the fact that van den Bergh had a deep-rooted suspicion of Rhodesia's British connection and wanted to satisfy himself that the individuals he dealt with in CIO were Rhodesians in their own right, and not British agents.

The assistance sought by and given to van den Bergh after his appointment helped dispel some of his doubts. I recorded the following in an office note in November 1968:[1]

Lt. General H. van den Bergh telephoned me from Pretoria on 28.11.68 to say he had a specific request to make, and was most anxious that I would consider it favourably.

He described how Mr Vorster had selected him for a new job, which was to head a new co-ordinated 'Intelligence Agency'. He said he had taken over the previous 'Military Intelligence' and that he was actually speaking from the office of Major-General Loots, the previous Chief of Military Intelligence, who would now be working as his second-in-command.

General van den Bergh said he had heard so much about my Organisation that he was tremendously anxious to know how it worked ... (he) was quite eulogistic in his praise, and seemed really anxious to pick our brains!

He said he could not possibly afford to visit Salisbury immediately, but wondered whether I could send him a senior officer with a comprehensive brief ... he would (then) make a point of seeing me in Salisbury ... he said he would appreciate it if my officer would bear in mind, when preparing his brief, that he (van den Bergh) was still to remain in charge of the Security Branch of the South African Police, and in addition, had been appointed as 'Special Adviser to the Prime Minister.'

We gave the General what assistance we could but, at his end, things did not work out quite as he had hoped. The Security Branch remained with the Police and was never brought under his command, nor did he take over any aspect of Military Intelligence. Instead, he made problems for himself rather than resolving them, and as the years went by I realised that his compelling patriotism was too much for those around him. He ended up with more enemies at home than abroad, where his reputation grew in Intelligence circles. It was depressing for us on our visits to South Africa to have to listen to 'Boss' reviling the Military, the Military berating 'Boss' and, towards the end, 'Boss' railing against the Police – in short, almost everyone denigrating almost everyone else.

Even when all the South African services became Afrikaner dominated, there was little change; the serious defects of Afrikaner tribalism emerged and the arguments continued with no apparent solution in sight. In 1970, in an attempt to achieve better co-ordination, the South African government appointed Judge Potgieter as a one-man commission to examine the functioning of South Africa's Intelligence services. Potgieter paid us the compliment of visiting Rhodesia to study our system before examining the South Africa problem or travelling to Europe and America to study the systems there. I spent several days in discussion with him, but to little avail, for internal jealousies continued to dominate the South African scene and no South African government dared implement the Judge's recommendations, based as they were on foreign experience.[2]

Taking into account the splits in the South African camp, CIO concentrated its liaison on BOSS, and van den Bergh became our most useful ally. His usefulness lay partly in his close friendship with Vorster, with whom he had shared a detention cell for four years during the Second World War, and partly in the strength of his influence in South Africa, which we had noted in 1967 when, virtually alone and overnight, he had sent us the first substantial contingent of South African Police to help guard the Zambian border.

Van den Bergh could be erratic, unpredictable or just plain embarrassing, and it took all our goodwill to appreciate the strength of conviction with which he served his Prime Minister, BOSS and his country. On one occasion, when I was driving him to Salisbury airport at about 70 mph and our relationship had worn a little thin, I commented that if Rhodesians were pushed too far in South Africa's search for detente and if he continued to allow his man in Salisbury to cause tension between our two services and between the Rhodesian and South African Military, he would end up the most hated man in Southern Africa. To my horror I suddenly noticed an ashen-faced General desperately trying to open the passenger door apparently trying to commit hari kari, so incensed was he at my accusation.

He was proud of the rank of 'General', which he had acquired despite having no background of military service and lacking all conception of military matters. During our many disagreements I found it difficult to refrain from making a typically British Service remark about 'Generals Without Troops', but Afrikaners' ways are different from ours and no one dare denigrate the Boer Commanders, promoted direct from burgher to General, who nearly conquered the might of the British Empire.

Our disagreements became particularly heated when the subject of British motivation was raised and I once provoked him into saying:

'There was nothing that Hitler did to the Jews in Europe in the last World War that was anything like as bad as the British did to our peoples in the South African War.'

'You cannot mean that, Hendrik!' I retorted. 'Hitler's Gestapo and SS acted deliberately in perpetrating genocide. All you can really say against the British in the Boer War is that they made mistakes and women and children died in the camps as a result. But those camps were not "concentration camps"....'

'Oh yes they were!' shouted van den Bergh. 'And you show your bias by calling it the "Boer War". It's typical of you Pommies to blame the other person ... everyone knows it takes two to make a fight – or you should call it the "English War". But why don't you call it the "South African War", as I did, or the "Anglo-Boer War"?'

I remember another occasion during which he demanded to know of me where my political sympathies lay. I tried to gloss over this as being irrelevant in my official position, but he would have none of it.

'You are failing in your responsibilities to your government and your country by shilly-shallying on such a vital issue! At least I know that I have a divine mission to ensure that the National Party will remain in power in South Africa for ever.'

He said this in all seriousness, just as he claimed with equal sincerity in 1972 that he had been restored to life through divine intervention after he had been electrocuted in a welding accident on his farm. I happened to call at his office shortly after the accident, and was told:

'I could feel I was dying. Nothing could have released me from clinging to that electric cable. Then I realised I was dead, and on the other side, for I heard God say "Hendrik, your life's work is not finished – I need you back on Earth", and I was restored to life.'

'But, Hendrik, you must surely acknowledge the part played by your servant, Johannes? By all accounts he had the sense to run several hundred yards to throw the switch, and that was how you were saved!'

'No, Ken, I have told you what happened. And how could any Bantu have had the sense to do what he did unless God gave him the right instructions?'

The problems in our dealings with van den Bergh and with the disparate South African services are evident in some of my reports on liaison with South Africa.[3]

During my visit to Pretoria in March 1976 the discussion with the General revolved around the Cuban invasion threat:[4]

... (there were) mutual queries concerning Mr Brand Fourie's intepretation of Zambian attitudes – for instance, his motivation in reporting that President Kaunda might be unable to resist the entry of the Cubans into Zambia, to be positioned at forward bases previously used by our terrorists. Immediately, General van den Bergh exploded that there was never any truth in such allegations.... We discussed at length the South African Military assessment of Cuban plans to attack Rhodesia.... (van den Bergh) appealed to me to commit to the wastepaper basket all reports received from their Military Intelligence!

Van den Bergh's consistency in his condemnation of Military Intelligence for the quality of their production was matched by his consistency in condemning their unwillingness to aid Vorster in his moves towards detente with black Africa. The significance of these moves for Rhodesia had been hinted at in 1967, when Vorster began to exert a little pressure on Smith to settle the Rhodesian problem.[5]

As pre-arranged last week, the Prime Minister saw me on the morning of 10th April, 1967, to advise what had been said during his recent meeting in Cape Town with Mr Vorster ... Mr Smith believes he (Vorster) is really anxious to ensure stability in Southern Africa and permanent compatibility between the races. Apparently, Mr Vorster mentioned that he was under criticism from his extremists because of the friendly approach he had made to Lesotho, Malawi, Botswana and the Africans generally, but he realised that the 'wild boys' – he even called them 'mad men' – must be ignored.

Mr Smith says he told Mr Vorster at this juncture that he was lucky: Mr Vorster only had a few madmen in his Cabinet, he (Mr Smith) had a much higher proportion in the Rhodesia Cabinet.

The most urgent and important impression that Mr Vorster obviously wished to convey was one of deep disappointment that Rhodesia's feud with Britain remained unresolved....

Mr Vorster went out of his way to impress Mr Smith with the extremely delicate situation which South Africa considers herself to be in because of South West Africa. Mr Vorster used the phrase: 'South West Africa is South Africa's Achilles' heel,' and he went on to say that 'Rhodesia could turn out to be the Achilles' heel of Southern Africa'.

Time and again in the ensuing years van den Bergh asked me to convey a message from Vorster to Smith to the effect that South Africa was anxious to get the Rhodesian question settled before they were forced into a settlement over South West Africa, and that Smith would be in a less favourable position if he continued to procrastinate while South West Africa became Namibia. I remember van den Bergh saying there were only 40,000 whites of Afrikaner stock in Rhodesia compared with 75,000 in South West Africa, which meant that Rhodesia's future was of less importance to South Africa than the future of South West Africa. In any event, he was adamant that Rhodesia's destiny must differ from that of South Africa or South West Africa, for Rhodesia had opted out of their future in 1922, and he maintained that whereas the separation of the races was entrenched in South Africa's national policy, the RF's pursuit of apartheid in Rhodesia was 'an embarrassing anachronism'.

Looking back on it now, it seems I did not appreciate the full significance of what Vorster and van den Bergh were saying at the time and cannot blame Smith, therefore, for ignoring the signs that South Africa would not continue, regardless, to support the whites in Rhodesia. And it was not until 1976 that Vorster, for his part, realised that he would have to twist Smith's arm to the last painful gasp if he was to make any progress in Africa.

The key to Vorster's detente was Kaunda, aided by his personal adviser, Mark Chona, an agile customer and a product of the University of Rhodesia. But Vorster and his emissaries in the detente exercise, Brand Fourie (Secretary for Foreign Affairs) and Hendrik van den Bergh, seemed to misread Kaunda's character, for he was no more genuine in his approach to detente than he was in adhering to the philosophy of 'Humanism'. He no doubt considered Vorster's concept of detente as hypocritical (for it was designed to do in black Africa what was not being done in South Africa itself) and thus answerable with hypocrisy.

But hypocrisy is not one of the Afrikaner traits, whereas faith and religious zeal are.

The Lusaka Manifesto of 1969, which became the cornerstone of black attitudes to the white south, and the failure of the Pearce Commission in 1972, pushed Vorster to even greater efforts in his pursuit of detente through Kaunda.[6] In a memorandum in November 1974 I wrote:[7]

Since (October) there have been two meetings of the Rhodesian and South African Prime Ministers.... Prime Minister Vorster made it clear to Mr Ian Smith that he must get a settlement, and get it quickly, or South Africa would cut off our water....

The South Africans believe the Zambians are genuinely anxious for detente and to get a settlement of the Rhodesian issue.... Prime Minister Smith took the opportunity whilst in Pretoria of protesting over the South African military withdrawal from their promise to transfer troops from the Caprivi and Mr Vorster (said) there was so much pressure on them against retaining the SAP in Rhodesia that they just could not commit themselves any further.... Mr Gaylard [Secretary to the Prime Minister] is convinced and he says Mr Smith now recognises it, that South Africa is virtually Rhodesia's only remaining friend and we could not afford to reject whatever offers they are making now.... Rhodesia must accept South Africa's participation in the settlement procedures.

CIO was asked to follow up the points raised in these discussions. On 6 December 1974, in a letter to Gaylard, I outlined the results of our follow-up:

I requested Air Vice-Marshal Hawkins to sound out Mr Brand Fourie; and for my man (in Pretoria) to sound out General van den Bergh on the so-called 'Vorster Proposals', particularly insofar as they refer to the attainment of majority rule in Rhodesia within the period of the lifetime of one Parliament (5 years)....

The answers that I have now received are to this effect:–

AVM Hawkins says that Mr Brand Fourie responded emphatically to the effect that neither Mr Vorster nor anyone else in a position of responsibility had ever indicated anything of the sort ... they had been scrupulous in avoiding any references to possible time scales ... General van den Bergh's go-between says 'no specific criteria was set out as a basis for discussion or negotiations between the Presidents and our nationalist elements. The only possibility is that Mark Chona outlined some proposals for Mr Vorster and the latter merely responded with a comment "that seems reasonable"'.... He believes Mr Vorster would not readily have suggested any sort of timetable. He went on to say that Chona had mentioned to him several times that nothing like 'one man one vote' was ever envisaged – just reasonable progress towards majority rule.

I had also put down some thoughts in my diary on the state of the South African–Rhodesian relationship:

1st December 1974: South Africa, in search of 'detente' with Black Africa, is prepared to ditch us. And with Mozambique gone we would be entirely dependent on South Africa for our economic – and to a great extent, our security – survival.... Moves towards Black and White rapprochement have intensified in recent weeks to the extent that some of the detained nationalist leaders were encouraged to go to Lusaka and Dar-es-Salaam for talks with the four African Presidents ... Who would have thought it possible at any time over the past decade that 'Smithy' would have been involved – virtually forced into involvement – with Black Africa (with South Africa pushing) to settle our constitutional problems and move towards majority rule?

The relationship between Smith and Vorster broke down irreparably at their meeting in Cape Town on 16 February 1975. They had both finally got the measure of each other. The notes I have of the consequences of that meeting emphasise the South Africans' dismay over Smith's reversal of stated policies:[8]

I gave General van den Bergh a briefing on certain prevailing attitudes in Salisbury on the settlement issue.... He made some biting comments on certain Rhodesian Cabinet Ministers ... he had conclusive evidence that some of these people would be the first to flee Rhodesia in order to enjoy their investments in South Africa.... General van den Bergh then reported what had happened at the conclusion of the last Prime Ministers' meeting in Cape Town on 16 February. He said he had never known Mr Vorster 'so shaken' as at the end of that meeting. After the Rhodesians had gone, Mr Vorster called in General van den Bergh and Mr Brand Fourie for a discussion with himself and Ministers Muller, Botha and Kruger. Mr Vorster advised them that Mr Smith had completely reversed his policy of qualitative franchise and the eventual sharing of power in Rhodesia between Black and White. By so doing he had undermined the fundamentals on which he (Mr Vorster) had 'sold detente' to Black Africa.

The following day, Monday, they were called to a special meeting of their Security Council on which occasion General van den Bergh says the proceedings were conducted in such solemnity that 'it was like a funeral'.... General van den Bergh said that America, France, Germany, Japan and Britain have been in close touch with Mr Vorster and have acknowledged his lead in getting Black Africa to accept Mr Smith's qualified franchise and moves towards 'responsible government'. He (Mr Vorster) is now made out to be a liar and the ground has been cut from under him ... (I said) I could not believe that the South Africans were so naive as to have misunderstood the true nature of Rhodesian government policy over all these years. General van den Bergh responded to this by saying 'But Mr Smith even said they were not prepared to reach parity – let alone majority rule.' I indicated that this statement might have been made to test what support would flow from a policy of 'go-it-alone'. The General felt that support in such a situation was out....

The possibility that Rhodesia would move to majority rule under Black Government was not regarded by South Africa with any alarm. If we wanted South Africa's support we had missed the bus in 1923.... If military action was eventually required then it would be for a limited duration not exceeding four-teen days...

(Mr Fourie said) his Prime Minister no longer knew where he stood with Rhodesia as Mr Smith had reversed all their previous understanding of Rhodesia's intentions ... Referring to the political differences between South Africa and Rhodesia he said that Rhodesia was making a grave mistake if they thought South Africa could support a policy of 'Baaskaap'* as South Africa had already moved away and would be moving further away from such a policy.

Smith never discussed this report with me, presumably because he found the South Africans' criticism of himself unpalatable. He might still have believed that his personal appeal to white South Africans would prevail over their government's formal attitudes. We had had a reminder of that appeal on a recent visit to Pretoria when 75,000 whites at Loftus Versfeld Rugby ground had given him a tumultuous welcome compared with the barely polite applause accorded Prime Minister Vorster. But there was no doubt in official circles that the relationship between Smith and Vorster, and between Rhodesia and South Africa, would never be the same again. One immediate side-effect of this state of affairs was that henceforth the South Africans manoeuvred things whenever they could to have David Smith, the Minister of Finance, standing in for Ian Smith, which gave them the added advantage of being able to discuss economic issues to mutual satisfaction.

Van den Bergh's references to Rhodesian Cabinet Ministers planning to emigrate southwards led me to put just that sting in the tail of one of my Cabinet briefings, with the comment: 'The South African Connec-tion has all those manifestations which indicate that it will prove to be Rhodesia's greatest strength if fostered with mutual confidence – or it will prove to be our greatest weakness.' Only one Minister, the Rhodesian-born Afrikaner Wickus de Kock, seemed to understand the significance of what I was saying.

'You're quite right,' he said to me later when I elaborated a little on my comment. 'I would never have believed that South Africa would constitute a weakness, but that is what it will be if they abandon us here or if they encourage whites to leave Rhodesia for South Africa.'

South Africa now started pressurising Rhodesia by withholding material aid and hinting at the withdrawal of the South African Police, whose morale had suffered through a tragic incident during the ceasefire coin-ciding with the release of African nationalist leaders in November 1974. Four of their number had been stopped on the Mazowe bridge by apparently peaceful ZANLA whom they presumed to be observing the

* Afrikaans word for the policy of control by whites of 'non whites'.

truce. On request they put down their arms – and were promptly murdered in cold blood. Then, to conform with the idea of detente, and to prepare for the Victoria Falls Conference, the withdrawal of the SAP was agreed in principle. It was shortly translated into action through a bizarre incident in which a Konstabel Kriel, stationed in the Mount Darwin area, had grabbed a black baby from its mother's back and slit its throat in what appeared to be a momentary aberration.

The local BSAP had arrested Kriel and were preparing to prosecute him under Rhodesian law when the Deputy Minister of the SAP, Jimmy Kruger, took me to task for the alleged breach of faith between friendly Police Forces; Kruger appealed to me whilst I was visiting Cape Town to use my influence to arrange for Kriel to be sent back to South Africa. I argued that the Rhodesian authorities must go through the formalities of judicial enquiry because the killing was so blatant and had come to public notice. Kruger countered by saying Kriel had a history of mental illness, to which I replied by asking why was he therefore serving in the Police. Kruger burst out: 'You Rhodesians have never understood us. We're in Rhodesia trying to help you and this is what you do to one of our men! It was your people – your Jameson and your Police – who started the Boer War with the Jameson Raid, but President Paul Kruger was magnanimity itself in handing back Dr Jameson "to do with as you would".'

This left me with little to say other than that Dr Jameson and the men he commanded were Britishers rather than 'Rhodesian' in the modern acceptance of the word. Our encounter ended in mutual recrimination and the SAP were soon withdrawn in their entirety.

Finally, Vorster exerted enough pressure on Smith to persuade him to participate in the Victoria Falls Conference of August 1975. The Conference, held in a South African railway carriage on the Victoria Falls Bridge which was opened for the occasion by the Zambians, was doomed to failure because neither the Rhodesian government nor the nationalists were willing participants in a staged attempt by Vorster and Kaunda to promote their concept of 'detente'. Aggravating factors were the presence of such intermediaries as Mark Chona, the intrusion yet again of Lonrho and Smith's deliberate inclusion in his delegation of Van der Byl, who could be relied upon to upset the South Africans, the Zambians and the ANC.

After the failure of the Victoria Falls Conference I felt that CIO should place a priority on trying to maintain South Africa's interest in our affairs. I quickly learnt how difficult this was going to be when I visited South Africa in September and held discussions with Fourie and van den

Bergh. Fourie's views, as outlined in the report of the discussion with him, were:[9]

At the Victoria Falls, agreement had been reached on all important points ... This had been a case for a demonstration of practical statesmanship, but none had been forthcoming. Since the Bridge, Zambia's position with Africa and the OAU had become more untenable ... RSA (South Africa) was in a quandary and did not know where to go from here ... Fourie felt that as the economic pinch developed in South Africa her ability to assist us as they had done in the past would be severely circumscribed ... One piece of advice which Mr Vorster had specifically asked B F to pass on to us was: 'Be careful with Mozambique.' He was referring to the repercussions which might flow from our breaching their territorial integrity.

Van den Bergh did not paint quite so pessimistic a picture. Indeed, he seemed to be making a genuine attempt to introduce a positive note into the situation, as my report to the Prime Minister indicated:[10]

The main theme emerging was that General van den Bergh is planning for the South Africans to participate in an anti-Communist grouping against MPLA in Angola and that if Rhodesia played her cards carefully (the emergence of Nkomo as the new head of ANC and the continuation of negotiations) we would retain South Africa's support within the same grouping as South Africa, Zambia, Botswana and the other relatively 'anti-Communist' countries.

Despite the encouragement received from the General, I placed more weight on what Fourie had said and in my report to Smith, quoted above, I summed the situation up thus:

The general picture painted by Mr Fourie could not have been more depressing; and he seemed genuinely dejected when seeking our suggestion as to what could be done from now on. The crux of his message was:
– The four African Presidents have washed their hands of us;
– There will be no more negotiations, therefore we are faced with the alternative of armed conflict;
– In view of Rhodesia's intransigence and our indication to them to 'get off our backs', South Africa could now wash their hands of us as well.

The situation continued to deteriorate during the closing months of 1975. The new year began inauspiciously with a report in the Johannesburg *Sunday Times* on 4 January alleging that a force of 12,000 ZANLA/FRELIMO guerrillas were about to invade Rhodesia. This was news to CIO, and we checked with the South Africans to see what game they might be playing. My request to van den Bergh that I visit Pretoria to discuss this 'invasion' with him coincided with a request from the General himself to see me before he flew to Cape Town for a meeting with Vorster. The lengthy discussion between us in Pretoria on 21 January opened with my putting him straight on the *Sunday Times* report, to the effect that, substantial as the guerrilla threat was from Mozambique, it was not overwhelming. The discussion then moved on to the recent badly mishandled South African raid into Angola, with the General lashing out, once again, at Military Intelligence.[11]

He maintained that he had always been opposed to South African military involvement (in Angola) and that, largely on his advice, they would now be withdrawing completely on Friday 23rd January. The main point made was that South African involvement in Angola could only be justified if seen to be with full Western support; and in the event this had not been forthcoming...

In trying to convince his Prime Minister that it was wrong for South Africa to involve themselves in Angola, General van den Bergh says he queried time and again what South Africa's attitude would now be towards Rhodesia. Having withdrawn the SAP from Rhodesia to avoid too great an involvement, but having subsequently gone uninvited into a fight against the Marxist MPLA, in a Black versus Black war, what excuse could South Africa offer for not going to Rhodesia's assistance if we were invaded, say, by Marxist orientated ZANU/FRELIMO?...

I queried whether South Africa's prospects for achieving detente in Black Africa had been affected.... The General responded with a firm 'No'...

At his request we discussed the talks then proceeding in Salisbury (between Smith and Nkomo) ... (he said) Britain and America had displayed surprising optimism concerning the talks. I thought it inadvisable to query this. It emerged that Foreign Affairs had got certain aspects wrong, such as South Africa's representation at the talks, and whether or not Nkomo really wished to meet Lord Carrington. This produced some surprising evidence from General van den Bergh on the part being played by Lonrho...

I re-iterated the need for regular meetings of our senior staff to keep the developing position in Mozambique under constant review ... He displayed every intention of complying ... but when I suggested that we needed to bring in the Military, Police and other advisers for planning, he was utterly adamant in saying that there would be no military participation with himself in South Africa, although he could see the merit of inviting Police to participate when appropriate.

A number of factors were now conspiring towards a final showdown between Vorster and Smith: Machel's closure of the Mozambique border had made Rhodesia entirely dependent on South Africa for economic survival; Rhodesia was turning increasingly to military raids into Mozambique and Zambia; detente *had* been affected by the failure of the Victoria Falls Conference and the Angolan raid; and the United States of America, having failed to support that raid, were now, by way of recompense, assisting South Africa in applying pressures on Rhodesia.

In mid-February I noted in my diary that the situation had deteriorated further 'not, as before, through politicians' intransigence –

although this is still relevant – but because of the fast-riding events in Angola, Mozambique and elsewhere in Southern Africa.' By June I was writing: 'The South Africans have been withdrawing their support in various spheres ... and van den Bergh has been deliberately undermining us with the Americans.... The "total and unrelenting" pressure, as threatened by Dr Kissinger, is now being applied to us.'

It took three months for Kissinger to come out in the open, three months during which he was preparing his quid pro quo with Vorster: American support for anti-Marxist forces in Angola and no further pressure on Vorster over Namibia, provided that Vorster increased his pressure on Smith and thus cleared America's name in black Africa.

On the morning of 14 September 1976 Vorster put to the Rhodesian delegation in Pretoria the proposals he and Kissinger had agreed upon during their meeting in Geneva the previous week. He told the Ministers present – Ian Smith, David Smith and Roger Hawkins – that the proposals represented the 'last chance'. He and his colleagues were gravely worried that the Rhodesians might not accept the proposals and that sanctions under Chapter VII of the United Nations Charter would be invoked against South Africa, particularly if there was no coincidental settlement over Namibia; the South African economy was worsening rapidly, mainly because of America's deliberately contrived pressure on gold. In short, as van den Bergh said to me while Vorster and Smith were talking: 'It is not Ian Smith who is being pressurised so much as it is a case of John Vorster having his arm twisted.'

I and the other officials who accompanied the Rhodesian delegation, Gaylard and Hawkins, were brought into the discussion in the afternoon during a 'pause for reflection'. I detected a surprising readiness on the part of the Rhodesian Ministers to settle once and for all. From what they said, it was clear that Kissinger's proposals were British-based and that full British participation could be expected in their implementation; following his visit to France and Germany, Kissinger also expected E E C support for the economic guarantees which were a part of the proposals and for massive investment to revitalise the economy and thereby encourage whites to stay in Rhodesia.

What was not so clear was the extent of America's pressure on South Africa, for Vorster did not hand over to the Rhodesian delegation the paper from which he had been quoting when outlining his proposals.

Argument ensued as to whether Mr Vorster should pass to Mr Smith the paper.... The South Africans appeared justified in withholding the whole paper as it included references to South West Africa and was an Anglo-American preparation, not authorised for further distribution. However, Mr Vorster seemed anxious not to indicate bad faith – although it became apparent that the South Africans must have represented some of the proposals in too favourable a light – and it was finally agreed to extract the material which the Rhodesians needed and to have it passed to them as an edited version of the original.[12]

The details of the proposals are included in the record of these meetings.* In essence, the proposals involved a return to legality in Rhodesia with an Executive-type government being appointed under the constitutional authority of the Queen. The country would be governed by decree from a Council of State comprising three blacks and two whites, or two blacks and three whites, with a white Chairman. This Council of State would function as a transitional government and prepare a programme for majority rule without a specifically pre-determined time scale. However, when taxed on the time scale issue, Vorster replied: 'In two years.' Roger Hawkins' comment on the same subject was: 'As we are being asked to commit political suicide, we should be allowed to do it in our own time!' Obviously, Roger Hawkins, David Smith and Ian Smith were going to have a problem selling the proposals to their Cabinet colleagues. But they had been left in no doubt that they must show willingness to go along with the proposals, in which case Dr Kissinger would take the matter one stage further, in direct discussion.

On the night of Tuesday 15 September I flew to Athens, and thence to Paris two days later. I held meetings with French and British contacts, to check on their knowledge of the proposals and to seek second opinions. The flight back to South Africa on the Friday night was delayed, and as a result I did not reach Pretoria until dawn was breaking on the Sunday morning. I was greeted with the news that the Kissinger meeting would begin in a few hours' time, which had little appeal for me after several nights on aeroplanes and no prospect of catching up on lost sleep.

The Rhodesian and American delegations, and accompanying officials, met in the American Embassy. Kissinger manoeuvred a quiet chat alone with Smith and then addressed the two groups, saying he regretted the circumstances that brought us together. He was not meeting us in any spirit of confrontation, rather one of impending tragedy, nor was he there to prove points or support moral issues; the Rhodesians should make their own assessment of the Security situation and judge the consequences for themselves. He would do what he could for the whites, but there was a point beyond which he could not go. Rhodesia faced a

---

*Report 'Notes on discussion with American Secretary of State at US Embassy Pretoria on Sunday, 19th September, 1976' and 'Notes: Second Meeting held on Sunday, 19th September, 1976 at "Libertas"'. The latter is reproduced in the Appendix.

bleeding guerrilla war, which would become unmanageable without foreign assistance. As the war continued Rhodesia would have to raid further and further into neighbouring countries, with dire results, and there was no basis whatsoever for United States aid.

Smith responded to Kissinger's opening remarks by thanking him for his interest and assured him that they shared the same objective – the achievement of a satisfactory settlement. Kissinger said he had been taking the British with him, step by step, and that although he could not enter into a bi-lateral agreement he would stand behind whatever was agreed. Smith said the Labour Government in Britain was bitter over UDI and would seek revenge. Kissinger pointed out that he himself could be out of office in six weeks and the alternative administration in the United States would be less favourably disposed towards Rhodesia.

The issues were discussed and papers exchanged. Some points had varied since Kissinger and Vorster met in Zurich; for instance, the original paper had the Council of State as being appointed by the British, to which Vorster had objected in the belief that the British government would appoint only those in opposition to the Rhodesian government. Kissinger said that Prime Minister Callaghan would not accept a white majority in the Council of State but might accept parity if the black Front Line Presidents agreed to this. The British had also inserted a provision that either side could veto the choice of the other, but Kissinger thought this was unworkable and that it was better for each side to nominate its own representatives. There were five points of note:

Point 1: 'Rhodesia agrees to majority rule within two years'

Smith asked for a definition of 'majority rule', suggesting that the word 'responsible' be inserted before 'majority'. Kissinger said he could not sell this; all Americans agreed there was nothing wrong with one-man-one-vote. If we had someone more radical than Nkomo as a negotiating partner we would have an even greater problem. He said there would have to be separate ZAPU and ZANU nominees selected by the African Presidents, pointing out that he would have no basis for argument if he was seen in the United States as disagreeing with the Presidents. The Russians were already saying he was attempting to instal puppets, when all he was trying to do was to get non-communists involved.

Point 2: 'Rhodesian representatives would meet immediately at a mutually agreed place with Black leaders to work out an interim Government until majority rule was implemented'

Kissinger said that Russia had a greater capacity to back their chosen groups than did the United States. Stopping terrorism when the talks began had not been discussed. However, Nyerere had told him that Russia had offered full support for ZANU but that he and the other Black Presidents had rejected the offer. There were other reports that the Russians had offered MIGS to ZAPU. Kissinger had been asked if he would give aid to the liberation movements if the talks failed; he had replied that the United States did not deal with liberation movements.

Point 3: 'The interim Government would consist of a Council of State, half of whose members would be Black and half White, with a White chairman who would not have a casting vote'

Kissinger said the British would accept only what the Black Presidents agreed, and at this stage the Presidents appeared to be adamant that there must be an African majority. Musset said that if the case could not be sold to Rhodesians, the RF Government would be out, there would be an election, terrorism would increase and the consequences would be severe. Kissinger said in that case our Prime Minister could be accused of rigging his own defeat.

Kissinger thought Rhodesia should accept a majority of Blacks and ask for the Ministers of Law and Order and of Defence to be White. David Smith said he had doubts regarding the ability of Blacks to handle the economic Ministries. Kissinger said he had told Vorster he accepted that Rhodesia would not be as well run as she was at present.

Point 4: 'All members will take an oath that they will work for rapid progress to majority rule'

Smith asked if this was necessary. Kissinger said it was not but it had been in the British paper; however, he felt it could be dropped.

Point 5: 'The United Kingdom would enact enabling legislation for progress to majority rule. Rhodesia would also enact such legislation as may be necessary'

Smith said he could not repeal Rhodesia's present Constitution until a new one was ready to replace it. Kissinger said we could either blow things up in this way or Smith could put forward a coherent plan on which Kissinger could stand. He did not want to trace the road to majority rule, only to have it rejected by the Russians. If Rhodesians did not want to fight it out they should put forward an alternative proposition which could be the dominant one. Either way, it was a high-risk course, but it would be a mistake to 'get into a three-week haggle'. If Rhodesia put forward something that had not been discussed with Britain then 'the United States would be naked'. David Smith remarked that if we returned to legality and called a constitutional conference it would be a feather in Kissinger's cap. Kissinger disagreed, saying that if his present initiative succeeded all he would get would be 'two weeks of favourable news stories' and two years hence he would be blamed even if the situation then was better than it would have been without his efforts. He would be depicted as the victim of a 'Smith trick', adding that he had been warned beforehand that the Rhodesians would trick him.

As the record shows, Kissinger was of the opinion that neither Nyerere nor Machel wanted a rapid political settlement; they would prefer a military-terrorist victory. He said that Mugabe favoured a slow takeover so that he could get people on his side as he moved ahead. He was aware that none of the blacks expected his mission to succeed and that in our deliberations we must bear in mind the 250,000 white lives which were at stake; Ian Smith added there were also many moderate black lives at stake.

In response to David Smith's query as to whether an acceptance of the proposals would mean that sanctions would fall away and terrorism would end, Kissinger affirmed that sanctions would be off as soon as the interim government was formed and that he would use all the influence he could to stop terrorism. Ian Smith asked what would happen if the Rhodesian government renounced UDI, to which Kissinger replied that although the United States could not back such action, they would not oppose it either. Ian Smith explained the essence of the 1961 Constitution and Kissinger responded by saying it was inconceivable that 'majority rule under Ian Smith' would be acceptable to the British. He knew the key British Ministers, some of whom were his personal friends despite what they had done to him in the past month, and he did not think that such a counter-proposal would work.

The meeting adjourned for a lunch-break during which we officials had a good chance to express our views, to considerable avail. Talks resumed in the afternoon at the South African Prime Minister's official residence, with Vorster, Muller, 'Pik' Botha and Fourie attending. Discussion ensued as to how the black leaders should be chosen. Kissinger affirmed that it would be done by the black Presidents. Ian Smith said the 'Security' Ministers should be white; Kissinger said we had convinced him on this point at the morning meeting. Ian Smith went on to say that his delegation needed more details about the economic support schemes. Kissinger replied that two documents had already been agreed with the British; and a three-way group comprising South Africa, the United Kingdom and the United States was to work out the details. Vorster said the South Africans could drop out of the financial arrangements but the Rhodesians must be represented.

The discussion then switched to the public statement that should be issued. Ian Smith made yet another attempt to get approval for renouncing UDI and going back to square one. Kissinger said he had tried this out on the British Ambassador who felt sure his government would be unwilling to accept the responsibility. Kissinger feared that the Soviets might give extra arms to the black militants and possibly one of the Front Line Presidents. If the Rhodesians accepted the scheme in principle he would go to Kaunda and Nyerere and say that, subject to a satisfactory plan for interim government, the stoppage of the guerrilla war, and the ending of sanctions, the Rhodesians should be clear to make their statement; but he added that it would help if we made the fewest possible conditions in public.

Smith said he would consult his Cabinet immediately, then his caucus. Kissinger warned that the Black Presidents would produce different proposals if there was any delay. He believed Smith should make a statement as soon as possible on what he was willing to accept. Smith repeated that he saw great problems in selling it. Kissinger said we were committed to the paper he would be taking to Kaunda and Nyerere. Smith said he was clear on this, and on that basis he would try and sell it; but added, once again, that 'some may still talk of renouncing UDI', to which Kissinger replied that Smith would lose all psychological impact if he tried that.

There was renewed discussion – increasingly acrimonious – on the statement to be made, with underlying attempts to get Smith committed to the proposals as if they were of his own choosing. Agreement was finally reached on how much Kissinger would tell the Press that evening, mentioning the timetable by which Smith would proceed later in the week.

Kissinger exuded charisma. He evoked tragedy – not conflict. Luck had run out for his President, he said, and they would probably both be out of office in a few weeks. He remarked that he was liable to be 'beaten to death by demagogues in the United States' for his efforts. He said more than once that his wife, Nancy, expected Smith to fight, not give in. All the indications were that his concern was genuine and he behaved with restraint; but as the drama unfolded we realised this was the end of the road for Smith. Whatever he did was fraught with danger, and with that realisation he conducted himself with dignity. To accept majority rule was to renounce UDI. There was no longer any hope the British would assist. The best prospect was to rely on American support even if Kissinger was out of office before anything could be achieved. There was no certainty that the Front Line Presidents were speaking

genuinely, or on behalf of the African Nationalists. They would almost
certainly renege on their promises to Kissinger. In the last analysis, it
was South Africa's attitude that would affect Smith's decision. Vorster
had achieved more than anyone else by getting Smith together with
Kissinger. If Smith refused to respond it would mean the end of South
African support – with defeat in the terrorist war staring him in the face.

We arrived back in Salisbury in the early hours of Monday morning. I,
for one, was too tired to sleep, so I turned to my diary:

Seven hours of talks with Kissinger and his team. Most impressed with K's grasp
of the situation. He was well ahead of his staff in providing answers on debating
points as they cropped up. His twenty minutes alone with the PM at the start
had a marked effect, for I have never known the PM respond so readily when we
moved into plenary session. As we broke for lunch Kissinger kept saying how
much he appreciated Rhodesia's position: how he would not know what decision to make if he was in Ian Smith's shoes. He left us, literally with tears in his
eyes. Maybe a touch of conscious drama. Or play-acting; but it did not appear
so; concluding a week of foreboding and near-tragedy.

Kissinger told us that his wife, Nancy, of Irish/Scotch descent who loves a
fighter and is a great admirer of Ian Smith, would never forgive him if she
missed seeing her hero. And he saw to it that she was produced immediately on
return from Cape Town, during the afternoon session at 'Libertas' – rushing in
and embracing Smith at some embarrassment to all of us.

Running through it all the deepening realisation by the politicians that they
would have to face the inevitable – a renunciation of UDI, surrender to black
majority rule and the political defeat of the white man in Rhodesia.

Towards the end, I detected some relief amongst the two PMs and Ministers,
except that Lardner-Burke's contribution was entirely negative; and if it had not
been for us officials – Gaylard, Hawkins and I – the thing could still have swung
the other way. Now the fateful decision has been made, let's hope it is as
represented, because I personally hold much responsibility for this, as a choice
between peace and war in Southern Africa.

On Friday 24 September 1976 Smith publicly announced his acceptance
of the Kissinger proposals. In a radio broadcast he said:

The American and the British Governments, together with the major Western
powers, have made up their minds as to the kind of solution they wish to see in
Rhodesia and they are determined to bring it about. The alternative to acceptance of the proposals was explained to us in the clearest of terms, which left no
room for misunderstanding.

He explained the advantages of what he called the 'Package Deal': sanctions would be lifted; there would be an injection of development capital;
an international trust fund would guarantee pension rights and investments and would assist in development; assurances had been received
that terrorism would be halted.

Then he began the backsliding which had been such a feature after the agreements reached on *Tiger* and *Fearless*. He offered his own interpretation of 'majority rule':

It will be a 'majority rule' constitution and this is expressly laid down in the proposals. My own position on majority rule is well known. I have stated in public many times, and I believe I echo the views of the majority of both black and white Rhodesians when I say that we support majority rule, provided that it is responsible rule.

In the following few days there were enough winks and nods to convince the electorate that whatever change there might be would be ephemeral. Behind closed doors Smith began to wriggle out of a dilemma that was not of his own making. In the meantime, as Kissinger himself had warned, the Front Line Presidents were beginning to indulge in dubious manoeuvres on the sidelines and there was, as ever, division in the nationalist camps. The Russians were feeding in whatever disinformation they could to discredit the American initiative. Generally, accusations and counter-accusations became rife. Small-minded men resented Kissinger's achievement and decried his success where everyone else had failed.

The two new players in the Rhodesian game, Callaghan and his Foreign Secretary, Crosland, were desperately anxious not to participate in yet another failure and thus, in an atmosphere heavy with doubt and suspicion, the British government attempted to implement the proposals by convening a conference in Geneva.

CHAPTER 10

Internal Agreement

Of all the delegations at the Geneva Conference only one – Smith's – could be described as solid. Sithole went there as the rejected President of ZANU; he had been excluded initially by the Front Line Presidents, who had been given the task of selecting the nationalists' representatives, but Nyerere had then changed his mind and had persuaded his colleagues to re-instate Sithole. Muzorewa led the 'United' ANC, but could not find enough supporters to complete his delegation; as it was, he kept two empty seats on either side of him at the conference for Enos Nkala (still in detention) and Edson Sithole (missing since October 1975), neither of whom would have been likely to join Muzorewa had they been available. The Patriotic Front (PF), a newly formed alliance between Nkomo's ZAPU and Mugabe's ZANU, was united only in its opposition to the Kissinger proposals and to other nationalists. The men in Smith's delegation – P. K. van der Byl, Mark Partridge and Hilary Squires – were all hardliners and as such presented a united front.

The odds against a successful outcome of the conference were heavy, not only because of the disunity among the nationalists but also because the only group genuinely trying to get a settlement were the British. Their efforts to do so, however, were severely handicapped by the man they chose to chair the conference, Ivor Richard, who was shown scant respect by Mugabe, and the other nationalists soon followed Mugabe's lead.

The Geneva Conference began on 28 October 1976. Within less than a week the Anglo-American initiative was heading for a dead end. The frustration I felt at this point was such that, for the first time since the rise of African nationalism in the late 1950s, I found myself more in sympathy with the British than anyone else (Diary):

Guy Fawkes Day 1976. Having returned from Geneva with the PM and his party yesterday, after a frustrating ten days ending up with a white-black confrontation at the Palais de Nations. Trying to cope with the aloofness of the Rhodesia delegation, particularly PK; meeting with Kenneth Dube, qualified in medicine in South Africa and surgery in Heidelberg, married to a German girl, anxious to help and so pleased to see Robbie and I but waiting in vain in our hotel to see whether PK would buy him a beer ... I experienced a definite cooling off of relations with Jack Gaylard and others of our delegation. It ended with me walking the streets of Geneva in despair one evening ... (and) who should I meet in a similar state of mind but my old Portuguese friend, Preza, with whom I had traversed Angola and learnt about the Portuguese. And we hit the town together – just a shadow of the rip-roaring times we used to have in Luanda, Lisbon and Lourenco Marques, for there is little soul in Geneva, or the Swiss as a people, compared with the Portuguese.

The aloofness of the Rhodesian party towards me probably arose because I appeared too anxious to accommodate the British and too close to the five 'White Presidents', the name given to the leaders of agriculture, commerce and industry in Rhodesia who had travelled to Geneva to do what they could to promote settlement. Their efforts behind the scenes at the conference to reconcile the RF leaders with the nationalist leaders represented an entirely new development in Rhodesia's political affairs. They encountered for the first time the deep-rooted hostility of the nationalists towards everything the RF stood for and, inevitably, clashed with the members of the Rhodesia delegation, who still accepted Ian Smith's belief that Rhodesia was inhabited by 'the happiest Africans in the world'. My open association with other Rhodesians who took the trouble to go to Geneva added fuel to the fire. Among these people were the Reverend Gary Strong, who preached reconciliation between the races, and Hardwicke Holderness, a Battle of Britain ace and long-time liberal who was opposed to everything Smith represented.

I found myself in yet another of those no-win situations. The Intelligence I produced was unwelcome because it was unpalatable. Smith and his colleagues acquired the sort of 'Intelligence' they wished to hear from various Rhodesian and British right-wingers in Geneva at the time, including Sir Frederick and Lady Crawford who entertained the Rhodesian delegation at their nearby chateau. My diary entry for 5 November continued:

Those of us who started this jaunt with Kissinger have moved from one cul-de-sac into another, and I fear we are no nearer finding a solution than we have ever been. So much for my optimism on 20th September – 'This could go down in history as the week that changed Rhodesia!'... I rested up yesterday which would normally be enough for recovery – and far more than I am used to – but I lapsed into slumber this afternoon when discussing Geneva with Daantjie Olivier.... Then at the Police Mess (I listened to) some utterly anachronistic ideas for fitting 'moderate' Africans into the political scene provided no whites realised what is being done.

Smith believed that the conference had been called to implement the Kissinger agreement. The nationalist delegations all rejected the Kissin-

ger proposals, except as a basis for negotiation. In their view, the conference was convened simply to arrange the transfer of power to a black
government on their terms. In the opening weeks the conference dealt
mostly with a projected date for 'Independence', with Smith adhering to
Kissinger's two-year period. When I returned with him to Salisbury on 3
November he said:

'I'm leaving because nothing is taking place in Geneva and I have a
country to run.' Van der Byl was left in charge of the Rhodesian delegation.

On 15 November Richard announced a compromise formula: 'Independence' after twelve months if this were technically feasible, or fifteen
months at the latest. Mugabe and Nkomo rejected the offer and demanded that the British government commit itself to 1 December 1977 as a
positive date for the hand-over of power. Nkomo then weakened in his
demands and Richard offered another compromise, calling it 'The British Government's firm position'. It was by no means firm, for the offer
was to grant 'Independence' on 1 March 1978 as long as all the necessary processes could be completed by that date. Smith returned to Geneva at this point, to find that the only measure of agreement among the
nationalists was that a British presence would be desirable during
the transitional period. This was promptly rejected by the Rhodesian
delegation.

On 14 December the conference adjourned until 17 January 1977, but
it was never resumed. Richard remained in the act for the following six
weeks or so in the hope that something might be salvaged from Kissinger's initiative. He visited Rhodesia and South Africa and, at Britain's
request, I briefed him on each of his visits. I believed that it was vital that
Britain continue to hold the ring, not only because of the mutual distrust
between the nationalists and the RF but also because the RF had convinced themselves that Rhodesia could survive without a settlement,
despite the increasingly vociferous advice from OCC to the contrary.
The RF stand on the Kissinger deal was 'all or nothing', while the British
were intent on exploring ways and means of implementing any aspect of
the package they could. On 23 January I wrote in my diary:

Ivor Richard is here for the second time, and I excelled myself by sending him to
sleep in his hotel suite; so much so that his snoring interrupted my train of
thought when I was trying to brief him. At least I seemed to convince him how
important the essential professionalism of our Commanders was to Rhodesia's
survival, for he indicated before he went to sleep that he would vary his intention forthwith, which had been to replace the Commanders with political
figures.

Twenty-four hours later I wrote 'finis' to the Kissinger initiative. In a traumatic meeting between Richard on the one hand and Smith and van der Byl on the other, the Rhodesians reacted to suggestions of further British involvement with uncustomary rudeness and bitter accusations of bad faith. Richard queried whether he should take this back to London as a final rejection of British participation in settlement negotiations. The Rhodesians backtracked a little, saying that it was not a rejection as such, merely a hiatus in the long process of negotiations. My diary entry for 24 January reads:

The final breakdown in the current negotiations. Talks ended after a traumatic meeting and the Brits were sent packing with an unanswered question: 'When is a rejection not a rejection?' I had hard words with Jack Gaylard – immediately regretted but taken to the point where I could see he was again wondering on whose side I was. At least I may have helped change the British attitude from one of walk out to their parting decision to 'keep the structure of Geneva intact against the possibility that someone will want to talk again before long.' The PM [Smith] broadcast tonight – not quite up to Richard's masterly performance of the night before, but with a very fair explanation of the causes of the breakdown. And what are we left with? Renewed moves towards internal settlement?

There had been no let up in the war during the Anglo-American initiative. If anything, it intensified during the long months of the Geneva Conference. ZIPA, ZIPRA and ZANLA launched campaigns based on the assumption that Rhodesia's guard was down but, with the black leaders occupied in Geneva, the campaigns were poorly co-ordinated and were undermined by rivalries. Tongogara and others unjustly implicated in the murder of Chitepo had been released from Zambian gaols to attend the Geneva talks and it would take some time before they were back in control. Hundreds of ill-prepared guerrillas were sent into Rhodesia, and there they were killed by the hundreds.

The RF interpreted this as a sign that Rhodesia was on top of the war again, ignoring the fact that the pace of recruitment had long since made such 'encouraging' kill rates irrelevant. In OCC there was little doubt now that the 'no-win' war was becoming a 'losing' war. Something of OCC's despair at the lack of political direction was beginning to seep through into the Security Forces, and the morale of the Forces began to cause almost as much concern as guerrilla recruitment. The minutes of the War Council meeting on 15 December record the following:

The Chief of Staff, Army, reported that most of the officers in the field were of the opinion that the vast majority of men currently serving on indefinite call-up would leave Rhodesia as soon as they were released from continuous service and it was suggested that a measure of reassurance, preferably in the form of a

statement by the Prime Minister, might assist in minimising the predicted increase in emigration.

In discussion it was confirmed that, whilst the problem had been caused in
part by the call-up system, this was strongly allied to political uncertainty ... as
there could be no purely military solution to Rhodesia's problems and as the
political portion of the solution was not in evidence, there was a general feeling
that the military effort was to no avail.

The Commanders understood the political situation well enough. The
politicians, on the other hand, were showing a marked reluctance to get
to grips with either the military or the political situation. And the general public was, as ever, given so little information that it could not begin
to understand the overall position. CIO tried to enlighten the public a
little by passing carefully processed but factual Intelligence to the Press.
An article headed 'The terror war four years on' which appeared in the
Rhodesia Herald on 22 December, for example, was based on such
Intelligence. The dramatic rise in the death toll was featured prominent-
ly, the editor making the point that the numbers of Security Force,
guerrilla and civilian deaths were rising in approximate proportion and
outlining disturbing new features of the war, such as urban terrorism,
the sabotage of railway lines and firing on civilian aircraft.

CIO also tried to spread the word overseas, and came to an agreement
with the Ministry of Information on a joint procedure for vetting foreign
journalists who could be granted special access to the Security Forces.
Some were given the status of 'War Correspondent' and among them
were a few, including Lord Richard Cecil, who were allowed to carry
arms whilst on assignment with the Security Forces. In Cecil's case this
caused some jealousy and led to accusations that he was contravening
the journalist ethic of 'neutrality'. He was a Guards Officer with a
distinguished record of service and in all my dealings with him he
evinced the same sentiments in search of glory in the world of journalism
as had Winston Churchill, similarly armed as a war correspondent in the
Boer War at the turn of the century. Cecil took too many risks and was
killed in action within a year.

All in all, a fair cross-section of journalists' reports began to find their
way into print. At times, when I grew tired of saying the same thing
again and again to Cabinet, I would draw on such reports to say it for
me, in the hope that a new voice might make more impression on Smith
and his colleagues. In my briefing to Cabinet on 11 January 1977, for
example, I quoted extensively from a well-researched article in *The
Times* (London) on 29 December 1976 headed 'Can Rhodesia's confident troops really stop the black guerrillas?', written by Michael Knipe.

On the day preceding this Cabinet meeting I and my colleagues in OCC had confronted the Prime Minister personally to voice our concern about the military situation (Diary):

Wednesday 12th January 1977. We had our face-to-face with the PM on Monday afternoon. Sticky to start with, and I had to open the batting although we had expected Jack Gaylard to do that for us. Got the message across after a couple of hours – even to the point where Ian Smith said he agreed with us – having pointed out the necessity for a political solution because our military/security situation could only worsen ... Then on Tuesday I briefed Cabinet and gave them the bleakest picture they've ever had ... David Smith saw me this afternoon and said that I had had a bigger impact on his Cabinet colleagues than ever before; and from what else he said I got the impression that they had made the fateful decision to go for a political solution and accept the inevitability of black majority rule, perhaps under Bishop Muzorewa ... At least, that's how it seemed to be. But I was told shortly afterwards by Jack Gaylard that the Ministers had adopted a hard line in 'Informal Cabinet' (Ministers meeting without officials present) yesterday evening.... The fact of the matter is that we still do not know where we stand ... On the one hand, the political scene has been set better (following the Front Line Presidents' decision to support only the Patriotic Front) giving us a better opportunity to produce a settlement; on the other hand the PM may feel he has no option but to close his party's ranks and fight it out regardless.

Having confronted Ian Smith on the Monday, and the Cabinet on the Tuesday, the third prong of OCC's attack took place in the War Council meeting on Friday 14 January:[1]

Council was advised that the OCC assessment of the military situation was that the country was losing so much ground militarily that even with general mobilisation, which would have a detrimental effect on the economy and which should be introduced only as a last resort, matters could only be prolonged ... it was stressed that action was required very soon, as the Security Forces would be unable to hold the position indefinitely. The Prime Minister informed Council that he was well aware of the fact that there ... would be no end of the war until a political solution was achieved. It was vital, however, that Rhodesia remain in a strong position militarily in order to enable the Prime Minister to negotiate from a position of strength and it was stressed that all would be lost if Rhodesia's enemies thought for a moment that the country's security was on the verge of collapse.

Despite all our efforts, however, we ended up with the same mixture as before. Even if Smith believed, secretly, that a negotiated settlement was preferable to the bloodshed he could now see all around him, he dare not admit it to his political colleagues. His mentor, Dupont, remained implacably opposed to any form of settlement, while Lardner-Burke, in an attack upon me during a sundowner at the Royal Salisbury Golf Club, spoke for the hardliners when he said:

'Don't you ever get tired of all that drivel you keep serving us? For years now you've warned of things that never happened and never will happen. Doesn't it bore you to keep repeating all the same old guess-work? And for what? To try and frighten us off the only course of action that we have! To frighten us? You only serve to frighten yourself!'

Such outbursts did not deter CIO or OCC from continuing to make the point time and again in War Council that the war could not be won militarily. But we were faced with a group of politicians in that forum who could not have been more retrogressive. Among the officials there were one or two weak links but overall it was a team that might have been able to stop the war running away with itself had it not had the misfortune to serve under what must have been the most abysmal political direction Rhodesian officials had ever suffered.

Despite the lack of political direction, the War Council did everything it could to keep the troops happy. It intervened, for example, over the delay in the production of Security Force medals in 1977. Of the 35,844 General Service Medals awarded by the beginning of that year, only 18,284 had been issued because the Treasury had cut the financial allocation for minting on the grounds that medals were less important than the purchase of arms and other materiel. The effect of this delay on Security Force morale was such that the Treasury's decision was promptly reversed by the War Council.

There was no shortage of political strategists to advise Ministers, or of experts in counter-insurgency to serve the OCC or Joint Planning Staff (JPS), whose task it was to examine any tactic that might bring the war to a successful conclusion. The JPS examined the problem of guerrilla recruitment, but could find no military solution. The War Council debated the concept of 'Sterile Zones' – to sterilise an area not for anyone's health but to cause death and render the area uninhabitable. The JPS produced a memorandum 'Sterile Zones and Food Control'[2] that so upset the Prime Minister because of its negative nature that he took me on one side and said: 'There are more holes in this report than there are in a mosquito net. I intend to appoint a team that will produce quite different answers.' Archie Wilson, ex-Commander of the Air Force, now a Deputy Minister, was appointed captain of the Prime Minister's team. The team recommended that sterile zones be created in areas where guerrillas were known to be operating with local support, so that suspects could be evicted for 'assisting terrorists' and anyone found thereafter in the zone could be shot on sight. Unfortunately for the Prime Minister and Wilson, the new Secretary for Internal Affairs, Dennis Connolly, was a more independent character than his immediate predecessors and he came out strongly in opposition to the recommendation. He said the[3]

creation of sterile zones would have a considerable effect on tribesmen. Land-owners would lose their land, stockholders would lose their grazing, which would be unobtainable elsewhere, and the population, consisting mainly of old men, women and children would lose their homes. Many of these people repre-sented the families or relatives of serving members of the Security Forces or Internal Affairs ... A number would probably leave Rhodesia and there would be increased sympathy for the terrorist cause.

Of far more consequence at this stage than deliberations in the War Council or the OCC was an event in the secret war which had passed virtually unnoticed in Rhodesia. On 22 January, J. Z. (Jason) Moyo, ZAPU's most militant advocate of continuing the war and of achieving unity between ZIPRA and ZANLA, had been killed in Lusaka. I wrote guardedly in my diary: 'Sunday 23rd January ... the war goes on. J. Z. Moyo was killed by parcel bomb yesterday, with the usual allegations that we master-minded it. But so much is under way in so many theatres that I just couldn't be sure what might or might not be the degree of our involvement.' The death of Jason Moyo spelt the end of attempts at unity between the fighting forces of the nationalist movement, and thereafter ZIPRA went its own way.

The collapse of the post-Geneva discussions between Ivor Richard and Ian Smith left little room for optimism. In its wake, however, a host of new participants appeared on the scene and hopes of settlement were revived. Among the new faces were Dr David Owen, British Foreign Secretary, and Cyrus Vance, American Secretary of State; Ivor Richard and Andrew Young brought up the rear. But well ahead of them in the attempt to salvage something from the Anglo-American initiative was the familiar face of John Vorster. My diary entry for 12 February 1977 reads:

There may be hope of an internal settlement after all. OCC having got the PM to the point of settlement – and the sooner the better – we paid a quick visit to Pretoria for discussions with the top South African military; then back to im-press on the PM his need to see Vorster early, and this has now been done.

I was back in Pretoria on Monday and down in Cape Town on Wednesday, ready for the meeting of the PMs that afternoon. I honestly believe that Harold Hawkins and I went a long way to achieving the best possible stage-management, first of all with Brand Fourie the previous evening and then with the PM and David Smith during our 'working lunch'. Be that as it may, Ian Smith virtually said it all to Vorster that afternoon – majority rule, as promised, within two years; working with a freely elected interim government, following democratic processes; allowing African nationalists back into the country and permitting them to canvass; encouraging other countries to supervise elections – and so on. Even on the subject of racial discrimination he promised to move further than the Quenet recommendations. At the end, there was virtually nothing left to offer!

We still have the problem of convincing the outside world that it is all genuine and practicable; and this is what Vorster promised to achieve with the British and Americans. I relayed this to T.Y. (our British colleague) and I am pleased to say we seem to be back on a better relationship; and I hope, working together, not against each other.

Vorster outshone everyone at that meeting in Cape Town. He appeared vastly superior in intellect and cleverer in politics than any member of his delegation, who spoke only when spoken to. Smith's performance, by comparison, was second-rate; and there was little support that the Rhodesian Ministers and officials present could give him in the face of Vorster's dominance. In an exchange of personal views with Harold Hawkins after this meeting I wrote on 18 February in reply to a comment he had made concerning opinion in South Africa of Ian Smith:

It is difficult, if not impossible, to get realisation here of how our top man is mistrusted outside. More than this, it keeps coming back to me that he – and I regret to say, Jack (Gaylard) as well – remain 'persona non grata' with virtually all the Africans with whom we have to deal.

My letter continued with an outline of ideas CIO had been feeding into British and American Intelligence circles in the hope that they would help the moves towards settlement. I believed that Smith had now committed himself to an early settlement, 'bringing in as many of the African Nationalist leaders as possible through valid democratic processes and with no suggestion of deferment or of trying to reverse the processes now started'. In the light of this I put the case forward for backing Muzorewa, not only because of his orientation towards the West, and towards America in particular, but also because he was 'already in the pound seats and he ought to be in the driving seat and end up as the first black Prime Minister of Rhodesia'. Events were to prove me wrong. Smith was not genuinely committed to 'valid democratic processes' and Muzorewa would end up as a puppet Prime Minister, not the real thing. I was not alone in being wrong, but that does not detract from the fact that on this sort of issue I should have been right.

Almost immediately, the government showed signs of backsliding on the subject of allowing African nationalists to return to the country. The government had shown strong reluctance over Nkomo's proposed return to Rhodesia and only the fear of an unfavourable reaction from

South Africa had persuaded them not to detain him, as the Minutes of the War Council meeting of 17 December show:

The Minister of Law and Order reported that discussion had taken place on how best to deal with Joshua Nkomo on his return to Rhodesia on Sunday, 19th December. Whilst many Rhodesians expected some sort of action to be taken against Nkomo, this would create considerable adverse reaction in South African Government circles ... Rhodesia's lifeline through South Africa could be jeopardised if the South African Government was antagonised by precipitate action.

Within a month of my letter to Hawkins, CIO was helping to arrange the return of Ndabaningi Sithole from Malawi. The government's ambivalence over the matter is evident from the Minutes of the War Council meeting on 9 March:

The Minister of Law and Order referred to a newspaper report that his Ministry had refused to state whether it would take action against the Rev. N. Sithole if he returned to Rhodesia and advised Council that a fresh statement would be issued informing the public that the Ministry had declined to comment as it was not the practice of government to rely on news reports ... Although the public would expect action to be taken in the event of Sithole's return it was pointed out that Government would be unwise to commit itself at this stage.

I had felt frustrated before but I thought this was the limit. A month previously Smith had promised Vorster that African nationalists would be allowed back into the country; now he was deferring to Squires' opinion that government commitment on the issue would be 'unwise'. The uncertainty over Sithole's return continued for another four months. On 11 July I gave vent to my feelings in my diary:

I almost despair of ever seeing anything resolved ... Robbie (Derek Robinson, Deputy 'Internal', CIO) and I; Peter Sherren (Commissioner of Police) and I; or just I alone have been subjected to political chicanery like never before. First, the PM or Ministers accusing us of trying to influence them (against their better judgement!) to let Ndabaningi Sithole back into the country; then the PM telling McK that he couldn't come back because this was contrary to the advice of his 'Security Chiefs'; then the PM telling Gaylard, Robbie and me that he must be back – and the sooner the better; then a reversal within twenty-four hours when he failed to sell it to his Cabinet; then another reversal, with compromise attached; and so on.

Sithole returned in July. He was so conscious of white opposition that, against my advice, he went out of his way to placate the whites by abjuring terrorism. This ruined whatever political chances he had left, and black Africa turned on him.

In the meantime, the tide of South African sympathy for Rhodesia had turned. Vorster, as promised in his meeting in February in Cape Town with Smith, had been seeking to convince the British and Americans that Rhodesia was now genuinely in search of a 'majority rule' settlement, and had come face-to-face with members of President Carter's new administration. He met Vice-President Walter Mondale in Vienna in May. Mondale's attitude bore little resemblance to the delicate and diplomatic handling of Southern African affairs displayed by Kissinger. He tried to browbeat Vorster into coercing Smith into an unsupportable settlement, and earned instead the wrath of the South African Prime Minister. The change in South Africa's attitude towards Smith was apparent when R. F. ('Pik') Botha, the Minister of Foreign Affairs, stopped over briefly in Salisbury in early August:[4]

Mr Botha said he wished to consult the Prime Minister about the way things were developing. He had had a message from Dr Owen last week inviting him to meet Mr Vance and himself in London on 12th August.... He wished to state clearly and firmly to Vance and Owen the real problems pertaining to settlements in South West Africa and Rhodesia. The West was making strenuous efforts to wage economic war on South Africa. Dr Owen had accused South Africa, holding it responsible for Rhodesia's survival.... Mr Botha referred to Russia's achievements in Africa and said his Government believed that the US would not assist in countering this.... He wished to say to them (Owen and Vance) that Mr Smith was proceeding in accordance with his previously stated policies and that he was not deviating from them.... (Smith said Botha's) aim should be to try to get the UK and the US to face up to their responsibilities to help us get through the present phase.... (Mr Botha sought permission) to say that in the circumstances Mr Smith might reach a stage where the only option was to obtain agreement among local Black leaders and proceed with an internal settlement.... The Prime Minister said that the internal Black leaders believed that if an internal solution could be found, terrorism would slowly wither away. We had information that there were many terrorists outside, waiting to surrender, and we were in touch with these people.* Mr Botha said this would be a tremendous propaganda boost for us.... Mr Botha also said he would indicate that time was of the essence and that he was concerned about the demands being made by certain factions. To help stress the warmth of contact and understanding between Mr Smith and his Government, he would indicate that further discussions would be held in the very near future.

Sympathetic as Pik Botha was, he appeared to shock Smith to the core when he looked him straight in the eye and said:

'A peaceful settlement is no longer possible and there will have to be losers.'

The implication was, of course, that Smith would be among the losers.

---

* CIO never discovered where Smith got his 'information' from; in such circumstances the royal 'we' was usually meant to include his Intelligence and Security advisers, but on this occasion it was probably based on the sort of thing he was hearing from Sithole.

I could not help wondering at the time whether Botha would one day be saying the same thing to his own Prime Minister.

In my letter of August 15 to General Walls accompanying my report of the meeting with Pik Botha, I commented: 'If we are reading the signs correctly, John Vorster and those who count in South Africa have come to the conclusion that "enough is enough" and that they are neither going to apply more pressure of any sort on Ian Smith nor give way to further pressures on themselves.'

The Anglo-American initiative continued but the proposals Owen and Young produced at the end of August were seriously flawed. In their proposal that a British Resident Commissioner should rule Rhodesia while majority rule elections were held, they had not looked closely enough at the problems of whose troops would be used to enforce the necessary cease-fire. Neither side would agree to the other's force being in control, and to suggest integration at that stage was unrealistic. Owen went so far as to suggest that the interim forces should be 'based on liberation forces'; worse still, his proposals contemplated Ian Smith's 'surrender' of power. On their visit to Salisbury to assess the reaction to the proposals, Owen and Young displayed considerable naivety in their understanding of the situation on the ground and appeared oblivious to all that their predecessors had achieved. They certainly ignored the most vital factor – that without Vorster's arm-twisting neither Kissinger nor anyone else could have got Smith to concede majority rule, and that advantage had been thrown away by Mondale.

While Owen and Young were coming and going Smith held elections designed to smash the right-wing revolt posed by the Rhodesia Action Party. True to form, Smith swept the board. Although he was as equivocal as ever on the subject of majority rule, he secured a mandate from the electorate to pursue 'settlement' – even with Owen and Young.

Before Smith committed himself to negotiations with Muzorewa, who saw himself as the only nationalist leader who could achieve unity (a fair enough assumption while he had the support of the Front Line Presidents but Nyerere had changed his position again and had influenced the OAU to back the PF), he decided to make another attempt to win over Nkomo. Through the ubiquitous 'Tiny' Rowland a meeting between Smith and Nkomo was arranged and Smith flew to Lusaka in September. The talks might have progressed, had not CIO sounded a note of warning during the secret sessions that both Nkomo and Kaunda were wrong in presuming they could proceed towards settlement without Mugabe. Overall, the talks succeeded only in upsetting Muzorewa and Sithole, who believed that all parties should work within the Anglo-

American initiative; in upsetting Nyerere, because of the surreptitious exclusion of Mugabe (although Mugabe would never have participated in the discussions); and in ruining whatever slim chance the PF might have had of working together within the Anglo-American initiative.

On 16 September the OCC discussed with the Prime Minister the 'Safe Return' of nationalists and we learnt to our surprise that Smith had already agreed to the return of James Chikerema 'as an indication of good faith'. But it looked more likely that he had been talked into Chikerema's return by Chief Chirau or 'Tiny' Rowland, for Chikerema shortly appeared as my near neighbour in a country house provided by Rowland. The OCC were also concerned to show 'good faith', having suffered widespread opposition from government Ministries to any form of safe conduct offered to guerrillas who would otherwise be shot or hanged, and we wished to know where we stood with the government:[5]

The Prime Minister said it was essential that Government action should be developed in parallel with what we (OCC) would be doing with the African Nationalist leaders....

He had agreed to the return of Chikerema because he believed he could assist in the same direction. I pointed out certain snags in this regard (primarily the fact that we believed Chikerema had lost all influence with guerrillas in the field) and tried to indicate that it would have been desirable for the Prime Minister to have discussed with us before agreeing to Chikerema's return, but he said that the decision in this regard had only been made yesterday and he had had no time to discuss with us....

(He said) at one juncture that he would never have considered agreeing to Chikerema's return as recently as six months ago, but that he was fully satisfied now that it was politically expedient and could be advantageous in the national interest.

On my copy of the memorandum I wrote: 'We stumbled haltingly ... and timing is so important.... It would have been politically unacceptable to both sides to have offered peace terms at any earlier stage; but my own belief is that now we are offering too little too late, which will weaken our position and prolong – not shorten – the war.'

Into this lions' den strolled a gladiator, Field Marshal Lord Carver, the prospective British Resident Commissioner. He flew via Dar-es-Salaam where he was told categorically by Nkomo and Mugabe that there would be no cease-fire unless their guerrilla forces were placed in absolute control. A report from my Deputy on a conversation with Carver at a dinner on 7 November contained a reference to the meeting between Carver and Nkomo and Mugabe:[6]

In a meeting with Nkomo and Mugabe in Dar-es-Salaam, it was fairly clear that he had little time for either of them and accepted the fact that Mugabe had virtually no support within Rhodesia and that Nkomo enjoyed almost universal support from the Matabele, but that his support in other parts of Rhodesia was minimal.... I got the impression that he treated Nkomo as a bit of a joke and said that it was on the cards at one stage that he might have to travel south with them in their Hercules aircraft, and if he did, he could not see how Nkomo could possibly fit into the plane's lavatory, which was minute in the extreme.

Carver arrived in Salisbury on 2 November in Field Marshal's uniform, outranking the Rhodesian Commanders. He explained that he wore uniform as a mark of respect, not because Rhodesia was in 'rebellion' against Britain, and yet I could not help remembering that British generals of the stature of Montgomery had thought it neither respectful nor appropriate to wear British uniform when among a fiercely independent command. Carver's choice of dress gave rise to much adverse comment, and his austere, unsmiling manner did not endear him to those of us who confronted him in the BSA Police Officers' Mess, a venue chosen specifically because it had more tradition in its rafters than any other building in the country. Surprisingly, Carver omitted to sign the Officers' Mess book, whereas Lieutenant General Prem Chand, who accompanied him as the representative of the United Nations, signed the book as a matter of course, saying: 'But of course, old boy, it's the first thing we should do.' Taken bit by bit, these were minor issues, but the overall picture they painted was of a man who was unlikely to appeal to Rhodesians, and thus of a man whose mission would fail. In my brief to Cabinet on 15 November I said:

The visit of Field Marshal Lord Carver and Lieutenant General Prem Chand to Rhodesia has done nothing to advance the prospects of settlement under the Anglo-American proposals. Carver's insistence that the Commanders should discuss the formation of the Zimbabwe National Army and then work back to a discussion upon the practicalities of a cease-fire was as a direct result of influence brought to bear on him by President Nyerere and the Patriotic Front in Dar-es-Salaam on Sunday, 30th October.... The meetings between Carver, Muzorewa and Sithole had as their main theme, the ability or otherwise of either faction to end the terrorist war. The British team was impressed with Sithole's oratory.... They were not impressed with Muzorewa who struck a particularly sour note by asking for a one-hour adjournment in the middle of the meeting to consult with his Executive – and then had nothing to say....

On 19 November Ian Smith dismissed Lord Carver and his entourage as a 'travelling circus' and within a week announced his intention to proceed directly with Muzorewa, Sithole and Chief Chirau towards an 'Internal Settlement'.

The year 1977 had seen several fundamental changes in Rhodesia's conduct of the war. The country had passed the point of no return in its struggle against African nationalism – no political settlement, no answer to the war. Early in the year the Commanders had convinced the government that all available whites should be conscripted to serve in the Security Forces on a basis of one-month-in and two-months-out of uniform. Inevitably, this meant greater military domination, coupled with the demand for the conduct of the war to be moved from a joint command to a single commander.

The OCC system had been designed from the start to co-ordinate all civil, police and military activities and was not geared for the pattern of direct military command which had proved such a failure with our Portuguese neighbours in Mozambique. Successive Army Commanders had become increasingly obsessed with the desire to command other services, but this had been resisted by the rest of us in OCC, particularly when the Army Commanders had made it clear that they would not serve under Police or Air Force command although the personal qualities of senior Air Force and Police officers were frequently superior to those of the Army; the BSAP were the senior Force; and the Air Force had developed into our most efficient weapon in counter-insurgency. I believed that once the Army took over, the war could be considered lost. At one point during a debate on the issue in OCC, Walls stated that I was the only person under whom he would agree to serve. His statement lacked validity, because I was a 'non-person' – it was made simply to negate the claims to overall command by the Commissioner of Police and Commander of the Air Force.

Armchair theorists in the Ministry of Defence added their voice to the clamour for a supreme commander and political pressure was generated through Territorial Army commanders who indicated that they wanted to serve under an Army general as commander-in-chief. Eventually, Smith bowed to the pressure. He ruled that the OCC forum should be enlarged into a 'National Joint Operations Command' (NATJOC) and then settled on a compromise, the formation of 'Combined Operations' (COMOPS), over which Walls assumed command but in the same rank as the other Commanders.

In 1977 OCC was replaced by COMOPS under a new Ministry of Combined Operations, separate from that of Defence which remained responsible for the Army and the Air Force. Lieutenant-General Walls was appointed Commander, COMOPS, and on retirement from the Air Force, Air Marshal M. J. McLaren was appointed Deputy Commander, COMOPS, with a small body of officials, mostly planning staff. The former members of OCC, and the enlarged NATJOC, attended COM-

OPS meetings as required. Inevitably, the influence of the new body on government was weakened because a single Commander under a separate Ministry could never exercise the same authority as the four of us working together in OCC. The move also weakened the resolve of the Police and the Air Force to give of their best under an Army command. In addition, a single Commander came under greater pressure to be seen to be winning the war, which was now more likely to be fought to a standstill, thus lessening the prospect of peace.

It was civilian morale that sustained Rhodesia, not military professionalism. Civilians in all walks of life did much of the fighting and most of the dying, but as military domination increased so the image of the military was exaggerated. The RLI troopie on parade was applauded and his senior officers appeared more frequently on television, were quoted in the Press, or acclaimed as the 'saviours of the nation'. There were many in the Army, from the lower ranks to the 'top brass', who reacted to these plaudits by behaving as elitists. Sometimes they went too far. I was asked by the Prime Minister and the Minister of Defence to report on the alleged sexual indiscretions of no less than three Commanders. I indicated that this should not have concerned me in my official capacity. Their behaviour did not appear to prejudice the security of the state, and I pointed out that illicit liaisons had not harmed the reputation of Horatio Nelson or Napoleon Bonaparte; but the Minister of Defence persisted. He dismissed my argument by saying that past heroes had behaved as gentlemen of their day, but our Commanders were becoming the subject of gossip which affected that precious commodity – morale. I had no answer, save to suggest that he sack a particular general, but this he did not wish to do unless I could arrange an exposure, which I was not prepared to do – hence stalemate.

Meanwhile, the clamour for 'Special Operations' beyond our borders grew. By the middle of the year it had reached a crescendo (Diary, 25 June):

PM and Ministers Hawkins, Partridge and Hilary Squires met with OCC and our Combined Op (six officials in all, to four politicians, with Gaylard to some extent holding the ring). Peter Walls outlined the Military/Security situation accurately and with great skill – that we were not winning – not even containing the threat ... that there were external operations that we might have been prepared to recommend, but these were politically unacceptable.

In no space of time at all our discussion led Partridge (as Acting Minister of Defence, mind you!) to say that the only thing to do was to start a conflagration and strike hard and deep into Zambia. Hawkins, new Minister of COMOPS, nodded his head vigorously in agreement. PM then invited the Service Chiefs to say whether this was practicable, when quickly it was explained that we could only sustain an attack on Zambia for two or three days – and at the expense of our widespread internal operations.

Gaylard then sounded a solemn note of warning (which should have been well enough known to all our politicians) that the South Africans had told us that the United States would apply sanctions – and worse – to them if they did not immediately cut off oil and other supplies to Rhodesia if we were extending our war into neighbouring territories. But still the discussion went on, with the PM doing nothing to bring his Ministers to order....

It was a CIO responsibility to assess the inherent risks in all external operations. Sometimes we had held out in OCC (and later COMOPS) against the sort of retaliation being demanded by Partridge and subsequently pursued even more persistently by Sutton-Pryce and others. Eventually, however, the pressure on the Commanders to extend the war externally – political pressure and pressure from their subordinate officers – became overwhelming. Nevertheless, while approving in principle that external operations would be pursued, CIO and the Commanders continued to stress that the only measure that held out any prospect of survival for Rhodesia was a political settlement. The 'Military and Police Implications' of CIO's Quarterly Threat paper for the period 1 April-30 June 1977 included the following conclusions:[7]

a. A concerted national effort must be made to contain the intensified terrorist effort and halt recruiting.
b. The necessity to increase all force levels with immediate effect is of greater importance than ever before.... Urgent consideration should be given to ways and means of utilising African manpower.
c. External operations should be pursued in order to counter the terrorists' ability to escalate the war on all fronts. In carrying out these operations it must be accepted that opposition within applicable neighbouring countries will be more determined and may also include enemy air...
The overriding implication is that an early political settlement to the Rhodesia dispute is essential.

This paper was signed by Walls, Commander of the Army and Commander, Combined Operations; Air Marshal M. J. McLaren, Commander of the Air Force; P. D. W. R. Sherren, Commissioner of Police; and myself. It was then discussed at the War Council meeting on 21 April, the Prime Minister summing up his reaction to the paper thus:[8]

In commenting generally on the matters raised ... the Prime Minister informed Council that Government recognised that the obvious answer to the problems being voiced was a political settlement. No effort was being spared by the Government to bring about a settlement in the interests of the country. At the same time it was essential that Rhodesia remained as strong and economically viable as possible, so that a satisfactory settlement could be reached. It was absolutely necessary that both the security and economic efforts must be maintained and that a balance be struck between the needs of both sectors. Within these parameters and until a settlement was achieved, the best use must be made of the country's manpower resources.

The concern about manpower levels and the need for a political solution appeared again in the conclusions of the subsequent 'Implications' paper dated 25 July, signed by Walls, as Commander, Combined Operations; Lieutenant General J. S. V. Hickman, Commander of the Army; Air Marshal F. W. Mussell, Commander of the Air Force; Sherren, Commissioner of Police; and myself: *

Of overriding concern is the present inadequate and diminishing force level with the resultant urgent need for additional manpower to even contain the situation, let alone prevent its inevitable deterioration.

No successful result can be attained by purely military means. It is now more vital than ever to arrive at an early political settlement before the point of no return beyond which it will be impossible to achieve any viable political or military/political solution.

The paper was discussed at the War Council meeting of 3 August, the first to be held for three months. The reason for the gap was that Smith, who was beginning to pave the way for 'Internal Settlement' talks by bringing Africans into the top ranks of government, did not want to draw attention to the all-white composition of the vital War Council. Far from being critical, most of us in OCC were only too relieved that Smith appeared to be moving towards some sort of settlement – or so we thought until the 3 August meeting:[9]

In discussion attention was drawn to paragraph 13 of the ('Implications') memorandum where reference had been made to a 'political settlement'. It was suggested that the unqualified use of this phrase could mean that sight was lost of the different problems and aspects of the current situation for which remedies needed to be found. If the phrase were to be more precisely defined and the alternatives flowing from the different types of settlement were to be detailed, this would make it more clear what sort of action would be necessary in each event and consequently would clarify what steps should be taken at this stage in the security situation. However, it was suggested that, whilst OCC had taken the view that any political settlement must be both responsible and acceptable, it (War Council) did not consider that it (OCC) should intrude upon what was essentially a political matter.

In the margin of the minutes I wrote: 'It is not a question of "responsible and acceptable" settlement – but the best settlement offering – or no settlement at all, with the disastrous consequences that we have tried to

* Military and Police Implications of the Quarterly Threat: 1 July 1977 to 30 September 1977, 25.7.77; reproduced in the Appendix.

spell out.' What the politicians were attempting to do was to stifle O C C, particularly myself, and keep us in our 'proper place'.

This marked the end of attempts by O C C to persuade the government to settle. Outside the O C C (and subsequently, C O M O P S) forum, however, the Commanders were developing a tendency to air their views on public platforms. On 6 July, in an article entitled 'While Rhodesia Bleeds...' in the *Daily Telegraph*, two Rhodesian generals were quoted:

As General John Hickman, Rhodesian Army Commander, said at the weekend, the most important battle the guerrillas could win would be the destruction of national morale.

General Hickman, one of a new breed of increasingly vociferous military commanders, warned the politicians that while morale of troops in the field was very high, when they returned home they were given a different picture....

Today, General Peter Walls, Commander of Combined Operations, and another of the military school which feels increasingly obliged to speak out, says the whole of Rhodesia must be regarded as an operational area.

I sent this article to the Prime Minister to warn him of the publicity being accorded our military Commanders and of the trend towards militarism that could change the nature of government in Rhodesia. With tongue in cheek I also sent a copy to Walls and Hickman, with the comment: 'Knowing Christopher Munnion and the general editorial policy of the *Daily Telegraph*, we can say that the article is meant to be helpful even if it draws certain unhelpful conclusions – not least, that we are bleeding to death.'

The article also contained a reference to the 'right-wing rebellion' in the R F. The rightest of the right-wing rebels was Reg Cowper, who resigned as Minister of Defence, followed by Ted Sutton-Pryce, who left the R F to join the extreme right Rhodesia Action Party. Both men propounded a total strategy for war, something beyond 'martial law' or 'martial licence' and more suited to the ideas of a military command in South Africa than to the concept of 'counter-insurgency' in Rhodesia. Some time after their departure from the R F I wrote in my diary:

M R relayed a story that I know only too well to be true, having listened to Reg Cowper giving his version of why he had to resign as Minister of Defence, including a diatribe against Ian Smith, the liar, the near-communist; and how the rest of Rhodesia has been misled that South Africa would not readily come to Rhodesia's aid under virtually any circumstances. The story now goes that Ian Smith was, in fact, misled by Ken Flower, and Ken Flower, a fellow-traveller, runs the country! (Perhaps Ian Smith is listening to me?) The same evening, after hearing M R's account, we dined at 'La Fontaine' at the table next to the Sutton-Pryces, senior and junior, with the atmosphere frigid between us, and I couldn't help thinking how welcome S-P's advice would be to his new

masters, the South African Military, now that Hendrik van den Bergh has gone
– Ken Flower misleading Ian Smith over South Africa; Ian Smith lying to save
his skin; Ken Flower and Ian Smith running the country – to damnation!

The split among the whites into pro- and anti-settlement groups had
been accompanied by the emergence of black groupings in favour of
alliance with the whites and opposed to the PF. For some months Hickman and Walls had been approached by what we called 'friendly
nationalists' in the country, and from time to time the generals would
seek my advice as to how far they should become involved in such
matters (Diary, 17 July):

John Hickman has just come to see me, late at night, seeking advice on what to
do in response to approaches from the Nationalists. Peter Walls is more heavily
involved: all of which is symptomatic of the desperately uncertain time in which
we live because Government won't give a steer as to where we're supposed to be
going. Or, to be brutally frank: they're determined to hang on to power at any
cost.

In the light of this development, CIO looked unfavourably upon the
proposals then being put forward by John Graham of the British Foreign
Office and Stephen Low, America's Special Representative on Rhodesia,
who were trying to keep the Anglo-American initiative alive, for within
the proposals was the suggestion that in the transition to majority rule
government the 'Security Chiefs' should be replaced. This could only be
regarded by our Commanders as surrender, something that was absolutely unacceptable at that stage of the war.

Meanwhile, the Commanders had been left in no doubt that although
the government appeared to be indecisive about which political direction it was going in, it was determined to intensify the war. The newly
appointed Minister of COMOPS, Roger Hawkins, said: 'Until now it has
been accepted as basically a police operation with military support
against criminals. Now it is to be a military operation, mainly by the
army, with police support.'

The intensification of the war during 1977, with a growing tendency on
both sides to indulge in indiscriminate shooting and the consequent
disproportionate increase in civilian casualties, was brought to a head
within days of Lord Carver's 'dismissal' by Ian Smith. On 23 December
COMOPS launched 'Operation Dingo', the biggest raid yet into Mozambique.

The targets were two ZANLA camps at Chimoio and Tembue, holding
bases for recruits on their way north for training and launching pads for
trained guerrillas re-entering Rhodesia. Chimoio, 60 miles inside

Mozambique and thus twice as far from the Rhodesia border as the site at Nyadzonia/Pungwe attacked in 1976 by Selous Scouts, covered an area of about five square miles and was well protected by anti-aircraft positions, personnel trenches and bunkers; in addition, there was a fortified FRELIMO base with Russian T 54 tanks situated nearby to assist in the defence of the camp. Tembue, at 140 miles from the Rhodesian border, posed even greater problems. It would have been asking the impossible for a sufficiently powerful force to get into either camp undetected, as in the case of Nyadzonia/Pungwe, had not our Intelligence been good and the preparations well laid. To maintain the element of surprise over considerable distances and to ensure safe evacuation, refuelling and administrative bases had to be prepared within Mozambique, one for 'Zulu 1' (Chimoio) and two for 'Zulu 2' (Tembue). CIO was in a position to offer invaluable help through elements of the MNR who had been our 'eyes and ears' in these areas for more than five years and could assist the officers of Special Branch and Military Intelligence employed on these operations. In one way or another, the gathering of Intelligence for 'Operation Dingo' had been in train for almost a year.

In military parlance, the plan for 'Operation Dingo' was one of vertical envelopment by parachutists. An added element was that a jet plane would fly low over the camps ten to fifteen minutes before the first strike, giving time for the enemy to dash to their trenches and then return to the parade ground in disorder, believing that they had been subjected to a false alarm, perhaps caused by a stray aircraft; subsequent aircraft movement would therefore be regarded as false, and they would not run for cover a second time. The air-armada comprised 42 helicopters, 8 Hunters, 6 Vampires, 3 Canberras, 6 Dakotas and 12 Lynx – a formidable effort for Rhodesia to sustain late in the war. The attack on Chimoio was started by Canberras bombing; then the Hunters and Vampires struck with rockets, followed by the Dakotas flying at 400 feet to offload the parachutists who formed stop-lines on three sides of the camp. This took two minutes. Within five minutes every aircraft over the target area had been hit, including the command helicopter, but not fatally. One hundred SAS and 50 RLI formed the stops, followed by 40 heli-borne troops of the RLI. The fourth side of the camp was boxed in by fire from K-cars ('Kill cars': Alouette helicopters with 20 mm cannons and a well-armed complement of soldiers). Chimoio was obliterated, and within twenty-four hours the attack on Tembue began. Tembue posed greater problems because of time and distance. One forward base was established on a mountain top and another on an island in Lake Cabora Bassa; the element of surprise was maintained and Tembue was also destroyed.

'Operation Dingo' was a brilliantly executed joint Security Force operation. Vast quantities of arms and ammunition were destroyed and it took Special Branch several months to absorb documentary and other Intelligence recovered. More than 2000 ZANLA guerrillas were killed and at least twice that number were incapacitated through wounds or desertion. The Rhodesian forces lost one soldier and one airman, and eight men were wounded. David Owen described the raid as a 'savage and pretty brutal attack' but added that that 'it might show the PF that the Rhodesian Defence Force is not on its back'. Understandably, Muzorewa reacted badly to the news of the raid and he complained bitterly to me that many of his kinsmen from the Eastern Districts had been killed in the two camps. He publicly announced his intention of breaking off negotiations with Smith and sought sanctuary in his rural parish, making it extremely difficult for us to get him back into the world of politics.

The political scene was changing, if only by fits and starts. Smith continued his search for an internal settlement but his vacillation over his commitment to any African nationalists, even the relatively compliant Sithole and Muzorewa, put everyone in a quandary: whether to support the Anglo-American initiative, Smith's initiative or indeed any initiative at all. By December 1977 the involvement of the generals in the political to-ing and fro-ing had leaked out. An article headed 'Rhodesia: Furtive support for the internal option?' appeared in the 16 December issue of *Africa Confidential*; it mentioned that 'there had been successful unofficial contacts between senior Muzorewa aides and senior Rhodesian army officers'. I sent copies of the magazine to Walls, Hickman and the Secretary to the Prime Minister, with a covering letter which contained a veiled warning that either British Intelligence was aware of the generals' involvement or that someone had been talking.

Much as the members of the Rhodesian government would have preferred things to stand still, the deterioration of the security situation was now pushing them towards settlement. In my brief to Cabinet on 17 January 1978 I outlined the position:

The overall picture is sombre. Our Half-Yearly Threat Assessment, just completed, confirms the steadily deteriorating internal security situation, as forecast, and holds out little prospect of improvement other than through the achievement of a political settlement. Time is no longer on our side. Like never before, it is vital to our interests to secure effective African allies against the Patriotic Front before they become disinterested or are swamped by numbers and the overall spread of terrorism throughout the country. . . . The main focus of internal African nationalism has been the settlement talks. The leaders of each Nationalist delegation have expressed optimism and have stated that they do not wish the talks to break off unless this is unavoidable. There is a growing belief amongst the great majority of White Rhodesians that an early settlement must be achieved. . . . There are grave dangers in the internal Nationalist leaders leaving Rhodesia at this crucial period of time. Once outside the country, they fall prey to suggestion and coercion. It would appear that neither Britain nor America expected that the internal talks would last as long or achieve as much as they have. It is essential, therefore, that an agreement be reached as quickly as possible to pre-empt action by external forces to disrupt the present initiative.

I was guilty of over-simplification in trying to get the message across to Cabinet, but the point was made: we had to secure effective African allies against the PF before it was too late. Sithole and Muzorewa were trying to keep their options open with Nkomo and Mugabe; even when it was against their own interests they remained insistent that the PF had to be invited in to join the internal settlement or compete in the elections that would follow it. The trouble was that Mugabe saw better prospects for his movement in fighting it out, and Nkomo, who might have been prepared to double-cross Mugabe, was afraid to commit himself to the internal settlement. By 22 February I was able to write in my diary:

> We have now reached agreement in principle on six out of the eight main points at issue, with a real prospect of achieving internal settlement.
>   Sure, the Patriotic Front under Nkomo and Mugabe are remaining aloof, or hostile, but there are emerging prospects of perhaps doing a deal with Josh (Nkomo) and persuading him to return and participate in the transitional arrangements. Sure, the Anglo-Americans are hanging on to their proposals, but the Conservative Party in England are showing signs of trying to force acceptance of what we are doing in Rhodesia, and our circle of foreign friends is widening. I made six trips to Europe last year and have progressed our liaisons, particularly with the British and French. I visited King Hassan of Morocco and was well received. The day after tomorrow I am off to break the ice with the Shah of Iran. . . .

The reaction abroad to progress in the talks between Smith, Muzorewa, Sithole and Chirau had been cautious but encouraging. The *Daily Telegraph*, in a feature article on 10 February, said: 'The chances in Salisbury are fragile, but not, as they seemed six months ago, forlorn. . . . What is desperately needed is a signal from the United Kingdom that some at least have faith in these endeavours, wish them well and will try to see them through.' An editorial in *The Times* on 16 February concluded with: 'Everything that successive British negotiations, and Dr Kissinger's intervention, sought to obtain, appears broadly within grasp . . . if the essentials of majority rule, reconciliation and an end to race discrimination are there, then whoever may demur, it must not be Britain.'

Agreement was finally reached on all the points at issue and on 3 March Smith, Muzorewa, Sithole and Chirau signed what the government described as a 'Document That Will Change a Nation'. The preamble to the official publication of the details of the document said agreement had been reached because 'the present constitutional situation in Rhodesia has led to the imposition of economic and other sanctions by the international community against Rhodesia and to armed conflict within Rhodesia and from neighbouring countries', making it necessary for an agreement that would 'lead to the termination of such sanctions and the cessation of the armed conflict'. Among the provisions of the agreement was a new Constitution that would ensure majority rule on the basis of universal adult suffrage; a justiciable Declaration of Rights to protect the essential freedom of individuals and provide for protection of property; and an independent judiciary. There was also provision for Executive and Ministerial Councils to control a Transitional Government until free elections could be held.

An editorial in the *Argus*, a Johannesburg-based newspaper, summed up the hopes and doubts surrounding the agreement thus: 'The agreement in Salisbury has been greeted with a mixture of suspicion, scepticism, and ire in Britain and the United States, but it has not been rejected out of hand ... it would be tragic if Britain and America wavered in seizing the opportunity to endorse the exciting progress made by Black and White Rhodesians, working together in a meaningful way for probably the first time in Rhodesia's history.'

CHAPTER 11

Zimbabwe-Rhodesia

The immediate objective of the Transitional Government established by the 3 March Agreement was to seek international support. Ian Smith argued that his new deal was almost identical to the Kissinger package which had been supported by Britain and the United States. His black colleagues claimed that they were party to an agreement which would achieve majority rule in the shortest possible time – by 31 December 1978 – and in the months that followed Muzorewa frequently exhorted those around him to abide by the Agreement while Sithole took to quoting liberally from his book *A Power Promise*, showing faith where others lacked it.

The objections raised outside the country – that whites would be left in control of the Administration, the Security Forces and the economy during the transitional period – were no more valid than they had been at the time of the Kissinger deal. David Owen said the most serious omission from the agreement was the lack of any arrangement for a cease-fire, but no cease-fire had been guaranteed in any earlier agreement. Owen was determined to preserve American participation and the team of Graham and Low intensified its efforts, trying to narrow the gap between the internally based Africans and the PF.

The PF had not been excluded from the agreement – they had excluded themselves – and the gap between Nkomo/Mugabe and Muzorewa/Sithole was widened by Britain's deliberate exclusion of Muzorewa and Sithole from the talks in Malta arranged by Owen in January 1978. At these talks Owen tried to reconcile PF objections to the Anglo-American proposals and, hopefully, achieve a cease-fire. Mugabe and Nkomo attended, Owen was supported by Carver and Chand, with Young and Moose, the American Assistant Secretary of State for African Affairs. The PF accepted a United Nations role during the interim period, and the formation of a Governing Council of ten formed by two representatives from each of the five delegations who had attended the Geneva talks.

By the end of March 1978 Young had met Nkomo and Mugabe in the company of the Front Line Presidents in Dar-es-Salaam. Nyerere advised Young that the remaining differences between the various Rhodesian parties were of no great consequence and should be rapidly resolved. Young returned to Washington with this advice and persuaded Carter to pursue the American initiative with all vigour. In mid-April 1978 the high-powered team of Owen, Vance, Carver and Young visited Africa. They went first to Dar-es-Salaam for what became known as 'Malta Two', but in spite of Nyerere's assurances that the Front Line Presidents had persuaded the PF to accept the fundamental elements of the Anglo-American proposals, they found themselves listening to the same old tune – the PF were demanding a complete re-negotiation of the proposals. It was not surprising, therefore, that the team found on arrival in Salisbury that all four members of the Executive Council were more determined than ever to adhere to the 3 March Agreement.

Vance and Young were at odds with each other over their interpretation of the meeting with the PF leaders, just as they differed in their attitude towards Russian involvement in Africa. After Vance had held talks with Brezhnev in Moscow on Russian intentions in Africa, he had said in London that Havana and Moscow were 'unwilling to recognise that African countries wished to resolve their problems without outside intervention'. Young, however, said that 'the Cubans are a stabilising influence in Angola' and added that 'efforts should be made to include Russia in Southern African peace efforts to prevent them from obstructing Western-led settlement initiatives.'

Young's tendency to shoot from the hip meant that he often misfired, but there were occasions when he came nearer to the truth than most others, as I observed during the Owen/Vance discussions in Salisbury. In a letter to a member of the American Conservative Group, I wrote:[1]

(When) Bishop Muzorewa and others asked for some explanation as to how (Vance and Young) assessed Mugabe's position, Andy Young was absolutely honest and forthright in saying 'he is fighting for personal power.'
    Two other things that Andy Young indicated:
(i) American policy in Africa is based more on commercial interests than on human rights or democratic principles – you could grow to like that guy, for he's reasonably honest!
(ii) He had expected the Front Line Presidents (particularly Nyerere) to exert a helpful influence on Nkomo and Mugabe – the very thing that the more experienced Kissinger warned us we could never expect to happen!
    With this – and much else – in mind, you must not blame us if we remain totally mystified as to America's policy on Rhodesia!

In the British Parliament the Conservatives were more encouraging than before. On 26 April the Parliamentary Report in *The Times* included statements by Lord Carrington, then Leader of the Opposition peers, and Lord Home:

(Carrington) It must be said that there (has) been inadequate recognition of the remarkable achievement of the internal settlement and too much support for its opponents.... If in the end the Patriotic Front (refuses) to be associated with a settlement which (is) in accordance with the conditions laid down by both Conservative and Labour governments, if these two leaders (insist) upon force as the only means of settling the issue, there (is) only one honourable course for the British Government to take and that (is) to support the internal settlement however difficult that might be.

(Home) In Rhodesia they (are) faced with a new prospect by Mr Smith's action which (has) dramatically reversed previous attitudes to African majority rule. Why (are) there hesitations and doubts?... Dr Owen and Mr Young (want) to bring Mr Nkomo into the settlement because that (is) the way most likely to end the war ... in their view Salisbury should make the concessions to Mr Nkomo and his army, and concessions to force and communism.... The United Nations put the responsibility for the future of Rhodesia on the British Parliament. It (is) therefore Parliament's responsibility and no one else's, and Russia should be told plainly that Britain (will) not tolerate intervention in a country for whose future the responsibility (lies) with her.

I wondered whether Smith appreciated the irony of the situation now facing him. He had got away with UDI because of a British Labour government's refusal to use force; now another Labour government's acquiescence in the use of force seemed to be determining the future of Rhodesia. Wilson may have been wrong to refuse to use force in 1965 but when he said that the effect of UDI would be to internationalise the Rhodesian issue, events were to prove him right, largely because of Russia's support for Nkomo. Kissinger's interest in Rhodesia arose from America's desire to prevent Soviet expansionism in Africa. Carter's approach was fundamentally different from Kissinger's in that it stemmed from considerations that had little to do with the actual situation inside Rhodesia. By aligning himself with African rulers outside Rhodesia and taking a stand on human rights against 'white racists', he hoped to attract the negro vote in the United States. Accordingly, Young had to oppose the internal settlement and support the PF regardless of the merits of any settlement.

From all appearances, Rhodesia had landed in the middle of a Black Power struggle and it was important to do whatever was necessary to keep the Americans on side. We talked to Carter's representatives and we talked to a group of American 'conservatives' who visited Rhodesia at this time. I submitted a report illustrating the considerable misunderstandings between the Americans and ourselves on the way things were going in Rhodesia:[2]

I saw Mr Stephen Low, American Ambassador to Zambia (and America's Special representative on Rhodesia) ... (who) agreed – but without committing himself – that American policy was based on beliefs outlined in paragraph 1 of my aide memoire but he put the emphasis on 1(a) – that the interim government could not stop the war – and added, forcefully, that they also believed we would not be able to hold elections in internationally acceptable conditions.... Mr Low gave it as his assessment that Nkomo still commands enough political power – let alone military power – to make nonsense out of elections which do not include him.... We talked about the prospects of Nkomo's return to the political scene in Rhodesia and I made it clear that the Patriotic Front, as such (including Mugabe) would be utterly unacceptable. Mr Low retorted that he believed quite frankly that we had been wrong about this throughout (he had previously indicated that the alternative to an internal settlement – a hand-over to a Patriotic Front government which would create a Marxist regime – was acceptable to the Americans in the belief that the 'New Zimbabwe', although Marxist orientated, would be forced for reasons of economics to accept American aid and would be 'no more Marxist than Mozambique').... I offered some adverse comment concerning British proposals for the interim period – particularly Lord Carver's part in it as being virtually 'authority without responsibility', but he said quite sharply that the Americans did not see it that way. They believed we needed British political surveillance and that it was better to have a 'politically sensitive General' for, even if he was a General-without-teeth, at least he was highly intelligent and would know what to do to the overall advantage of Rhodesia.... He said, with conviction, that they would now sign the Patriotic Front into the Anglo-American proposals and hang on in the hope that we would still have to fall back on them.

Stephen Low and I disagreed about many issues but we understood each other and I appreciated his frankness. The fact that we had common interests may have contributed to the mutual understanding. Whenever he visited Salisbury he borrowed a 'cello from the College of Music and played in his hotel room, which appealed to me as one who had played the violin alone in the Somali wastes.

To gain international recognition the Transitional Government had to stop the war. The attempt to do this comprised a number of elements, in particular the amnesty and 'safe return' policies aimed at guerrillas operating within Rhodesia or in neighbouring Zambia and Mozambique. To this end, Sithole submitted a well-reasoned case to the Executive Council to lift the ban on ZANU, stating that since the first banning of ZANU and ZAPU in 1964, they had remained 'very much alive in the minds and consciousness of the African people who belong to these organisations' and that lifting of the ban 'would bring about a reconciliatory attitude among the ZANLA forces and thus facilitate their co-operation in the matter of the cease-fire' and 'undermine the very basis of the Patriotic Front'.[3]

A few days later CIO's recommendations in favour of lifting the ban were submitted to the Executive Council.[4] The paper opened with the observation that two parties then operating openly in Rhodesia, ANC(Z) and the People's Movement, were in fact ZAPU and the Mugabe faction of ZANU respectively, and lifting the ban would simply turn *de facto* recognition into *de jure* recognition. It might also enhance Rhodesia's international image, improve the prospects of making the safe return policy effective and sow some dissension in guerrilla ranks, and it was suggested that these advantages outweighed such considerations as the effect upon white morale of a lifting of the ban.

But these efforts were to no avail. Muzorewa, Smith and Chirau were not impressed by Sithole's argument and made no comment on CIO's views. I remember saying to my staff at the time that the pattern of nationalist politics was so well established inside and outside the country that it would not be changed by the cosmetic action of lifting bans; I recalled making the same point during a confrontation I had had in June 1977 with Squires when, in response to his demand that ZAPU be re-banned, I had replied that the banning or un-banning of nationalist parties for political reasons had never worked in practice.

Despite such differences of opinion, however, CIO's relationship with the new leaders in the Executive Council seemed to be improving (Diary, 9 and 19 April):

9th April: Things are beginning to move more positively, though much of it from Ian Smith's side is the mixture as before with prevarication the order of the day and general uncertainty as to where we are going – if we are going anywhere! The Brits and the Americans are back in the game and we are due to have top-level talks including Vance and Owen next week – forced on them because of their attempts to get the Patriotic Front in on the act.

19th April: The British and American Foreign Secretaries, Owen and Vance, have come and gone, accompanied by 'big mouth' Andy Young, Lord Carver, et al; but with no real movement towards a re-negotiation. But strangely, the Internal Settlement may be beginning to work.

Our National JOC – egged on by myself – presented themselves to the Executive Council yesterday, and again today, to try and impress upon them the urgency of movement towards achieving a cease-fire. For, it will be the acid test of the willingness and effectiveness of the new Transitional Government whether or not they can bring the war to an end.

In session with the Executive Council one was soon impressed with the genuineness of Bishop Muzorewa, the facility of the Reverend Sithole, and the overall spirit pervading the four of them; with no indication that Ian Smith was any longer directing – not even taking a lead, except when patently required of him. And with Chief Chirau completing a quorum that may definitely be destined to achieve the near-impossible – Settlement in Rhodesia. . . . Sure, there are already signs of developing inter-faction strife – or worse – but the spirit of co-operation displayed at the top is impressive, as is the apparent intention to shape a genuinely non-racial State.

Exhilirating as it was to sense the 'new spirit of co-operation' among the Transitional Government leaders, this spirit was not matched by their experience and drive and I soon found myself hammering away at them on issues CIO considered of vital importance, as illustrated by my notes for a brief to the Executive Council in mid-April:[5]

Britain, America – and most of the world – believe we cannot secure a cease-fire – and because of this the Internal Settlement will fail.... They even doubt we can de-escalate the war sufficiently to be able to hold elections.... Nkomo, Mugabe, currently committed to continuing – even intensifying – the war (and) refusing to join the Internal Settlement because they believe they will win anyway before the end of this year. If they are interested in you (Muzorewa and Sithole) at all they believe you might join them – not the other way around – or you will be eliminated.... Everything points to the fact that our very survival depends on stopping the war – and stopping it quickly.... We officials need authority from Executive Council so that the Working Party (on cease-fire) can get moving with COMOPS now. We need direction from the top. You, as leaders, should be tied in to the 'cease-fire' as an essential part of the Internal Settlement.

The need for cohesion in action was the subject of a subsequent address given jointly by myself and the Commissioner of Police to the Executive Council, for we were now becoming increasingly concerned about the development of factionalism and the potential threat of lawlessness posed by inter-faction fighting.[6] Towards the end of the address we reminded our listeners of Nkomo's forecast that the Shona-speaking members of the Executive Council would end up fighting each other, and we warned that if the scene continued to be marred by political in-fighting Nkomo would be proved right.

The first personal test that Bishop Muzorewa had to face was that posed by his UANC colleague, Byron Hove, Co-Minister for Justice and Law and Order in the Transitional Government. Hove had made a number of statements which, according to Police Headquarters, were affecting Police morale. Some of his statements were relatively mild: 'We must bring in a situation where the laws reflect the broad interests of all the people in this country.... I am aware that in this country the Police Force has been used as an instrument to enforce the Rhodesian Front Laws which it has done enthusiastically. This has got to stop.' But others outraged white Rhodesians: 'The white community and all law enforcement agencies need to adjust to a new situation. Blacks do not need to because they have always wanted fairness and justice.'

Everyone waited to see how the Transitional Government would handle the situation. Hove could not have had a more incompatible counterpart as white Co-Minister than Squires who, at the Geneva Conference, had been incensed by the mere thought of 'co-ministering', let alone majority rule. Like most whites, Squires had not accepted the reality of the changes inherent in the Internal Settlement.

Before the Executive Council had had time to react to the Commissioner's complaint, Hove spoke out again, this time against the slow progress of Africanisation in the government, and warned that unless blacks were given evidence of real reforms the internal settlement would fail: 'To win over the black people, we have to be seen to be making changes. We can't just sing the praises of the settlement. We have to do something.' He also said it would not be possible to hold free elections under the existing laws. The Executive Council asked Hove to withdraw his remarks, which he refused to do. Muzorewa was present when the matter was first discussed in the Executive Council and it was apparent that the other three members' desire to discipline Hove was not necessarily for the sake of unity but rather to disadvantage Muzorewa. The Bishop agreed to discipline Hove, who was then issued with an ultimatum threatening dismissal unless he retracted his statements (Muzorewa later denied that he had agreed to Hove's dismissal).

At this point the Special Branch officer who was CIO's permanent representative in COMOPS submitted an urgent request for me to get the Executive Council to reconsider the matter:[7]

There is increasing awareness amongst the Central Executive of the UANC that the removal of Minister Hove from the position of Co-Minister of Law and Order might place the entire settlement issue in jeopardy ... they point out that to continue on a course of removal of him from office would cause a split within the ranks of the UANC.... It has become apparent that the terrorists in the field like what Hove has been saying, and to remove him from office at this time will show the entire (settlement) exercise to be a sham because although on the one hand the Europeans sign an agreement to hand over to majority rule, any African who speaks out against the Europeans is automatically dismissed, indicating that the members of the Executive Council have been 'bought' and are 'lackeys' of the whites.

I was also advised by Special Branch Headquarters that Hove appeared to be the only Minister in the Transitional Government who might be able to make the cease-fire effective. But before I could make any representations to the members of the Executive Council they had gone their separate ways for the weekend, while Hove had accepted dismissal and flown to London. It was some time before I had the opportunity to raise the matter with Muzorewa who had taken refuge in his rural retreat. In discussing Hove's dismissal, it became clear that he had realised too late what damage the action would do to his party and to himself. He said he would demand Hove's reinstatement but that he had little hope of success unless he threatened to pull out of the Transitional Government, which he was not prepared to do. We also discussed what needed to be done to make the Internal Settlement more effective (Diary):

Sunday 7th May: 'Settlement' – maybe! The latest debate in the House of Commons has not advanced the situation. The Conservatives, still pushing for recognition of the Internal Settlement, or the uplifting of sanctions. But Dr Owen and Government not budging, except to produce a promise that recognition and the uplift of sanctions will come as soon as the Internal Settlement is seen to be acceptable to the people of Rhodesia as a whole – the famous Fifth Principle.

Meanwhile the Bishop's UANC is rent by demands and counter-demands (much of it stimulated by the unfortunate affair of Hove's dismissal) and the Bishop sits less serenely in charge with every day that passes.... I have been to see the Bishop twice at his home, trying to help him and move the cease-fire along, but only to become even more frustrated; for good guy as the Bishop is he lacks most of the qualities of leadership, and his political acumen is virtually non-existent.

The Bishop had failed his first test. He had failed his colleague and the chances of his recovering his position within the UANC, let alone in the country at large, seemed slim. Nevertheless, I believed that he was the best hope for peaceful transition and that he had to be helped as far as humanly possible.

In COMOPS we were now concentrating every effort on the cease-fire, although it was apparent by this time that no one in the Executive Council could help very much. From the outset Chirau had disassociated himself from the operation and laid no claim to any guerrillas in the field. Sithole's oratory was as impressive but as empty as ever. On 5 May his Publicity Secretary, Joseph Masangomai, announced that peace would come to Rhodesia within three or four months, adding: 'We say this because we are fully acquainted with the guerrillas on the settlement agreement.... When our President participated in the decision to call for a cease-fire, he knew what he was doing and talking about.' David Mukome, the UANC's Publicity Secretary, cast doubts on Sithole's claims and said enough to indicate that the UANC had little control over guerrillas in the field. The minutes of the 13th meeting of Executive Council, held on 2 May, just two months after the 3 March Agreement, reflect something of the lack of control over any guerrillas by the Executive Council members:

The Director-General, CIO, reported that it was vital that regular progress reports on the cease-fire be submitted to the Executive Council. On 16th April Council had approved a plan submitted by the Working Party for handling the guerrillas. It had been thought that the plan would be well received and no major difficulties had been anticipated. However, many claims regarding the support of the guerrillas had been false and the freezing of certain areas in March had not been very effective ... the chances of implementing the plan would be remote unless guerrillas could be reassured that the settlement was genuine. Some guerrillas had indicated that they would only lay down their arms once a majority rule government had been installed and in many areas guerrilla commanders were encouraging their followers to dissociate themselves from the internal settlement. It had been noted that as soon as plans were put into effect to encourage guerrillas to return home, counter-measures had been taken to frustrate the exercise. Politically suspect guerrillas had been eliminated and others who were considered untrustworthy had been recalled to Mozambique. There was a stronger concentration of effort in the recruitment of private armies rather than in the conversion of guerrillas into law-abiding citizens, and it was essential that this practice be halted.

The recruitment of 'private armies' by Muzorewa and Sithole brought them into conflict with Smith and Chirau, but they had to embark on such a course if they were to have anything like the same chance as Nkomo and Mugabe in 'politicising' the people. And they were soon faced with the reality of conflict in this politicisation. Many of Muzorewa's followers were murdered in rural areas of Mashonaland. Four envoys sent into the Fort Victoria area to promote cease-fire were taken prisoner by ZANLA, labelled as 'sell-outs' and shot dead before a crowd specially assembled for the spectacle. Over forty of Sithole's supporters were gunned down in the company of unarmed envoys sent to the Wedza area. In an attempt to combat this CIO agreed to arrange the return of fifty of Sithole's guerrillas from their training grounds in Idi Amin's Uganda. Most of them proved too tough to handle and had to be eliminated by the Security Forces before they could do too much damage. These killings were chalked up by COMOPS as 'terrorist' deaths but they were prophylactic killings intended to save the lives of countless civilians who might otherwise have been subjected to the worst forms of 'politicisation'.

The increasing violence being perpetrated by all sides – accelerated by the emergence of many splinter groups, practised in banditry – gave the leaders of the Rhodesian Security Forces little satisfaction. Where loss of life offended, COMOPS was quick to condemn it. There was a night-time attack by Security Forces on a village in Gutu when guerrillas were due to address a captive audience. The Security Forces were obviously too quick on the draw. Of the seventy-four villagers killed or wounded, only

one was a guerrilla which, in the opinion of COMOPS, was pushing the
excuse of 'Killed in Cross-Fire' much too far.

The guerrillas' campaign of terror for the sake of terror was intensified. The most horrendous example of this was the raping and butcher-
ing of thirteen white missionaries and children at Elim Mission, near the
Mozambique border, on 23 June. It was a meaningless atrocity, as all
atrocities are; perhaps it was revenge for the wholesale killings of blacks
at Nyadzonya/Pungwe and Chomoio. Whatever the case, it was part of
the systematic terror which was used extensively against unco-operative
missionaries who provided the softest of targets in the remote areas of
Rhodesia.

The African nationalists had a decided advantage. They could destroy
schools and clinics, or kill teachers and abduct medical orderlies, without losing the support of the population because the actions of blacks
upon blacks could be made to appear as releasing the chains of colonialism, whilst anything done by the whites appeared as an extension of
colonialism. The guerrillas could even invite civilian casualties, knowing
that they would gain the psychological advantage if the Security Forces
killed civilians in their counter-action.

On the Rhodesian side, junior commanders could shelter under the
Government's 'Get Tough' policy or the stark necessity of punishing
villagers who were helping guerrillas, but no one could commend their
actions. The phrases, 'Killed in Crossfire' or 'Killed whilst Running with
Terrorists', in official communiqués had been used accurately to start
with, but as the violence mounted they became code-language for deaths
that should not have happened, and for this all of us who were in
positions of authority must take responsibility. No one was blameless.
Much of the responsibility for the killings lay with the Anglo-American
decision not to recognise the Transitional Government. This in turn
encouraged a solution through the use of force.

I got away whenever I could, garnering Intelligence, seeking international support and attempting to defeat sanctions (Diary):

Sunday 9th April 1978: A successful trip to see the Shah of Iran. Teheran,
Isfahan (that superb mosque!), Shiraz (the grandeur of Persepolis!) back to
Athens, Paris, London and home. Arrived in Teheran with trousers for three
suits but no jackets – hurried packing on my part! Fortunately, the Shah was
most understanding (shades of that tea-party in Jigjiga for Emperor Haile Selassie in 1942 when all I could offer were leaking cups). The Shah talked sense: no
oil sanction, no support for Nkomo, Ian Smith, or any particular leader at this
stage.

25th June 1978: Returned two days ago from four weeks of hectic travel. First of all, with Olga to Paris and London; then by myself to Cairo, Muscat, Khartoum, Morocco, Lisbon and London again, before returning to Salisbury with Olga. Not much change in Cairo – merely to confirm that they still have the best belly-dancers in the Arab world. Pleasant enough, but ineffectual as far as inter-service relationships are concerned, or any prospect of development until there is a change of regime in Rhodesia.

In Muscat the Omanis were their usual helpful selves (although theirs is self-interest through investment in Rhodesia). At least, they showed great interest in representing to the Chinese the need for them to swing their support from Mugabe to Sithole – and from the more harmful associations with communism to some sort of co-operation with the West. Broke new ground in Khartoum where General Niemeri should be prepared to handle awkward aspects of our case during his tenure of office as chairman of OAU.

Morocco: General Dlimi attentive and particularly helpful in pursuing the same line with the local Chinese Ambassador as we managed to establish in Muscat.

Back in London, and an interesting encounter with the Saudi Sheikh KA, arranged through the good offices of our French friends – all veering towards Nkomo's return into the act. In between, discussions with Brit colleagues and entertainment into the small hours. . . .

I seem to have done a lot, but how is anything likely to work unless Smithy & Co do something positive to break the log-jam now that it appears the Internal Settlement will not work because of the failure of the internally based Nationalist leaders to secure anything approaching a cease-fire?

On the one hand we talk with the French and the Moroccans about the type of 'African solution' they can support. We talk to the Omanis – and now the Saudis – about oil, and seek their support for the Internal Settlement but the Saudis say it must have American backing. We manoeuvre to get Nkomo back, but he cannot return in a privileged position within the terms of the Anglo-American proposals; nor even as part of the Internal Settlement. And so it goes on.

I arrived home to find Muzorewa struggling to make his presence felt in the government. He had submitted a paper to the Executive Council for the dismantling of 'Protected Villages' as a matter of urgency, but he weakened his case in the opening sentence: 'It seems to me to be imperative that we take an urgent decision to abolish the *principle* of Protected Villages.'[8] He italicised the word 'principle' himself, as if it were more important to abandon the principle than abolish the substance of Protected Villages. However, he did go on to say that the continued existence of Protected Villages militated against international recognition of the 3 March Agreement and provided the PF with useful propaganda.

The UANC was not impressed with the Bishop's efforts and produced a loosely worded appeal that he should pull out of the Transitional Government rather than suffer humiliation because 'your pleas for disbandment of the PVS have been rejected'. The UANC document was 'lifted' by Special Branch and, unsophisticated though it was, it contained some telling points:

The people are sceptical of the bona fides of the Interim Government and since the dismissal of Mr Hove have become positively antagonistic.

As far as the proceedings of the Executive Council go it is abundantly clear from what the President has said that the UANC finds itself in the minority on major issues ... the leadership of the UANC is being questioned on the buses – an infallible guide to popular African political feeling. The murmurings have been heard that the UANC is becoming a Smith political puppet.... At present Smith needs the UANC. The UANC does not need Smith.... The idea is spreading that the Interim Government is more concerned with European confidence than African progress.... The political assessment is whether the UANC will be stronger and with a better future in or out of the Interim Government.

I showed Smith the document. He dismissed it, knowing that the Bishop could no more make up his mind to leave the government than to stay put. In the event, it was easier for him to stay, hoping against hope that his position would strengthen despite the warnings of his party advisers. Although all of us in a position to help wanted to give the Bishop every chance to succeed, it was clear that if he did not make the grade we would have to try to get a stronger African leader to participate in the Internal Settlement and, to this end, I began working secretly on a plan to get Nkomo back in on the act.

Meanwhile, the Commanders and I continued to hammer away at the Executive Council. The main thrust of my brief to them on 21 July was that their lack of leadership was having a serious effect on national morale. A few weeks later the Commanders and I addressed a joint session of the Executive Council, the Ministerial Council and the National JOC:[9]

The scene is more than sombre. It's pretty desperate and needs desperate remedies.... So far we have failed – and none of us should be surprised if the rest of the world looks at it as failure ... there are fewer Ministers, White and Black, dedicated to your survival as a Government than there are undermining it by default.... Our professional assessment is that, individually and collectively, all four members of EXCO have lost support, and will continue to lose political support unless the trend is reversed; whereas the Patriotic Front, and particularly the Mugabe faction, has gained and is gaining support.... There is hardly anything on record indicating that any faction represented in the Executive Council has achieved anything effective against the Patriotic Front ... you have proved more effective in fighting amongst yourselves than in any way getting to grips with the common enemy – exactly what Nkomo forecast.... As things are now, it will be impossible to hold the sort of elections that will be recognised elsewhere – or if you can hold them, Mugabe's supporters may win.... The

security situation has never been so desperate.... Over 6000 terrorists within
Rhodesia with plus or minus 30,000 lined up against us, and their numbers
probably growing to about 40,000 before the end of the year – with more
support and sympathy internally and externally than they have ever had. Meantime, our White Security Forces diminish in numbers and effectiveness.

The record of Walls's address included the following:

Time was of the essence and unless something positive and effective was done by
Government within the next two or three weeks, then it was the view of the
Security Chiefs that some political solution other than that now being pursued
would have to be found.... He identified the major failure as being that of a
lack of success in the cease-fire.... The Commander also drew attention to the
conflicting and contradictory statements made by officials of nationalist parties
which did not accord with the decisions taken by their leaders in the course of
governing the country. He stressed that such statements tended to add to the air
of uncertainty and doubt prevailing in Rhodesia today. He stressed, however,
that contradictory statements were not necessarily the prerogative of black
politicians and officials and that the public was also confused by statements
made by white Ministers.

The minutes of the Executive Council meeting two weeks later recorded that:[10]

No real progress had been made (in the cease-fire position). There had been
innumerable contacts with members of guerrilla units, but their commanders
and those serving under them, together with large segments of the population in
the tribal areas, were adopting a neutral position until there was some form of
political motivation which would persuade them it was worthwhile to declare
their support for the Transitional Government. By contrast, hundreds, if not
thousands, of blacks were leaving the country as recruits for the Patriotic Front.

Muzorewa and Sithole reacted to this assessment by clutching at
straws. The Bishop said that 'a large number of people were returning to
Rhodesia from Mozambique.' CIO could not confirm these reports, nor
could we back his statement that 'there were substantial numbers of
Rhodesians in Mozambique who wanted to return' or Sithole's claim
that 'FRELIMO have decided to evacuate camps near the Rhodesian
border and have told the Rhodesians living in them that they must
return.' To cap it all, when speaking of the general situation, Sithole said
'the tide of events is flowing in favour of the Transitional Government
and there should be encouraging developments within the next fort-
night.' The meeting closed at this point, with officials glancing at each
other in disbelief. From my left came the comment: 'I don't know about
you but I'm finding it difficult to remember whether I'm Arthur or
Martha.' I suggested a drink or two might refresh my colleague's memory, so we retired to the COMOPS Mess.

Two days later I wrote in my diary that 'the best prospect (for a political solution) is to encourage the return of Nkomo, even if it means he must take over as boss-man.' Because I knew only too well how equivocal Smith could be on an issue such as this – prepared to do something, but not necessarily anything of consequence – my deputy and I continued with our secret trips to Zambia. 'Tiny' Rowland played his part in the proceedings once again, this time using an emissary, Brigadier Garba, former Foreign Minister of Nigeria, to arrange talks between us and Kaunda and Nkomo. Kaunda was keener than ever to promote a settlement in Rhodesia in order to rid himself of involvement with ZIPRA and halt Zambia's declining fortunes by officially re-opening her trade routes through Rhodesia. As for Nkomo, he could see by now that only he or Mugabe could stop the war; he paid no heed to Muzorewa's contention that because the Internal Settlement included a genuine prospect for majority rule there was no point in continuing the war. Being more interested in power than in majority rule, the decision he had to make was based on whether he could more easily obtain power for himself in partnership with Mugabe, or in coalition with Smith, or through the barrels of his guns.

In mid-August, Smith met Nkomo at a secret venue in Zambia. To our surprise they reached agreement on the next vital step to be taken – that Nkomo should take over the chairmanship of the Executive Council. It was left to Smith to explain to his black colleagues in Salisbury why Nkomo had to supplant them, while Kaunda was faced with the even more difficult task of explaining to Mugabe why a secret agreement had been reached behind his back. Neither my deputy nor I believed Mugabe would accept the deal or be prepared to subordinate himself to Nkomo in any internal settlement, but Kaunda and Nkomo appeared confident that he would. It also seemed likely to us that Nyerere and Machel would resent their exclusion from Kaunda's diplomacy and the exclusion of Mugabe from the deal. The reaction to the premature disclosure of the secret negotiations confirmed our beliefs. A fracture appeared in the PF that would never be healed. Nyerere avoided public censure of Kaunda but cursed him privately, and he castigated Smith, saying: 'He has destroyed the Bishop and Sithole. He's ready to dispose of them and now he's looking for others.'

While the negotiations were going on, Smith was indulging in another piece of deception – the banning of the *Zimbabwe Times* and the restriction of journalists – unknown to either the officials or his colleagues in the Executive Council. The Executive Council had sought the National JOC's views on the banning of the *Zimbabwe Times* and we had expressed the opinion that such a move was neither wise nor necessary. When Smith's stance became known things came to a head. I was prepared to chuck my hand in, realising the near impossibility of keeping the Executive Council on an even keel when there was such blatant deception between the members, with the added difficulty of conducting secret negotiations on behalf of one of the four against the interests of the other three. On 28 August I wrote in my diary:

> We had a vile session earlier in the day, with Ian Smith trying to lie his way out of the banning/proscription exercise he had initiated against the press, blaming it on others. C M told me of the state of play they had reached on the fringes of government, comparable to the situation in Germany when Hitler should have been overthrown but wasn't, to try and save thousands of lives; and of how people of his persuasion had been convinced for some time that Smith should go, to give impetus for new (white) leadership.

On 3 September an incident occurred which put an immediate end to the Nkomo/Smith negotiations. This 'stroke of fate', as Smith described it, forced all the players in the Rhodesian game on to a different course. An Air Rhodesia Viscount was shot down by Nkomo's ZIPRA guerrillas, using a Russian SAM–7 ground-to-air missile, shortly after take-off from Kariba to Salisbury. Eighteen out of the fifty-three people on board survived the crash; ten survivors, while still dazed and shocked, were massacred by ZIPRA guerrillas before rescuers could reach the scene of the crash. Nkomo compounded the crime when, in a BBC interview, he appeared to boast about the attack. Only twenty-four hours earlier white Rhodesians had welcomed the official release of news of the Nkomo/Smith negotiations. Now they demanded an end to negotiations and military retaliation on ZIPRA forces in Zambia. Any illusions they might have retained that they were fighting a war, not terrorism, were shattered, and as they waited in vain for condemnation of ZIPRA's action from Britain, the United States or anywhere else, they began to realise they were completely alone in their grief and anger.

I well remember Smith's double-edged reaction to the 'stroke of fate': firstly, great relief and a sudden release of tension for, ironically, settlement with Nkomo had by 3 September been there for the taking and Smith might have had to grasp it, to his own embarrassment and the condemnation of many of his party; and secondly, righteous shock and horror.

Coincidentally, NATJOC were scheduled to meet Smith on the morning following the atrocity because of his expressed concern that the war was not being conducted aggressively enough. In private discussions he had had with me, he had developed the theme of complaint he intended using with NATJOC, based partly on the increasing hardships suffered by white farmers and the need to keep them on the land, but it had been pretty obvious that he was under considerable pressure from his political colleagues to step up the shooting war to its absolute limit. ZIPRA's attack on a civil aircraft strengthened his argument that NATJOC no longer needed to abide by the 'Queensbury Rules' of waging warfare. Walls, however, managed to keep the discussion within bounds, making it clear he would not commit himself to 'Martial Law' or to any advance into unbounded licence by way of military retaliation. He held his ground without too much difficulty, arguing that only the military Commanders should decide military tactics, and that their actions would be based on military necessity. Two other significant points were made during this NATJOC meeting with Smith:[11]

The over-riding impression was that the white Ministers concerned (Hawkins and Squires) and Caucus still believed that we can win the shooting war, and it seemed significant that the Prime Minister made several references to the 'Facade' when referring to the Executive Council – he also indicated that the whites were still in command.

We had a follow-up discussion in the National JOC, debating amongst ourselves whether this new line of approach of the Prime Minister does not indicate a reversal to 'War Council' or 'Security Council', cutting out the Black members of the Executive Council and the Black Ministers from the more vital aspects of the war?

The sense of outrage at the Viscount incident took some time to develop, and was more evident in the subsequent meeting between the National JOC and the Prime Minister, on 9 September (Diary):

We suffered a 'hairy' session of NATJOC this morning, following the Air Rhodesia disaster and the strongest possible political pressures on us to agree to martial law, military strikes into Zambia and all that would follow from this.

Right at the start (with only Hilary Squires present amongst Ministers) Peter Walls was quite magnificent. With eyes flashing, he said: 'If you really want martial law in the true sense of the phrase we will take over from the President and Government, and rule as a Military Junta!' A chastened Squires was joined by Hawkins, and again we went through all the long, long explanations of what 'martial law' really means; compared with no martial law; retribution or no retribution; licence or no licence; with every one of the twelve officials there being opposed to every course of action proposed by the Ministers.

Squires and Hawkins couldn't handle it and had to ask the Prime Minister to join us. When the PM arrived it developed into a sorry occasion, for he had obviously committed himself to Caucus and his Ministerial colleagues in expectation that we would all go ahead with martial 'licence' regardless.

It took my mind back to UDI, when the officials (with two of our number more with the politicians than the rest of us) made all their representations – opposed to UDI – only to be told that a political decision had to be taken –

hence UDI. But that was at the apex of white (RF) rule and we were all allowed
our say *before* the decision was taken. Today *all* the officials were solidly
opposed to the course of action proposed, only to learn that the political decision had already been taken – this time by white Ministers ignoring the black
Co-Ministers of the Executive Council – two of the three of them being abroad
at the time.

In essence, then, Smith and his fellow politicians had lost the initiative
and were offering it to the military. It was to the Commanders' credit
that they realised their limitations in a losing situation and would not
become politically involved. The politicians continued to demand martial law, by which they meant 'martial licence', but the military continued to stall, saying that the Emergency Powers legislation gave them
all the legal authority they needed for tough action and that it was still
better to plan for a political settlement. Of course, there were exceptions
to the rule. Some junior commanders were more politically attuned than
others and permitted more licence than they should have done or turned
a blind eye to excesses under the new 'get tough' policy. Among these
was a Brigade commander who was heard to comment: 'If we carry on
this way the country will soon have a white majority and its political
problems will be solved.'

The lack of unity in the Transitional Government over political and
military issues was reflected in their approach to security matters. An
example of this arose in October, at the 38th and 39th meetings of the
Executive Council, when there was a debate as to whether a certain
Peter MacKay should be deported as an alleged KGB agent.[12] The issue
brought into focus the diametrically opposing attitudes to communism
within the Executive Council and the Ministerial Council.

Bishop the Hon A. T. Muzorewa reported that he had been surprised to learn
that Mr Peter MacKay had been declared a prohibited immigrant and was to be
deported immediately. In the past he had had a close association with African
Nationalist movements and this could well have brought him into disfavour
with the authorities. However, he had been enthusiastic about the changes
which had been brought about by the Rhodesian Constitutional Agreement and
it was thought that on this occasion his past activities could be disregarded. In
view of this it was questioned whether his deportation was warranted at this
stage.

In reply the Hon Dr M. E. Gabellah, as joint Minister of Information, Immigration and Tourism, stated that the evidence submitted by the security authorities provided an irrefutable case for deportation and he and his colleague,
the Hon P. K. F. V. van der Byl, concluded that they had no alternative but to
authorise the deportation.... The Hon P. K. F. V. van der Byl read out a
prepared statement which set out in considerable detail MacKay's political
associations....

The Hon J. F. Chikerema stated that in his view, the deportation of Mr MacKay would cast grave doubt on the Transitional Government.... The Minister had known Mr MacKay personally for thirty years. When the Minister was in exile Mr MacKay had worked under his directions. This had undoubtedly required him to make contact with communist elements. However the Minister was convinced that Mr MacKay had never had any genuine association with communist aims.... The spirit of the Rhodesian Constitutional Agreement required that the past activities of those who supported the Agreement should be set aside.... If Mr MacKay was deported because of his past record, it would be interpreted as meaning that any white person who was sympathetic towards any Nationalist party must be a Soviet agent.

For many years now the consensus of opinion in CIO and Special Branch had been that it was more important to accommodate African nationalism than to over-concern ourselves with the communist threat as it was represented in parts of the Western world. As far as the MacKay affair was concerned, therefore, we considered that if it had been acceptable for Smith to make a deal with Nkomo (who was dependent primarily on the Soviet Union for his support) it should be equally acceptable to accommodate any Soviet connection that would help the attainment of a solution which would be in the national interest. But a solution seemed as far away as ever. On 15 October I wrote in my diary:

Our political situation is awash. Ian Smith and the rest of EXCO are now in the States trying to drum up support.... But the end is no nearer in sight, though things begin to point to the possibility of Muzorewa, at least, making something of the Internal Settlement. Nkomo probably ruled himself out following the 'Viscount' tragedy, whilst some of the power has swung towards Mugabe. And there are emerging signs of political re-alignment.

Because Rhodesia was losing the war at home, the military planners in COMOPS turned outwards in frustration, to strike beyond our borders where the inhibitions that restrict an army fighting on its own ground need not apply. There was also the score of the Viscount to settle with ZIPRA and a readiness to please the politicians by getting tougher. My advice on external operations had prevailed for many years, but henceforth it was over-ridden or simply ignored. The Joint Planning Staff formulated a plan of retaliation that could not be delayed until the return of Smith from the United States. The plan entailed an air-borne strike against ZIPRA deep into Zambia, with a vital part of it so close to Lusaka that there could have been involvement with British, Russian or other aircraft, or Kaunda might have sought Russian or Cuban assistance if the strike over-exposed his weakness.

As 'D' day drew nearer everyone except myself seemed to be raring to go. Eventually I decided not to quibble further and merely insisted that Walls and I should see David Smith, then Acting Prime Minister, to ensure that he had a full appreciation of the military, political, economic and other implications before the attack. During a most friendly discussion, I reminded David Smith that all our allies or advisors (the British, the Portuguese, the South Africans and the Americans) had warned Ian Smith not to extend the war, saying, in effect, that once we started external military raids into neighbouring territory we would be bound to raid further and further afield until we involved all our neighbours and internationalised the conflict. But David Smith gave his assent to the plan and I withdrew my reservations. Walls, it would appear, then told the Joint Planning Staff that I had put every obstacle in the way of their plan, with the result that they believed I had tried to sabotage their efforts. This brought about a crisis of confidence between Walls and myself, and affected my subsequent relationship with the staff at COM-OPS.

Thanks to the effectiveness of the Rhodesian Air Force, the strike (subsequently known as the 'Green Leader' raid) was successful in terms of the immediate objective envisaged in the Joint Planning Staff plan. Between 18 and 20 October the ZIPRA camp at Chikumbi, 12 miles north-west of Lusaka, was flattened and two camps in the Mkushi area 90 miles to the north-east were occupied by heli-borne troops. At least 1600 'trained terrorists' and other members of ZIPRA were killed and the Lusaka hospitals were inundated with wounded. A proportion of those killed in the Mkushi area were women under military training who gave a fair account of themselves but whose sex could not have been identified through aerial reconnaissance or the more remote intelligence on which we had to rely. Over 30 civilians and ZIPRA 'dissidents' being held in underground bunkers were released. Thousands of weapons were destroyed on the ground and tons of war materiel blasted from the air.

A Zambian Air Force MiG observed the action from a safe distance whilst the Rhodesian Air Force controlled the Zambian air space, preventing any hostile reaction.[13] Nearly 100 Zambian Army and Police entered the Mkushi camp too late to be effective and about half their number were killed together with an unknown number of Cuban instructors. Helicopters and ground troops were ferried in and out, using a Zambian air strip en route. One helicopter crashed, injuring its two-man crew, and one Rhodesian soldier was killed in action.

The strike provided a tremendous boost for the Rhodesian Air Force pilots who had been given an opportunity to display their skills in a dramatic operation. In Zambia, however, a state of panic prevailed for weeks after the raid, with ZIPRA shooting at all low-flying aircraft, including civilian planes trying to land at Lusaka airport. Kaunda had to ask Britain to refit Zambia's Rapier SAM system which had fallen into disrepair and he was forced to continue the humiliation of sending most of Zambia's foreign trade through Rhodesia, much to the dismay of Nyerere and Machel who could no longer provide alternative outlets because of the inefficiencies of their rail and port systems. Nkomo asked Moscow to replace the equipment ZIPRA had lost but, significantly, saw to it that ZIPRA made no more attacks on the Victoria Falls-to-Bulawayo railway line. A simultaneous raid had been launched against ZANLA in Mozambique. Walls described it as 'enormously successful' and went on to say: 'I do not give a damn what the rest of the world says about Rhodesia's raids into neighbouring territories.'

The raids were successful insofar as they were an increasing source of irritation to Kaunda and Machel and, as such, made the two Presidents more likely to welcome an end to the war. Nkomo became even more concerned to keep his troops out of the firing line and thus unwittingly passed the advantage to Mugabe who was now recruiting at a greater rate than Nkomo and was filling the areas contiguous with Mozambique with men of his own persuasion. Whites in Zambia, including some CIO agents, suffered through the raids because the Zambian authorities found it easier to implicate or punish those near at hand than admit their own inadequacies.

Walls knew as well as I did, however, that despite the apparent success of the raids the war could not be won by military means. Political mastery had to be established but there was still little sign of such mastery among the internal leaders. Smith, who had started the war, could not stop it. Sithole and Muzorewa had managed to attract so few 'turned terrorists' to their side that they had resorted to recruiting their own men-with-guns – 'Auxiliaries', 'Pfumo re Vanhu' (Spear of the People) and so on. Muzorewa's men were no match for the PF guerrillas, while Sithole's 'Auxiliaries', under the guidance of Kadzviti, co-Minister of Defence in the Transitional Government, embarked upon such a reign of thuggery that they had to be removed from some areas by the Rhodesian Security Forces; Special Branch threatened Kadzviti with court action on a murder charge and he left the country. Then the adherents of the various internal parties began to kill each other. The situation was further confused by clashes occurring within the PF itself. While the Rhodesian Security Forces were able to curb some of the excesses of Muzorewa's and Sithole's men, their capacity to control ZANLA or ZIPRA had long since passed.

Action by Special Branch also tended to be aimed at the internal parties rather than at PF supporters. Special Branch was in fact more averse to action against the PF than were the politicians, as can be seen from the minutes of the Executive Council meeting on 24 October, when Squires queried Special Branch's failure to act against members of Mugabe's family. Special Branch stated that:[14]

With regard to the members of Mugabe's family, there was not sufficient evidence against them – a brother and two sisters – to justify their detention, but the fourth member was being sought and once apprehended he would almost certainly be detained ... (In discussion, Squires said that) the members of Mugabe's family were completely committed to his cause and were actively engaged in promoting it. Whilst acknowledging that Special Branch had to differentiate between legitimate political activity and subversion and that the dividing line was not easy to determine, it nevertheless appeared that the attitude adopted was over-cautious having regard to current circumstances and the consequences of failing to deal effectively with the country's enemies.

In similar vein the Executive Council went ahead with plans to conscript blacks as 'Territorials' in the Armed Forces against the strongest opposition from CIO. We considered that the timing of such plans seemed 'to ignore the overwhelming weight of African opinion ... (and that) the passive or active hostility it is likely to provoke amongst Africans could seriously impair the goodwill previously engendered by African members of the Transitional Government.'[15] We illustrated our point by referring to Special Branch reports of initial reaction to the plans, one of which stated that: 'Following heated discussion amongst Black students at the University on the subject of military call up, a total of 51 of these students have left the Campus, 20 stating their intention of going to Botswana to contact Mugabe representatives and 31 to Mozambique to hand themselves over for training there.'

As the Executive Council continued to stumble on, it became clear that the elections scheduled for January which would turn the government of Rhodesia over to black rule would have to be postponed (Diary, 7 January):

I went over to Britain again in November, via Athens and Paris, and returned in December, feeling more depressed than ever, because of the news that reached me of the so-called 'Government of National Unity' – and all the indications that Good Old Smithy and Co have once again squeezed every concession out of the Black leaders; which made me think that we could never get this thing resolved.... Having been at rock bottom, I'm now beginning to believe that Ian

Smith is finally committed to the April elections and – after so many deferments – to his own departure from the political scene.

I had the doubtful pleasure of telling him in the presence of the National JOC that, far from supporting their own Agreement of March 1978, with every step taken recently the Whites have undermined the position of the Black leaders – so what hope of holding successful elections!

Smith's political manoeuvrings continued and my relationship with him deteriorated further (Diary, 17 February):

The war continues and the standard of life deteriorates, but it is still not so bad that it will force any political change of consequence. Indeed, Muzorewa, Sithole and Co have less chance of forming a strong government after April – mainly because Ian Smith is up to his old tricks again. Smith using the prospect of his departure from the political scene as a 'bargaining point' – ostensibly to try and demand recognition for 'Zimbabwe-Rhodesia' and the uplift of sanctions? As if this would be acceptable anywhere!

During this worsening period of transition when a monolithic white government is supposed to give way to a majority-rule black government, we in the National JOC control more and more of the reins of power. But will the situation develop where we can actually use that power? I wonder.

Peter Walls attracts the public eye, and much of his effort is genuinely in the public interest, but he has not really formed a team which he can command. If anything, we were more united under the old OCC without a chairman, so how can we achieve what most of us already realise must be done within a system that does not provide for unitary, military control; without the slightest inclination that any of us would stage a coup; and with few of us (excepting Peter himself) who would lend ourselves to political aspirations?

While things deteriorated at home, we seemed to be attracting more friends abroad despite the attitudes of the British and American policy-makers towards the Internal Settlement. The Transitional Government's objective of a moderate, democratic and anti-communist stance attracted support from Europe, America and the Arab world, and we responded to offers of help from wherever they came.

Among those who offered assistance was King Hassan of Morocco. Pursuing a policy opposed to Russian expansion into the Afro-Arab world, the king had said he could support the Internal Settlement 'as soon as new political guidelines for African rule are drawn in Rhodesia' which would not conflict with his plans and influence as far south in the continent as Zaire and Angola. I had had no difficulty convincing Moroccan Intelligence of our community of interest, and towards the end of January accompanied Sithole to Morocco so that he could appeal to King Hassan for financial assistance for his election campaign. My formal report of the visit contained everything that the Executive Council was entitled to know about the venture.[16] But my diary digs a little

deeper into that other world in Africa where men die willingly in defence
of Islam or assert the centuries-old superiority of Arab over African:

7th February 1979: Sithole and I went to Morocco to meet King Hassan – to
break entirely new ground between an Arab and African leader. First, Mar-
rakech, an oasis of palm trees, and 'naartjies' [tangerines] interspersed with
'Zimbabwe Creeper' (just as the creeper grows in Zimbabwe Ruins), against the
backdrop of the Atlas Mountains – snow in Africa. But sun in January, with
sparkling cold air.
   We stayed in the Mamounia Hotel where Winston Churchill often went to
relax and paint, a well chosen venue. The essential part of our visit was well
rehearsed, resembling a scene out of the 'Arabian Nights': the long walk
through the palace courtyard with the American General, Dick Walters (former
Deputy Director, CIA, who resigned at the time of Watergate), saying this was
done to ensure that supplicants were sufficiently awed, and how he had known
the King since he was a boy of thirteen and how he considered him the best
informed man in the world. (This may seem exaggerated, but I gained a similar
impression when the King first discussed Rhodesia, showing a total grasp of all
related subjects.)
   We waited at the far end of a magnificent room under a dome which opened
to the skies and was then closed, leaving a tiny bird fluttering in the vastness
between scores of electric light bulbs in a fantastic Moorish setting. The King
walked in alone, in western dress, and Dlimi (within days of our visit promoted
from 'Colonel-Major' to General in order to command the war against the
Polisario) almost devoured his hand in a frenzied display of loyalty. We sat
silent and remote in the vastness until the King led Sithole by the hand, unusual-
ly diffident but apparently calm and collected. Came the time when the King
asked what we wanted. Sithole strangely backward, so I said: 'Your Majesty,
Sithole needs money – and now – to enable him to fight an election.' The King
said 'How much?' Sithole, still diffident, saying 'Five hundred thousand.' The
King looked surprised – he may have thought he was hearing 'Five hundred
million'. Intruding again, I said: 'The Minister is too modest in his request – he
needs more than half a million.' And the King, ending the conversation, said to
Dlimi, 'See that they get a million by Monday....'
   On the way out Sithole was overcome. With tears in his eyes he kept saying,
'A great stone has been lifted from my heart.' Subsequently, in the hotel, he said
to me: 'I have read of "King Makers" in history, but have never had the good
fortune to meet one. Now I have met someone even better – a "Millionaire
Maker"!' He sought my advice, showing a depth of reasoning which impressed;
but the old devilry was not far away. Assuming he had got me on-side with
flattery he was soon suggesting various forms of intimidation – not the 'intimidation' that the Police would need to act upon, but cunningly contrived,
that he must exercise if he is to win the forthcoming elections....
   We returned to Le Bourget in driving sleet: and as my colleague Max and I
climbed down the gangway carrying the cheap suitcases our friends had acquired in a hurry to pack the million dollars, the handles parted from the cases.
One fell and burst on the tarmac, half exposing its contents which started to
blow away in the howling wind! Then we flew back to Salisbury with 'my first

million' in a much stronger suitcase weighing well over one hundred pounds which I used as foot-rest – not trusting Ndabaningi with the money until we reached home.

Within a week of my return to Salisbury from Morocco another Viscount airliner was shot down on take-off from Kariba, killing all on board. Among the dead were my son-in-law's parents and members of five families within sight of my home. On this occasion Nkomo claimed that his troops had planned to shoot down Walls, who was in Kariba at the time. It was a palpable lie, but it pushed COMOPS into pursuing various attempts at assassination, despite my advice that 'dirty tricks' should be left to CIO rather than risk them being mishandled by uniformed soldiers unaware of the political implications. A daring attack on Nkomo's house close to State House in Lusaka was planned by the Selous Scouts but my closest advisers indicated their opposition to any further co-operation with the Scouts because of the frequency with which unsuitable agents of theirs had imperilled our valued connections. One such agent was under detention in Zambia at the time and this led us into months of humiliating appeals to the highest in the land before we could get him out, making it appear that CIO had played a key part in a mission of which we strongly disapproved.

The assassination plan was ill-conceived and had to be switched from the Selous Scouts to the SAS as a straightforward military attack. By this time, however, our well-tried system of 'jointery' in Special Operations had broken down. The timing went haywire and the attack went in when CIO were actually engaged in secret approaches to Nkomo as part of a last-ditch effort by Ian Smith to make the Internal Settlement work.

It was not long after the assassination attempt that the inevitable happened – COMOPS and the Army decided they had finally had enough of the Selous Scouts' activities. Reid Daly's telephone was bugged by Military Intelligence who suspected that the Scouts were gun-running, poaching ivory, or worse. Reid Daly discovered this, and I found myself in the impossible position of having to cover up for all sides at once: COMOPS, the Army and Military Intelligence, because their actions were unconstitutional; and the Scouts, because the loss of confidence between the Military command and Scouts operating in the field had already constituted a grave breach of security.

Many of us were anxious now to see the end of a unit whose *raison d'être* had died in the random killings its members had perpetrated without in any way stopping guerrilla recruiting. I say this whilst accepting that the initial mistake was mine, compounded by the Police who had declined to keep Special Branch up to strength and thus forced CIO to look elsewhere for manpower. We would have done better leaving the unit under the control of Special Branch, keeping it small and secret. Instead, we had created something which was always in danger of getting out of control, led by a man who frequently overstepped the mark, as in his exposure of the bugging affair. Then Reid Daly, as a Lieutenant-Colonel, had berated the Army Commander, Lieutenant-General Hickman, with other officers present. Hickman was not responsible for the bugging, yet Walls, who was responsible for the Scouts and the Military Intelligence activities in question, let his brother officer take the blame to the extent that he was dismissed on irrelevant evidence shortly afterwards, leading him to sue the Minister of Defence for wrongful dismissal. Simultaneously, Reid Daly sought to sue the Prime Minister, the Minister of Defence, the Lieutenant-General and others, leading to a series of inconclusive courts-martial symptomatic of the stress and strain of fifteen years of war. The strain was also evident in political circles (Diary, 3 March):

Olga and I had a week in Cape Town, hopefully on leave but I found myself flung into the fray following the visit there of an Anglo-American delegation whose principal aim appeared to be to try and separate the South Africans from us. If anything, their visit turned out to be counter-productive, for we have now received new offers of help from 'Big Brother' in the south ... Since returning to Salisbury I have found myself in the middle of a political struggle for power. The Caucus met to select a new white leader, but this was aborted by Ian Smith who reversed his decision to retire from politics since when sufficient has occurred to show David Smith that his accession – which appeared imminent – would not be automatic by any means. And two younger men are also in the running – Cronje and Squires.

Meantime Pik Botha got at David Smith, trying to hold him to a statement he had made some time ago to the South Africans about Ian Smith's retirement; and it appears that Cronje has made his own approach to them and is now in Cape Town. David Smith has seen me twice and has asked me to intercede with Ian Smith (shades of 1964 when Winston Field was ousted by Ian Smith!) and try and persuade him to fly to Cape Town to see P. W. Botha to get from him, 'eyeball to eyeball', precisely where the South Aricans will stand if he stays on – whether in fact they will withdraw from offers of help in the economic, military and political spheres.

David Smith appeared to be above intrigue. It was Ian Smith who had done a typical reverse turn and expected everyone to acquiesce in what appeared to most of us (and certainly to the British, American and South African governments) as a damaging, if not fatal, impediment to genuine majority rule. Without doubt, Smith's retention in any sort of office after the elections would damage the credibility of the black leaders. I thought it extraordinary that Smith should believe he could force a quid-pro-quo by offering to resign only on 'recognition for Rhodesia, the granting of independence and the uplift of sanctions'. I wrote in my diary that 'Ian Smith should have chosen a better time for bargaining over his departure. He could have used the recent proroguing of Parliament as the occasion, but instead he indulged in a bitter diatribe against the British and tried to put all the blame for Rhodesia's ills on them.'

Meanwhile, CIO had been developing its relationship with the black leaders, particularly Muzorewa, who seemed most likely to be Rhodesia's first black Prime Minister and thus potentially the Minister responsible for CIO. My diary describes the start of my personal relationship with the Bishop:

12th March 1979: R and I visited Bishop Muzorewa at his church home in Salisbury Park. Living in modest circumstances, I thought the atmosphere was much more genuine – more natural – than one knew of with any of his contemporaries ... the Bishop raised, with every semblance of modesty, his pressing need for money, big money, right away, if he is to conduct an effective election campaign in anything like the intensity it needs. Having established myself as Sithole's 'millionaire maker' I couldn't help thinking that we must do something equally positive to help the Bishop, without delay.

Either I was naive in this first assessment or Muzorewa's character changed on the assumption of power, for he later became vain, and prone to nepotism. Regrettably, his assessment of me, as reported to me by Special Branch, over-valued my capacity to help. On 18 March I recorded in my diary that 'SB confided a couple of days ago that Bishop Muzorewa had now assessed it that Ken Flower was the real government of Rhodesia'!

The security situation had by now slipped almost beyond repair. My brief to the Executive Council on 13 March included statistics that I hoped would shatter any illusions the Executive Council may have had over the possibility of a peaceful election. ZANLA had nearly 21,000 trained men at their disposal, while ZIPRA had about 20,000, with an additional 18,000 recruits, the highest number ever, waiting in Botswana to be moved to Zambia for training. I went on to say:

ZANLA tactics are to infiltrate maximum numbers, avoiding contact with Security Forces, to be in position to disrupt the elections. We can presume that ZIPRA have similar objectives ... The Security Forces are merely holding the situation to enable us to achieve two outstanding objectives – credible elections and the de-escalation of the war. We still need that political solution we have been talking about for some time.

If ZANLA and ZIPRA can still recruit, this means they are winning over the population, and not yourselves. It is absolutely essential that this trend is reversed. If they can get tens of thousands of youths and older men to follow them, why can't you (addressing Muzorewa and Sithole)?

But the Bishop continued to wallow in a slough of uncertainty, Sithole went his own way, which veered towards white rather than black interests, and Chirau could help neither white nor black. Their ineffectiveness was such that they were easily talked into agreeing to compromises which contributed significantly to their eventual demise. For example, while most whites in the Transitional Government would have been prepared to accept the change of the name 'Rhodesia' to 'Zimbabwe', Ian Smith and the hard core held on to the name 'Rhodesia' and produced the absurdity 'Zimbabwe-Rhodesia'. The Executive Council were then talked into a 'Government of National Unity' before the elections had made clear whether or not this was necessary or desirable. Finally, any chance the Executive Council members may have had of political survival was killed off by their acceptance of the Military Planners' 'Total National Strategy', a plan designed to please the South African Military more than anyone else.

The opening paragraphs of the Executive Council's directive for the plan, contained in a paper entitled 'National Strategy Guidelines for Zimbabwe-Rhodesia for the period of the Government of National Unity' illustrates the extent to which the Executive Council had succumbed to RF influences:[17]

The national security of Zimbabwe-Rhodesia is seriously threatened by communist imperialism on the one hand and on the other hand by an ultra-liberalistic philosophy of the present governments of Western powers, especially the United States of America and the United Kingdom.
The Communist Strategy: Zimbabwe-Rhodesia is an intermediate objective in the communist onslaught on South Africa aimed at expanding communist influence in the whole of Southern Africa at the expense of the West.... The destinies of Zimbabwe-Rhodesia and the Republic of South Africa are thus inextricably inter-related...

The document was sent to the South African Prime Minister *before* elections had been held to determine who, in fact, would constitute the new government of Zimbabwe-Rhodesia.[18]

The elections took place between 17 and 21 April. CIO judged them to be a success, in more ways than one. More than 10,000 PF guerrillas had been deployed to disrupt them, in particular to attack polling stations, but only 18 out of 932 stations suffered attack and none was put out of action. Landmines were placed on roads leading to polling stations and several vehicles were ambushed but 1,869,000 votes out of a possible 2,826,000 were cast. And the atmosphere at the polling stations was more relaxed generally than anyone could have hoped for. Muzorewa emerged as Prime Minister-elect, having gained 51 out of the 72 black seats in Parliament.

Most observers judged the elections to be as free and fair as could be expected in the face of an armed insurgency throughout the country. Inevitably, though, there were those whose bias against the Internal Settlement led them to condemn the elections out of hand. Among them was Dr Claire Palley, whose booklet on the subject, 'Zimbabwe Rhodesia: Should the Present Government be Recognised?', made much mention of 'intimidation' by Rhodesian Security Forces (in protecting voters being transported to the polling stations), by 'Auxiliary Forces' (in being present at the stations), by the government (in calling for a massive turnout of voters) and by white employers (in persuading their black employees to vote). But she made no reference at all to Nkomo's well-publicised campaign to ensure that 'every man with a gun is equal to one thousand voters'.

Lord Chitnis, representing a human rights group, went even further by citing unproved instances where the Security Forces had allegedly forced Africans to vote. He said a 'cowed and indoctrinated electorate' had been produced but he offered no proof to show that the electorate had voted against their inclinations. A few observers went so far as to suggest that Mugabe and Nkomo, by threatening to continue the war, were not practising intimidation but that Muzorewa, by promising peace, was.

Successful though the elections were, Walls spoke for all the officials when he warned the Executive Council on 9 May that no one should read too much into the PF failure to disrupt them. The minutes of that meeting show concern over the alarming rise in stock theft incidents and the effect of this on white farmers, as well as the effects of war, drought and lack of credit facilities on black farmers. The essence of Walls's message, however, was contained in the following paragraph:[19]

While the number of incidents of a really aggressive nature appeared to have declined recently, the number of ZIPRA and ZANLA terrorists entering the country was increasing. The number of terrorists captured was also increasing but there were very few defections from the terrorist ranks and no response to the amnesty offer. The success of the election had given rise to a mood of elation and optimism which was not justified at the present time. The overriding need for continued political initiative and momentum had in no way diminished.

Over the next few days I had to pay some attention to matters of less importance, dealing with honours and awards for my staff before the Transitional Government handed over to an entirely different regime – I was thus overriding CIO's normal practice whereby honours were accepted only on retirement.

Ian Smith came with his wife to say goodbye to CIO, fifteen years after becoming our Minister, during which period CIO developed from a handful of amateurs to a professional service with an international reputation – as I tried to get across in a brief speech when presenting our emblems and a picture by Joan Evans to Mrs Smith. I also compared my term in office with that of all other Heads of Service with whom I had been in liaison since 1963: only one had survived more than ten years without being disgraced or forced into retirement; four had been imprisoned; one had been executed. It was an emotion-charged affair and, as Gaylard commented during the course of the evening, Smith acted with dignity and a sense of the occasion. Mrs Smith and a number of ladies were tearful on departure. Later, in my diary, I wrote 'there seemed no doubt in anyone's mind that we were saying farewell to the old Rhodesia and living that bit of history for the last time'.

Back on the job, I had to try and help Muzorewa resist white demands that would damage him politically. I tried to fortify the Bishop against giving in over the 'Independence Celebrations'. For example, the question of raising and lowering the new and old flags generated much heat. Muzorewa wanted the Rhodesian flag lowered prior to the raising of the Zimbabwe-Rhodesia flag. The white Ministers argued that protocol did not require that the old flag be lowered before the new one could be raised. Then the Commanders, who had initially supported the Bishop, shifted ground under white political pressure and claimed that it would be regarded by the Security Forces as a defeat if the Rhodesia flag was *ever* lowered. At the height of the argument, which Muzorewa eventually lost, he turned to the Commanders and said: 'You may save the face of sixty thousand whites in the Security Forces but I will lose the respect and support of six million blacks and we will have another country.' Time would prove him right, of course, but he handled the argument badly and I left the room in disgust at his failure to stand up to white arrogance.

At midnight on 31 May Bishop Muzorewa took over from Ian Smith as Prime Minister. We thought at the time that this was the end of an era but the Bishop must have known that he had merely taken over the country in name and that the name of the 'other country' to which he referred would be different.

CHAPTER 12

Agreement at Lancaster House

The past was closing in behind us and the future looked obscure. Less than two weeks after Muzorewa's election victory the Conservatives had been returned to power in Britain, a result we had greeted with optimism. By the time Ian Smith had officially handed over to Muzorewa on 31 May, however, we had been shown that a Conservative government could be just as ambivalent as a Labour government in its attitude towards our country. I had travelled to London a few days after the Conservative victory to test the temperature there and, for the first time since UDI, I was received openly at the Foreign Office. The theme of much of what was said was that we were now all working together whereas previously we had been working against each other.

After this trip I felt confident in advising the Commanders that although the Bishop faced many problems not of his own making, there was also a great deal going for him.[1] On the question of political recognition, I considered that the Conservative Election Manifesto, published as recently as February 1979, should work in the Bishop's favour, as I was aware that the report of their Observer Group under Lord Boyd would state unequivocally that the elections which had brought the Bishop to power were 'free and fair'; that the six principles which applied to Anglo-Rhodesian negotiations were now fully satisfied; and that if the Conservative government were to abide by its own manifesto it had 'the duty to return Rhodesia to a state of legality, move to lift sanctions, and do its utmost to ensure that the new independent state gets international recognition.' On the question of sanctions, I indicated that I had passed to British, American, French and German intelligence services sufficient evidence of Russia's removal of Rhodesia's stockpile of chromite to convince their governments that they need prevaricate no longer in ending sanctions. Admittedly, there was a danger that before the British government acted it might use our evidence against its partners who had worked secretly in our support for many years, but now that we had incontrovertable proof of large-scale Russian sanctions-busting I hoped this would convince the British to lift sanctions immediately.

But the wheels within wheels of international politics rarely make for

a smooth ride and where we had expected strength – from Margaret
Thatcher, whom the Russians had dubbed 'The Iron Lady' because of
her belligerence in Opposition – we now found weakness. As Prime
Minister she seemed more anxious to mollify the Russians than fire any
sanctions-busting ammunition at them. As to the Americans, their reluctance to confront the Russians over the sanctions issue was based on
their desire not to upset their current re-negotiation of the SALT II
Treaty.

At the British Foreign Office I had learnt from Ministers and officials
that Lord Carrington hoped to dilute those feminine instincts of
Thatcher's which were considered too favourably disposed towards
Zimbabwe-Rhodesia and that the Foreign Office would encourage delay
rather than persuade the Prime Minister to 'grasp the nettle' now. One
of the officials put it this way to me: 'Don't be disappointed, old boy, for
surely you realise that when the FO has been forced into making a
decision it has been wrong on every major issue in Africa since before
and after Suez.'

The French and German officials I saw on this trip confirmed that
their governments would support Zimbabwe-Rhodesia against the
Patriotic Front and that they and other European powers would back
British government recognition of Muzorewa's government if Britain
led from the front rather than from behind. Their stance, and that of
the French-speaking Heads of State in Africa (who had all signified
support for Muzorewa provided they were backed from Paris), was
undermined by British diplomats in France who stated, too glibly, that
they did not expect French support for Britain's position over Zimbabwe-
Rhodesia.

I tried to put across to all the officials I saw that there was a real
danger of a serious escalation of the war if Britain did not commit
herself to positive action before the Commonwealth Conference, scheduled to open in Lusaka on 1 August. I added that Australia might be a
better venue, for it was not difficult to imagine the emotions that would
be generated so close to our border – the white/black border of Africa –
by a group of black Heads of State anxious to pre-empt recognition of
Zimbabwe-Rhodesia and intent upon getting their own nominees into
power.

By June the prospect of Britain leading the international community in
recognising Muzorewa's government was fading. And at home there
was little happening which could be viewed as an indication that anything had changed at all for the better, as my brief to Cabinet on 12 June
shows:

The new Government has been well received by all races throughout the country, although considerable disappointment has been expressed over the failure of ZANU (Sithole's party) to take their seats in the House of Assembly and Cabinet.... Terrorist initiated activity has increased.... The Amnesty programme has had little material effect on the terrorists.... A substantial number of FPLM have entered Zimbabwe-Rhodesia with members of ZANLA....

The failure of the United States (and Britain) to lift sanctions and recognise Zimbabwe-Rhodesia is depressing and damaging. On 7th June, President Carter stated that he would not lift sanctions as he had reservations about the Elections conducted in terms of a Constitution that was not endorsed by the Black majority.... It looks as if no decision on restoration of legality, recognition, or the lifting of sanctions will be taken by the British Government prior to the Commonwealth Conference scheduled to take place in Lusaka from 1st to 8th August....

Trying to offer a general assessment, I would say the heat is on – like never before.... You are right in pursuing a path of peace; but most of your enemies are planning to escalate the war. And that war is now costing more than 2000 killed or wounded a month....

With every month that goes by, sanctions become more debilitating. The war has gone on too long already. White and black morale will suffer grievously if there is not a reasonably early end to the present impasse.

The priorities must be to: (a) De-escalate the war; (b) Fight for the uplift of sanctions; (c) Gain international recognition.

For the moment we must concentrate on our amnesty within the country – but, please, it needs an all-out effort to achieve results: and if we do not get results, we will be seen to be losing.

CIO staff, working with every Intelligence agency with whom we could liaise, produced an analysis of the problem and suggested some remedies:[2]

In Washington, London and elsewhere the next few days, or weeks, will see an intensification of the struggle to uplift sanctions or to win or lose recognition. Any ammunition we can provide during this period to those who are fighting the battle for us, will be of great value.... To continue with sanctions now could literally kill the Bishop's chances of survival.

The external Nationalist leaders, Nkomo and Mugabe, are receiving all the help, materiel and financial, that they need from Russia and Russia's allies. The most serious effect of sanctions against Bishop Muzorewa's Government is to deny them the right to defend themselves, or to end the war....

The timing of President Carter's announcement (to continue sanctions) seemed sinister. He was not required to say anything until 15th June. Why bring it forward to coincide with the decision of the Front Line Presidents to escalate the war against Bishop Muzorewa's Government?....

The OAU, or member states, threaten strictures on America or Britain if they uplift sanctions, but not a word is said against Russia for consistently evading sanctions...

One must look at the insidious role played by Nigeria and the furtive link between Andrew Young and Julius Nyerere ... it is significant that Nigeria is now courting Mugabe with funds; Garba's [Brigadier Garba, ex Nigerian Foreign Minister] role appears to have been assumed by Andrew Young, whose personal interests might differ, but whatever those interests are, they are unquestionably linked with Nigerian/American commercial interests.... The whole history of the Rhodesian affair casts suspicion on the role played by Julius Nyerere ... he will seize any chance to destroy the prospects of settlement or to promote his own protégé – originally Nkomo, then Sithole, and now Mugabe; for we know (and it is known where it counts in London and Washington) that Nyerere and the other Front Line Presidents warned Nkomo and Mugabe during their meetings in Dar-es-Salaam before the holding of the Rhodesian elections that, if they were unable to prevent those elections, support might have to be withdrawn from them ... that support would have been withdrawn if a new opportunity had not presented itself – Britain deferring her decisions, giving more time for them to recoup, and President Carter clamping sanctions on Bishop Muzorewa....

In order to preserve at least a neutral position, Britain should consider ways and means of helping Bishop Muzorewa's Government now.... Moves towards the restoration of legality could be made now.

To help strengthen Muzorewa's position I made yet another trip to Europe, this time via America, bearing the message that the Anglo-American decision to continue sanctions would ruin his chances of survival. I found many more sympathetic listeners than I had expected to and no one argued that the Bishop needed a political success in order to consolidate his position; nor did anyone dispute that the prospect, slight as it was, of persuading the guerrillas to accept the amnesty would disappear altogether unless the Bishop could be seen to be winning at least something on the international scene.

As far as the Americans were concerned, I made use of an issue mentioned in the CIO Analysis concerning CIA activities in Africa. CIO were in the process of uncovering extensive CIA operations in Zimbabwe-Rhodesia and other African countries, designed to undermine Muzorewa. This indicated, in effect, that the CIA were helping the PF. We arranged the release of three of their agents under detention in Zimbabwe-Rhodesia on a promise from the Director, CIA, that Carter would be appropriately advised of our action and of Muzorewa's readiness to oppose communism in concert with the United States. I joined up with Muzorewa on his visit to the United States and accompanied him to Europe (Diary):

22nd July 1979: Arrived in Washington on the not-so-glorious 4th July – for it rained, the firework display had to be postponed to the following night when we almost froze in unseasonal weather on a launch on the Potomac.

But our official reception couldn't have been better. I was received after nine long years by Director, CIA, like a long-lost brother. Given a spy satellite photo as a parting gift, showing our home in Salisbury, recording changes in the surroundings every 103 minutes – perhaps to remind us that Big Brother is always watching!

Our recent actions in getting CIA out of a bit of a predicament have undoubtedly helped the Bishop get his interview with President Carter in as congenial an atmosphere as could have been expected....

Then to London. Well received once again at the Foreign Office, for a discussion between Lord Carrington and his team and Bishop Muzorewa and our team comprising four blacks, two whites (George Smith, the Attorney General, and myself). Then lunch at Admiralty House, though I fear the naval atmosphere was lost on most of the assembled company. A Petty Officer brought drinks: all 'soft' – cokes, sherries and not a gin in sight until I asked whether the Royal Navy no longer ran on pink gin. Carrington seemed taken aback, but the PO responded with alacrity and, I thought, renewed interest in serving us.

Immediately after lunch the Bishop went into a huddle with his team before going to see Mrs Thatcher, seeking our assessment of where we stood with our hosts. George started denigrating – doubting their genuineness – to the extent that I believed I had to intervene ... I said we couldn't possibly reject what little the Brits were offering at this stage if we expected more from them later on and wished to retain their interest. There was no current pressure on the Bishop. Indeed, Lord Carrington had gone out of his way to say that the Brits could not expect the Bishop to accept any changes that might undermine his position. It was a question of trust. If we were prepared to believe what the Brits were telling us, at least it would tie them into the final solution. If we rejected them now, we were stuck with a war situation that neither the Brits nor anyone else could help us with.

I got the right responses from the blacks, but it was made patently clear to me thereafter that none of the whites connected with our party would trust the Brits and I began to wonder whether I had been too trusting; whether the Bishop might regret it; whether I would appear back in Zimbabwe-Rhodesia as someone who had lent himself too readily to a Munich-type solution....

Since returning home I believe I have taken the Commanders with me in supporting the Bishop and trusting the British. But the fear grows that the Bishop will be undermined, casting a blight on an otherwise successful sortie by him....

On the one hand some of us have been doing what we can to fortify the Bishop – and ourselves – in the belief that the next three months should see the uplift of sanctions, and recognition. On the other hand there has been enough weakening of the Bishop's position already, through defections from his party. And the white politicians have been up to their old tricks of divide and rule – a luxury which we can no longer afford when the country is bleeding to death – someone killed each hour of the twenty four, and the war costing a million dollars a day.

The Commonwealth Conference duly opened in Lusaka on 1 August and the Zimbabwe-Rhodesia problem assumed priority on the agenda. From the other side of the border we watched the week's proceedings and waited for the outcome, aware throughout how easy it would have been to embarrass both Kaunda and the British, with the Queen in residence, by striking at Russian-backed guerrilla bases and exposing the weakness of British defences by hitting guerrilla bases near Lusaka. But we held our hand in the hope that the British would give Muzorewa full marks for correct behaviour and support him against the political blackmail of African Heads of State in no way devoted to the democratic ideal. Long after the event I realised that we had underestimated how close Kaunda and Machel were to throwing their hand in, and that another raid or two might have made them force the PF into any sort of agreement that would end the war.

By the end of the week Mrs Thatcher and Lord Carrington had reached agreement with other Commonwealth representatives that Britain should assume responsibility for calling another all-party conference at which a constitution comparable to those granted to ex-colonial (not 'Self-Governing') territories should be agreed; that a cease-fire should be negotiated; and that new elections should be held in Zimbabwe-Rhodesia under British authority with other members of the Commonwealth as observers.

In reaching this agreement, Thatcher's government had finally reneged on all its election promises to Zimbabwe-Rhodesia and as such was responsible for the greatest betrayal in the history of Anglo-Rhodesian relations.

Neither Muzorewa nor any other respresentative from Zimbabwe-Rhodesia had been invited to the Lusaka Conference. No explanation was offered for rejecting Muzorewa's claims, but it became obvious that Britain's decision to renege was not taken on any objective view of developments in Zimbabwe-Rhodesia; it was forced on Britain by outside influences with little or no relevance to the situation in Zimbabwe-Rhodesia. Above all, it was the influence exerted by Kaunda and Nyerere in support of their protegés Nkomo and Mugabe that changed the nature of things. Although Nkomo and Mugabe had declined to participate in the elections that brought Muzorewa to power they were to be given another chance to achieve power on terms acceptable to themselves.

Preparations proceeded for the conference to be held in London and I made myself increasingly unpopular when it became known that I had helped persuade Muzorewa to attend and was insisting that he choose only the most compatible Ministers and officials to accompany him so that he could clinch the best deal and bring an end to the war. The Bishop was keen to include white Ministers in his delegation. I queried the wisdom of this but he made it clear that he needed David Smith for his knowledge of economic affairs, just as he believed that his best constitutional advisers would be certain white lawyers he had in mind. Unfortunately, David Smith was adamant that he could not go unless his political senior, Ian Smith, was included in the delegation; most of us around the Bishop thought this would damage his standing and undo the good he could otherwise achieve through a predominantly black delegation. (In the event, the Bishop's official delegation numbered twelve, including the two white Ministers named, Ian Smith and David Smith. Prominent among the black delegates were Silas Mundawarara, Ndabaningi Sithole, Ernest Bulle, Francis Zindoga, Kayisa Ndiweni, Simpson Mtambanengwe, David Zamchiya and George Nyandoro. Two white Deputy Ministers, Rowan Cronje and Chris Andersen, went to London in support of the delegation, while the number of white officials varied according to the subject under discussion, and included George Smith, for constitutional drafting, David Young as economic adviser and Dennis Connolly on election proceedings.)

At the time there were also problems in NATJOC, caused by political interference in the conduct of the war, but there was not much any of us could do about this whilst Smith and the white Ministers responsible for defence and security were still more powerful in the War Council than the Prime Minister. After airing my views somewhat guardedly in the War Council, I wrote in my diary:

4th September 1979: The day after the 40th anniversary of the start of the Second World War, which brought back a flood of memories! Our war continues, and in some respects, escalates. We officials in War Council have had to listen to insistent demands for 'Militia-types', more 'Security Force Auxiliaries' and the rest, with Ian Smith for the first time strident in his demands. Yet, how many years ago was it that I was advocating just that – a 'Home Guard', or what the Bishop now calls 'The Presence of Men-with-Guns in the Tribal Areas' – advocating to deaf ears and against the bitter opposition of Smith's Ministers who swore 'only over our dead bodies would we agree to munts being armed!'

Unfortunately, our NATJOC–COMOPS system is proving less workable in many respects than the old OCC. We certainly spend an unconscionable time reaching decisions, with Peter Walls and others busy trying to reassure themselves and others who serve them. Perhaps I've been around too long. Experience is not necessarily what is required; and it just doesn't pay to be right, for you can never profit from 'I told you so'. More likely to get the blame for anything that misfires.

Meantime, I plan to go to London tomorrow, in advance of the Conference, to meet up with Harold Hawkins whom I got the Bishop to accept as principal Foreign Affairs adviser in his delegation; to face what British Intelligence say may be 'some bitter pills we will have to swallow'. Already, then, doubts and suspicions arise. Have I been too pushing with the Bishop? Should we have relied on what Lord Carrington and Co told us in London – that the main purpose of the exercise was 'to see the Bishop confirmed in office as Prime Minister of a moderate, pro-Western government', when the later news out of London is that Maggie Thatcher actually changed course – was not just veering in the wind – during the Lusaka Conference and is now ready to sacrifice the Bishop in order to please Nyerere, Kaunda and Co. Exactly what I warned them in London last May would happen if they were ill-advised enough to try and get a fair settlement of the Rhodesian problem with Nyerere in on the act.

The scene now shifted from Salisbury to London where, at Lancaster House on 10 September, an all-party conference began that differed from all earlier conferences in that discussions on the constitution were more or less academic. The real argument was over the control of the instruments of power in the run-up to the elections. Britain, and white Rhodesians, would be holding the ring but the participants would be fighting it out themselves, either anxious that their opponents should disengage from the conflict or that they would be given sufficient time and opportunity to achieve success for themselves.

Carrington and his highly efficient team were intent on what they called a 'First Class Solution', into which all parties would be tied. We would have preferred a 'Second Class Solution', where the PF would have opted out, and there were many occasions when we had reason to believe that some members of the British team were helping towards that end.

The PF was under pressure from Nyerere, Kaunda and Machel to settle, but not at any cost. They could obtain greater concessions for themselves by threatening to walk out and continue the war than by too ready an acceptance of the British proposals. The Bishop's sponsors, however, edged away from him and he had little option but to stay and make the best of whatever arrangements the British would offer. Ironically, the greatest weakness in the Bishop's position was the British intention to do the right thing by him, for this meant that he had to conform to their wishes where otherwise he might have fought the issues involved.

Carrington's tactics were masterly. He decided to dispose of the consitutional issues first, then to discuss matters such as the cease-fire during the period of transition and finally to implement what had been agreed, including the holding of elections. He took the issues one by one, getting agreement on each before proceeding to the next stage. If either side lagged behind, he would first of all threaten to impose a deadline and then report that he had the support of the British Prime Minister to proceed without further argument. No doubt there was a considerable amount of bluff, but the brinkmanship paid off.

During the first week of the conference some time was taken up with formalities. There were really only two controversial points in the proposed constitution: a reduction in the number of seats reserved for whites in Parliament (finally reduced from 28 to 20); and the consequential removal of all blocking mechanisms attached to the reserved seats, leaving it to a simple majority of 70 members in a Parliament of 100 to permit any changes to entrenched clauses in the constitution. The protection of minority rights appeared in a Bill of Rights which was fully entrenched against any amendment for ten years; this was designed to allay white fears and compensate for the removal of the blocking mechanism.

The constitutional proposals were accepted by Muzorewa on 21 September. This acceptance in fact represented the Bishop's greatest success at the Lancaster House talks, in that he forced his delegation into line by ignoring consensus and insisting on a vote on the proposals. The delegation had been split in several directions over whether or not to accept the proposals and after days of disagreement and no apparent prospect of getting a favourable consensus the Bishop had summoned a meeting of the full delegation and all the senior officials. He opened by saying, quite simply, that he believed we had no option but to accept the proposals and move on to the next stage; the alternative was to go home now and carry on unaided, fighting a war with no end in sight.

David Smith then got to his feet and said we had wasted too much time already and that if the delegates were not prepared to accept Muzorewa's leadership and work loyally as part of his team, they should not have come to London. He, for one, wished 'to stand up and be counted' in support of the Bishop. He paid deference to his old political leader, Ian Smith, but said it was no good continuing to bar progress at the conference on points the British could not concede. He pointed out that our main objective was to reach a settlement and that if we rejected something sponsored by the British which they could not amend in our favour it would be the end of the conference. It was a fine speech, just right for the occasion, and drew rounds of applause from the black delegates. Sithole and Mtambanengwe then spoke in similar vein, giving the Bishop the opportunity to ignore convention and insist on a vote to be taken then and there. Eleven delegates voted in favour of acceptance; only one, Ian Smith, voted against. Within an hour Muzorewa had conveyed his decision to Carrington.

The valuable time wasted by the whites arguing over constitutional niceties such as the retention of a white block in Parliament had caused the British team some concern, as my 'Notes' taken at the time show:*

The British representatives impressed on us that delay will only complicate matters or destroy their initiative. They were worried that if the likes of Mr Andersen continued with their legal nit-picking over minor matters, we would still be talking next year, by which time we would have suffered serious losses of whites from our Security Forces and a general decline in morale throughout the country. Delay could only help the P F who would try and drag out the talks, or their subsequent implementation, as long as possible.

Clearly, the British team had as much of a problem handling our delegation as they did the separate groupings within the P F. We were far less homogenous than the P F, for our delegation comprised Muzorewa's U A N C, Sithole's Z A N U, Smith's R F and a newly formed party led by Ndiweni, with the result that the British dare not disclose the real nature of their plans to anyone other than the Bishop and the three or four of us working closely with him. Another result of this division in the Zimbabwe-Rhodesia delegation was that at the plenary sessions the Bishop, who had no hope of matching Nkomo and Mugabe in the cut and thrust of debate, could make little use of the ablest debaters in his delegation, the eloquent Ndabaningi Sithole and the vastly experienced Ian Smith. He had to rely on the British chairman to see fair play, whether that chairman be Lord Carrington or, in his occasional absence, Sir Ian Gilmour or Sir Antony Duff who had varying success in keeping the debate within bounds, particularly when Mugabe was at his brilliant best. On more than one occasion I noticed the Bishop casting envious eyes across the conference table when Nkomo or Mugabe were holding forth while the British chairman seemed unable to intervene to the Bishop's advantage.

Back in his hotel the Bishop would lapse into fits of depression, realising that the P F were too smart for him, that he could not rely on his own delegation and that the British might let him down. I went to try to cheer him up, but to little avail, and was finally forced to say to him:

'Can I ask you this, Bishop: are you not spending too much time in your bedroom? No doubt much of your time is spent in prayer, but are you not losing your grip of the situation?'

He looked at me hopelessly and replied:

---

* 'D G C I O: Notes in Connection with the Lancaster House Conference, London: September–December, 1979', 31.12.79; further extracts reproduced in the Appendix. (The Official Record of the Conference was contained in Conference Papers and the exchange of telex and other messages with the government in Salisbury, but much of this was later destroyed.)

'How can you really expect me to keep my spirits up when I'm living on vichysoisse and carrots, the only food I like in this hotel!'

His accommodation was costing the British taxpayer £150 a day. I was luckier than the Bishop, having managed to stay in that fine old hotel, The Hyde Park, when the Bishop and the rest of his delegation had been moved a couple of hundred yards down Sloane Street to a hotel recommended by Scotland Yard, allegedly because they would be safer there but no doubt because British Intelligence had comprehensively bugged the place.

Three days after Muzorewa's acceptance of the constitutional proposals the PF gave way on the main issues and by 3 October Carrington was able to publish the full details of the constitution. The PF leaders then changed their minds and rejected the constitution in its entirety, putting forward alternative proposals which were totally unacceptable to Muzorewa. On 15 October Professor Claire Palley, acting as Nkomo's constitutional adviser, gained considerable support for the PF by publishing an article in *The Guardian* which declared the constitution to be 'unworkable'. The PF were also getting infinitely more time on British television, whereas most of our delegation kept away from the media, although Ian Smith, who was lionised on arrival, continued to be popular with the London crowds.

With the PF remaining adamant against acceptance, Carrington announced that he would proceed to discuss the transitional arrangements with Muzorewa, without the PF if necessary. On 17 October the PF accepted the constitutional proposals.

While the constitutional wrangles had been going on, the British had been sounding some of us out on the transitional arrangements. In lengthy discussions during September with Foreign Office officials I had been given a fairly clear picture of their intentions. During these discussions Sir Antony Duff mentioned several times that he believed the military problem was 'virtually insoluble' and that all they could hope for was to make the best arrangements possible. He added that there would have to be a pre-condition of cease-fire before the PF could participate and a corresponding agreement from our Forces to disengage.

My 'Top Secret Draft' outlined as much of the British plan as was evident at this stage:[3]

At a private dinner party given by Sir Antony Duff shortly after my arrival in London on 6th September, 1979, he re-iterated their serious intention of 'working it all out with us'. He expected at that stage that the Patriotic Front would opt out sooner rather than later. . . .

Again, at a small dinner party on 20th September, 1979, with Mr Derrick Robinson and I, Sir Antony said he was thinking of sending someone to Salisbury to reassure our Security Force Commanders that the 'British intentions were honourable' and that they intended to see this thing through to our mutual advantage.... Sir Antony mentioned that they dare not disclose the real nature of their plans in that same forum as Mr Ian Smith, the Reverend Sithole, and others, as they would try and get political advantage from it and the Patriotic Front would accuse them of collusion with us.... At this particular stage it was becoming more apparant that the Patriotic Front would *not* opt out, sooner, nor maybe, later; and Sir Antony Duff mentioned how they (the British) were surprised – even impressed – with the reasonableness of the Patriotic Front delegation....

On 25th September, 1979, Sir Antony Duff and Mr Renwick had a return dinner with AVM Hawkins and myself.... Mr Renwick did most of the talking to start with, explaining that they had a plan which they preferred to call 'Pre-Independence' so that emphasis could be placed on the granting of Independence, and to show the seriousness of their intention to uplift sanctions. He went on to explain that as soon as agreement was reached on the Constitution – or as soon as the British 'imposed a constitution' – they would have to ask the Bishop to 'stand down'....

They expect to appoint a 'British Controller' or 'British Administrator' in charge of elections. He would not be a military man, and they have no intention of interfering with the existing command or control of our Security Forces; but as the Police would have to appear as an acceptably impartial force, they were thinking that the Commissioner would have to stand aside, and they thought the Force could be run by his senior Deputy, with the Commissioner possibly continuing as Police Adviser to the Administrator. I pointed out certain objections to this which they seemed to absorb in their thinking.

Co-incidental with the appointment of a British Administrator – or whatever he is to be called – they will declare a 'return to legality' and announce an immediate uplift of sanctions; for, as one of them put it, how could they continue with sanctions against their own administration in any shape or form?....

Clearly they have a problem in trying to fill the vacuum created by asking the Prime Minister and Government to stand aside, but they expect the Commanders and Heads of Ministries to continue to function – in effect, to run government during the interim period.

They proposed that a small team of Day, Byatt, and Reilly should visit Salisbury within the next few days to explain something more of their plans to the Commanders....

On 26th September I saw the Prime Minister to seek his approval for proceeding with the British on lines indicated above.... He said he would welcome a visit by the British to Salisbury to brief the Commanders, but that he wished me to accompany them.

He said that he supported the British plan and could only wish it success, but that there was one serious defect, and that was their belief that our forces could 'disengage'. Under no circumstances should any of us agree to this, because it could not be a genuine dis-engagement. The PF would merely take advantage of it: they have their boys everywhere and they would immediately dominate the *what does this mean?*

elections through intimidation ... (I said) we ought to insist that any party that broke the ceasefire or indulged in intimidation would be proscribed.

The report went on to describe how, as a result of consultations with British Intelligence, it was decided that to avoid accusations of collusion I should go back to Salisbury alone and prepare the Commanders for discussion with Byatt. In essence, the British were showing how deeply concerned they were to take the Commanders with them.

The most significant point arising from these meetings, however, was the British request that the Bishop should 'stand down'. Muzorewa had participated in the conference with as much, if not more, claim to legality as Smith's government with whom the British had been negotiating on equal terms for fifteen years. As such, Muzorewa's government was the only constitutional authority entitled to administer any process of transition required by the British; and he had formed his delegation on a multiracial, non-tribal basis, only to realise that the PF would score more heavily against him if they developed their campaign on a tribal basis with Black Power as their objective. And the British were now giving way to PF demands, allegedly so that all parties would enter the elections with equal standing! It was a preposterous request. Such a derogation of status would not have been expected of any government anywhere in the world, certainly not in Africa where no nationalist leader had ever been known to relinquish power voluntarily and would lose all support if he gave way. The Rhodesian Security Forces under Muzorewa could be relied upon to disengage, or submit to British supervision, but the PF forces owed no such allegiance to Muzorewa's government or to the British and they could divest themselves of all responsibility because most of their forces were based in Zambia and Mozambique, beyond British supervision.

At about midnight on the day after the British demand had been passed to the Bishop I returned to my hotel to find a personal message from him asking that I go to see him, no matter what time it was. I did so and found him anxious to discuss the dilemma which the British demand had created for him. He said:

'I want to remain steadfast to my colleagues in the Transitional Government; and I in no way feel inclined to renege on the 3rd March Agreement, but I'm convinced, after much thought and prayer, that I must give something – perhaps it is what I am now being asked to do – in order to get a settlement and the benefits that should flow from it.'

I sat on the edge of his bed and communed with him as well as I could. And then he put the vital question point blank:

'Should I move ahead for the greatest good of the greatest number?'
After a slight delay I replied:

'Yes, Bishop, provided you realise that if you do that – if you do what
appears to be the right thing for the country – it will damage the credibility of your delegation and will be disastrous for you personally. There
is absolutely no precedent in the history of Africa where any African
leader has relinquished power voluntarily and ever been able to recover
it. You know better than I do that your delegation will believe you have
abandoned them – whereas it's the British who are prepared to betray
you, and you'll never be able to explain that, privately or publicly. Your
friends as well as your enemies will look on your retirement from office
as a fatal weakness on your part and will take full advantage of it.'

I am sure he expected an answer of this sort but he looked very upset.
Perhaps I should have added that a few of us, close to him, would regard
his action as a display of strength, but I just could not see it that way at
the time. He had been elected by a majority of blacks in Zimbabwe-
Rhodesia but was now being asked to betray them and cede power to his
enemies, for there was every possibility that the British, following the
least line of resistance, would not work effectively enough to ensure his
return as Prime Minister; in fact, they might destroy the Bishop politically once they realised that all advantage would pass to Nkomo or
Mugabe.

I left the Bishop in no doubt that he was being martyred and that the
choice he had to make was agonisingly unfair. With a look of despair on
his face, he told me that all the key members of his party had implored
him not to agree to the British request, for they saw it as a PF demand
which would have only one result – the death, politically, of the Bishop
and his party. I replied that the decision must be his alone. If he said
'yes', he would be finished; if he said 'no' the conference would be
finished and the bitter war would continue. It was no comfort to him,
and I was not surprised to learn later that he had spent the rest of the
night in prayer. By dawn he had arrived at the decision that he must say
'yes'.

Walking back to my hotel in the small hours of the morning my mind
was full of vengeful thoughts. What right had the British to impose this
on him? What right had they to kill him off politically when on every
appropriate occasion they had pretended to be working out a future
with him? I felt angry with myself that I had not given him more positive
support at a time when he needed it most. This sense of personal failure
was compounded by the nagging thought that the British would double-
cross him and that it was I, more than anyone else, who had impressed

upon him that a Conservative government would be as good as its word. I could only guess then at British double-dealing behind the scenes; it was to be several years before something of the extent of their duplicity emerged, such as the revelation that a senior Foreign Office official was given the job of handling a Foreign Office press campaign to discredit the Bishop and push Thatcher towards Mugabe. I reached my hotel in deserted Knightsbridge, but instead of going in I turned right and went into a nearby casino so as to have something other than the prospect of betrayal to occupy my mind until dawn broke.

A few days later the Conservative Party held their annual conference. Sifting through the rhetoric it was clear that Thatcher was not going to grant independence as promised. She was even baulking at doing the easiest thing of all – an immediate uplift of sanctions. No mention was made by her or by Carrington of how Muzorewa would be sacrificed. I noted the tremendous applause given Julian Amery for his statement that 'we all want peace in Rhodesia, but not peace at any price', which seemed to me to be nearer the 'Conservative Truth' than anything else said at the conference. Later, Carrington tackled me about the loyalty of some of his colleagues:

'I hope you're not being misled by those right-wingers, Julian Amery, Steve Hastings and Co.'

We were alone, and I lashed out, which I should not have done:

'Not at all. They're only trying to be helpful, which is what I thought the Conservatives were meant to be over Rhodesia. And they've never failed to speak well of you – or of Mrs Thatcher – so there's nothing wrong with their "loyalty" and I'm astounded you should query their actions rather than those of other members of your party like Edward du Cann and Duncan Sandys who appear to be working against your and our interests by remaining on the Board of Lonrho after an earlier Conservative Prime Minister (Edward Heath) called it "the unacceptable face of capitalism".'

The recital of these facts is not meant to imply that our view of Lord Carrington in any way resembled that of the American Secretary of State, General Haig, who in his anger over the Falklands war labelled Carrington a 'duplicitous bastard'; Carrington resigned during that war on a point of honour (over the mishandling of Intelligence). In our case, I believe Carrington did what he believed to be best for Britain and his party, a judgement upheld by Lord Home when I went to see him in Scotland during the early stages of the conference. Lord Home conducted Harold Hawkins and me around his ancestral estate, recounting something of the turbulent history of the Black Douglases and of terrorism and treachery in the Middle Ages; later, he gave us the soundest advice we were likely to receive anywhere in Britain and spoke highly of Carrington. Shortly before our departure Lady Home commented that her husband had always felt deeply about Rhodesia and would not die happy unless there was a satisfactory resolution of the problem.

On 27 September, the day before I was due to fly to Salisbury to brief the Commanders on British intentions, I went to the Foreign Office to meet the British team, Robin Byatt and Colonel Reilly, who would be flying out a few days later. My 'Top Secret Draft', cited above, recorded something of what was said at the meeting:

Sir Antony Duff went through the need to reassure the Commanders that the basic British intention was to preserve our Security Forces, and to be able to present a plan for 'Pre-Independence' towards the end of next week, or at the beginning of the week starting 8th October at the latest.... They are prepared for a confrontation on the P F plan for a transitional period – which Sir Antony classified as 'nine-tenths unacceptable', and went on to say the British would have no option but to 'throw it out of the window'; whereafter they expect to put their own plans on the table on a take-it-or-leave-it basis. In advance of all this, they must know that what they hope to do would be generally acceptable to the Commanders.... (I said) most Rhodesians had a built-in resistance to British control in any shape or form, but I believed that the Commanders could accept their plan as providing the best prospect offering.

The British had changed their minds about asking the Commissioner of Police to stand down and this, among other things that were said, reassured me as to the sincerity of their purpose. It was late in the evening when the meeting ended and Duff accompanied me out through a side entrance, appealing to me to return to him at any stage that I thought things were going wrong. Standing alone at the corner of a deserted Downing Street and Whitehall I was suddenly struck with a sense of destiny. We had now reached a stage where we could get it right at long last, or go into oblivion, having failed for the last time; and my role in it was vital.

I saw the Bishop shortly before going to the airport. My 'Top Secret Draft' contains an outline of our discussion:

I mentioned some of my apprehensions concerning the 'return to legality' involving as it does a transfer of loyalties by the Commanders and possible opposition by the White politicians. It was vital for me to know whether he still supported the plan as we understood it. He said he did.... He made a touching appeal for loyalty from the Commanders.... He had just had an hour alone with Lord Carrington and was convinced that the British wanted him to be returned as Prime Minister.... His assessment was that the P F would go right through with the elections, otherwise they were finished as far as the Frontline Presidents were concerned and would be forced into permanent exile. He appreciated the enormous problems that we (the Rhodesian officials) faced, but had complete confidence in us.

It was not until I was flying back to Salisbury that I began to realise what a serious problem the British had set for themselves. They could fill the vacuum created by Muzorewa's resignation only if the Commanders and the Heads of Ministries continued to function with full effect; in other words, key Rhodesians would have to run the country for the British during the transitional period without political direction at home or from abroad. As to the Bishop's problems, they were greater than anyone else's. He had already lost valuable support in the party and would be further denigrated at home and elsewhere in Africa when his agreement to step down became known, for his action would not be seen as self-sacrifice but as weakness. My thoughts then turned to the Commanders, of whom I was about to ask the near impossible, to transfer their loyalty to a transitory authority that had no more power than they themselves had; or, to put it another way, to give everything up for nothing without knowing where it would lead them.

I later recorded in my diary:

Back in Salisbury and meeting the Commanders alone, subsequently with Byatt and Reilly, we got a fair consensus of opinion in favour of the British plan, but the Commanders were opposed to the suggestion that the Bishop should have to stand aside and fight a new election. . . .

With enough knowledge of their inner feelings I could tell that they were more pro-Bishop (and one at least was pro-Smith) and more anti-British than I was, which made for a very tricky situation when my mission was to get them to abandon the Bishop, say goodbye for ever to Ian Smith, and support the British.

Whilst I was in Salisbury Peter Walls exceeded his authority by visiting South Africa and briefing their Prime Minister concerning the British plan, and coming back with strong objections from the South Africans if they have to deal with our Commanders in a political vacuum. Meantime, I had got no reassurances out of London that they (the British and the Bishop) were prepared to change plans to suit. But Peter Walls sent off an 'exclusive' to the PM in London which, ironically, he used as a weapon to convince all who saw it that the Commanders had accepted the Constitutional proposals otherwise they would not be concerning themselves about the next phase! An undue intrusion into politics. . . .

Then we had to cope with Ian Smith's untimely return to Salisbury, stirring up the White Caucus in opposition to the British proposals. And I've had to listen to P. K. van der Byl talking of leading an exodus of his constituents through a white corridor to South Africa – fighting every inch of the way if need be – and other pretty crazy conspiracies. But what better plan has Ian Smith or anyone else to offer?

It is only fair to Ian Smith to say at this juncture that his apprehensions proved well founded. Some five years later, in the Granada Television series entitled 'End of Empire', he said:

I could see through the Lancaster House agreement early on. I remember telling them – including Carrington – that the Constitution they were trying to sell us would give us a PF government.... They accused me of being alarmist – this was the talk in the corridors. I remember Lord Carrington saying to me: 'But my dear Mr Smith, the whole thing has been planned to ensure that that will not happen.'

I returned to London on 10 October to find that relationships between the members of Muzorewa's delegation had deteriorated further during my absence (Diary):

Some of the Bishop's own Ministers have turned against him because of his acceptance of the need to 'stand aside'. And if we are not arguing amongst ourselves within the delegation – with Ian Smith the most disruptive element – we are arguing with the Brits, although they have tried to work the whole thing out as one massive exercise in collusion, having failed to recognise the Bishop's government when they could have done so.

The conference was about to discuss the cease-fire and I advised Muzorewa that he should now enlarge his 'Think Tank' by calling in key members of NATJOC, particularly General Walls and Peter Allum, the Commisioner of Police. Hitherto, there had been only three members of the 'Think Tank' – Harold Hawkins, myself and Dr James Kamusikiri, who had abandoned his professorship at the University of Southern California to act as the Bishop's Secretary – and we had met daily or sometimes twice daily with our opposite numbers in the Foreign Office. Walls and Allum arrived in London three days later but during the preliminary session that our enlarged Think Tank had with the Bishop there emerged such a marked mood of depression that we all began to wonder whether our efforts over the past month had been worthwhile.

Matters deteriorated further at the next meeting of Muzorewa's delegation. Ian Smith was particularly virulent and talked of putting NATJOC (especially me) in its place; George Smith suggested that as the British had effectively torn up Rhodesia's constitution we should in turn tear up their new Zimbabwe constitution. A further complication arose when the South African Minister for Foreign Affairs, Pik Botha, appeared on the scene. My 'Top Secret Notes' contain the following:

Mr 'Pik' Botha arrived, blustering at the start, but was corrected. As Dr Kamusikiri said, 'his representations were two-thirds concoction.' He saw Mrs Thatcher who was quoted as saying: 'You must be mad if you really intended to withdraw support from Zimbabwe-Rhodesia.'...

AVM Hawkins and I dine with the Reverend Sithole and Minister David Zamchiya on the evening of Friday, 19th October, when the Reverend Sithole is taken away after dinner in 'Tiny' Rowland's chauffeur-driven car.

On the morning of Saturday, 20th October, we had an extremely rough meeting of delegates, with Minister Zindoga and Deputy Minister Andersen accusing AVM Hawkins of being 'grossly misleading' in his report-back on the previous day's meeting of the Legal Constitutional Committee, even before the Minutes he had taken were studied. Andersen and Adam (Ishmael Adam, the UANC Secretary for Finance) attacked the British and their plan with venom. Anyone who argued in favour; or suggested that there was no better alternative, attracted the stigma of 'British Agent'. At the end, without reaching any conclusion, the PM (Muzorewa) appealed to the meeting to face reality and not induce a situation where we 'would go back to our war empty-handed'....

Subsequently, we had numerous ups and downs within our own delegation, ending in another 11 to 1 vote on 25th October – this time in support of the interim arrangements as approved by the Bishop. On this occasion Deputy Minister Andersen spoke well in favour, and it even seemed at one stage that Mr Ian Smith might have voted 'Yes'....

At our 'Think Tank' meeting in the Foreign Office on 24th October, there was a sudden flare-up between General Walls and Sir John Graham (recently returned from Tehran to replace Sir Antony Duff and apparently not in touch), followed by an inflamed outburst by Dr Kamusikiri: all of which was set more or less right by Mr Robin Renwick, followed by Lord Carrington seeing General Walls. Apparently, Graham had thought he was back in the dreary months of 'non-negotiation' after the style of Ian Smith and Jack Gaylard. We never saw him again, as he was posted straight back to Tehran – indicative of Lord Carrington's determination to have people working readily with us.

In the meantime the Chief Justice of Zimbabwe-Rhodesia, Hector Macdonald, had flown over to London of his own volition to offer his services to the Bishop's delegation. He joined our discussions at a time when Ian Smith was arguing that Parliament must approve the Lancaster House proposals. Warming to his self-imposed task, Macdonald advised the blacks in our delegation that there was nothing to prevent them by-passing Parliament just as Smith had done, and reversing UDI in any way they wished. This amused the blacks and startled the whites, for Macdonald had the reputation of being an RF supporter and yet here he was, the highest legal authority in the land, persuading the blacks that justice should prevail against the RF.

The Conference continued. Nkomo, the practised politician who had come as the senior partner on the PF, livened up proceedings at plenary sessions, whereas Mugabe's unsmiling performance caused apprehension amongst our delegation through its sheer efficiency. Only Tongogara appealed to white sensibilities across the table, and at tea breaks would often chat with Walls and me while most other delegates on both sides sheltered behind self-imposed barriers. By half time Mugabe had taken a clear lead. His intellectual superiority gave him the edge in debate over Nkomo and over the Bishop and his team; on some occasions he seemed even to outsmart the British chairmen. Mugabe's skill in debate served only to increase the gloom in Muzorewa's delegation, but there were occasions when it inspired a little humour. After a particularly frustrating plenary session during which Mugabe and his team had seemed intent on obstruction, Sithole said, 'The PF's attitude is not that of virile obstruction. It's more like feminine indecision in a love affair when the lips say no but the eyes suggest yes.'

At the beginning of November it became apparent that the PF were considering circumventing the British by negotiating directly with us. My deputy had arranged for Walls and me to meet Nkomo and his Chief of Intelligence, Dumiso Dabengwa, in his hotel. Nkomo was keen to discuss mutual matters and· spoke forcefully of ZIPRA's difficulty in accepting what they knew of the British plan unless there had been a prior integration of the guerrilla armies and the Rhodesian Security Forces, which Walls could not have conceded at that stage. Nkomo then made a half-hearted attempt to get us interested in bi-lateral discussions with the PF, leaving out the British, stating that otherwise we would all be left at the end of the day in separate camps or opposing each other in the field. Again, Walls could not respond to this, for he could hardly say that he had been promised by the British that control would remain in the hand of the Security Forces.

There were no futher attempts by the PF to by-pass the British and on 15 November, against the expectations of the key members in the British team and our top negotiators, the PF accepted the transitional arrangements.

The news from home was that our Security Forces were striking with apparent recklessness into Zambia and Mozambique, hitting both military and economic targets. Much of Mozambique's transport system in Gaza Province was severely damaged by the destruction of road and rail bridges, while the rail link between the port of Beira and the coal-mining district of Moatize, north of the Zambezi River, was also cut. Then the SAS blew up ten vital road bridges on either side of Lusaka and destroyed a major railway bridge across the Chambesi River in northern Zambia, severing the Chinese-built Tanzam Railway from Dar-es-Salaam. With the Benguela Railway linking Zambia to the Atlantic still blocked, and the Kazangula ferry linking her with Botswana destroyed, this meant that Zambia's only link with the outside world was, once again, through Zimbabwe-Rhodesia.

The Security Forces struck with customary efficiency but at a greater cost than ever before. ZIPRA defences had been improved through Cuban, East German and Russian instructors, while ZANLA had acquired more effective Soviet equipment, including anti-aircraft weapons. In a three-day raid into Mozambique in September the Security Forces lost thirty men, including thirteen shot down in a helicopter. Then a South African 'Puma' assisting the Security Forces was shot down by missile fire, killing the three-man crew. Later, ZANLA's 'New Chimoio' base was overrun, but in the face of fierce resistance, and there was one occasion when an RLI unit, one of the toughest elements in the Rhodesian Army, had to beat an uncharacteristic retreat.

Then it appeared that COMOPS in Salisbury had devised a new strategy — 'Total War' — to please our South African allies and to take effect within the period of six weeks that the Lancaster House Conference had originally been expected to last. This strategy might have succeeded, if only by escalating the war so as to bring in the major powers on both sides and thus provide relief for our hard-pressed military forces. But COMOPS were in no position to get political clearance from a government or War Council half of whom were in London. Nor could their strategic plan be fully implemented, and unrelated parts of it appeared more suspect than in fact was the case, causing unneccesary friction between Walls, who could not be adequately consulted in London, and the rest of COMOPS in Salisbury.

The irony of it was that Britain's non-recognition of Muzorewa's government meant that Britain could not hold Muzorewa or any other consitutional authority responsible for COMOPS' action. The NATJOC members in London (Allum, Connolly and myself) would normally have been consulted but we could not remain conversant with the developing situation as seen by COMOPS, and the tendency grew for COMOPS to strike first rather than risk a refusal from any of us in London. We were not necessarily opposed to the new strategy. Indeed, it seemed appropriate on several occasions to give our support in retrospect rather than criticise the remainder of the team in Salisbury, particularly when the main effect of the external military raids was to impel the British negotiators towards a more rapid conclusion of the Conference; Kaunda declared that Zambia was now 'in a state of war with Rhodesia', therefore he would apply greater pressure on Nkomo to settle, and President Machel appeared ready to take whatever action he could to end the war in Mozambique.

This all increased the strain for those of us in London. As we approached the end of November I wrote in my diary: 'Nearly three months in hotels in London! With the traumas of the Conference driving our delegation up the wall and over. Not surprising that young Giles committed suicide.... [contrary to speculation that he was a victim of some Intelligence operation].'

Among the issues which led to a strain in relations was one concerning a promise Carrington had made to Walls while discussing the cease-fire. Carrington had frequently invited Walls to his flat for an exchange of confidences and had offered certain assurances which he said he was prepared to commit to writing. He had, for example, assured Walls that the Security Forces could continue cross-border raids under certain circumstances and that Walls, as Commander, COMOPS, would not be subjected to the control of a British Governor, adding that if he encountered problems in that regard he would have the right of direct access to Thatcher. Subsequently, Carrington changed his mind, saying that an exposure of such guarantees could bring down the British government and he was prepared only to acknowledge an unwritten gentleman's agreement. Walls would not accept this. In my 'Notes' cited above I made the following observations:

General Walls and I had a torrid hour or so over a bottle of whisky in Duff's office after a two-hour joint session with the others – with Tony Duff trying to talk us out of 'that bit of paper' which had been promised General Walls by Lord Carrington, assuring him – amongst other things – that our Security Forces could continue cross-border raids under certain circumstances. I said that if Lord Carrington had gone back on his word, he must be prepared to offer us the equivalent, if not something better, in oral reassurances or guarantees, and I suggested that this could only be done before Mrs Thatcher and those of us who are primarily concerned – i.e. General Walls, Mr Allum and myself.

Unfortunately, I was in Paris, discussing the progress of the Conference and the prospects of France uplifting sanctions, when the appointment with Thatcher materialised. Fog prevented me returning in time to join the meeting, but within an hour of its termination I had been de-briefed by Walls on what had transpired at No 10 Downing Street. Walls maintained that Thatcher had endorsed what Carrington had proposed and had confirmed that Walls could have direct access to her if he was not satisfied with the way things were going in Rhodesia under Soames, but that neither she nor Carrington could be expected to commit this to writing; he must take it as a gentleman's agreement. My own interpretation was that Thatcher had to support Carrington as her Foreign Secretary but not to the extent of diminishing what little authority Soames was expected to exercise as British Governor in Rhodesia. No Rhodesians could be placed under the direct command of Soames, but Thatcher must have hoped that we would all support him as far as we could, and that only in extreme circumstances should Walls, or anyone else, have direct access to herself.

Walls was not the only one who had started showing signs of tension. Smith's patience had run out and he accused the British in plenary session of deliberately causing delays which would lead to unnecessary bloodshed in Rhodesia. But Carrington cracked back: 'If there's blood on anyone's hands, Mr Smith, it's on yours.'

On 11 December, with so many issues still unresolved, the British advised our delegation that we were now in 'Lacuna' because Muzorewa had officially stood aside as Prime Minister and no longer represented any constitutional authority. Soames had flown to Salisbury to assume the responsibilities of a British Governor. To send out a Governor with little or no constitutional authority or military or executive control was a desperate move on Carrington's part to try to force an early end to the Conference. He was gambling once again that if he moved forward with Muzorewa's delegation, the PF would not want to be left out.

I sought out the Bishop's deputy, Dr Mundawarara, and said as forcefully as I could that someone representing the Bishop's government – preferably himself – should return to Salisbury without delay, for the longer the Prime Minister and his deputy remained in London, with a British Governor in Salisbury, the more their political prospects would be diminished. The advice I was receiving from Salisbury at this time seemed to indicate that the only hope the Bishop had of recovering lost ground was to push for elections as quickly as possible. The advantage of time lay entirely with the PF as they could infiltrate hundreds, running into thousands, of armed men into Rhodesia to secure support for themselves through force.

The PF were given till 11 o'clock on 15 December to accept the ceasefire terms. We did not expect them to agree for, among other things, their spokesman, Eddison Zvobgo, had said on 14 December: 'The answer is a clear and eloquent "No" to Carrington: the answer is "No" and he and his Governor can go hang.' We learnt later at a meeting with Foreign Office officials that Mugabe had been en route to catch a flight to New York, intent on rejecting the cease-fire terms and attracting support to continue the war, when he had been recalled to take a phone call from Samora Machel. Machel had virtually ordered Mugabe to sign, indicating that if he did not the most he could expect back in Mozambique was political asylum or a villa on the coast. We

were also told of the serious effect our continued military raids and
MNR activities were having on Machel, whose country was now suffering from extreme problems caused by damaged communications and
food shortages. One official quoted Machel as saying that it was no
longer a question of 'a luta continua' (the war continues).

On 14 December I returned to Salisbury to assess the situation on the
ground, and on the following day received the news from London that
the PF had accepted the cease-fire arrangements.

The time factor became even more crucial in the discussions in which I
was involved after returning to London on 20 December. My official
record notes:

During the next few days we had one argument after another with the British on
the time factor. Whether, for instance, four to six weeks were needed after
registration (of political parties contesting the election), or whether it had to be
a clear two months period before the PF could compete in the elections or
whether the Government would proscribe the PF in certain circumstances....
We held up signing the agreement for two days and General Walls threatened
one of his periodic 'walk-outs'. I reckoned there was a limit as to how far we
could get the Bishop to delay signing when he is represented as The Man of
Peace and the PF might get the advantage of the Bishop prolonging the war and
they are the only party capable of stopping it.

It was clear that the war was now moving Mugabe's way. The Security
briefing I received from CIO after my return to London made dismal
reading:[4]

The current situation is not good owing to the terrorist presence which has
made itself felt to a greater or lesser extent throughout the country with the
possible exception of the major urban areas. The influx of greater numbers of
trained terrorists under ceasefire proposals will further adversely affect the
situation unless the ceasefire arrangements are adequate, the returning terrorists
are properly monitored and those in neighbouring countries are prevented from
infiltrating.... The ZANLA High Command are reported to believe that, in
many cases, junior commanders would challenge any ceasefire instructions.
Reports emanating from some groups of terrorists operating in Rhodesia, particularly ZANLA, indicate that they do not intend to abide by any ceasefire ...
(but) a ZIPRA commander recently produced a letter which he alleged was
signed by Joshua Nkomo, directing every effort be made to promote the election, adhere to any ceasefire and co-operate with ZANLA.... The following
figures illustrate assessed ZIPRA and ZANLA strengths:

	ZIPRA	ZANLA
Deployed internally	4055	10275
Held in external bases (trained)	16000	3500
Under training externally	2950	14000
Totals:	23005	27775
Grand Total	50780	

Forecast election results
Bishop Muzorewa and his UANC Party swept to power with an impressive majority in the April elections and his Party is confidently predicting a repeat performance. However, an assessment – based on careful analysis of the previous election returns and current Intelligence – indicates that the Patriotic Front could well gain a marginal election victory over the UANC, but the assessment may radically change once campaigning gets under way.... It must be emphasised that tribal allegiance will play an important part in the election and this could cause a re-alignment of the existing political parties.

Rhodesia, as ever, was a political football, but after three months at Lancaster House the stuffing had been knocked out of most of us and the Bishop was utterly deflated. Whatever leadership he had attempted to display had been undermined by Smith's disruptive tactics and by the incessant arguments within his delegation. Significantly, however, these arguments had more often than not been white against white or black against black, rather than black against white, for during the sojourn in London a fine relationship had developed between black and white members of Muzorewa's team. I was touched by James Kamusikiri's oft-expressed concern that I was overdoing things and needed to relax, when he had not the slightest idea how to relax himself, and was pleased to hear David Zamchiya and Dr Mundawarara saying at the end how much we had all benefited from our association and that this proved that black and white Rhodesians could work satisfactorily together.

The job at Lancaster House was not quite finished, as my Top Secret Notes disclose:

In discussions between us (Foreign Office officials, Walls and I), we agreed that it would make it easier for everybody if the split in the PF were widened.... Our FO friends re-iterated that it was no part of the British plan to have Mugabe winning the elections. The difference now is that Machel and not the British has been making the running.... We received other confirmation that Tongogara and Dabengwa were now trying to make the process (of calling guerrillas into Assembly Points) work....
I took the opportunity to comment that we still lacked proper interchange of Intelligence with our professional British colleagues. In fact, more was volunteered in half an hour at the Foreign Office than we had had offered in routine exchanges with British Intelligence....
On the morning of 21st December, 1979, I accompanied Bishop Muzorewa, Dr Mundawarara, Chief Ndiweni and General Walls to see Lord Carrington, before the Bishop moved on to see Mrs Thatcher, and was surprised to listen to the Bishop complaining to Lord Carrington that he needed money to fight the elections, and Lord Carrington confirming with him that they had agreed to do just that.
We attended the signing ceremony (the Constitutional agreement had been signed on 6th December; what was being signed on 21st December was the

agreement on ceasefire and transitional arrangements) and the immediately following reception at Lancaster House.

Subsequently, travelling back to Salisbury with General Walls and myself, Chief Ndiweni offered to stay in the game provided he was given sufficient funds to compete in the election. It became apparent during the discussion that [as an Ndebele Chief] he would not really expect to be able to compete against Nkomo on a ZAPU ticket, but that if Nkomo competes on a PF ticket, it will emerge that Mugabe has virtually no political following in Matabeleland. . . . (he went on to say) that neither Nkomo nor Mugabe can possibly expect a clear run. It is more likely that the major issue will be fought out by Tongogara and Dabengwa.

We arrived home to little applause for our efforts. Instead, there was deep suspicion and widespread concern over the pitfalls in the Lancaster House Agreement. In London and elsewhere, however, Lord Carrington and his team were being congratulated on having engineered a solution to a problem which had plagued successive British governments for half a century.

CHAPTER 13

Rhodesia under Soames

Settlement at Lancaster House brought a sense of relief and a semblance of peace. A new course had been set and there was an overall awareness that the control exercised by the old Anglo-Rhodesian establishment was fading. Yet while much was changing, much remained the same. Ian Smith continued to play a negative role, lashing out at the British for imposing a solution he considered unworkable; Abel Muzorewa continued to count on the British to see him right; and the British were as anxious as ever to relieve themselves of the last vestiges of responsibility for Rhodesia, for the Bishop and for any of us caught in the middle. We had no more sanguine anticipation of the outcome than we had had over the past fifteen years and were as troubled by doubt, frustration and argument as we had ever been.

Lord Soames had been in Rhodesia for five weeks when I wrote the following in my diary:

Sunday 20th January 1980. Virtually the same traumas apply! The same sort of arguments as filled much of our time in London continue to frustrate and annoy.

The process of 'Assembly' of guerrillas has proceeded remarkably well; but the doubts grow apace that the Bishop may be losing out; because the Patriotic Front have returned as 'Liberators' – which was never intended, and Mugabe's people have deliberately broken the cease-fire.

' The sharpest point of confrontation is with the British. Will they or will they not proscribe, or otherwise act effectively against ZANLA? Having inveigled us into agreement through various phases of finesse – in particular that we had nothing to fear in asking the Bishop and his government to stand aside as they were certain to be re-elected – we are now faced with growing reluctance by the British to do anything about ZANLA's flagrant contraventions of the cease-fire agreement. And, once again, the blackmailing tactics of the Front Line Presidents outweigh in effectiveness the British desire to do the right thing by us, for it's more important to them that Mugabe should be seen to compete in elections and fail, than that the Bishop should be at risk, or that we might end up without a viable government; or that everything is left in chaos. Meantime, Peter Walls fluctuates between threats and sullen silences. All of which adds to the considerable stress and strain. His latest threat was to 'blow' the cease-fire: start the war again, and throw ourselves on the mercy of the South Africans: as if such a tactic could possibly work!

The cease-fire arrangements had been accepted reluctantly by the Rhodesian Commanders, and it is to their credit that they tried hard to make them work even when it was against their own interests to do so and when all other parties were displaying a more partisan approach. Against this background, Walls' 'threats and sullen silences' were understandable. In his effort to assist in the peaceful implementation of the Lancaster House Agreement he was faced with a number of major problems. ZIPRA complied with the cease-fire arrangements as far as its forces inside the country were concerned but kept most of its armed forces in Zambia. ZANLA would no doubt have observed the cease-fire under the leadership of Tongogara but his untimely death in the last week of 1979 had placed ZANLA under more direct political control of the ZANU(PF) party leaders known to be opposed to the cease-fire and any settlement other than victory in the field.* And within the Rhodesian forces Walls and his fellow Commanders were faced with an apparent determination by some junior officers to force events in the direction they believed they should go. Like many white Rhodesians, these officers had grown to detest Nkomo following the massacre of the air crash survivors and had developed an intense fear of Mugabe following the publication in November 1978 of the ZANU(PF) 'Death List'.[1] My diary entry on 4 February 1980 makes mention of an incident which illustrates the attitude adopted by such officers:

Over the weekend R sought my approval for eliminating Mugabe according to three different plans – all of which I vetoed, explaining that the Powers-that-be were determined to make the cease-fire work and hold successful elections. But this did not prevent R and some others from contacting me the following morning (Sunday) to say there was no means of stopping Plan No 3 – as if this could have been true when we had agreed to stop it the previous day! But when I said categorically that it had to be stopped or I would go out and stop it personally, and that there was no other authority to whom they could appeal – R demurred, obviously having ignored everything we had agreed and still gone ahead with his plans.

In the event I managed to stop the original plans, but not the massacre of fifteen or more wedding guests who should have played no part in this.

Now we have a stark confrontation. Myself adopting the line that fair is fair, God-dammit, whilst some of the military have tried to get away with doing their own thing: although the responsibility – or the blame – is still being passed to me.

In this very tricky game one should have absolute confidence in one's associ-

---

* Josiah Tongogara, Chief of Defence in ZANU's 'Dare-re-Chimurenga' and Commander-in-Chief of the ZANLA forces, was killed in a road accident in Mozambique. The Mozambicans subsequently invited Walls and myself to check the facts surrounding his death and we were satisfied that there had been no foul play.

ates, but that confidence has been desperately breached by the lies and deception to which I have been subjected. Apart from this, it has never been our practice to approve the killing of innocents.

The pace was hotting up and a subject now of vital concern to us all – intimidation and the effect it was having throughout the country – led to a confrontation between COMOPS and the Governor, the opening round of which occurred in early February.

The subject of intimidation in all its manifold forms assumed such significance that it held priority over any other, for it threatened the very emergence of the new State of Zimbabwe. But the British were in an extremely difficult position. Through force of circumstance, they had to rely on the Rhodesian Security Forces to maintain order but could neither assume responsibility for Rhodesian military action nor avoid censure for the failures of the administration they had imposed on the country. The lightly armed Cease-fire Monitoring Group (CMG), commanded by Major-General Acland and comprising British and Commonwealth (Australian, New Zealand, Fijian and Kenyan) troops, was the only military force under the direct control of the Governor but, as its title implied, it was there only to monitor the cease-fire, not to enforce it. The CMG did perform a valuable function in organising the Assembly Points at which the guerrillas were required to report with their arms and maintained a commendable impartiality between the innumerable bodies of armed men throughout the country, but it was broken down into small groups which could not have done much more than defend themselves if the numerically superior guerrillas at any of the Assembly Points had turned against them.

The CMG presence was therefore little more than a gesture of precarious British responsibility, utterly ineffective against the widespread intimidation which continued unobserved around it. Similarly, the Commonwealth Observer Group (COG) which flew in later had no responsibility to do anything but 'observe' the election proceedings, leaving it to a British Governor with minimal powers to guarantee the fairness of elections being conducted by the white agencies of the old Rhodesia.

In CIO and COMOPS none of us had any doubt as to the effectiveness of ZAPU/ZIPRA 'politicisation' throughout rural Matabeleland. This was Nkomo's domain and no other party dared intrude upon it and expect to get out alive. Only in the urban area of Bulawayo, where there were thousands of migrant Shona workers, could a non-ZAPU voice be heard. For a while, Sithole's followers managed to survive in fringe areas of Matabeleland, using whatever counter-intimidatory methods they could to establish themselves, but as the election campaign swung into top gear they became an insignificant factor. Muzorewa, as a 'Man of God' and a 'Man of Peace', attracted support from the women of Mashonaland and Manicaland but he realised too late that such support was ineffective in a male-dominated society faced with the ultimate threat that the war would continue if those waging it were not voted into power. And his Auxiliaries were quite unable to match the intimidatory tactics used by hardcore ZIPRA and ZANLA forces in the field.

All of this posed serious problems for Lord Soames. While other parties could ignore the Lancaster House Agreement with impunity, he was left to shoulder the blame for tardiness in fulfilling the terms of the Agreement, and where he needed co-operation he had to rely solely on the goodwill of the officials serving Muzorewa's 'set aside' government. A typical example of his predicament concerned the release of political detainees. Many detainees in Zambia had been released by Rhodesian Security Forces. Those in Mozambique, such as Mukutu Hamadziripi and others detained by FRELIMO at the instigation of ZANU(PF) following the Nhari rebellion and the assassination of Chitepo, were beyond Soames's control although the Lancaster House Agreement had specified that they should be released at the same time as those in Zambia. In Rhodesia, however, the release of 'political detainees' was subject to the normal processes of the law and a not unwilling Police Force found it difficult to differentiate in their recommendations between criminals who had capitalised on the upsurge of lawlessness in the country (murder, robbery and stock-theft) and the comparatively few genuine political detainees. Soames suffered international condemnation for his apparent failure to release what the world called 'political detainees'.

On similar lines, Soames had hoped to persuade Walls to withdraw Muzorewa's Auxiliaries, which were attached to the Rhodesian Security Forces, or to cancel their deployment in the field. But Walls was reluctant to take such one-sided action when it was suspected that ZANLA had deployed thousands of their guerrillas throughout the Shona-speaking areas in defiance of the cease-fire conditions. Indeed, the more-or-less licensed intimidation which developed so sharply on all sides, and the threat that the Rhodesian Commanders might respond to ZANLA's violations of the cease-fire by attacking the Assembly Points, forced Soames to accept the re-deployment of Rhodesian Security Forces throughout the operational areas.

It was clear that the advantage in this set of circumstances lay with ZANU(PF), not least because of their numerical superiority and the ease with which they could deploy guerrillas throughout the north-eastern and eastern areas contiguous with Mozambique. But it was the south-eastern area, centred on Fort Victoria and inhabited by the Karanga, the largest ethnic group in the country, that really mattered. In CIO we were of the opinion that the election results would be determined by the 'silent majority' and the hitherto uncommitted Karanga people. Nkomo, Muzorewa and Sithole all laid claim to Karanga allegiance, but as time went on only Mugabe's party were able to produce effective political leaders among the Karanga, such as Simon Muzenda, Eddison Zvobgo and Emmerson Mnangagwa. All the other parties soon discovered that their representatives were unable to survive in the Fort Victoria district, let alone canvass there.

The counting of heads was the factor which would dominate all others, and in the end sheer numerical weight would in itself prove the most effective form of intimidation. In CIO we knew enough of what was going on to realise that the pending elections would be subject to intimidatory practices, but it was not in the nature of things that we could have known of the more sinister nature of underground intimidation. As far as we were aware, Rex Nhongo, the ZANLA Commander, had instructed 7000 or more guerrillas to ignore the cease-fire and hide their weapons throughout the central and eastern electioneering areas, to be used to persuade the people to vote for ZANU(PF). Several years later, in the Granada Television series 'End of Empire', Zvobgo put it this way:

British Intelligence repeatedly said that there were something like six to eight thousand ZANLA guerrillas inside the country. But when we were asked to declare how many guerrillas we had, we chose to declare 20,000. If everybody thought we had 8000 and we were willing to deliver 20,000, then clearly we didn't have anybody else left. In fact, we had a very large army left, who remained as political commissars in the country simply to ensure that we would win the election.

It is worth noting the views given in the same television series by the other principal participants:

Joshua Nkomo: It was not just 'intimidation'. We lost people. We lost a candidate. We lost eighteen to twenty party workers killed by the young men who were deployed by ZANU outside the Assembly Points. We learnt later that they were never committed to Assembly Points. They were given a task that during the elections they would see to it that everyone in that area voted ZANU.

General Walls: They (ZANLA) sent in (to the Assembly Points) their Mujibas [young boys] with a few ant-eaten old muskets and a few rusty old weapons that couldn't possibly have been the terrorist weapons and equipment. Meantime, the terrorists themselves mingled with the population and made damn certain which way they were going to vote in the forthcoming election. . . . The massive intimidation had its intended effect. There was no way this was going to be a free and fair election.

Lord Soames [speaking on arrival in Salisbury]: I want to see the freest, fairest elections possible in this country ... but intimidation is rife, violence is rife, and I've got to do everything I can to minimise this.... You must remember this is Africa. This isn't Little Puddleton-on-the-Marsh, and they behave differently here. They think nothing of sticking tent poles up each other's whatnot, and doing filthy beastly things to each other. It does happen, I'm afraid. It's a very wild thing, an election.

On 4 February the members of COMOPS went en bloc to Government House to confront the Governor and his staff on the subject of intimidation. I had been delegated to set the scene. My aide mémoire read:[2]

All know that all parties to the Lancaster House Agreement committed themselves to free and fair elections – to campaign peacefully – not through intimidation – and to observe the cease-fire....

Our side at Lancaster House fought for you (the Governor) to have the authority to proscribe a party that flagrantly flouted the rules. We would say that there is more than enough evidence of violations to justify proscription ... it is imperative that the main offenders are not seen to be winning through foul means – because if they are, it can only attract more support to themselves as the bulk of our more primitive population will either climb on to the band-wagon, or support the man they believe to be winning.

All parties were supposed to renounce the use of force, but Mugabe's spokesmen are saying that only they can end the war – which means that they will continue the war if they do not win (the most potent intimidation of all).

While I spoke, my mind went back to the last occasion, nearly fifteen years previously, when in the same room in Government House the Rhodesian Commanders and I had discussed UDI in a gentlemanly style, but surreptitiously, with Sir Humphrey Gibbs. Now there was more of an edge on things and the Commanders were poles apart from the Governor. Gibbs had represented the Queen and the Commanders stood by their oath of allegiance, but Soames represented a British Government to whom the Commanders owed no allegiance. Gibbs had stood against UDI on constitutional principles and would not have tolerated political interference from Salisbury or London, whereas Soames was presiding over the death of UDI, a political act, on behalf of a British government that seemed to have abandoned constitutional niceties for peace at any price.

As the discussion developed, most members of COMOPS became so belligerent as to be insulting in their demands upon the Governor. I felt saddened by the fact that ninety years of Anglo-Rhodesian association which both sides had been proud to sustain through war and peace had come to this.

While the subject of intimidation continued to absorb much of my thinking, significant developments were taking place south of our border (Diary):

Sunday 10th February: Two further attempts on Mugabe's life at Fort Victoria yesterday and today, both of which aborted. How crazy can you be! And how I wish I were out of it!

In between, more traumas with Peter Walls. Rows over his latest speech, with senior Brits thinking the Governor would have to sack him if he continued criticising in public, or tried to force the Governor's hand. But in the event, the lion, Peter, roared and to most people it sounded like the moo of a cow.

As it emerges now, Mugabe's party must try and force their way to power or continue the war: and they should be banned on both counts....

Peter Walls and I are off to see the South African Prime Minister, at their request. It seems they are working it out that they should continue to give us the utmost assistance, or face the prospect of a Marxist regime on their borders. This may give us the protection we need, but will it provide the political settlement without which the war will continue?

Rhodesia's relationship with South Africa had changed since P. W. Botha had become Prime Minister in 1978. In March 1979 a high-powered military delegation headed by Magnus Malan, the South African Defence Force Commandant-General, had visited Salisbury. The delegation held discussions with NATJOC. Essentially, the attitudes the South Africans were promoting were that military influence would now dominate their domestic and foreign policies; that because of vacillation by the Western Powers there would be no further compromise over Namibia, where they expected to be in control for at least another decade; that UNITA posed a greater threat to the Angolan government than SWAPO posed to the South African government in Namibia and it would therefore suit the South Africans to keep the situation in southern Angola destabilised, thus helping UNITA and further hindering SWAPO; that they expected Mozambique to become an active base for the SAANC poised to strike against South Africa and would respond accordingly; that the main threats facing South Africa were the possibility of sanctions and of international pressures created by her association with Namibia and Rhodesia; and that they considered that Russia was working to a five-year plan to establish domination in Africa but before the end of that period Russia would have to repair her relationship with China.

When Walls and I visited Pretoria in February 1980 we were given an unexpectedly friendly reception. Walls was highly regarded there, but we had often been in conflict with their representative at Lancaster House and I was known to have had a strong commitment to the previous regime of Vorster and van den Bergh, both of whom were now in disgrace. Botha and his colleagues displayed a surprising reasonableness in their attitudes, going so far as to say they would be prepared to accept a PF victory in the forthcoming elections, preferably with Nkomo heading a coalition government. Their earlier condemnation of Nkomo as a committed communist no longer applied and they saw him as the best prospect for a balanced pro-Western government.

The South Africans went on to say that while the cease-fire remained precarious they would maintain their current force levels in Rhodesia, which stood at about 800 military personnel. The deployment of these forces in the the south-eastern and Limpopo border areas could provide stability against the deteriorating situation in Mozambique and at the same time be available to protect Rhodesian whites if there was a large-scale exodus to South Africa. They were quite prepared to confront the British on any points affecting the security of Southern Africa and had already reached agreement with Soames that South African troops would protect the vital connection between South Africa and Rhodesia at Beit Bridge.

This meeting in Pretoria was significant in that, clearly, the South Africans were not concerned to try to influence the political outcome of the elections. It also marked something of a turning point in the orientation of Rhodesian military personnel. Those who wished to continue their careers in uniform began to look primarily to South Africa, rather than consider staying in the new Zimbabwe forces or joining the British forces. The subsequent southward migration of servicemen was facilitated by the Rhodesian Commanders' decision to promote what was known as the 'Incentive Scheme'. Designed to offer white servicemen a greater remittability of pensions abroad for every year they continued to serve, the 'Incentive Scheme' had been formulated under Smith's government with the aim of keeping a substantial white nucleus in the armed forces. At that time it had received little support from the Zimbabwe-Rhodesia Treasury but at Lancaster House it attracted considerably more support when it was broadened to include civil servants. Unfortunately, it was made operative immediately, without imposing any obligation to continue in service and regardless of the effect it would have on an incoming black government, which would see it as encouraging whites to desert their posts with a golden handshake.

The 'Incentive Scheme' cost the country dear. White servicemen found it attractive, as did a range of civil servants, from judges to office clerks. On my return from Lancaster House I found that senior members of my staff had arranged for CIO personnel to be included in the scheme, thus undermining years of negotiation with government to ensure independence of action for the organisation. Many of my own staff left saying they could not afford to miss out on such an attractive inducement to leave. Servicemen who had been expected to maintain national security left with tens of thousands of dollars, denuding the country of much needed foreign currency. The scheme destroyed any remaining obligation of national loyalty once the majority of government servants left, and it was difficult to understand why it was allowed to continue when its perversion became so apparent. The problem was compounded by South Africa's ready acceptance of all and sundry, whereas previously they had promised to discriminate and to avoid draining Rhodesia of whites. To add salt to the wound, many of those who fled to South Africa, at the expense of the Zimbabwean taxpayer, turned themselves into agents of destabilisation, bent on ruining the country that continued to provide their pensions.

My subsequent diary entry added a footnote about my trip to Pretoria, and then went on to describe events at home after my return:

Apart from the top South Africans, I met my old friend 'Y' from CIA HQ who waxed enthusiastic over our performance in CIO and mentioned how impressed George Bush had been when Director CIA....

Sadly, when I got home, I was again involved, in-or-out-of 'Special Operations', mostly unauthorised, half-baked and more damaging to us than the enemy – even the near destruction of three churches including the old Presbyterian Church in the centre of Salisbury where Kennedy-Grant and my father had been minister: as if the members of that congregation could possibly have been victims of a terrorist attack, or in any way involved! And the death during urban sabotage of two members of the Selous Scouts. All of which led to sharp confrontation at top level – rapidly resolved I'm pleased to say – between Peter Allum, Peter Walls and myself.

It was not long before Walls and I were again flying across the border, this time to Maputo. After more than five years of trans-border raids, with our Security Forces striking deeper and deeper into Mozambique at ZANLA/FRELIMO bases and lines of communication, it was with some trepidation that we responded to an invitation by FRELIMO to visit Mozambique to discuss the new relationship (Diary):

Sunday 24th February: Peter Walls and I made a quick trip to Maputo yesterday – the first since my abortive trip to see General Costa Gomes in Lourenco Marques following the coup in Lisbon. Now everything has changed. Silent, near empty streets. Long queues at the only shops with anything for sale.

On the way down P W asked me whether we should avoid having lunch in
case they poisoned our food. Maybe I've been around too long, or am just too
trusting, for I said I would eat whatever was put in front of us – as we did: cold
(meant to be hot) prawns; hot (meant to be cold) something else, served in not
unreasonable style but not to compare with living in the old Lourenco Marques.

Even the revolutionary General Sebastio Mabote treated us like long lost
friends, beaming smiles at us whilst insisting we address each other by first
names – overlooking his own lack of English or anything other than basic
Portuguese as a language we could use between us.

At least we found mutual respect between enemies; and much hilarity when
we compared our unavailing attempts to kill each other!

While Walls discussed military subjects with FRELIMO's High Command, I was taken to see Joaquim Chissano, the Foreign Minister, with
whom I had a tête-à-tête which turned out to be surprisingly helpful.
Chissano tried to persuade me to influence opinion in Rhodesia in
favour of Mugabe, the man he considered to be the only leader to have
popular support. He ignored my interruptions to the effect that this
support was 'politicised' rather than 'popular', and brushed aside my
comments on Mugabe's ideological stance:

Mugabe is not a Marxist as we are. He is not even a Communist. And you
whites must not allow him to repeat the same mistakes that we made here in
getting rid of most of the whites ... although this was not our fault. We did not
want the Portuguese whites to go; it was the right-wing backlash in Lourenco
Marques shortly after the coup that forced their exodus. It was something
falsely staged by a few conspirators whom you must have known![3]

He knew I knew, or he would not have addressed me with such persuasion.

I listened, most interested in Chissano's attempt to repair some of the
damage that we had inflicted upon each other and fascinated at the
remarkable resemblance between him and the bust of his hero Lenin
which peered at me over his shoulder. Clearly, Chissano was keen that
Mugabe should win the election. He saw no hope for Muzorewa because he did not command the confidence of Machel; during the months
the Bishop had stayed in Maputo they had got to know him well and
saw him as incapable of governing except as a puppet. Despite my
attempt to portray the Bishop as a unifier, Chissano was in no doubt
that if the Bishop got into power the war would go on, for both Mugabe
and Nkomo were fighting against the Bishop's government.

Other than this oblique reference to Nkomo, Chissano seemed reluctant to consider him a possible ruler of Zimbabwe. When I insisted that
he must be considered, Chissano said there was a slight hope that
Nkomo could be acceptable to Machel if he emerged as the leader after

the elections and that this could end the war out of Mozambique. But we agreed that Nkomo's tribal support was less than Mugabe's and was based in areas more remote from Mozambique.

To my surprise, Chissano warned several times against 'political assassinations' and said how worried they had been to get reports that a number of attempts had been made on Mugabe's life. There was little I could say to this, except:

Mugabe had become a target for attack from all sides; and I told Chissano what Mugabe had said to the Governor when he explained he had decided not to go to Bulawayo for his major rally there because he had learnt that Nkomo's minions were planning to assassinate him.

It emerged during our discussion that neither General Walls nor I had ever exchanged words with Mugabe, although we were on satisfactory personal terms with Muzorewa, Sithole, Nkomo and most of the African political leaders, in which respect, Chissano was critical; but I felt the best reply I could offer was that any relationship of that nature had to be reciprocal and it was a simple fact of life that the others were pleased to be working with us, whereas Mugabe had made no gesture in that direction. . . .

General Walls told me (later) that there had been a query concerning our personal relationship with Mugabe, as a result of which they had said Honwana would bring back a message to Mugabe from Machel, ordering him to contact General Walls — which was subsequently done.

Not surprisingly, Chissano also had something to say about the MNR, presuming that I would now disassociate myself from it:

Chissano inferred that all of us were puppets of South Africa, which I disputed. He seemed genuinely concerned over the imminent threat by South Africa to intervene in our affairs if the (election) result was not to their pleasing, but I reassured him that this was just not on.

He talked intensely of the 'Resistance' (MNR) and our alleged support for it — almost to the extent that we fell out — but I did what I could to gloss over it by saying there had never been anything like the support for Mozambique 'Resistance' from our side that there had been by Mozambique for those attacking our country. And, surely, we must let bygones be bygones and hope that an incoming Government in Salisbury would be acceptable in Maputo, and therefore should not be concerned to support any 'Resistance' in Mozambique. . . . We ended our discussion by Chissano saying that I could assist tremendously if I was that way inclined.

Of course, I was flannelling, avoiding the main issue, but enough was said during this visit to convince me that the time had come to divest ourselves of the MNR. In General Mabote's presence FRELIMO's military personnel scoffed at the MNR as 'just a bunch of bandits', implying that their demise was near at hand, but Chissano was much more serious in his analysis of the movement. Two of the three main points which emerged from my talk with him were that Mugabe would be victorious and that he owed much to Machel. The third was that the MNR should be disbanded. Accordingly, I arranged for all those serving in the movement to be advised to revert to civilian life; those who wished to continue in operations on their own account were to be told that there would be no further link with Zimbabwe; alternatively, they could be transferred to South African control.

To my great surprise, the vast majority not only preferred to continue in the field but took no exception to being placed under South African control. Unfortunately, the principles that had guided us when controlling the MNR could not be applied when arranging the South African take-over. We had resisted the intrusion of any white Portuguese or Mozambicans who might subvert the movement and had avoided military involvement for fear that the MNR would be turned into just another group of foreign mercenaries. Now we had to deal with the South African military who had assumed the controlling interest in all external operations and were the only Service that could offer the MNR the viable alternative they seemed to desire.

The South African response was immediate and enthusiastic. It was decided that some of their military officers should live for a while with CIO staff, picking up the ropes and making preparations for the transition. Within days, the final arrangements were completed and the MNR was transferred lock, stock and barrel. In the meantime I had told the British a little of CIO's involvement with the MNR (they were not unaware of it) and had advised the Governor's staff that we had cut all links with the movement. Subsequently, the MNR seemed to go from strength to strength, and I began to wonder whether we had created a monster that was now beyond control.

The election campaign was nearing its close and the doubts and prognostications were multiplying. On the day after my return from Maputo I wrote in my diary:

We had a quick series of meetings this morning, with Antony Duff, with David Smith and with COMPOL at Police HQ where we discussed the destruction of the Mambo Printing Press in Gwelo: another outrage by the Selous Scouts? And then lunch with Evan Campbell at his home and a bevy of Knights from the British team of Observers, including Johnston who was the last High Commissioner at UDI, Glyn Jones of Malawi and others.

The consensus among the British group seemed to be that the election results would be finely drawn – to be followed by intense jockeying for position.

By this time the Bishop was floundering, not knowing which way to turn. On several occasions he discussed with me the possibility of applying more pressure to Soames to proscribe ZANU(PF) or to postpone the election. But I believed that the election was running away with itself, that the British were committed to it come what may, and that the Front Line Presidents would loudly denounce any move which might obstruct the course of Mugabe and Nkomo. I began to feel that the British would rather accept the worst result than no result at all, and that all Muzorewa could do now would be to use his right of direct approach to the British Prime Minister in the form of a protest. Muzorewa responded positively to this suggestion and asked me to prepare a note which he could use in a personal letter to Thatcher. He wanted the letter to concentrate on the sorry trail of broken promises, particularly Carrington's promise at the end of the Lancaster House conference concerning the proscription of parties that practised intimidation. My note for the Bishop read, in part:[4]

The Conservative Government assumed office in May, 1979, having promised the British electorate that they would recognise Bishop Muzorewa's Government, lift sanctions, and grant constitutional Independence; but they changed their minds....

The Lancaster House Conference passed through all its phases ... with Bishop Muzorewa offering the greatest readiness to co-operate; although certain decisions, such as the need for his Government to 'stand aside', were only achieved after considerable anguish and after promises, oft-repeated, that neither he nor his Government would be unduly disadvantaged....

Before the cease-fire came into force, the Mugabe faction of the Patriotic Front had planned and had begun to implement wholesale breaches of that Agreement. Indeed, there is ample evidence that Mugabe was forced into the Agreement without the slightest intention of complying....

Suffice to say that ZANU(PF) *never* had any intention of entering peacefully into elections; nor have they any intention of abiding by the election results unless they end up in a winning position....

All facts and evidence have been made available to the Governor, but, so far, he has decided not to act, and we must ask ourselves whether any greater accumulation of evidence can possibly suffice.

Will 'enough' ever be enough to satisfy the promise made by Lord Carrington in his concluding address at Lancaster House on 21st December, 1979: 'Our commitment is to fair elections. Having committed themselves to campaign peacefully and to comply with the Ceasefire Agreement, *no party or group could expect to take part in elections if it continued the war or systematically to break the Ceasefire and to practise widespread intimidation.*'

It was all I could do to bolster the Bishop's sagging position, but CIO had by this time reached the conclusion that Soames' inaction against parties practising intimidation was right. This assessment was contained in a telex I sent on 26 February to Air Vice-Marshal Hawkins, our ADR in Cape Town, in response to a query he had raised concerning the advice the British were giving the South Africans.[5] I also told Hawkins that CIO's election forecast was 'something like plus or minus thirty seats each for Muzorewa and Mugabe and about twenty for Nkomo. . . . Sithole and lesser groups may net something like four or five seats altogether, but this looks doubtful.'

Within a week, however, the forecast had to be considerably revised (Diary, 2 March):

> The reasonably confident predictions we gave a week ago have turned to dust. Massive intimidation has had its effect; or there has been a revolutionary swing to Mugabe's ZANU(PF), with the sombre thought that they might win an over-all majority on their own . . . four of us confronted the Bishop yesterday and warned him of his possible elimination unless he went into coalition with Nkomo. This he decided to do – reluctantly, at long last, and probably too late – and gave me the task of preparing the ground with Nkomo, which I tried to do later last night, after I had got the blessing of Lord Soames; seeing Nkomo secretly at his home. But he did not want to know of anything so fanciful as that he would not win outright victory for himself. We ended up in disagreement: myself telling him that he would win no more than 20 seats out of Matabeleland. And Nkomo claiming that he would also win many seats in Karanga-land. Then myself saying he would win none at all there.
> All rather sad, particularly as we appear to have let the Bishop down all along the line.

This entry in my diary opened with the comment that 'we have been sitting on a powder box since the elections started.' The 'powder box' was a plan to manipulate the elections by substituting polling boxes where the votes seemed to have gone too much one way. It was as watertight as it could be, but the decision as to whether or not to embark upon it was left to me. In the last forty-eight hours before the election results were announced, however, it was clear to me from all the advice I sought that a Mugabe victory was inevitable and that substitution in any degree would raise too many suspicions. The key figures in the plan were patently as relieved as I was that it was off.

Simultaneously, other attempts were being made to alter the course along which the country was travelling. One such attempt involved many Members of Parliament, with the notable exception of David Smith. On Sunday 2 March all available members of NATJOC were summoned at short notice to Muzorewa's official residence to meet this group. Muzorewa spoke first, on the theme that the British had man-oeuvred him out of his position of power obtained in the 1979 elections and had now broken their latest promise that the current elections would be as free and fair as those in 1979, by allowing ZANU(PF) to practise massive intimidation without let or hindrance. Various Members of Parliament added their comments in support of this theme and, in an atmosphere heavy with irony, the Bishop then asked Ian Smith to speak to the suggestion that a joint delegation from those assembled should ask the Governor to postpone the election so that the trend of events could be reversed, by force if necessary. At this point the senior officials present – Walls, Connolly and myself – made it clear that under no circumstances would we lend ourselves to the use of force. We expressed the opinion that matters must now take their own course, for the situation was too difficult for Ministers or ourselves to handle. Within a few minutes, the meeting was dissolved and everyone went his own way, disconsolate.

Later that day Walls summoned Sir Antony Duff and Robin Renwick from Government House to the Headquarters of COMOPS. There Walls allowed his juniors to blow off steam in the presence of Britishers whom they had been advised had broken all the promises Walls had relayed to his subordinates. Some of the junior officers exceeded the bounds of decency in their outright condemnation of the British, while Walls, obviously under considerable stress, sat morosely in his chair and Duff and Renwick listened uncomfortably. In the Granada Television series 'End of Empire' five years later, Walls and Renwick described the encounter thus:

Walls: We reminded the Governor's staff of the terms of the Agreement. And we asked that the elections be set aside, declared not free and fair.

Renwick: We said that we had promised a free and fair election – there has been an election which, broadly speaking, was free and fair, and we are going to help the government which emerges from it in every way we can.

Walls: Typical diplomatic language as to why nothing could be done; a wringing of hands and a 'We can't do anything, you know. And it's terribly difficult. The United Nations have been here and people from all over the world are watching us now and how can we possibly stop it at this stage?' We certainly felt that the people we were talking to were beneath contempt.

The British were put through such a grilling that they left the meeting with the belief that a coup was imminent, while Walls let his subordinates believe that they could stage a coup to reverse the order of things. But the confrontation was simply a face-saving exercise on Walls's part and the last opportunity for his juniors to give vent to their anger against the British. The possibility of a coup was never discussed in COMOPS or any other responsible forum, and Walls was well aware that many senior officers would not have participated in a coup and that at least one essential service, the Police, would not have supported it. It merely suited Walls's purpose to let the British believe a coup was imminent, otherwise he would have had to admit failure in the field, which no self-respecting general should do.

It was untypical of the British to be deluded or to ignore the advice being given them, and they should surely have seen the unlikelihood of a coup being implemented when the prospect had been ventilated before the very people against whom it would have been staged. The British media gave the 'threatened coup' undue publicity and some military credence.

None of us left the meeting in a happy state of mind. Some spiteful things were said, some petty minds relieved, but none of it should obscure the fact that most of the rank and file of the Rhodesian Services had fulfilled their tasks honourably and with as much tolerance as they could muster during the election period, realising that they could be working themselves out of a job.

In an equally well publicised attempt to reverse the order of things, Walls sent a message to Thatcher asking her to abrogate the elections because of systematic intimidation and to rule in Rhodesia through a Council of Ministers until free and fair elections could be held. He did not advise the inner forum of COMOPS of his action until after the message had been sent, at which point he explained that he had acted in terms of his personal agreement with Thatcher that he could appeal to her at any time if he was dissatisfied with the way things were going. Nor did he inform Soames, with whom he was hardly on speaking terms by this time, and he thus ignored the diplomatic/military convention to use proper channels of command. He compounded this fault by using South African Military Communications to ask the South African Ambassador in London to convey the message to Thatcher.

Predictably, no reply was received until Walls had to eat humble pie and ask Duff what response there was to his message. Mrs Thatcher, true to convention, had sent her answer – which did not answer Walls's assertions – through Lord Soames, the British Governor.

While the principal figures in the Rhodesian game played out their parts, the people of the country cast their votes. Polling began on 27 February and closed five days later. The polling process was conducted in an exemplary manner. The fact that there were no hitches was due in some part to the calming influence of the 500 British Bobbies specially sent out who provided a sight never seen before at polling stations in Rhodesia – blue uniforms and helmets in the humid heat of February.

Nyerere might have caused a hitch by his statement two days before polling was due to start that 'the results that are going to be announced by the Governor, Soames, are rigged results', but Mugabe reacted quickly to this potentially disruptive intervention by flying to Dar-es-Salaam to correct Nyerere. Machel, on the other hand, had adopted a more co-operative stance, having advised Soames through Honwana, his representative in Salisbury, that he would accept the poll as valid, whatever the outcome.

On the morning of 4 March the results were announced on radio and television. Out of 80 African seats in Parliament, Mugabe had won 57, Nkomo 20, Muzorewa 3 and the other contenders – Sithole, Chikerema and Ndiweni – 0. In the 100-seat Parliament in which 20 seats were reserved for whites Mugabe therefore had an outright majority. The immediate effect on the whites was cataclysmic. Not only had all hope of a 'moderate alliance' between Muzorewa, Nkomo and the whites vanished, but they were now faced with what was to them the worst possible result – a black Marxist government. Near-panic prevailed in the Civil Service and precipitate plans were made to flee to South Africa, Britain or Australia. Estate Agents had a field day and put hundreds of houses on the market.

The winners and the losers were summoned to Government House, and supplied the Press with such comments as:

Mugabe: 'Lord Soames has been magnificent. I had not expected him to allow the elections to go unhindered, and the fact that he did said much for his courage.'

Nkomo: 'You give them one-man-one-vote and look what they do with it! We (the PF) should have fought the election together. Mugabe let me down.'

Muzorewa: 'The most important thing is that we don't have persecution of the losers.'

To everyone's surprise and many people's delight, Soames and Mugabe chatted together in relaxed and friendly manner, indicating that a satisfactory rapport had developed between them. That evening Soames, Mugabe and Walls broadcast to the nation. Soames spoke first, saying: 'This is a solemn hour for Zimbabwe. There must be no violent action or reaction of any kind. . . . My purpose is to bring about an orderly transfer of power to a stable Government.' Walls said: 'I appeal to you all for calm, for peace. No hatred. No bitterness.' And then the Prime Minister-elect appeared, calling for reconciliation and national unity: 'Let us join together. Let us show respect for the winners and the losers. . . . There is no intention on our part to victimise the minority. We will ensure there is a place for everyone in this country. I want a broadly based government to include whites and Nkomo.' He strove to allay white fears, promising the business community that there would be no sweeping nationalisation, promising Civil Servants that their pensions and jobs would be guaranteed and assuring house owners and farmers that their property rights would be respected. To the South Africans he said: 'We offer peaceful co-existence. Let us forgive and forget. Let us join hands in a new amity.' And to the world at large he said: 'Zimbabwe will be tied to no one. It will be strictly non-aligned.'

Mugabe's speech, delivered in an impressively sincere and articulate manner, had a significant impact upon his white listeners and by the end of the week, when he had begun to honour some of his promises by naming David Smith as Minister of Commerce and Dennis Norman as Minister of Agriculture and indicating his intention of retaining Walls to preside over the integration of the armed forces, the white electorate began to see light at the end of the tunnel. A new consensus was apparent – that there was too much at stake to abandon their homes and that they should give the new rulers of Zimbabwe a fair trial. All but a few resignations from the Civil Service were withdrawn and scores of houses were taken off the property market.

To allay Ndebele fears, Mugabe, with the British pushing behind the scenes, offered Nkomo the Presidency. Nkomo made the mistake of rejecting the offer, indicating that he wished to be Minister of Defence and then, when that was refused, asking for the Home Affairs portfolio in the belief that he could control Special Branch through the Police, not realising that Special Branch was part of CIO and thus responsible to the Prime Minister. In spite of these manoeuvres, Nkomo's party were given four seats in Cabinet and three posts for Deputy Ministers.

Nkomo's confused handling of Mugabe's reconciliatory moves stemmed no doubt from the fact that he, like all the principal African participants, had been unprepared for the result of the election. His rejection of the necessity for a coalition was based on his firm belief that ZAPU would win an overall majority. Sithole, too, had oozed success during the elections despite CIO warnings that our official analysis gave him little or no chance, and was taken aback by the result. Even Mugabe was surprised. He told Soames after the announcement of the result that few of his party were sufficiently experienced in the art of government to make satisfactory Ministers and that he would like Soames or another British representative to continue in a guiding role for up to two years. I was informed of Mugabe's request and went to see Soames to implore him to respond positively to it and thus help establish Zimbabwe as a pro-Western nation. But the British rejected the request, although I believed that what Mugabe was asking for was perfectly reasonable and the subsequent criticism of his pro-Marxist leanings should be offset again the British rejection. Why did the British refuse? It seems that they were so relieved to have fluked a solution that their only consideration now was to get the hell out of Zimbabwe while the going was good and relinquish their responsibility for a country which had been a thorn in their side for so long.

The leader who was perhaps the least prepared for the outcome of the elections was Muzorewa. I wrote the following in my diary on 9 March:

No one has properly analysed why it was that the Bishop lost so abysmally. But he told me, literally with tears in his eyes, how he had gone to Mabvuku (a densely populated African 'township' on the outskirts of Salisbury where there had apparently been very little political intimidation) during the elections, where thousands of happy cheering 'supporters' greeted him, many of them running back to their rooms to put on his T-shirts as soon as they saw him. And of how he learnt subsequently that not one of them had voted for him! Muzorewa had become too beholden to Rhodesian whites, but ironically he was seen as a stooge of the Brits who betrayed him.... The overwhelming desire for an end to the war — which Muzorewa had failed to achieve — was the dominant factor. Those who continued to express sympathy for him did not intend to do anything more than just that — sympathise. The symbolism of the ZANU(PF) cock also counted tremendously; conveyed by gesture and hidden meaning.

English phrases such as 'Cock-a-Hoop' and 'Cock-a-Lorum' convey something of the symbolism of the crowing cock chosen as the ZANU(PF) logo; in the Shona language there is a more sensual connotation and the added symbolism of heralding a new day, a new era. The massive turnout of voters (estimated at over 90 per cent of those eligible to vote) was achieved in part by a herding of the voters and a shepherding of the queues at polling booths by young men who flapped their elbows up and down to signify a rampant cock after sexual conquest, much to the amusement of men and women alike.

My diary entry quoted above ended with the comment that 'nothing untoward' had happened: a reference to what I knew to have happened to my contemporaries who had headed a Secret Service when a change of regime had occurred, and to the horrors that had followed the end of civil wars, in Europe as well as Africa, where the losers had been killed in their thousands by the winners. Any residual fears were soon allayed. I responded to a suggestion made by Walls that the members of NATJOC should call on Mugabe to pay our respects. McLaren (Deputy Commander, COMOPS), Maclean (Commander of the Army), Mussell (Commander of the Air Force), Connolly (Secretary for Internal Affairs) and Denley (Deputy Commissioner of Police) followed suit. Only the

Commissioner of Police declined to accompany us, having decided to approach Mugabe alone. To Walls's credit, he was now doing everything he could to create the right climate for whites to accept Mugabe as Prime Minister, and he led the rest of us in a small procession of motor cars to Mugabe's temporary residence in the suburb of Mount Pleasant; on the previous night the house had been subjected to an attack and was now heavily guarded.

The seven of us waited, ill at ease, until Mugabe appeared, accompanied only by Emmerson Mnangagwa. Walls spoke first, offering to serve Mugabe with the same loyalty and dedication as he had served previous Prime Ministers. Then, one by one, the rest of us conveyed the same sentiment. Mugabe responded with warmth and gave every indication that he genuinely welcomed our continuation in office. Overall, a strong sense of mutual respect prevailed at this meeting.

On 13 April, five days before the official birth of Zimbabwe, I wrote in my diary:

I have a new Minister of State for Security, Emmerson Mnangagwa, and what would seem to be a more remotely placed Prime Minister, Mugabe, to work for in CIO. And it *is* very much a matter of working *for* them, rather than the uneasy arrangement during the transitional government and the Bishop's term as PM, when, as one looks back on it now, the whites were not really working *for* the blacks – almost the reverse.

We live with reasonable expectations. And most of the whites are staying on a wait-and-see basis.

At one minute after midnight on 18 April the Rhodesia flag was lowered, the Zimbabwe flag raised and Britain's last African colony became independent. I attended the official Independence celebrations that night in Rufaro Stadium in Salisbury, and on the following evening joined other officials at a reception given by Lord Soames. My diary takes up the story:

20th April 1980: Olga and I attended the receptions at Government House when we were introduced – twice – to the Prince of Wales. On the first occasion the Governor praised my single-handed efforts and the Prince commented: 'A sort of one-man effort?' On the second occasion he said to Olga: 'Were you not here last night?' To which she answered 'Yes', and with a smile he said 'Bad luck!'

I exchanged a few words with Malcolm Fraser, the Australian Prime Minister – not a typical product of that country, trading on the sanctity of race relations when all Rhodesians knew over the years that the Aussies were more determined to Keep Australia White than we ever were to Keep Rhodesia White. Lord Carrington came across for a private chat, saying quite frankly that the British Government were lucky to have fluked a solution at Lancaster House – with which I agreed – and now they could only hope that all of us in Zimbabwe could make a success of it.

Prior to that the Governor asked me to go to Government House so that he could thank me personally for my help and advice. At one stage he said it was virtually the only advice he had got from Rhodesians which never had a cork-screw in it! And he went on to say that Mugabe should benefit similarly, as he understood Mugabe would keep me in my present position for a while and then continue with me in an advisory capacity....

The Captains and the Kings depart, having come from a hundred countries. Now we are on our own again.

Epilogue

I counted myself fortunate after Independence that Mugabe and Mnangagwa were content to keep me as Intelligence/Security Adviser and Head of CIO, although we had been so clearly opposed to each other throughout the pre-Independence era. When Mnangagwa asked me to stay in office for at least the two-year period it would take to reconstruct CIO, I agreed but maintained there was little need for change, particularly if they wished the organisation to retain its professional standards. Only once did Mnangagwa pass me a written instruction outlining some of his thoughts on reconstruction. As the main purport of that instruction was CIO's alleged need to develop Intelligence liaison with certain European countries with whom we had maintained effective liaison for many years, I confronted the Minister of State and explained that we would be unable to work together satisfactorily if our relationship was so formalised that we could not sort out any problems, man to man, in a few minutes of discussion; and that if we wished to keep our Intelligence secure the less we committed to paper the better.

The point was taken. Mnangagwa left the professional control of CIO to me, while he provided the political link with the government. This made for very little change in Intelligence functioning, and as far as the rank and file of CIO were concerned there was virtually no change in executive or administrative control. Obviously, Mnangagwa had to apply the government's policy of Africanisation, and he introduced into CIO some of his comrades from the guerrilla ranks, including a few who had been gaoled in earlier days by the very members of Special Branch now working as their colleagues in CIO. Some of these newcomers had received low-grade training in Intelligence techniques in communist countries, but Mnangagwa found there was no need to push the claims of his protégés because we had long since accepted the principle of Africanisation in CIO.

It soon became clear that neither of us wished CIO to be infiltrated by subversive agents or destroyed from within. Sadly, the damage done during the opening weeks of Independence by a few white officers in the middle ranks of Special Branch/CIO, exposed as South African agents, was greater than any damage done by blacks adhering to a communist ideology.

Mugabe was conciliation personified, and as we got to know each other he proved to be the most appreciative of all the Prime Ministers I had served during the previous twenty years in Rhodesia, or the other African potentates I had known elsewhere, responsible for so much of the death and destruction that preceded or followed their seizure of power. It was a strange experience working for an African leader whom whites had been taught to hate and whose assumption of power we had forecast to be catastrophic.

I volunteered to Mugabe at one of our earliest meetings that I had handed over the MNR to the South Africans, rather than have him learn the facts from other sources. He expressed no great surprise, indicating that he already knew that I was responsible for the MNR. What came as a greater surprise was to hear Mugabe say that President Samora Machel had commended me as an adviser on whom he could rely.

'But Samora Machel and I have never met!'

Mugabe replied: 'He knows a lot about you, otherwise he would not have recommended you to me.'

'Does he know that I started the MNR, which is causing him so much trouble?'

'Yes,' said Mugabe, 'and I imagine that is why he has so much respect for you!'

Mugabe had returned from exile in Mozambique as a professed 'Marxist' – but the term is relative. ZANU(PF) had sought aid wherever they could, but had been rejected by Russia in favour of Nkomo's ZAPU. This no doubt explains the early advice I received from Mnangagwa: to accept foreign missions as friendly or 'non-aligned' until proved otherwise, but in the first instance to make life as difficult as possible for the Russians. The principle of non-alignment obviously appealed, enabling the new rulers of Zimbabwe to choose as friends those who responded most readily to their appeals for aid; whilst Mugabe made it clear in our discussions that his greatest mentor was Marshal Tito of Yugoslavia, the founder of the Non-Aligned Movement, from whom he had learned that adherence to communism does not necessarily mean subservience to Russia.

Realising that the changes we were facing were drastic enough by any standards, I wondered who might have been Mugabe's other mentors, and discovered that he was taught as a youth by Jesuit priests. But his later academic successes were achieved through self-education. Clearly, he was his own man: intellectually superior, independent in thought and

action. Above all, I found him a good listener, careful in his considerations, a fine judge of any man's worth. In particular, I remember his
whole-hearted response when I had the temerity to ask how he intended
to implement his public promise to produce 'as broadly based a government as possible'. For instance, would he agree to the appointment of
outstanding Zimbabweans irrespective of whether they were supporters
of his party? Immediately he said:

'Whom have you got in mind?'

Not to be caught out in a vague generalisation, I said: 'First of all,
Prime Minister, have you considered Bernard Chidzero who has an
international reputation at the United Nations but may not be committed to you politically?'

Mugabe replied without hesitation: 'I have already written to him in
Geneva and hope he will agree to head one of the government's economic ministries. Who else?'

'I would have thought it would help prove your policy of reconciliation to bring someone like Enoch Dumbutshena back from Zambia (a
man who had appeared on ZANU(PF)'s "Death List").'

'Yes,' said Mugabe, 'I am hoping that he will become our first black
Judge in this country. Who else?'

'You will have seen for yourself, Prime Minister, what good work
David Zamchiya did at Lancaster House. Could he not be fitted in
somewhere?'

'Yes,' said Mugabe, 'I would like to see him as Chairman of Parliamentary Legal Committees or something of that sort, but he has been
so closely attached to Sithole that I would not try to get it through
ZANU(PF) Central Committee just now ... perhaps a bit later.'

Having apparently scored two out of three, with the third a probabil-
ity for the future, I thought it wise to move on to discuss something else.

The most enduring lesson learnt in Intelligence is that the highest degree
of professionalism can be based only on that policy of 'political indiffer-
ence' that we tried to follow in CIO. This principle of good Intelligence
was propounded by the German Chief of Intelligence, General Reinhard
Gehlen, after a dramatic confrontation with Hitler. It seemed as natural
to be working for Mugabe as it had been working for Haile Selassie
forty years previously. At least, we were now Zimbabweans together,
serving the same nation. But not everyone saw it that way. My continued service, well beyond the allotted span, was condemned as 'survival' – a dirty word in the world of Intelligence where any one of us could
be accused of double-dealing or called a defector in any move he makes.

I suddenly found myself accused of being a 'top level British mole' – not that that mattered – and of perpetrating some of the more outrageous actions, such as the sabotage of churches and unspecified assassinations that had occurred during the elections. Erstwhile allies such as the South Africans and the Portuguese lashed out wildly, determined to incriminate me in any way they could – which probably had the opposite effect to what was intended, for as I became the victim of South African attack I appeared more readily acceptable to Mugabe. It seemed sensible not to pay too much attention to this sort of thing; and to ignore the loss of a war that had been unwinnable. I consigned the past to my diary and looked hopefully to the future:

I have found relief in some of the simple things in life that not many of us had realised were missing until they were restored: civil aircraft flying north and south over our home for the first time since UDI, where only warplanes had flown for fifteen years; different news on the air, and genuine anticipation of peace. As one of my doctor friends observed: 'There is a new look on the faces of Africans. For the first time you can see them "walking tall" in the streets of Salisbury.' Some palpable injustices – alleviated when Bishop Muzorewa came to power, but too little, too late – are now removed for ever. The political pendulum is swinging, possibly beyond Mugabe's reach, but hopefully to settle into a steadier rhythm later on.

Within CIO we concentrated for a while on a general review of Intelligence that had been so painfully garnered over the years, and when we added it all together it was with some relief that we could see that no one had done any better than us. Of what value, then, had the Intelligence been to either side? I would say, of no value when nothing was done with it whilst time still held: or of little value, say, when warning the Bishop of the calamity ahead of him, for his fate was beyond recall. Winston Field may have been justified in trying to insist on 85 per cent, or better, in the accuracy of our estimates; but other politicians were uninterested in Intelligence that baulked their plans. There was no kudos and no advantage in one's Intelligence being proved correct – if anything, it made politicians more obdurate in trying to establish their political theories. For a while after Independence it was respected by Mnangagwa and others who knew its value from the other side. And it could be of value again, particularly as there was no limit now on how CIO's functioning could be expanded around the world.

The settlement signed at Lancaster House left a legacy of unsolved problems, not least of which was the integration of nearly 80,000 ZANLA, ZIPRA and Rhodesian Security Forces, all with different backgrounds of recruitment, of training and of motivation. ZANLA Commanders had proved the efficacy of Chinese methods and were intent on forming a People's Army. ZIPRA's strategy was based on Russian military concepts. The Rhodesian Security Forces were engaged in a holding operation wished upon them by the British.

In order to offer the best advice I could, I travelled to the United States to learn how they had integrated opposing forces after their Civil War, only to find that their problem had been considered insoluble and that no real attempt was made to integrate forces wearied by slaughter. But one perceptive student of international affairs in the State Department suggested that I would do better by studying what the British achieved through General Monck at the Restoration in 1660, after the English Civil War had ended. And with what surprising relevance to our situation! For Monck served both the Royalists and the Parliamentarians. He supported Cromwell as 'Protector of the Commonwealth' but was the principal architect in restoring the Monarchy. Indeed, he founded the Coldstream Guards which still serve the Queen as living proof of the 'Restoration'. Three hundred years later Lord Soames, a former Coldstream officer, faced an equally difficult task in trying to persuade Africans of opposing political views to serve together in a small well-knit force. But African politicians believe that a large Standing Army is the key to national stability – although nowhere in Africa has stability been achieved through such means. One had to accept that it was more important for Mugabe as a new ruler in Africa to produce an African solution by providing as many jobs as he could for the thousands of supporters who were his comrades-in-arms.

Then occurred what could have been a much more serious affair, undermining the position of whites and illustrating the widening gap between General Walls and the rest of the 'Old Guard' remaining in government (Diary):

20th August 1980: Peter Walls hit the headlines with his talk on BBC of a coup that was not a coup. And the threat of civil war – divulging promises from Margaret Thatcher that were intended for the two of us alone.... It seems he has 'talked himself out' at last, in the sense that he can do not greater harm, but he does not seem to have appreciated the harm he has already done. By criticising Mrs Thatcher for not reversing the election results he has let the whole world know that he resents serving Mugabe, or is serving him under false pretences ... It seems that his frustration got the better of him; or his egotism; or his abiding immaturity; or he was merely trying to justify himself to his 'Troopies' before departing for South Africa. Sad that we have this back-biting amongst the whites, when blacks have shown understanding and surprising generosity.

Sunday 31st August: I went for a farewell chat with Peter Walls who spent the best part of an hour justifying himself; during the course of which he did have the good grace to say that if I'd been available to give advice – like in the good old days – he may not have made such damaging comments on BBC. In another context he mentioned how the South African Military had pressed Intelligence briefs on him to the effect that Mugabe was merely following the classic communist line – deluding those who serve him and preparing to strike when it suits his purposes. (The old, old tune, played to death by the SA Military, with Peter not realising they have been wrong so often in their prognostications – and when is a 'communist' not a 'communist'!)

Sunday 7th September: Had two hours alone with Mugabe yesterday, talking mostly about Peter Walls. There will be no recovery there. Mugabe believes that Peter betrayed him: having sworn a personal loyalty but still living in the past and not really serving him as Prime Minister, although Mugabe described how he had done everything he could to win his friendship. The rest of our talk dwelt on the need to get the relationship between Police and ZANU(PF) right – the future control of SB – the South African relationship (we have broken off diplomatic relations) – what to do about SAANC infiltration into Zimbabwe...

Sunday 28th September: The Peter Walls affair has finally become a national issue. He will be deprived of his Zimbabwean citizenship. As MH said: 'He presumed too much. I know from my own experience how insulting his behaviour was toward Lord Soames, and how he would have seen himself as the one and only saviour of Rhodesia.' But the Cabinet Minute shows there was also a mercenary touch, in that he tackled Mugabe about his promotion to full General from Lieutenant-General, which explains Mugabe's earlier questioning and my reply to the effect that two previous Prime Ministers (Muzorewa and Smith) had turned down the same request because our system did not provide for a Commander-in-Chief and there would have been problems with the other Commanders – Air Force, Police and Army – and if he was not entitled to the rank of 'General' when fighting a war as Commander, COMOPS, how could he be so entitled in an administrative post on semi-retirement?

Time and again Mugabe asked whether I thought his government's actions might induce civil war. And on each occasion I said that he was showing understandable tolerance, and the likelihood of civil war was diminishing with every week that passed regardless of whether ZAPU/ZIPRA kept aloof from government or not. Unfortunately, the white Commanders who were still in office at that stage believed that civil war between ZIPRA and ZANLA was inevitable – probably because they gave ZIPRA too high a professional rating and thought, wrongly, that Mugabe was deliberately heading for trouble. His policy of reconciliation had not been fully reciprocated by some blacks and by many whites; but that was hardly his fault. Mugabe did not push ZAPU to the brink, nor did he force ZIPRA's disarmament, for tactical reasons which seemed sound enough to me. He was fully appreciative of the dangers of allowing malcontents to remain at large; he knew that no African could subscribe to the concept of 'Loyal Opposition' and therefore there would be militant opposition. As a Father of African Nationalism, Nkomo deserved well of his country, but his political career was littered with mistakes and lost opportunities. Mugabe's decision to fight the elections alone had destroyed his chances, and Nkomo's decision to keep most of the ZIPRA forces in Zambia was politically unsound and potentially treasonable. One way or another it would be force that would decide the issue, as had been the case elsewhere in Africa: armed force, or force of numbers once it came to counting heads.

Fortunately it is not in the Zimbabwean's nature to indulge in extremes, although aberrations occur. No serious attempt was made to implement ZANU(PF)'s 'Death List'; but Bishop Muzorewa was committed to prison after Independence on charges that were never disclosed. Major-General Hickman, ex-Commander of the Rhodesian Army, was detained for several months in the maximum security prison on trumped-up allegations that he would have lent himself to an invasion by South African forces – the last thing he was likely to do. Air Vice Marshal Slatter and Air Commodore Pile, Commanding the Zimbabwe Air Force, were detained on scant evidence, acquitted before Chief Justice Dumbetshena, who bravely censured the authorities, only to see the men he had discharged immediately re-detained with no further evidence being led, illustrating open contempt for the rule of law.

Amidst all these changes I suffered the most serious domestic crisis:

Sunday 2nd March 1981: Return from Cape Town after three weeks, racked by concern for Olga. She survived operation at Groote Schuur and everyone at the hospital was quite wonderful – but there is no guarantee that the cancer is removed or contained.

Monday 23rd March: Had a session with Mnangagwa, explaining my commitment to Olga and my need to phase myself out. Thanked him and Mugabe for their humanity – I had not been better treated by any previous Prime Minister, and it seemed a poor response to ask to retire, but I felt I must put Olga first after years of neglect of my home; nor was it fair to continue in a privileged position, in charge of CIO, without taking full responsibility. Better to let me go, at the latest, on my anniversary on 30th June...

We had a happy holiday in Britain and America, but further treatment of my wife's cancer was to no avail and she died in November, shortly after returning home to Zimbabwe. My services were retained for a while after retirement because Mugabe, while adamant that no black member of his government should associate with South Africa's white regime, saw practical advantages in continuing the association via a white like myself. However, I had no hesitation in declining, which was as well because I got things badly wrong, right at the start of my association with Mugabe. He had asked me on several occasions whether I believed that South Africa would pursue a policy of destabilisation towards Zimbabwe and I assured him time and again that they would not be so stupid or so short-sighted as to do that – still believing that Vorster's policies of 'detente' would apply. How wrong I was! What could anyone like myself really do to help whilst South Africans believe that they must ensure the failure of black government because this confirms the superiority of white government?

I should have remembered my mother's determination in 1924 to take her six children away from Aliwal North on the Orange River to be educated in England 'to escape the tragedy that will strike this land'. I should have remembered, too, the prescience of Sir Patrick Duncan, Governor-General Designate of the Union of South Africa, when he addressed those of us destined to join the B S A Police aboard the *Carnarvon Castle* in 1937, on the need to change the black-white relationship south of the Limpopo to accord with Rhodes's dictum of 'equal rights for civilised men south of the Zambezi' – but this ideal brought only tragedy to his family, for his own son, beside us then, would die in a South African gaol fighting for racial equality.

Now the blacks in South Africa can learn for themselves the lessons of Angola, Mozambique and Zimbabwe where independence was achieved through the unremitting demand by the majority of blacks to be governed by other blacks, regardless of irrelevancies such as constitutional democracy. The struggle in South Africa, as elsewhere, is simply a struggle for black power. Sanctions will only serve to unite the whites and make the white rulers less amenable to change; some African states will be the main defaulters, thus increasing black Africa's dependence on South Africa; neutral countries who would not otherwise support South Africa may do so in order to promote their business interests.

In Kenya and Malaya we saw the pre-eminent role that can be played by Special Branch in counter-insurgency. In Rhodesia and then in South Africa the appropriate role for police was replaced by an inappropriate role for the military. Vorster's detente with Black Africa gave way to Botha's destabilisation of surrounding territories in preparation for what the soldiers call the 'total onslaught'. Fighting our sort of war it was necessary to keep reminding our Military Commanders of their favourite axiom – a war of counter-insurgency is 20 per cent military and 80 per cent political – which implies that greater force is needed against politicians to settle a dispute, than against 'terrorists' in the field, or government will shelve its responsibilities and the military ignore theirs.

The achievements of colonialism took visitors such as Nyerere by surprise on their first visits to Zimbabwe. He said: 'You have inherited a jewel in Africa, don't tarnish it.' Signs of neglect and disrepair are indeed to be seen all over Africa, and there is no doubt that the mistakes made by whites in Rhodesia will be multiplied by blacks in Zimbabwe – if only because there are more blacks to make mistakes; more theorists, and far fewer doers; and every educated black aspires to a white-collar job. Kissinger warned Ian Smith in 1976 that his package-deal, or any other negotiated settlement, would result in a lowering of standards, such as the decline in the efficiency of telecommunications, whereby one may be able to speak to a non-existent relative in China but cannot contact a member of one's family living in an adjoining suburb in Harare. But the deterioration we should expect in Zimbabwe is relative: not to be compared, say, with that in Uganda, Tanzania or Mozambique. The modernising influence has been so much stronger in Zimbabwe than elsewhere in black Africa; and enough Zimbabweans have been through the crucible of Independence to have faith in their destiny.

Appendix

All Top Secret and Secret papers were either destroyed or pruned after a certain fixed time. Exceptions were made to allow for a more permanent record in the Prime Minister's Office. CIO was constituted as the 'Prime Minister's Department' and I was granted authority to hold papers after normal dates for destruction. Because of constant pruning, more material was removed from the older files, and more documents remained in newer files. As the political situation developed and it became likely that there would be a change of regime, I held on to greater numbers of my own files and kept more CIO files under my personal care. I could extract papers more easily from them, or counter what I believed to be excessive pruning or destruction happening in other offices. I could also counter what I believed to be an unconstitutional decision to send Cabinet, War Council and other Top Secret papers out of the country during 1979 and 1980. In the final, rather rushed circumstances in which I collected some of the papers here used, it was much easier to lay hands on the newer files, with one firm exception – the immediate run-up to UDI, and UDI itself. I had decided to keep these latter papers as no other member of CIO who had been personally involved was still in office.

Those Top Secret and Secret papers either quoted from or referred to in the text are listed in the Source Notes on p. 318. A selection of some of the most important papers is reproduced in this Appendix, two of them in facsimile.

Extract from Minutes of Meeting of Security Council, 19 October 1965

TOP SECRET

1. BORDER: ZAMBIA, RHODESIA, BECHUANALAND AND CAPRIVI STRIP.

(previous reference s.c.(S) (65) Fifth Meeting – minute 5.)

Referring to discussion recorded under minute 5 of the Fifth Meeting, the query was raised as to the progress being made in the attempt to settle the meeting point of the borders of Zambia, Rhodesia, Bechuanaland and the Caprivi Strip. It was understood that the Ministry of External Affairs had written to the South African Government but, beyond that, progress was not known.

The Security Council instructed the Secretary to obtain an up-to-date report on developments from the Ministry of External Affairs.

2. RHODESIAN INDEPENDENCE.

The Security Council was given a verbal Intellignce appreciation of the implications of a U.D.I. and reports on the implications of such unilateral action on the three Security forces.

(a) *Intelligence Appreciation.*

The Director, C.I.O., after explaining the difficulty of presenting an accurate picture without knowledge of the political exchanges at the highest levels, emphasised that the intentions of the British Government should not be underestimated. Although economic action only was proposed at this stage, military action should not be discounted in circumstances of (a) internal disorders on a scale justifying direct intervention, (b) the destruction of Zambia's lifelines to and from Rhodesia and, (c) a failure of sanctions. Of these three possible motives, the greatest threat was posed by the position of Zambia. The Government of that country would feel obliged to cut itself off from Rhodesia and, on its own initiative, refuse to continue drawing supplies of coal and power from Rhodesia and making use of railway facilities. An appeal for assistance to the United Nations might succeed, notwithstanding that the crisis would have resulted from its own choosing, and this could result in limited intervention at Wankie, the Victoria Falls and Kariba. It was not impossible to foresee the British Government artificially accelerating such a situation. The United Nations would be bound to take up the Rhodesian question though this would not be initiated by the United Kingdom. The use of force was not likely unless Zambia was threatened. The threat from the Organisation of African Unity or from individual African states could be discounted. It was believed that the United States of America would not act independently against Rhodesia.

Internal strife was not likely and what did develop could be handled by the Police. An increased infiltration of trained terrorists and of material could be expected, and terrorism was likely to spread over a wider area than at present and to include attacks on isolated European settlements and Government-owned property. Industrial unrest would probably be fomented, and there was a possibility of attempts being made by restrictees to abscond from their places of restriction and by prisoners to break out of the gaols.

It appeared possible that less positive steps than hoped for could be expected from the South Africans and the Portuguese who might find it difficult to assist Rhodesia openly. At present, South African residents in the country were showing the most signs of 'panic' and this would increase if the South African Government was not seen to be backing Rhodesia. Assistance was unlikely to be forthcoming if armed intervention was undertaken by the United Nations.

On the general question of timing, doubt was expressed as to the wisdom of early action to declare independence. It was suspected that the country was not psychologically prepared to move onto a 'war' footing at short notice and morale would suffer if setbacks were experienced without previous conditioning. Over the past few days, heat had been generated all over the world, which ought perhaps to be allowed to cool down. It was known that Britain was pressurising friends and enemies of Rhodesia and plans existed for closing the Zambian border and the railways through Bechuanaland. Early action would compel Britain to retaliate, where a delay would force them to take the initiative which might suit Rhodesia. The United Nations was at present in session. In all the circumstances, a delay might be to Rhodesia's advantage.

At this point, the Prime Minister intervened to bring the Security Council up to date on certain factors which were contributing towards the general consideration of a unilateral declaration of independence. There was no doubt at all that circumstances were favourable for an early decision and, with every day's delay, the prospects deteriorated. Massive support for Rhodesia existed in the United Kingdom which would be the target for erosion from now onwards. Support on the Continent, and particularly in France, was growing, whilst in the United States of America the Rhodesian 'problem' had now reached the table of the President, and some criticism over its past handling had been directed at Mr. Mennan Williams and the State Department. The American Service Chiefs were sympathetic. It was quite clear that a campaign of intimidation and fear had been mounted against Rhodesia with the object of steering the people away from U.D.I. In regard to the positions of South Africa and Portugal, their backing was assured but for obvious political reasons, they could not come out into the open for the present. The Government was convinced that unless a decision was taken soon, Rhodesia would 'lose out'. Even under the worst conditions, a U.D.I. would be worthwhile in the long run.*

In discussion, the question of the effect of public opinion in Britain on the British Government's reactions to a U.D.I. was raised. There was little doubt that this factor was worrying the British Government because they would have to take immediate action in the event of U.D.I. and could not afford to wait for a weakening of the present opinion favouring Rhodesia. Indeed, this was one of the points supporting an early decision by Rhodesia. So far as public opinion in Rhodesia was concerned, it was true that a section of the people was not in favour of U.D.I. but there would be a general rallying if and

---

* Handwritten marginal comment made by the Author at the time: 'My brief, p. 5, "Under the most favourable circumstances chances may be no more than even." '

when the decision was made.** Commerce and Industry came into this category.

On the question of timing, it was true that rapid progress was being made in finalising emergency regulations. There was a risk, however, that the British Government, sensing that U.D.I. was imminent, might take action before Rhodesia was ready. Although this might be to Rhodesia's advantage in that unprovoked interference by Britain would be justification for unilateral action by Rhodesia, the initiative would then have been wrested from Rhodesia. The Government's present intention to act legally by declaring a state of emergency under the present Constitution and by legally bringing emergency regulations into operation might thus be prevented. Timing, from Rhodesia's point of view, rendered it essential that the first step should be the declaration of a state of emergency and the promulgation of emergency regulations.

** Marginal comment by Author: 'There would also be some defections.'

Minutes of Meeting of Rhodesian Cabinet, Item 1, 1 November 1965

TOP SECRET

Z. 533 (PM)

TOP SECRET

Annexure to
R.C.(S) (65) 59th
Meeting

1st November, 1965

Distribution:
1. Standard File
2. Prime Minister
3/13. Ministers
14. Secretary to the Treasury
15. Secretary for Law and Order
16. Secretary for External Affairs
17. Secretary to the Cabinet
18. Director, C.I.O.

SECRETARY'S STANDARD FILE:

1.   RHODESIA INDEPENDENCE

        (previous reference R.C.(S) (65) 58th Meeting - minute 1)

        CABINET had before them the Note by the Secretary R.C.(S)
(65) 305 distributing for consideration the following documents:-

     (1) A report to the British and Rhodesian Governments on the
independence of Rhodesia and the proposed Royal Commission.

     (2) Text of a letter sent by hand of the Rhodesian High
Commissioner in London from the Prime Minister of Rhodesia
to Mr. Harold Wilson dated 31st October, 1965.

In addition the Prime Minister gave Cabinet an oral report of discussions
which had gone on over the weekend since the departure for Britain of
Mr. Wilson himself on Saturday morning. The report referred to in
item (1) above was the result of those discussions which had been
between the Ministers of External Affairs, Internal Affairs, Commerce
and Industry, Law and Order and Labour and Social Welfare and Mr.
Arthur Bottomley, the Commonwealth Secretary, and Sir Elwyn Jones,
the British Attorney General, and their advisers.

        The Prime Minister declared that in his opinion nothing had
been achieved by Mr. Wilson in leaving Mr. Bottomley and Sir Elwyn
Jones behind in Salisbury because they had been unable to reach
decisions and it was evident that they had no authority to decide
anything. In an attempt to close the gap the discussions had been
a failure. The report merely recorded points outstanding between
the Governments and identified the respective points of view. It
had now to go back to the British Government for a decision. He had
asked Brig. Skeen, the Rhodesian High Commissioner, to return to London
last night and he had sent his message of the 31st October to Mr.
Wilson with Brig. Skeen and had asked the High Commissioner immediately
on arrival to deliver the message. The High Commissioner was also to
make immediate contact with the Conservative Opposition and to see

TOP SECRET

TOP SECRET

2.

what support could be raised in Rhodesia's favour on the political stage. The Prime Minister said that he felt that Rhodesia's position was today stronger than it had been before Mr. Wilson's arrival, but he had no idea what sort of response would come from the British Government. To his way of thinking the British Prime Minister would find it difficult not to accept the recommendation for the appointment of a Royal Commission which would have the task of putting Rhodesia's case to the people. If he refused to accept the suggestion this would be tantamount to his saying that the British Government was not prepared to trust their own commissioners. As matters now stood it was for the British Cabinet to consider the report and to give their reply at the earliest possible moment.

CABINET then discussed the situation under three headings as follows:-

A. The British Government's likely response to the report.

B. The action which should be planned in the event of an unfavourable reply.

C. The position which would be created if a favourable reply were received.

A. The British Government's likely response:

The Minister of External Affairs informed Cabinet of certain worries which the Portuguese appeared to be having about these new developments and their tentative impressions that the Rhodesian Government were beginning to retreat from the final decision under pressure from the British Government. It was reported, on the other hand, that the Government of South Africa were very concerned at the possibility of there being a declaration of independence without the agreement of the British Government. They had made their position clear. There was also some uneasiness on the part of Rhodesians about certain Portuguese manoeuvres that appeared to be designed to turn the situation to their own advantage. Yet the situation probably was that the Portuguese could not afford to see Rhodesia collapse economically and politically and therefore at the present moment, whatever may be their business and trade interests, they could be relied upon to give full support; otherwise, if Rhodesia collapsed the future of Mocambique would become extremely serious.

TOP SECRET

TOP SECRET

Z. 533 (PM)

3.

In discussion the following further points were made:
The British Government, in considering the report, might decide
to play for time and therefore they might avoid giving a categorical
answer this week; indeed, they might attempt to put up further
proposals in the hope that these would continue discussions indefinitely. It had to be brought firmly to their notice that this was
now the time for decision. On the other hand, the Rhodesian Government had declared that it was not going to be deviated from the
course which it was following. There was every indication that
during the talks of last week it had already been brought firmly
home to the British Government that the Rhodesian Government was
serious about its request for independence and that if the negotiations for a settlement failed the Government would take action to
declare independence. This was an important bargaining position for
the Rhodesian Government; but at the same time it was very necessary
that no impetuous action should be taken and that full scope should
be left for negotiations so long as they hold out any hope at all
of success. It was the duty of the Government in the circumstances
to take the wisest course for the good of the country. Moreover,
there was likely to be an immense tactical advantage for the country
now that the proposition of a Royal Commission on Rhodesia's conditions
had been put forward. Good effect might be made of this with the
official Opposition in Great Britain. By attending to every
possible chance of negotiation the Rhodesian Government had gained
a moral ascendency in this matter. But at the same time, the
consequences of a refusal on the part of the British Government should
be kept to the fore and while the Rhodesian Government should not
indulge in any threats it should firmly stand by its position and
make it clear that it required a decision one way or the other at
least this week.

CABINET agreed that it was not the correct thing now for
the Rhodesian Government to retract from the position as set out
in the report and that it should be prepared to wait for an answer
and to suspend a final decision pending the receipt of that answer
but, at the same time, it should take every opportunity to press
for an early reply, and invited the Prime Minister to proceed on
these lines.

TOP SECRET

TOP SECRET

4.

B.   Action to be planned in the event of an unfavourable response:

The Prime Minister informed Cabinet that he had received advice from several sources, including the Rhodesian High Commissioner in London, that it would be the right tactics, in the event of the Rhodesian Government having to take the extreme step, first to introduce a general state of emergency and thereafter to let the impact recede before taking the next step. The advantage of this course would be that while most people would appreciate that a general state of emergency was but a prelude to a declaration of independence, it was still a legal proceeding and when the actual declaration did come people generally would have been resigned to it. During the state of emergency no country could take active legal steps to impose sanctions, least of all the British Government and, therefore, the Rhodesian Government would be in a stronger position to plan and to prepare for retaliatory action that would be resorted to once independence was declared.

The Minister of Law and Order informed Cabinet that instructions had already been issued for all the preparations for the declaration of a state of emergency to be completed. All planning had been done so that only twenty-four hours notice was required by his Ministry. The other Ministries concerned were preparing their own arrangements for immediate action.

In discussion it was felt that the gradual assumption of independence after a declaration of a state of emergency was likely to minimise the impact overseas. It would have the additional advantage of not disclosing until the last minute Rhodesia's hand. The declaration of independence would then be chosen at a time to suit the Rhodesian Government and, having regard to the security situation. During this interval it would be brought home to the British Government that the last stages had been reached. Britain may be induced to come a further step forward to prevent the ultimate decision being taken by Rhodesia. There was a psychological aspect also; that people overseas would become resigned to the decision before it was actually taken. A state of emergency, moreover, being legal, left Rhodesia in control of the situation. On the other hand, Great Britain might accept this warning as the last step itself and put immediately into operation such action as it may have determined upon. They might take action in this interval to persuade other countries to come out against Rhodesia and to support Britain's

TOP SECRET

TOP SECRET

Z. 533 (PM)

5.

sanctions. It was believed, from what had been learned during last week's discussion in Salisbury, that the British Government's final decision of the action to be taken will be made on their assessment of the effects which the declaration of emergency would have on the British Commonwealth.

CABINET agreed –

(a) that there were two alternative courses to be taken and that a final decision should stand over until the actual response from the British Government had been received and assessed;

(b) that these two alternative courses were as follows:-

(i) to delay matters in such a way as to draw the British Government's final answer; the best procedure for this might be, on receiving the British reply, to return immediately an answer making ti clear that the Rhodesian Government could not accept the reply nor comment any further and that this was the end of negotiations, and so leave it to the British Government to come back with such further final proposals as they think necessary; or

(ii) to send a reply rejected the British proposals but answering any counter-proposals that they might have made and giving them an ultimatum to the effect that unless the Rhodesian Government heard from them within a specified time, which would be a short time not exceeding at the very outside a week, the Rhodesian Government proposed to declare a general state of emergency;

(iii) in the event of alternative (ii) being adopted, the Rhodesian Government would wait for developments after the state of emergency before taking the final step of a declaration of independence;

(c) that they would discuss all these matters further as soon as a reply had been received from the British Government.

TOP SECRET

TOP SECRET

Z. 533 (PM)

6.

C.   In the event of a favourable reply:

If the British Government's reply was favourable and would result in the appointment of the Royal Commission on the terms dictated by the Rhodesian Government, serious consideration would have to be given to making absolutely certain that the Commission could carry out its task without interference. This may then mean that the Rhodesian Government ought to declare a state of emergency in any event in order to take all precautions to prevent intimidation or any action to undermine the standing and approach of the Commission.

CABINET agreed that this aspect would be further considered when the time came.

CABINET then gave consideration to the public relations aspect of the phrase 'unilateral declaration of independence (U.D.I.)'. The Cabinet Committee on Information and Propaganda had decided that this phrase should be dropped in all public references and communications and that an alternative description of the possible ultimate action should be found. Various suggestions were made and the one most favoured was 'assumption of democratic rights' to be abbreviated as 'A.D.R.'

CABINET agreed that Ministers should consider this aspect and be prepared to discuss it again at the next meeting when this question of independence for Rhodesia came up for further consideration.

- - - - -

TOP SECRET

SECRET

Present:

Hon I. D. Smith M P	Prime Minister
Hon V. W. Dupont, M P	Minister of External Affairs Minister of Defence
Hon W. J. Harper, M P	Minister of Internal Affairs Minister of the Public Service
Hon J. H. Howman, M P	Minister of Information, Immigration and Tourism
Hon D. W. Lardner-Burke, M P	Minister of Law and Order Minister of Justice
Hon I. F. McLean, M P	Minister of Labour and Social Welfare Minister of Health
Hon B. H. Mussett, M P	Minister of Local Government and Housing
Mr J. Armstrong	Secretary for Labour and Social Welfare
Mr F. E. Barfoot	Commissioner of Police
Mr T. A. T. Bosman, Q C	Attorney General
Mr A. M. Bruce-Brand	Secretary for Law and Order
Mr G. B. Clarke	Secretary to the Prime Minister and Cabinet Office
Mr K. Flower	Director, C.I.O.
Sir Cornelius Greenfield	Secretary to the Treasury
Air Vice Marshall H. Hawkins	Chief of Air Staff
Mr E. G. G. Marsh	Secretary for Local Government and Housing
Mr W. H. H. Nicolle	Secretary for Internal Affairs
Maj General R. R. J. Putterill	Chief of General Staff
Mr E. C. W. Trollip	Secretary for Defence

The Prime Minister, opening discussion, stated that it was Government's intention to declare a country-wide state of emergency, with the least possible delay. He emphasised that the reasons for this action were quite unconnected with a unilateral declaration of independence, a decision on which had not yet been taken. It was clear that forces were already mounting to undermine the work of the Royal Commission which, if it was set up, must be given every chance of carrying out its task successfully. The threat posed by terrorist activities was also sufficient justification for action by the Government sooner rather than later. Government's hope was that the state of emergency could be handled as quietly and as calmly as possible so as to avoid any panic reactions and certainly to prevent any misconceptions as to the reason for its declaration. Indeed, it was hoped that, so far as the detention of persons hostile to the Government was concerned, this could be confined to the 'security risks' only, leaving those persons untouched, for the time being, who were hostile in the political sense.

The Commissioner of Police confirmed that, on purely security grounds, there was justification for a state of emergency to be declared.* The Security Forces had been lucky, to date, in apprehending terrorists and unearthing arms caches but, with several hundred trained terrorists known to be waiting to enter the country, this good fortune must end sometime. Steps to minimise the serious situation which would then arise must be taken now.

In general discussion, it was accepted that the need for a state of emergency was justified. It would, however, be restricted to the requirements for maintaining law and order, all the remaining emergency provisions which related to a U.D.I. situation and which were already covered by legislation in draft form being held over until a final decision was taken by the Government. It was recognised that the state of emergency would have to be played down in order to prevent unnecessary alarm and despondency, and consequently much would hinge on the nature of the public announcement to be made. The Service Chiefs were authorised to take their unit commanders into their confidence immediately. The timing of the type of emergency envisaged would present no complications for the Armed Forces though if it were to be extended in scope to a full-scale one, the minimum of 24 hours notice previously agreed would still be necessary. Recognising the limited nature of the proposed emergency, army and air force units would not be activated, nor would the Prime Minister's Information Room and Communications Room.

THE SECURITY COUNCIL endorsed the need for an immediate state of emergency along the limited lines mentioned in discussion and invited all authorities involved to complete the necessary planning.**

---

* Handwritten marginal comment made by the Author at the time: 'Mr Bruce Brand said that had it not been for political considerations, they (Compol, his Minister and he) would not have been likely to make representations for a state of emergency. No-one else spoke on the subject.'

** Handwritten marginal comment by the Author: 'No mention made of the A G's strong attack on Govt for trying to keep the proclamation "on ice" after the Governor had signed it. The A G's objections were the main reason for rushing through the proclamation the same day.'

ANGLO-RHODESIAN NEGOTIATIONS

I feel that Provincial Commissioners and District Commissioners, as the Senior Government Representatives in Provinces and Districts, would find it useful if they had a clearer picture of the situation in regard to our negotiations with the British Government and this knowledge could assist them in their dealings with the public, both white and black, and also counter some of the wishful thinking and adverse propaganda which appears to be floating around.

We can start from the position immediately prior to the Declaration of Independence on 11th November, 1965. This reflected a situation in which many people were leaving Rhodesia and the overall economy was beginning to decline, because people could see no clear future and, it seemed that sooner than later, a black Government would take over in terms of the policy Britain sought to impose. Experience elsewhere in Africa very clearly showed that if this happened in Rhodesia there would be a very early economic collapse; there would certainly be no future for the European and the future for the African would be bleak to say the least...

Since November, 1965, the confidence in Government policy, despite sanctions, has caused thousands of new immigrants to flock to Rhodesia and thus reversed the previous trend of a net outflow to a substantial net inflow. Even under heavy mandatory sanctions, Rhodesia has managed to hold the position and satisfactorily meet her balance of payments requirements; something Britain has not been able to achieve, despite devaluation last year and hence the severe economic measures she has recently been forced to take...

In these circumstances, some people enquire whether it is necessary or desirable to come to an agreement with Britain. The answer is 'Yes'; if the terms are such that we can see a future for Rhodesia, because if we can reach a settlement then we can get rid of sanctions and get our economy into top gear. Accordingly, Government has been negotiating with Britain with a view to arriving at a settlement. The results so far have not, from our point of view, been encouraging. In fact the *Fearless* proposals offered by Britain on the basis of a package deal are unacceptable for the simple reason that, taken as a whole, they must result in an African Government sooner than later and, in consequence, chaos and economic collapse probably worse than that which has been witnessed elsewhere in Africa where this philosophy of majority rule has been implemented...

Meanwhile, our negotiating position has not been improved by those who would be happy to sell our birthright for a mess of pottage and who seek to paint a current gloomy economic picture. They would have the public believe that acceptance of the *Fearless* package deal would result in placing the economy in 'over-drive'. They are not concerned by the fact that the 'gear box' would blow up almost immediately, because they plan and think that in the interim, they could make a fortune and pull out. It is no concern of theirs that there would be no future or economy for Rhodesia.

Similarly, there is the element, a familiar residue of the past, who despite the glaring examples to the north of us, think or believe that the African can successfully operate a Government with a sophisticated and enduring civilized economy. They seek to back their arguments with the theory that it is inevitable the African majority, by sheer weight of numbers, must submerge the European sooner than later. Therefore it is better to accept the position and come to terms with them now. The fact that the Africans' terms and only terms, are 'European get out', and that when this happens there would be chaos and ruin, is not a matter for concern because it is thought to be inevitable...

During the course of the [*Fearless*] discussions Britain introduced a string of fringe area matters obviously designed to strap flesh on the basic structure with a view to producing NIBMAR in another dress. However, in discussion of these various fringe points – many of the points were obviously over-dressed to allow them to discard superfluous items and permit them room for conceding points, yet retaining the main clothing and proceeding to argue that it was essential. Ultimately the original creature emerged in its newly bedecked finery and the creature was astutely re-christened 'Package Deal'. It soon became clear that the 'Package Deal' was nothing other than the 'Tiger', with a jackal substituted as a lead in the place of the previous hyena. Ultimately the so-called 'Package Deal' was put to paper and presented by the British as their offer under the title of the *Fearless* proposals. It is this document that formed the basis of the recent discussions with Mr Thompson. Examination of this document reveals that it contains over 14 points...

5. *Delimitation: (Proportional Representation)*

The British not only require the entrenchment of sections 37 and 38 of the Constitution which deal with the composition of the number of seats in each house and the normal Delimitation principles, but in addition they desire to override the Delimitation principles with a view to giving *Africans* proportional representation. In effect they require, for example, that if there are say 5000 Africans on the 'A' roll and 100,000 Europeans on the 'A' roll then the country must be delimitated to give the Africans a majority in 1/20th of the constituencies, i.e. in a House of 67 seats, at least 3 African seats. The fact that this might be impracticable because of the tolerance factor, community of interest, geographical distribution etc. (factors entrenched in sections 37/38) is to be overridden and the Delimitation Commission must either block scattered groups to form the required number of African majority constituencies or ignore the tolerance factor and delimitate a handful of Africans to form an African majority constituency. This blatant discrimination and jerry-mandering in favour of the African is argued by the British to be justifiable on the grounds of our so-called unique situation. The history of how this crooked formula was born does not react to the credit of the British but there is no purpose in relating it here except to record that it savoured of sharp practice and did not engender trustworthiness in the British from a negotiating point of view...

9. *Amendment of the Constitution*

This proposal envisages that the Constitution will be graded into two parts, one part would be termed 'ordinary' and the other 'entrenched'. In regard to the 'ordinary' part, this could be amended at any time by a Bill passed by a 2/3rds majority of the *total membership* of the Legislative Assembly. You will note, 2/3rds of membership, and *not* 2/3rds of those voting in the House at the time.

The second or entrenched part can only be amended through the operation of a mechanical process similar in principle to that used for the first part, but on a 3/4trs majority vote of the total membership of the *Assembly* and *Senate*, plus an ideological process outside the control or influence of Parliament and devoid of any mechanical or measurable factors. This double-barrelled device has been aptly termed by its inventors as the 'lock and chain technique' where the first mechanical process is the lock requiring a 3/4trs vote as the key and the second or ideological process is the chain which prevents the door from being opened until the 'witchdoctor' has satisfied himself that the amendment reflects that there is *no unjust discrimination* ... or that it *does not derogate from the principles of the Declaration of Rights contained in the Constitution*...

The proposal provides that this witchdoctor system is unamendable for at least fifteen years and thereafter it can be *modified* (not repealed) by going through the same system applicable to an entrenched clause. It is obvious that it will be strongly and successfully argued that the provision is immutable – in fact the British admitted that this would be the position. In short, therefore, when the British referred to this gadget as a chain safeguard, they in fact meant just that, and it is clear that if we accepted this requirement it would hold us as prisoners in chains for ever. In other words we would not enjoy sovereign independence because we would be at the mercy of some outside body which caused Parliament to be subservient to it....

This is not the end of this funny story, because in relation to the 'B' roll no referendum can be held until there are 200,000 people on the 'B' roll register – just a little device to force the Government to force people to get onto the 'B' roll, but as proverbial as "taking a horse to water cannot make him drink" so this little joke could well cause another laugh if those who are registered failed or declined to vote in sufficient numbers. And this does not complete the pantomime for, having hurdled all those obstacles, the two houses must again accord the matter a 3/4trs majority vote – this time at the Third Reading.

Assuming that this ingenious device was acceptable to Rhodesia, this alternative chain up is only offered provided Rhodesia is prepared to accept the Judicial Committee of the Privy Council as its final Court of Appeal ... The fact that the Privy Council has recently ruled that everything which has been done by the Rhodesian Government since 11th November, 1965 is illegal, and the fact that the Rhodesian Courts have just ruled in the converse, presents a field for legal argument before we can start on this fringe area. But leaving out the absurdities reflected by this proposal, nobody can argue that it does not infringe the sovereignty of Parliament and although the witchdoctor has now discarded his attire of skins, the bones and magic are still clearly evident and the witchcraft is merely being propelled by an armoured tank instead of an antbear. Little wonder that our Prime Minister was constrained to enquire from Mr Thompson after he had propounded his so-called alternative, whether this was a practical joke...

11. *African Education*
The proposal here is that Britain will provide £50 million over ten years to be matched by a similar amount by the Rhodesian Government over and above the currently planned annual expenditure for these purposes ... in total just a round £180 million of African Education over ten years. The primary British object being to ensure that in less than ten years sufficient Africans qualified *educationally* to get on the 'A' roll and thereby kick the European out of Rhodesia. *Education by itself* will not produce any economic development in Rhodesia and empty stomachs and no jobs will surely lead to chaos and disruption to assist in achieving the prime British purpose...

12. *Fifth Principle: Test of Acceptability*
On the assumption that these peculiar proposals which I have just described are deemed by our Government as being necessary for our unique situation, then what one might term the last hurdle must be overcome and here we see British current thinking as it operates 6000 miles away. The details envisage:
a) A British Government appointed Royal Commission sent to Rhodesia to test by some magical means, the acceptability or otherwise of the new Constitution by the people of Rhodesia as a whole.
b) While this magic is being performed, it is envisaged that it would be conducive to realistic results if:
i) there was no censorship
ii) normal political activities were permitted on condition that they would be conducted peacefully and democratically without intimidation from any quarter...
v) radio and television facilities were provided for *opposition* opinion to the satisfaction of the Commission...

13. *Subsequent Steps*
... inserted under this heading we find a most peculiar requirement, which the British subsequently rated as vital, and this is the proposal that Rhodesian public servants who had fallen for the British bait to desert or leave, should be reinstated. It is not necessary for me to tell you the Rhodesian answer to this one. All that I can say is, that as a senior Civil Servant, I am completely unable to accept the British definition that the word 'loyal' is synonimous (sic) with 'traitor'.

14. *Interim Arrangements*
The final *Fearless* proposal requires our Prime Minister to form a broad based administration which must include Africans and this would operate until a new Parliament was elected under the new Constitution. It replaces the *Tiger* "Return to Legality" requirement. It represents the only real British climb down from *Tiger*, and this is not surprising because it is relatively unimportant...

15. *General Summary*
It is clear from the Rhodesian point of view, particularly as this vitally affects our future, and in this context 'our' means European and African, that there is no future for either or both, if this fearful package is swallowed. It contains germs which sooner than later will cause the death of this country as a civilised and progressive entity and in the process we would endure the pattern of tur-

moil and suffering now so familiar wherever Britain has sought to impose her 'one man, one vote' philosophy. In these circumstances, it is difficult to understand or appreciate the British motives other than their declared aim of African majority chaos sooner than later.

And for those in the centre and on the fringes, I can but advise that this *Fearless* package taken as a whole, is a fearul and deadly poison capable of killing all Rhodesians, black and white.

It is possible that further negotiations with Britain may produce something more acceptable to Rhodesia, but this remains to be seen. In the interim the Rhodesian Government is going ahead with the drafting of its own new Constitution and this should be ready for final consideration early in the New Year.

W. H. H. NICOLLE
SECRETARY FOR INTERNAL AFFAIRS

Message from Sir Alec Douglas-Home to Mr Ian Smith

SECRET

Since my message to you of 8 April, I have again gone over Lord Goodman's reports. I know that you understand that we must have a settlement which fair-minded people will regard as being within the five principles and which will command the public support of responsible members of the international community. The most important of these principles is the first. A formula is needed as to how to get to parity in a reasonable but necessarily unspecified time scale and what to do at that point and beyond. No-one here is suggesting now the adoption of one man one vote and our thinking has always been that progress should be through a voting roll with significant qualifications based on merit and responsibility. Then in time it should be possible to proceed with confidence to majority rule in a stable society. I am looking forward to receiving your thoughts. In the meantime we are working hard on the problems in the hope that the next round will bring a real chance of agreement.

BRITISH EMBASSY
CAPE TOWN
16 April 1971
SECRET

'Flechas' and the Formation of the 'Mozambique National Resistance'*

why no vogue

TOP SECRET

The first Flechas ('Arrows', or pseudo-terrorists) were recruited in Angola during the 1960s by Dr São José Lopes, Head of DGS. Having been accorded the privilege of consultation with the authorities in Angola I could see the Flecha-concept being developed on the lines of the Illaloes we had recruited during the 1940s to safeguard the Ethiopian-Somali borders; although – not to put too fine a distinction on it – many of these 'Illaloes' became the 'Shifta' or bandits of Somalia's struggle for independence in later decades.

2. We put the Flecha-concept into practice in CIO during the late 1960s, trying to develop counter-terrorist groups as 'an African solution to an African problem'; but although we made some progress we failed to establish a tripartite basis with the South Africans. Subsequently, we argued that Flechas should be introduced into Mozambique but there was considerable resistance from the then Director, DGS, Mozambique – because DGS in Angola had thought of it first!

3. I saw the Portuguese Prime Minister, Dr Caetano, in September 1971 concerning the deteriorating security situation in Mozambique and to try and get his government to use its influence in developing Flechas in Mozambique. Unfortunately, my actions were misconstrued as being critical of General Kaúlza de Arriaga's conduct of the anti-terrorist war and were rejected by the Portuguese High Command in favour of General de Arriaga's alternative suggestion of forming anti-guerrilla groups (GEs and GEPs) from black Mozambican soldiers: but in our estimation this was merely an extension of failed military strategy, unlikely to be successful in countering subversion.

4. In the meantime, Flecha operations in Angola had proved increasingly successful, at one stage accounting for 60% of all terrorist kills, and had won a fair measure of favour with the then Commander-in-Chief, Angola, General Costa Gomes.

5. I saw Dr Caetano again in August 1972 and re-introduced the desirability of trying more unconventional methods in fighting the pattern of insurgency in Mozambique. At this stage the improved Portuguese position in Angola contrasted sharply with the deteriorating situation in Mozambique, and Dr Caetano made comment to the effect that they might have done better by offering more scope to the DGS in the earlier stages of the anti-terrorist war.

6. Dr Lopes was appointed Joint Controller of DGS Operations for Angola and Mozambique, and a belated move was made towards introducing Flechas in Mozambique as a cover for the small-scale pseudo-operations CIO had already started there.

7. Further tripartite meetings (DGS–BOSS–CIO) took place, during the course of which General van den Bergh promised support – particularly finan-

* MNR, MRN, or RENAMO, according to English or Portuguese usage.

cial support – provided that the Flechas to be formed within Mozambique would be based along the Zambian border; but I believed this would defeat the object of the exercise (re-introducing conscripts or mercenaries in a conventional operation that had already been tried and failed, instead of the non-conventional 'head-hunting' type operation based on personal or tribal affiliations).

8. I remained convinced that what we needed was a pseudo-terrorist operation directed from Rhodesia into Mozambique and I saw the South African Prime Minister to seek his authority for tripartite support. Mr Vorster showed every appreciation of our need and said that I could discuss the detail with General van den Bergh, but when I saw General van den Bergh the following day he claimed that he had no responsibility for participation in this type of operation. I reminded him that over a period of years he had always claimed that his organisation had the sole responsibility for external clandestine operations; and that his own Prime Minister had confirmed this with me the day before. He then said that our current proposals would only interest him under conditions which I believed to be unattainable.

9. The security situation within Mozambique continued to deteriorate, and in March 1974 I was invited to Lourenco Marques by the Director-General, DGS, Major Silva Pais, to find him and Dr Lopes utterly depressed but most forthcoming in that they made a new offer for Rhodesia (and South Africa if they wished to join in) to operate Flechas within Mozambique on the basis of what they called 'unconventional, clandestine operations by local Africans'. The following was then agreed between us:

Rhodesia must continue in 'Hot Pursuit' of her own terrorists;
there should be no international objection to Africans of the same ethnic grouping operating in adjoining territories;
there was little prospect that the Portuguese military forces could protect the electricity power lines betwen the Cabora Bassa dam and South Africa, but Flechas could help eradicate terrorists on either side of the Zambezi river and give Rhodesia (and South Africa) some stake in Mozambique.*

10. I visited Lisbon yet again in April 1974 and confirmed with the D-G, DGS, that he had cleared our trans-border operations with Dr Caetano: he expressed deep disappointment that we were not already operating in strength in Mozambique and that there appeared little prospect of obtaining South African participation.

I also saw General Luz Cunha, Chief of Defence Staff, who gave his approval for our Flecha-type operations and I discussed with him our Prime Minister's 'First Prize' – tripartite defence of the Zambezi River Line. I had similar discussions with the Minister of Defence, Silva Cunha, and the Foreign Minister, Rui Patricio, but the military coup in Portugal on 25th April put paid to our joint plans.

---

* The Cabora Bassa transmission lines were to have followed the direct route through Rhodesia to South Africa so that Rhodesia could benefit from that hydro-electric scheme; but the route was changed to omit Rhodesia, allegedly to ensure protection by the Portuguese military, and it was this route that the Portuguese now claimed they could not protect!

11. Irrespective of pending political changes we were left with the same defence requirements as before. Following the convention of 'Hot Pursuit', Rhodesian Security Forces had killed more FRELIMO in the Tete District of Mozambique than had the Portuguese military; and our chances of success against ZANLA/ZIPRA had also been considerably improved.

The alternative now was to withdraw – and perhaps withdraw unnecessarily – within our borders when no change of political consequence would occur in Mozambique for more than a year after the Portuguese coup.

It seemed that all of us in Southern Africa had to face the inevitability of action similar to that to which Israel had become accustomed – pre-emptive strikes against neighbouring countries – and our chances of succeeding with such action in Mozambique would be immeasurably improved if we acted under the guise of 'Hot Pursuit' in *advance* of any political change in Mozambique.

In other words, Rhodesia's (and South Africa's) security requirements would be better maintained by protecting our borders beyond our borders: at least, this was one side of the argument. The other side had been expressed by Dr Banda, for instance, who always advised that Rhodesia's war would be won or lost within Rhodesia. And we had found from experience that military planners quickly develop an obsession to strike at the enemy as far away as possible irrespective of cause and effect or the lessons of counter-insurgency; whereas the experience of Police and Special Branch indicated it was more important to safeguard internal security when the 'enemy' originated within one's borders.

12. In the event, CIO proceeded with the recruitment of Mozambicans who were encouraged to do their own thing in Mozambique without having to rely on support from Rhodesia.

The surprising ease with which the Mozambique Resistance Movement developed indicated that we were proceeding on right lines, particularly as we kept the movement small and clandestinely manageable during the first five years whilst it could provide the eyes-and-ears of our Intelligence in Mozambique.

The undoubted success of the movement also signified that FRELIMO in Mozambique (as between MPLA and UNITA in Angola) lacked that essential measure of support that they needed from the population: or the Portuguese had acted too hastily in transferring power to a liberation movement which could not establish popular support through free elections.

Top Secret
Director General, CIO
April 1974

Notes on Second Meeting with US Secretary of State Henry Kissinger, 19 September 1976

TOP SECRET

The meeting began at 1750 hours. As well as those present at the earlier meeting in the American Embassy the following attended:
    Mr. Vorster
    Dr. H. Muller
    Mr. B. Fourie
    Mr. Pik Botha.
Dr. Kissinger said he had dropped point 4 – the Oath – and also the one about repealing the constitution. This was best left to us. The P.M. asked how the Black leaders would be identified. Kissinger said this would be done by the Black Presidents. He was prepared to make strong representations about ZAPU and ZANU. The Council of State would be half-Black and half-White with a White Chairman without a special vote. Dr. Kissinger said he did not have British support for this but he would defend and support it. The numbers on the Council of State could be determined at the meeting referred to in paragraph 2. He would like to put forward a fairly general statement which the public could understand. He would go over Annexe C and we should detail one of our persons to go through it carefully so that we could then stick with it. This document was the basic proposal and was not to be too specific. He did not wish to leave misunderstandings and we would know what he was going to do. We should try to do this tonight. This was agreed.

Kissinger said if we asked for the two White Ministers in the Security Ministries he could not say what the British would do. He intended to write to France and Germany asking them to support what we put forward. He had not discussed this detail with Britain and France. If we could make a statement by Wednesday we would have put forward a clear-cut proposition. He could put it up for us but if we came forward quickly the U.S. could make a supporting statement which Western opinion would also support. If we started shopping around there would be confusion and the matter should not run on for weeks. When we get into negotiation the paper basis for settlement would be Annexe C which we will work out tonight. The groups designated by the P.M. and the Black Presidents would work on this, hopefully, inside Rhodesia. The P.M. said the Security Ministers should be White. Kissinger said we had convinced him of this at the morning meeting and the U.S. would support it. The P.M. said we would rather have these two security Ministers and give up equality. We could accept a majority of Blacks on the Council of Ministers. Mr. Mussett asked what would happen if the British did not accept the two White Ministers and parity. Kissinger said he preferred the British to be tied down to accepting a majority of Blacks on the Council of Ministers provided these two Whites were there during the two year transition. Decisions by the Council of Ministers required a 2/3 majority. With the "Oath" provision out, *a new para 4* said "The U.K. would enact enabling legislation" etc. The wording avoided amending our constitution and the P.M. agreed that we favoured the suspension of the constitution. Kissinger thought we could leave this to the negotiators. Kissinger said he understood we would wish to suspend the constitution. The P.M. agreed and said the document permitting this should now be re-worded. This was agreed.

Mr. Vorster said we should avoid raising a fuss with our enemies and Kissinger advised us not to raise anything new with the British. Mr. David Smith felt it would be alright as long as we here understood it.

Dr. Kissinger thought the five Presidents would meet to designate a negotiating group and we should decide where we would meet this group and when. The P.M. said we should have more precision about the economic support scheme. Kissinger said two documents had been agreed with the British. A three-way group comprising R.S.A., the U.K. and the U.S. were to work out details. Some points required further discussion. The higher figures however needed agreement. With individuals there was to be a limit (all figures in Rhodesian dollars) of $5000 if leaving in the first year but 10% per annum more for staying longer. Another equation was that a person could take 10% of liquid assets right away or $5000 whichever was the greater. Mr. Fourie had suggested this might be 10% or $25,000 but this was still in dispute with the British. Kissinger said the basic concept envisaged a fund to which the U.S. would contribute 40%, the British 25% (10% of which was a U.S. loan to them) and France had made a promise but provided no figure. If the fund were used for additional development in Rhodesia part of the earnings from those investments would go back into the Development Fund. Funds would always be an insurance cover for Whites. Mr. Mussett asked if the imposition by a future Government of Exchange Control had been considered. Dr. Kissinger and Mr. Fourie said it had been spelt out specifically that money could be paid outside Rhodesia and would always be available for either pay-offs or investment. The P.M. asked about funds for development in Rhodesia. Kissinger said part of the scheme was that the private sector would be encouraged to invest in Rhodesia. The three-way group was to meet next week, possibly in Pretoria. This would be the best venue and Rhodesian representatives could be available to it. He said he must have this in the hands of someone close to him and of course the British had to be involved. The P.M. asked if this was to help sell it and Kissinger confirmed this applied to the whole concept. Mr. Mussett said some people would accuse the P.M. of accepting the scheme without ascertaining all the facts. Mr. Fourie said he would communicate everything that had been worked on in a paper which had been received yesterday. Kissinger said he had to tell Kaunda and Nyerere what the P.M. would accept provided the final plan was implemented. Mr. Vorster said the finance aspects were none of their business. Both the P.M. and Mr. David Smith asked if Rhodesia could be in at the next three-way meeting. Mr. Smith drew attention to certain problems with regard to sterling, pensions and so on. He asked if the money would be adequate and said a huge sum would be needed. The P.M. said Rhodesians would look at it to see what was in it for them if they had to leave. Mr. David Smith also mentioned the Central Africa Pension Fund, and life insurances and said these were complex matters. Kissinger said suppose we put forward a scheme contingent on a worked out economic plan. Our enemies would see it as a device for delay. If we put it forward but would not guarantee to establish an Interim Government until the plan was worked out, this could be an incentive to speed matters up. There could be no rational objection to Rhodesian participation in working it out. His instinct told him he could keep better control in Washington than in Pretoria.

The P.M. would have enough to explain in this context and Kissinger would consult his colleagues privately later this evening.

The P.M. said there must be other points for inclusion in any statement, which would help us. For instance sanctions and terrorism must end. Kissinger said he could get a committment that these will end when the Interim Government is set up. He would have to discuss the committment and who gives it to whom, but the principle was accepted. If the Republicans stay in power and the Interim Government was attacked they would be diplomatically helpful and understanding to countries who would give us support. If Russia intervened it would require much effort. If the Democrats came in, and the Russian development happened early we would be worse off. Kissinger's object was to keep the Whites there and to set up a moderate anti-communist Government. He would like to see a structure which it would be possible for the U.S. to assist. The U.S. Congress was difficult today but we did have intelligence contacts which were of value. Dr. Muller said we must have the support of the front-line Presidents for we could be sure Soviets would try to take over. The P.M. said the British would also have a responsibility. Mr. Mussett asked if the Interim Government got going, sanctions were lifted and terrorism ceased and there was a manpower drain, would R.S.A. help us? Once we were "legal" could we expect assistance? This drew no discernable response. The A.D.R said that a bonus/incentive scheme might be considered, in addition to any other economic aid scheme, to persuade service personnel to remain in post. Dr. Kissinger said this could be something for us to work out for ourselves.

Mr. David Smith asked if it would be possible for us to buy arms and equipment for our defence in the U.S. Dr. Kissinger thought it might be possible after a while. Mr. Smith asked if Machel would actually stop the terrorists. If we had assurances on this point it would help us to persuade his Cabinet colleagues and our security forces. The P.M. felt that countries party to the agreement, should take on themselves, after the establishment of an interim Government, responsibility for ensuring we had the means to defend ourselves. Kissinger said the U.S. would not be a party to the agreement but she could recognise us. She was asking $45-million for Zaire – which was already facing Russian tanks – but only $28-million would be provided in 1976. When the Cubans show up in Mozambique the U.S. would have a base for assistance which she did not have now.* If he was in office it would be a legitimate enough basis on which to stand. Mr. Mussett asked if the French could be approached and Kissinger said he would be happy to do this.** The P.M. asked for something to help us to sell this. If the Blacks in the provisional Government were willing to step forward and the Black Presidents supported them we should have a good chance. We had a difficult domestic position at present.

---

* At this juncture Mr. Mussett said "We would not want that sort of assistance!" There was some misunderstanding because of the way the question had been put. What Mr. Mussett implied was that we should not have to wait until there were Russian tanks in Mozambique before America came to our assistance (K F).

** Not quite. The question was more one of whether we could expect interference if the French or anyone else wished to supply us with arms. Dr. Kissinger said again that we had our intelligence links and covert arrangements were possible and could be strengthened if there was no de-escalation of terrorism out of Mozambique (K F).

The P.M. referred again to the possibility of renouncing U.D.I. and going back to square 1. Kissinger said following our discussion this morning he had tried this on the British Ambassador this afternoon. The latter felt the U.K. would be unwilling to accept the responsibility and would get rid of it as soon as possible. Kissinger said again he feared Soviet recognition of what we were doing and they could possibly attempt to give extra arms to the Black militants and to, say, one of the Front Line Presidents.

The P.M. asked how Kissinger saw the mechanics of the situation from here on. Dr. Kissinger said it fell into three parts:

1. what we had in substance;
2. the procedure to be adopted;
3. what would be said in public.

If we accepted the scheme in principle he (Dr. Kissinger) will go to Kaunda and Nyerere and say that subject to a satisfactory fiscal plan, the stoppage of the guerilla war, and the ending of sanctions we would be clear to make our statement. He would take up the matter of our rail links to the Mozambique ports, with Mozambique, behind the scenes. What will help us is to make the fewest possible conditions in public.

The P.M. said he would consult his Cabinet immediately and then his Caucus. It would have to move through Parliament with a 2/3 majority. Kissinger said the Black Presidents would put up other proposals if there was any delay. The P.M. would need to make a statement on what he was willing to accept. The Provisional Government would not be set up until details were worked out. Some generous offer by the P.M. could be tied to the R.S.A., British, U.S. move. If we made a comprehensive proposal the U.S. cannot push too hard but will acknowledge that we have made a reasonable offer. Mr. David Smith saw the necessity for taking the initiative and felt we should try to get the Cabinet and Caucus together on two successive days. The P.M. said their colleagues would say they had an incomplete picture and want more details. Kissinger said we must go through our own necessary processes as soon as possible. The Front Line Presidents might then take three weeks to set up who the representatives were to be; probably they would first hold a summit meeting and then get ZAPU and ZANU together to hammer it out. If the final deal was to be put to the UN they would have to have the British with them. This was his worry about "shopping around". Once it had been taken up with Nyerere it would leak. He knew Nyerere sent around circulars to various African states concerning any discussions he had with Kissinger, and Somalia, for one, would let the Russians have it.

The P.M. said he saw great problems in selling it. If we can we would avoid delay. Kissinger said we are committed to the paper that he will take to Kaunda and Nyerere. The P.M. said we were clear on this. On that basis he would try to sell it but some may still talk about renouncing U.D.I. Kissinger said we would lose the psychological impact of the P.M. putting the proposal forward if we try this one. Mr. Vorster agreed. Mr. Mussett said it would be easier and more positive if Kissinger could say that the P.M. backed it and would take it to his colleagues on Tuesday. Mr. Vorster said this would show the P.M. was reasonable and going out of his way to seek a solution which would give him an advantage. Kissinger said if it failed people would say the P.M. had tricked him.

He understood that the P.M. was going to see Cabinet on Tuesdsay and Caucus on Thursday and would give a statement soon after that. Kissinger said that if the statement says that he has a tentative undertaking with the P.M. subject to this and that, the Press would only say that he was given a mandate by his Congress last week to settle. At this point Kissinger asked if he and his colleagues could withdraw for private consultations, and the U.S. party together with the South African party went into other rooms.

When they left the P.M. said that this was a gimmick to get us completely committed to a statement and we must resist it. Mr. Young could come down here, when the U.S. and other economic people arrived, for consultation by the members of the three party group.

Some time after this the P.M. and Ministers went to join the South African and U.S. teams and I do not know what took place thereafter. I understand however that agreement was reached on how much Kissinger would tell the Press that evening, and the timetable by which the P.M. would proceed this week.

Mr. George Smith stayed behind to collect and go through various papers.

Printed by the Government Printer, Salisbury.   60600-8 Z 535

SECRET

DCC/81   Copy No 12

20th July 1977   Reference: G/5/1

MILITARY AND POLICE IMPLICATIONS OF THE
QUARTERLY THREAT: 1ST JULY 1977 TO 30TH SEPTEMBER 1977

Reference A : Intelligence Co-Ordinating Committee Assessment of the
             Threat to Rhodesia for the Quarter 1st July 1977 to 30th
             September 1977.

INTRODUCTION

THE THREAT TO INTERNAL SECURITY

1.   Activity among the African political parties remains at a low
level with marked divisions between the nationalist elements, and
inter-faction violence and intimidation may occur if the tempo of
settlement negotiations increases.   The drift of rural Africans from
terrorist affected areas to urban townships causes concern and may
result in unrest.   Urban terrorism will continue in Bulawayo and may
spread to Salisbury.   No significant labour unrest is expected.

THE THREAT FROM EXTERNALLY BASED TERRORIST ORGANIZATIONS

2.   Terrorist recruiting has far outstripped the level of Security
Force successes.   ZANLA's numerical potential will enable it to
intensify and expand operations, especially in the HURRICANE, THRASHER
and REPULSE operational areas.   Present tactics of attacks on European
property, hampering Security Force movements, the severing of
communications and attacks on and subversion and intimidation of tribesmen
will continue, and ZANLA may resort to urban terrorism.   The high
level of recruiting in Matabeleland with training facilities in Russia,
Cuba and Angola should provide ZPRA with an expanding army of a higher
calibre.   This, combined with a recently resolved logistic problem
and Russian assistance, and because ZPRA terrorists remain undetected
in Northern Matabeleland establishing arms caches and an intelligence
network, is expected to spark off a long anticipated escalation of
terrorist activity along the whole of the Zambian border during the
next three months.

THE THREAT FROM HOSTILE OR POTENTIALLY HOSTILE COUNTRIES

3.   Mocambique and Zambia are determined to support the Patriotic Front
regardless of the consequences to themselves.   Zambia now presents a
major threat to Rhodesia, and like Mocambique, will not recognise a
settlement that is not acceptable to the Patriotic Front.   Both
countries will counteract transborder operations to the best of their
ability.   This will include raids from Mocambique by FPLM in support
of ZANLA terrorists, and with looting on the increase.   Zambia and
Mocambique may elicit foreign military support to assist in territorial
defence.   Tanzania will continue to maintain and intensify the terrorist
offensive.   Botswana will continue to maintain terrorist recruits in
transit but is unlikely to provide training or base facilities for
attacks against Rhodesia.

/ THE ATTITUDES ...

SECRET

Printed by the Government Printer, Salisbury.   60600-8 Z 535

SECRET

2

THE ATTITUDES OF THE REPUBLIC OF SOUTH AFRICA AND THE UNITED STATES

4.   There is no indication that South Africa's attitude towards
Rhodesia will change.   The US role in efforts designed to achieve
majority rule in Rhodesia will be maintained and selective political and
economic measures against South Africa are probable, as part of the
indirect pressure against Rhodesia.

OTHER ASPECTS

5.   The Anglo-US Consultative Group should continue its work despite
pressures to abandon negotiations, and sanctions will be more strictly
enforced.   The European community will support initiatives designed to
achieve majority rule in Rhodesia by 1978, assist Front Line States
financially, harden its attitude towards Rhodesia and give increased
material support to liberation movements.   Soviet pressures aimed
at the imposition of a Marxist government in Rhodesia will escalate
during the quarter.   The UN will consider proposals for increased
support for the liberation struggle at the next session.

THE MILITARY AND POLICE IMPLICATIONS

6.   Inter-faction Violence and Intimidation.   Settlement negotiations
and the marked division between nationalist elements demands a high
state of preparedness by SF if inter-faction violence and intimidation
is to be quelled at an early stage.   Possible implications are:

   a.   The Police will continue to be committed in countering this
        and any escalation could result in the re-deployment of
        Police away from the terrorist war.

   b.   Military assistance, if required, may have to be at the
        expense of deployed effort.

7.   Drift of Rural Africans to Urban Areas.   The prospect of urban
unrest is likely to be increased if the drift of rural Africans to
urban areas is not curtailed.

8.   Terrorist Recruiting.   It is impossible to prevent terrorist
recruiting by Police and Military means.   The continuation of this
trend together with the estimated training rate of the terrorists means
that the terrorists deployed and still alive in Rhodesia will probably
exceed the deployed bayonet strengths of the Security Forces by the end
of this quarter.

9.   Attacks on Property and Communications.   We are unable to prevent
attacks on property and communications because of the low level of
Security Forces.   The resultant abandonment of European farms and other
properties will make it easier for the terrorists to operate.

10. Terrorist Logistics.

   a.   Military.   The external harassment of terrorist logistic
        support lines is essential.

SECRET   / b. .....

Printed by the Government Printer, Salisbury.   60600-8 Z 535

SECRET

3

b. **Military and Police.** The continued and rapid construction
of PVs is essential if food is to be denied to terrorists
and steps should continue to be taken to control the
terrorist ability to obtain goods and cash internally.

11. **Classical War.** It is not anticipated that the Rhodesian Security
Forces will be involved internally in classical war during this quarter,
but transborder operations could escalate the situation towards a
classical war.

CONCLUSIONS

12. Of over-riding concern is the present inadequate and diminishing
force level with the resultant urgent need for additional manpower to even
contain the situation, let alone prevent its inevitable deterioration.

13. No successful result can be attained by purely military means.
It is now more vital than ever to arrive at an early political
settlement before the point of no return beyond which it will be
impossible to achieve any viable political or military/political
solution.

(J.S.V. Hickman)   (P.D.W.R. Sherren)
Lieutenant General   Commissioner of Police
Commander of the Army

(F.W. Mussell)   (K. Flower)
Air Marshal   Director General of Intelligence
Commander of the Air Force

(G.P. Walls)
Lieutenant General
Commander Combined Operations

/ DISTRIBUTION

SECRET

Extract from Notes taken by D-G CIO *in connection with the Lancaster House Conference, London, September–December, 1979*

TOP SECRET

1. On rejoining the Conference in London on 10th October 1979 the Bishop met me with the news that the African members of his delegation had got a new nickname for me which he wished to endorse – 'Sekuru', meaning uncle or elder.

4. I explained the need to call key members of the NATJOC to London, particularly General Walls and the Commissioner of Police, as soon as we entered into discussions on a ceasefire, with which the Bishop agreed; and they arrived over the weekend of 13/14 October, to join our Think Tank.
   Our 'Think Tank' consisted originally of Dr Kamusikiri, AVM Hawkins and myself, and met daily or twice-daily with representatives of the Foreign Office.

5. During the first discussions that our enlarged Think Tank had with the Bishop there emerged a marked sense of depression, expressed particularly by Mr Allum, and reflected in varying degrees among the rest of us, to an extent that one began to wonder whether anything in the whole enterprise had been worthwhile.

6. At the subsequent meeting of our delegation Mr Ian Smith was particularly virulent; talking of putting NATJOC (especially me!) in their place. And Mr George Smith held forth on 'tearing up the Constitution'.

8. The atmosphere in our morning meetings of delegates continued edgy. The Bishop had problems with his own Ministers, particularly over the requirement to stand aside during the election process.

11. It was regrettable that Zindoga and Mukome, two of the Bishop's most loyal Ministers, were most affected by the British proposals because of their portfolios of Law & Order, and Foreign Affairs. AVM Hawkins learnt later on that the PM had acquired evidence (through the tape-recording of a conversation) that Zindoga and Mukome were making plans against him, which accounted for him saying he would 'fix his Ministers, although it might take a little time'.

12. The British, for their part, appeared to be taking a more favourable view of our delegation's attitudes and supported a paper we submitted opposing the PF views.

14. Gen Walls made a trip back to Z-R with Dr Mundawarara, and returned at a stage when the atmosphere amongst key officials had fortunately improved – although the Bishop still favoured working through a 'dare' (Shona-type meeting, with prolonged discussions where everyone talks himself out).

15. Our Think Tank gave the Bishop dinner at my hotel, which got him out of his bedroom and provided everyone with the opportunity for relaxation.

18. Decisions taken by our delegation on 26 October should have helped the British to speed up the process of bi-lateral settlement (hopefully excluding the

PF), but on 29 October there was an adverse reaction from most of our black Ministers who had a sudden urge to go home.

19. The Bishop gave Sithole the chairmanship of our newly-formed Delegate's Committee.

21. The Chief Justice (Hector Macdonald) was now very much 'with it' and ready to sponsor the early dissolution of Parliament, if only David Smith, Rowan Cronje and others could get sufficient votes in the House and Senate to support this. The plan changed later on, based on the straightforward suggestion of the CJ to by-pass Parliament completely – thus reversing UDI. I had found myself on the same stage with him fourteen years before when he had argued with the Governor that he should either arrest the Cabinet or concede that the 'revolution' had been successful.

22. Ian Smith turned even more sour, and was doing his best – or worst – to undermine the Bishop's plans here and at home.

23. Our meeting of delegates on Friday 2 November, after the official photograph had been taken, was dramatic, starting with an address that the Bishop asked the CJ to make. The discussion moved in favour of rapid action, even if it had to be unconstitutional, to restore legality, uplift sanctions and the rest. There was much comparison with the circumstances of UDI. I said a few words which were immediately disputed by Ian Smith. The blacks applauded the CJ and later praised my contribution together with General Walls's; but it was a sad occasion for Ian Smith who was obviously hurt to the quick. Altogether, another ulcer-making occasion.

24. Ian Smith subsequently showed up in his true colours; pretending to come out in support of the Bishop, then switching on a personal appeal based on what the RF had done to get a settlement and maintaining that the Security Force Commanders were behind him!

25. Derrick Robinson, Gen Walls and I called by arrangement to see Nkomo who had Dumiso Dabengwa and one other with him. Nkomo dwelt on the impossibility of their accepting British proposals before there was integration of the Forces who would be left opposing each other, and where the real control was left in the hands of our Security Forces. He maintained it would be better for us to talk ceasefire, leaving out the British.

26. The South Africans – particularly van Vuuren – were calling on the Bishop at every opportunity, and the South African military (through John Erasmus of all people?) seemed to be planning external operations for the Bishop, through Minister Bulle. (An instance came to light through our LO Paris, when it seemed that Bulle had been trying to get an appointment for the Bishop to see King Hassan of Morocco – which I had to stymie.)

31. Through LO Paris, we try and get President Bongo's representative at the UN Security Council to firm up and support – or abstain from opposing – the British plan for uplifting sanctions.

33. As arranged through the good offices of Mr Anthony Layden in the British delegates' support team, I had a useful discussion with Seth Helper of the

American Institute of Strategic Studies, Georgetown University (where Dr Kissinger lectures). According to Helper, the middle-level British FO officials were thinking of calling President Kaunda in to fix some sort of deal with Nkomo now that it was known that Mugabe had returned from Addis Ababa with promises of continued support from Mengistu and there seemed to be a developing split with the PF.

35. As arranged by Rev Sithole, I saw Mark Chona, Kaunda's special representative, in Sithole's suite at Lonrho's hotel (The Waldorf) on 14 November, for what turned out to be a sparring match – not much more. I told Chona the PF had nothing to fear if their participation in the election was 'free and fair', particularly if their intentions were manifestly peaceful. He said that ZIPRA 'refugees' were returning from Zambia to Z-R in that spirit. There was no question of armed men crossing the Zambezi at this stage.

37. My encounter with Chona ended by him making an appeal for all of us to work towards a 'strong government' (with Nkomo no doubt?) in order to deal with the future problems of Zimbabwe; maintaining that no form of coalition could work and an indecisive government would lead to chaos.

40. Trying to get a point across about the ceasefire Chona said it would be better if neither side took up fixed positions. They could cease firing under separate flags and just wave to each other when there might be an encounter!

42. On 15 November the PF accepted the interim arrangements, to our consternation as neither the British nor ourselves had expected this. All the more reason now to get them to opt out over the ceasefire and to achieve this we must keep the pressure on the British to insist on as tight a time-scale as possible, together with all the other safeguards that we have discussed in Think Tank.

44. General Walls and I attend our first plenary session together on 20 November, from which it appeared that the British were keeping their plan on course; and that the PF – in an attempt to circumvent this – were anxious to be talking to us rather than in bilaterals with the British.

45. Meantime, our Security Forces carried out further raids into Zambia (contrary to the advice given by General Walls and me) and Kaunda announced his 'state of war', which must delay the outcome of the conference. Once again, the signs point to the PF opting out.

46. In discussion with British Intelligence on 21 November, they expressed deep concern that the conference could be aborted at the eleventh hour through escalations in Zambia. Obviously, they still hanker over the British 'First Prize', with the PF in, whereas we want the prize with them out. Gen Walls got the same play-back from Lord Carrington that afternoon.

47. If British Intelligence were genuinely concerned, it meant that they must believe we could not continue the war alone; but I argued that we would get more external support than previously – much more than the British say we would have got if they had recognised us unilaterally in May when the Conservatives came to power.

49. The next few days were spent waiting for the British to recover their international position following the 'hiccup over Zambia': also to put to the PF their remaining proposals over ceasefire.

50. Tempers got pretty frayed once more as we approached the end of November – nearly three months in London.

52. General Walls showed how mercurial he is when under strain; and AVM Hawkins and I had problems keeping him happy. Overnight he was telling us that he was looking forward to putting all those back in Z-R in their places when we returned and it was realised how much we had achieved on their behalf.

54. The scene unfolded into the 'second-class' rather than the 'first-class' solution preferred by the British. Obviously, the 'second-class' solution would suit us better, provided the British remained committed to the irreversible processes of Independence, up-lift of sanctions, recognition, etc. They are hoping now that the PF will 'board a moving train' in these processes. What we have to ensure is that nothing will be put into reverse if the PF decide to pull out and leave us to our own devices – what the British have sometimes referred to as 'the Aden solution'.

55. Sir Antony Duff mentioned to me on one occasion that he had believed for some time now in the internal solution in Z-R as being the only practicable solution.

57. I travelled overnight to Paris on 4/5 November, at the request of Count de Marenches, to meet M. Ceyrac, Patron des Patrons, one of the most powerful men in France next to the President and Prime Minister, to discuss the prospect of France uplifting sanctions; and received a confident assurance that France would immediately follow a decision taken in London and that all French-speaking African Heads of State should follow a French lead.

62. The 6 of December was no day for me! Having received an urgent call to present myself to Mrs Thatcher with General Walls at midday, and having requested the aircraft which the Count was kindly providing, to depart earlier than scheduled, we encountered one delay after another because of fog at Le Bourget. Then there were further delays at Gatwick before the traffic up to central London made me miss the interview. After all this we suffered a traumatic plenary session with the PF in the afternoon which dissipated any euphoria over ceasefire or any other agreement made earlier. In fact, the PF indicated that they had agreed to nothing!

63. The saga continued on 7 December, when Sir Antony Duff put on a slightly better performance as Chairman, but there were still plenty of threats by the PF, and it all ended on a theme that we should think again; stay in bases; cease firing; cease movement – but nothing else.

66. In the ensuing sessions there was much discussion concerning the desirability of making 21 December the 'cut-off date', after which the PF would be counted out.

67. Tony Duff made comment to the effect that he had been planning the British Government's policy on Rhodesia ever since 7 May, on which date Carrington had decided against unilateral recognition and had started getting his government 'on side' with the new policy they jointly formulated. (It was no comfort to realise I had had my first interview at the FO on 11 May but had been told nothing of this.)

68. Mr Renwick requested that I use whatever influence we had through our French friends to act upon President Bongo's representative on the Security Council – and this was done.

69. On 11/12 December we move into the 'Lacuna' where we would no longer appear to be representing any constitutional authority, Bishop Muzorewa having stood aside as Prime Minister and the British Governor in Salisbury having assumed whatever (unconstitutional) power he could. I represented to Dr Mundawarara that if we remain in London much longer it will diminish our constitutional responsibilities still further, and we will lose the confidence of those back in Salisbury who are relying on us.

70. The emphasis in our London discussions shifts, more and more, to that of 'numbers to be assembled', either from the PF or what we can agree separately with the British.

72. Although the train of our discussions is all towards squeezing the PF out, I learnt from British Intelligence that they and the FO were still thinking very much in terms of the PF remaining in. Now that it appears as if Lord Carrington has made a success of the Conference, neither he nor Mrs Thatcher would wish to slip to the 'second-class' solution if they can avoid this. Our view is that there will be less embarrassment in due course if there is a fairer appreciation of the implications of 'ceasefire' before, rather than after the event.

74. On return to Salisbury on 14 December we had it confirmed that the Bishop had lost support over wide areas. There was great apprehension lest the PF win the election. The stage seemed set for PF participation against all previous predictions, and it was with some dismay that we learnt of their acceptance of the ceasefire terms following what appeared to be British concessions – even deeper dismay when it appeared the PF were planning to contest the elections together on a PF ticket. (Not proved in the event. Assessments of election prospects at this juncture may have proved faulty and it was significant that on our subsequent return from London we were advised at Comops on 24 December that Home Affairs and Police assessments on where the the UANC stood in most rural areas were 'encouraging').

75. It was an emerging possibility that the bulk of the population might support the PF if the field were left clear for them, how could a handful of whites (presently controlled by NATJOC) appear to be reversing the political process or oppose the wishes of the majority? The British have engendered 'peace at any price' as a solution. Apart from this there is a widespread yearning for peace and we might find it difficult, if not impossible, to reject the PF. Another possibility emerging is the 'Mark one-and-a-half' solution as referred to recently by Sir

Antony Duff, whereby one faction of the PF competes peacefully, in which regard Nkomo's placatory approach as published in the *Herald* recently is significant.

81. At the first meeting we attended at the FO on 21 December we were told that Mugabe had been en route to New York, intent on rejecting the ceasefire and whipping up support to continue the war, when he was recalled to take a phone call from Samora Machel, virtually ordering him to sign, or not to go back to Mozambique; and indicating that if he disobeyed the most he could expect back in Mozambique was political asylum or a villa on the coast.

82. Tongogara had already taken the opportunity to return to Mozambique and it seemed to the British that he and Nkomo were now working things out together.

83. Indicating an intimacy with these people that we could only have suspected before, Charles Powell of the FO referred to the many hours that he or Robin Renwick – separately or together – had spent in the hotel bedrooms of Nkomo or Mugabe.

Other information passed to us by the British referred to Machel's extreme predicament caused through our raids into Mozambique, and the activities of the MNR. There was a desperate shortage of food over many areas and transport was precarious. As Renwick put it: it was no longer a question of 'a luta continua': they wanted the war to finish.

84. The British believed that the PF were more divided than ever and that neither leader had any intention of competing genuinely in the elections on a joint ticket. According to their reports, Nkomo would lose support even in Matabeleland if he was seen to be competing in favour of ZANLA.

85. In discussions between us, we agreed that it would make it easier for everybody if the split in the PF were widened; and that there would be decided advantages if one faction only – preferably ZAPU – competed in the elections; in which respect Mugabe has made enough public statements to show that he has no real intention of complying with the ceasefire – or any other requirements of the agreement. Following a particularly hectic session which the British had had with him, he was reported as having gone to bed for the day and they had called in Tongogara and Dabengwa to carry on the discussion. From that particular discussion, the British got the impression that Tongogara was anxious to comply and could even do so without the political leadership of Mugabe or anyone else.

86. Our FO friends reiterated that it was no part of the British plan to have Mugabe winning the elections. The difference now is that Machel, and not the British, has been making the running; and because of Machel's pressure over Mugabe, it has had the effect of keeping Mugabe in rather than forcing him out; which may be unfortunte, but the indications are that Mugabe should have lost authority and prestige in the process.

88. All seemed set for positive British support in sponsoring a satisfactory outcome of the election – a moderate, democratic government – but see the article 'The Thinking Man's Guerrilla' in the *Guardian* of 21 December.

89. We received other confirmation that Tongogara and Dabengwa were now trying to make the process of assembly work, because they realised the penalties of not trying, and we were passed a copy of what Tongogara said at a Press Conference given by him on 19 December.

91. We were also advised of the British plans for Trans-Border Monitoring Bases on three crossing points on the Mozambique border (which we argued should logically be increased to 5) and for Victoria Falls, Kariba and Chirundu on the Zambian border (which we argued should be increased to 4 including Feira/Kanyemba). We agreed that only one was needed for Botswana, Plumtree/Francistown, and better to look on that for control of refugees.

93. The British set little store on Kaunda being effective in his control over ZAPU, or even in doing the right thing toward normalisation across the border; and they descibed his behaviour in front of Mrs Thatcher recently as being 'unbelievably pathetic'.

97. We attended the signing ceremony and the immediately following reception at Lancaster House. I thought Mrs Thatcher conducted herself in an exemplary manner, but I happened to be with Lady Gilmour when she displayed what I can only describe as quite surprising friendship with Zvogbo, whom we learnt had been virtually ostracised by the British Press and others since his reference to Mrs Thatcher and Mr P. W. Botha as 'living in a state of concubinage'.

98. Field Marshal Lord Carver came to speak to me during the reception, starting in a very friendly vein, but quickly embarking on some mildly derogatory comments concerning Lord Soames and then markedly denigrating the Bishop as being in no way a leader of anything.

102. Later, on 22 December, Chief Ndiweni asked to see the Commissioner of Police and myself about a report he had received earlier in the day from Minister Bafanah that virtually all his Executive were threatening to resign because of intimidation. He said that he had received approaches from Mugabe for his Party to join with theirs but had given a flat rejection.

Top Secret
CIO ref A1
31 December 1979

Source Notes

CHAPTER 2, pp. 22 to 44.
1 Note, Portuguese Affairs, DG* CIO 17.7.64
2 Note, Portuguese Affairs, 'L' CIO 17.7.64
3 Office Note, Liaison with Portuguese Security Organisations, DG CIO 18.9.64
4 The Rhodesian Independence Issue: From a British Point of View: From an American Point of View, CIO Paper 29.9.65

CHAPTER 3, pp. 45 to 60.
1 Note, Independence Issue, DG CIO 11.10.65
2 Memorandum, Independence Issue: Report by Rhodesian High Commissioner in London, DG CIO 29.10.65
3 Memorandum, Service Instructions in the Event of UDI, DG CIO 8.11.65

CHAPTER 4, pp. 61 to 77.
1 Cabinet Note, Relations with South Africa and Portugal, Secretary to the PM 13.4.66
2 Minutes of Meeting of Cabinet 19.4.66 Item 13: Relations with South Africa and Portugal
3 Minutes of Meeting of Cabinet 19.4.66 Item 17: Economic Sanctions – Counter-Measures
4 Note, Relations with Portugal, DG CIO 25.4.66
5 Letter from Irl Smith to the author 29.12.69

CHAPTER 5, pp. 78 to 101.
1 Note, A Suggestion for Positive Action for the Termination of the Rhodesian Problem, CIO 30.3.66
2 Note, CIA Liaison: Political Negotiations, DG CIO 26.4.66
3 Note, Position of Sir Humphrey Gibbs, CIO 23.11.66
4 Note, Tiger Proposals, DG CIO 16.2.68
5 Note, Confrontation with Britain, DG CIO 9.5.67
6 Addendum, DG CIO 18.3.68
7 Memorandum, Anglo/Rhodesian Relations, DG CIO 1.10.68
8 Note, Anglo/Rhodesian Relations, DG CIO 14.10.68
9 Recapitulation of Points raised by Commanders at Interview with the Prime Minister on the Issue of an 'Illegal' Republic 4.1.67
10 Rhodesia: Republican Status, CIO 9.1.67

* Until the early 1970s, my official title was Director, CIO rather than Director-General (DG) CIO.

11 Note, Whaley Commission: Mr S. Morris: African Affairs, DG CIO 4.9.68
12 Paper, The Anglo-Rhodesian Dispute: and the Security Threat to Rhodesia, CIO 19.5.71
13 Paper, Anglo-Rhodesian Settlement Proposals: Security Situation in Rhodesia, DG CIO 21.1.72
14 Letter, Settlement from Rhodesian ADR 8.8.72

CHAPTER 6, pp. 102 to 119.
1 Paper, Rhodesia: Military, DG CIO 27.4.66 and 28.4.66
2 Message, Harold Wilson to Sir Humphrey Gibbs 17.12.65
3 Note, British Military Moves, DG CIO 29.12.65
4 Paper, The Evolution of Rhodesia's Africans and the Security of the State, DG CIO 27.8.68
5 Memorandum, The Evolution of Rhodesia's Africans and the Security of the State, DG CIO 21.7.69
6 RF Paper indicative of their membership's attitudes at the time: Unanswered Questions January 1967
7 Letter from Lord Graham to General Putterill 21.12.67
8 Note, Plan to Invade Malawi, DG CIO 5.2.69
9 Memorandum, Security situation: Tete – Interview with General Deslandes; Interview with Major Silva Pais, DG of the DGS; Interview with the Portuguese Prime Minister, DG CIO September 1971; Aide Memoire, Security Situation: Tete 27.9.71
10 Memorandum, DG CIO: Visit to Europe August/September 1972, DG CIO 21.9.72
11 Memorandum, Account of Director CIO's Meeting with Dr Caetano 30 August 1972, DG CIO

CHAPTER 7, pp. 120 to 134.
1 Memoranda, Arthur Guy Clutton-Brock: Proposed Deprivation of Citizenship, Minister of Internal Affairs 3.9.70 and DG CIO 7.9.70
2 Frederikse, J., *None But Ourselves: Masses vs Media in the Making of Zimbabwe*, Harare 1982
3 Paper, Commitment of Africans in the National Interest, DG CIO 2.9.75
4 Paper, A General Review of Our Security Situation, DG CIO July 1976
5 Paper, The Threat to Rhodesia, CIO 17.8.76. Paper, The Military and Police Implications of the Threat to Rhodesia PS 7.9.76
6 Letter, The Threat to Rhodesia, DG CIO to the Prime Minister 1.9.76
7 Note, Meeting of War Council – 7 September 1976, DG CIO
8 Minutes of Meeting of War Council 7.9.76
9 Minutes of Meeting of War Council 8.9.76

CHAPTER 8, pp. 135 to 152.
1 *Rhodesia Herald* 18.8.71
2 Brief, The Threat to South Africa, DG CIO 28.11.73
3 Brief for PM from DG CIO 27.5.74
4 Report, Security Situation in Mozambique: Approach to the Portuguese and South Africans, DG CIO 22.3.74

5 Report, DG CIO Visiting Portugal: April 1974 29.4.74
6 Brief for the Prime Minister, DG CIO 16.8.74
7 Reid Daly, R., *Selous Scouts: Top Secret War*, Alberton 1982
8 CIO Note DM Deskcoord to DG CIO 9.9.76

CHAPTER 9, pp. 153 to 171.
1 Note, CIO: South African Interest, DG CIO 28.11.68
2 Note, DG CIO briefing Mr Justice Potgieter 20.2.70
3 Report, Visit of DG CIO to South Africa: 24–26 September 1970, DG CIO 30.9.70
4 Report, DG CIO: Visit to South Africa 16–17 March 1976, DG CIO
5 Memorandum, Meeting between Mr Smith and Mr Vorster, DG CIO 10.4.67
6 Report, Visit to the Republic of South Africa: DG and Assistant DG (External) 26/27 September 1974 1.10.74
7 Memorandum, Detente South Africa – Zambia: Anglo Rhodesian Settlement, DG CIO 4.11.74. *See also* Report, Mr Vorster's Disclosures re President Kaunda ADR SA 7.5.71
8 Report, DG CIO: Visiting South Africa 25–28 February 1975
9 Report to the Prime Minister from Air Vice-Marshal Hawkins 23.9.75
10 Report, DG CIO: Visit to Pretoria: 22–23 September 1975, DG CIO 26.9.75. Memorandum, Discussions between DG, DDG (External) and General van den Bergh, BSS, at Pretoria on 23 September 1975, DG CIO 25.9.75
11 Report, DG CIO: Visiting Pretoria 21 January 1976, DG CIO 28.1.76
12 Report, Rhodesia and the United States: (1) and (2), DG CIO 20.9.76

CHAPTER 10, pp. 172 to 195.
1 Minutes of Meeting of War Council 14.1.77
2 OCC Memorandum for War Council, Sterile Zones and Food Control 16.2.77
3 Minutes from Meeting of War Council 11.2.77
4 Notes on Meeting at New Sarum at 0845 hours on Thursday, 4 August 1977
5 Memorandum, Safe Return, DG CIO 16.9.77
6 CIO Report, Lord Carver 7.11.77
7 Military and Police Implications of the Quarterly Threat: 1 April 1977 to 30 June 1977 12.4.77
8 Minutes of Meeting of War Council 21.4.77
9 Minutes of Meeting of War Council 3.8.77

CHAPTER 11, pp. 196 to 224.
1 Letter K. Flower to B. Engle 28.4.78
2 Report with aide memoire, American Attitudes to Rhodesian Settlement, DG CIO 11.4.78
3 Memorandum, Lifting of the Ban on ZANU and ZAPU, N. Sithole 12.4.78
4 Memorandum, Lifting of the Ban on ZANU and ZAPU, CIO 14.4.78
5 Notes for Brief to EXCO, Safe Return: Cease-Fire, DG CIO 18.4.78

6 Notes for Brief, Executive Council: COMPOL and DG CIO to represent Security Aspects 25.4.78; Minutes of meeting of Executive Council 25.4.78

7 Note, Removal of Minister B. Hove, SB COMOPS representative 28.4.78

8 Memorandum, Protected Villages, A. T. Muzorewa 13.6.78

9 Brief by DG CIO to joint EXCO, MINCO and NATJOC 3.8.78 and 8.8.78; Minutes of Meeting of Executive Council 8.8.78

10 Minutes of Meeting of Executive Council 22.8.78

11 Memorandum, National JOC Meeting with Prime Minister 4 September 1978, DG CIO

12 Minutes of Meetings of Executive Council 10.10.78 and 17.10.78

13 Transcript of Air Force tape recording of the raid

14 Minutes of Meeting of Executive Council 24.1.78

15 Letter, National Service for African Males, DG CIO to Secretary to Prime Minister and Executive Council 10.11.78

16 Report, DG CIO: Visit to Morocco with the Reverend Ndabaningi Sithole: January 1979 5.2.79

17 Executive Council Directive for Total National Strategy 3.4.79

18 Minutes of Meeting of Executive Council 3.4.79

19 Minutes of Meeting of Executive Council 9.5.79

CHAPTER 12, pp. 225 to 250.

1 Report to Commanders, DG CIO: Visit to Europe: 8–15 May 1979 16.5.79; CIO Aide Memoire for DG CIO 8.5.79

2 CIO Analysis 12.6.79

3 Draft, The British Plan for Pre-Independence, DG CIO 3.10.79

4 CIO Briefing: Security Council: 20 December 1979 19.12.79

CHAPTER 13, pp. 251 to 271.

1 ZANU Death List, issued by Dr Eddison Zvobgo, Deputy Secretary for Information and Publicity, In Maputo 13.11.78

2 File Note, Meeting with the Governor: 4 February, 1980, DG CIO

3 Report, Visit to Maputo: 23rd February 1980: Lieutenant-General G. P. Walls and Director General, CIO, DG CIO 28.2.80

4 Notes for Use by Bishop Muzorewa in a Letter to Mrs Thatcher, DG CIO

5 Telex to AVM Hawkins: Cape Town from DG CIO 26.2.80

Index